LANGUAGE AND HISTORICAL

REPRESENTATION

Language and Historical Representation

GETTING THE STORY CROOKED

HANS KELLNER

THE UNIVERSITY OF WISCONSIN PRESS

The University of Wisconsin Press
114 North Murray Street
Madison, Wisconsin 53715

The University of Wisconsin Press, Ltd.
1 Gower Street
London WC1E 6HA, England

5   4   3   2   1

Printed in the United States of America

Library of Congress Cataloging-in-Publication Data
Kellner, Hans, 1945–
    Language and historical representation.
    (Rhetoric of the human sciences)
    Includes bibliographical references and index.
    Includes index.
    1. Language and history. I. Title. II. Series.
P41.K4   1989   907'.2   88-40437
ISBN 0-299-12050-3

CONTENTS

Contents

PREFACE

Get the story crooked!

These are dangerous words, I recognize, to put into a book on historical discourse, especially if the author wants historians as well as literary scholars to read the book and to think about it seriously, as I certainly do. Just to get the story *straight* is the first duty of the historian, according to an influential tradition of scholarship, which presumes (a) that there *is* a "story" out there waiting to be told, and (b) that this story can be told straight by an honest, industrious historian using the right methods. On this view, to get the story "crooked" can only entail dishonesty, incompetence, or devious willfulness, none of which I endorse.

However, I do not believe that there are "stories" out there in the archives or monuments of the past, waiting to be resurrected and told. Neither human activity nor the existing records of such activity take the form of narrative, which is the product of complex cultural forms and deep-seated linguistic conventions deriving from choices that have traditionally been called rhetorical; there is no "straight" way to invent a history, regardless of the honesty and professionalism of the historian. Indeed, the standards of honesty and professionalism are to be found in precisely those conventions, both in what they permit or mandate and in what they exclude from consideration. All history, even the most long-term, quantified, synchronic description, is understood by competent readers as part of a story, an explicit or implicit narrative. The longing for the innocent, unprocessed source that will afford a fresher, truer vision (that is, the romantic vision) is doomed to frustration. There are no unprocessed historical data; once an object or text has been identified as material for history, it is already deeply implicated in the cultural system.

Getting the story crooked, then, is a way of *reading*. It means looking at the historical text in such a way as to make more apparent the problems and decisions that shape its strategies, however hidden or disguised they may be. It is a way of looking honestly at the *other* sources of history, found not in archives or computer databases, but in discourse and rhetoric. In other words, *this is a book about historical sources.* One must agree with Arnaldo Momigliano when he writes that the "whole modern method of historical research is founded upon the distinction between original and derivative authorities."[1] At the same time, we must recognize that this fundamental distinction between primary and secondary sources excludes from consideration the *other* sources of discourse, the sources that make representation in language (as opposed to the other arts) possible, credible, and ethically effective.

The first section of the book, "The Other Sources: History and Language," contains three chapters that address fundamental problems of historical representation. "The Deepest Respect for Reality" introduces a number of the motifs that will reappear throughout the book in various guises; it puts forth a case for the "other" sources of historical realism, the rhetorical conventions that are invisible to "straight" readings in which the text is ideally transparent. The next chapter, "Time Out: The Discontinuity of Historical Consciousness," deals with the fragmented nature of the so-called "historical record," which contrasts with the inherent continuity of narrative discourse. In the third chapter, "Boundaries of the Text: History as Passage," it is rather the *discon*tinuity of historical discourse, as it is constituted in a text that must inevitably begin and end, that contrasts with a sense of the past that has neither clear beginnings nor self-evident conclusions within it.

In Part II, "The Language of Historians: Four Shipwrecks," I look a bit more closely at certain historians and their texts. François Guizot is the canny social historian of civilization, using the poets to illustrate their time, and their time to explain them. His relation to language and the arts is rarely problematic, and has been much copied. But when his allegorical summations of social forces, institutions, and artistic works cannot be made comparable, his craft founders briefly, affording us a glimpse of his methods. On the other hand, Jules Michelet's endless wrestling with representation is quite different. For him, language is dangerous, like history itself; it is both "out there" and within himself. The antinarrative of the "Tableau of France" becomes a personal journey, a microscopic narrative without events that subsumes all of French history into itself synchronically, only to see it evaporate precisely because of its avoidance of the pain and labor of time and events—and diachronic narrative.

Despite the tremendous difference in their respective approaches to history, both Oswald Spengler and Fernand Braudel have unraveled

1. Arnaldo Momigliano, *Studies in Historiography* (New York and London, 1966), 2.

their own texts like Penelope's textile in the *Odyssey*. Spengler bases the substance of his vision of history on essentialized versions of cultures, which are governed by the logic of the rhetorical figure that represents things by presenting a part that is presumed to embody the essence of the whole; but his own culture, which enables him to envision all the others, is represented by the figure of Faust, whose essence is to have no essence at all, but rather to strive endlessly for an erasure of boundaries that will eradicate part/whole distinctions. Braudel finds a similarly uncomfortable situation in *The Mediterranean and the Mediterranean World in the Age of Philip II*. When he is writing about what strikes him as the most fundamental and meaningful level of history—the slow, long-term history of geographic and economic structures—language, in the form of names and straightforward statements, becomes inadequate, so that statements must be self-referential, about their own failure to capture what they represent. On the other hand, when Braudel is writing the history of events, which he considers of little fundamental meaning to those not involved in them, language works quite well. In each of their masterworks (and Spengler's *Decline of the West is* in its way a masterwork, regardless of fashion), the rhetorical structure that makes comprehension of the history possible is disassembled by its very functioning, raising serious questions about the possibilities of historical understanding at the very moment of making vast claims for such possibilities.

The third section, "Tropology and Narrativity," is devoted more intensively than the rest of the book to the subject of language, and in particular to tropology, the study of rhetorical figures as ways of thinking. This section addresses the relationship of tropology to historical discourse and sketches the sort of resistance to and defenses against the power of tropology found even among its most distinguished adepts. Chapter 8, "A Bedrock of Order: Hayden White's Linguistic Humanism," discusses White's *Metahistory* within a tradition of rhetorical humanism that aims to resolve intractable conflicts through close attention to the language in which these conflicts are waged. White's method, however, involves important, if unrecognized, consequences that are spelled out more fully and more technically in Chapter 9, "The Inflatable Trope as Narrative Theory: Structure or Allegory?" The possibility that the four-trope system of tropes derived from Vico may generate its own narrative forms, taking over the story, so to speak, is a danger from which White implicitly drew back in *Metahistory*. This fear of tropology's explanatory power, which threatens to make human meanings but a "moment" in the language system, is exemplified by Freud in *The Interpretation of Dreams*. Chapter 10, "Tropology Versus Narrativity: Freud and the Formalists," discusses how Freud represses the powers of his tropology of dreams in the interest of maintaining the authority of the psychoanalytic interpreter. Repression of the linguistic sources of psychoanalysis seems to derive from this same anxiety that interpretation itself may be no more than an allegory of processes found in the tropes.

The genre of *allegory* pervades the last section of the book, "Allegory and Anxiety," which discusses the confrontation of conventional historical thought and practice with profoundly different ways of conceiving historical representation. In Chapter 11, "Triangular Anxieties," the three forces of psychoanalysis, marxism, and structuralism confront the historian with powerful, often irresistible, explanatory systems that can scarcely disguise their invented, allegorical nature behind the façade of "science." Chapter 12 juxtaposes a number of the most radically "antihistorical" continental theorists with recent work in the philosophy of history. In both of these chapters, the allegorical nature of all interpretive ventures like history is stressed as the cause of an anxiety among historians. The principal symptom of this anxiety is the refusal to recognize the rhetorical sources of historical thinking.

Anyone writing about the general issue of historical representation will have an inescapable frame of reference deriving from professional training. My own background in modern European intellectual history clearly shows in the selection of examples and methods; the names of Kant, Michelet, Goethe, and Braudel make several appearances in the chapters that follow. Others working in the study of historical representation, the "new" philosophy of history, come from literature, philosophy, and various areas of historical study, but we all are united by a persistent attention to the *text* of history, a text that can only be seen by "getting the story crooked." The diversity of this group has led some to fear that crossing the disciplinary line between fields can lead only to arrest for poaching.[2] The boundaries of academic disciplines, particularly those as relatively youthful as history and literary criticism, are all the more bitterly defended when criss-crossing becomes prevalent, and books are written that (like this one) do not bear clear marks of affiliation. What is at stake here, besides the professional rewards reserved

2. Stephen Bann, "Analyzing the Discourse of History," *Renaissance and Modern Studies* 32 (1983), 61.

for insiders, is the larger cultural question, "Who owns history?" If one agrees with Huizinga that history is the way in which a culture deals with its own past, then historical understanding is a vital cultural enterprise, and the historical imagination an important, if neglected, human faculty. Because the sources of history include in a primary sense the fundamental human practice of rhetoric, we cannot forget that our ways of making sense of history must emphasize the *making*. To get the story crooked is to understand that the straightness of any story is a rhetorical invention and that the invention of stories is the most important part of human self-understanding and self-creation.

ACKNOWLEDGMENTS

Academic debts are many and varied, and mine are far more numerous than this list can indicate. F. R. Ankersmit, Robert Berkhofer, Richard Buel, Joan Burbick, Philippe Carrard, Jonathan Culler, Gregor Dallas, A. C. Goodson, Margaret Grimes, Joel Fineman, Micheline Herz, Herbert Josephs, Stephen Kaplan, Ruth Kimmerer, Dominick LaCapra, Richard Macksey, Wallace Martin, Allan Megill, James Mellard, Louis Mink, Linda Orr, Michael Palencia-Roth, Nancy Partner, DeWitt Platt, Murray Schwartz, Richard Stamelman, Richard Vann, and Bill Vincent have all helped me with this work. The American Council of Learned Societies, the Center for the Humanities at Wesleyan University, the Center for the Humanities at Cornell University, the National Endowment for the Humanities, the Porter Institute of Jerusalem, the Werner-Reimers Stiftung, and Michigan State University have provided financial support, direct or indirect. My wife, Ruth Gross, my parents, Florence and David Smith, and my children, Hans, Anneliese, and Gretel, provided love and encouragement.

Portions of this book have appeared in *History and Theory*, the *Journal of European Studies*, *Diacritics*, *Groniek: Gronings Historisch Tijdschrift*, and *Modern European Intellectual History: Reappraisals and New Perspectives*, edited by Stephen Kaplan and Dominick LaCapra (Ithaca, 1982). All previously published material has been revised.

The work and example of Hayden White have influenced every page of this book. It is dedicated to him.

PART ONE

THE OTHER SOURCES

HISTORY AND LANGUAGE

Continuity is the central intuitive certainty we have about history. From this moment back to the Reformation, or to the Magna Carta, or to the construction of the pyramids is an unbroken span of time, moment to moment. There is no rational reason to believe that Joshua (with God's help) could extend the length of a day in order to win a battle, nor that time would stop for decades around Sleeping Beauty's castle. However, this is only an intuition, and not provable, strictly speaking. History, furthermore, could never claim to be about the continuous past itself; at best, it is a reasoned report on the documented sources of the past, whatever form those sources may take. Yet these sources are clearly not continuous, nor is conscious human experience of time continuous.

What is the source of continuity, then? Why do we intuit and represent and defend the continuity and essential unity of history? The assumptions do not come from the documentary sources, from existing historical texts, or from our own lives. Rather, the source of the assumption that the past is in some sense continuous is a literary one. What is continuous is not so much reality, or the form in which reality exists (as artifact) in its obvious discontinuity, but the form in which our culture represents reality. Continuity is embodied in the mythic path of narrative, which "explains" by its very sequential course, even when it merely reports. A strong working suspicion arises that the intuition of historical continuity has less to do with either documentary fullness or personal consciousness than it has with the nature of narrative understanding. "This, then that" is a structure dependent on the amazing powers of the concept "then," which virtually sums up what seems to be the historical point of view. To promote "this, that" as a syntactic model of history would be to resort to the ostensibly prehistoric chroni-

1

cle (or worse, annalistic) form of representation, or to espouse the catastrophic, inexplicable transformations of apocalyptic thinkers, found to some extent in the work of N. O. Brown or the early Foucault. And there is still the comma ("This, that") and the order of presentation (not "That, this") to consider. It is hard to distinguish the boundaries between the intuited continuity of reality and the relentless powers of narrative to make things continuous.

Yet no narrative can seem continuous in its beginning and ending; there the fact that a narrative, a history, is a discontinuous thing in a world of discontinuous things becomes all too apparent. As a narrative fact, a fact of language, it points to the scandal of general discontinuity. It is the source of concern . . . about sources. At the boundaries of the historical text, the general problem of presenting an image of a past presumed to be continuous becomes evident. If beginning and ending a historical text are artful, literary acts, then are not historical periods, or historical events themselves, equally literary creations, composed by the same conceptual processes?

Champions of a more textual approach to historical writing are often attacked on moral grounds. "History"—the true and verifiable story of human experience—is the guarantor of reality, of the meaning of human society and values, and of human liberties, we are told. To suggest that historical representation has an inevitable basis in the cultural forms it takes is "reductive," aiming to show that the text is nothing but a fiction, a willful creation. The results of this dangerous form of activity can be only a wanton disregard for fact, abandonment of standards of verification, loss of cultural identity, rejection of past victims and their memory. From the beginnings of the critical study of sources (wherever that beginning is assumed to be), the social and political dangers of inquiring too deeply into the sources have been repeated. A morally decent community depends upon a respect for reality; and reality for us depends on a certain notion of representability, or so the argument goes.

Rhetoric, representation, and reality, however, cannot be separated from one another. To do so is to repress that part of human reality that accounts for our understanding, convictions, and values. The moral high ground of the historical realists (who are actually less proponents of the material reality of the past than opponents of the material reality of the historical text) is always won at the expense of language and its imperatives, the "other" sources of historical representation.

1   THE DEEPEST RESPECT

FOR REALITY

The purpose of an introductory chapter which focuses the sections that make up the book to follow is a questionable one; it is my contention from the start that *focus* is in a certain sense the enemy (albeit a valuable and necessary enemy) of any worthwhile discussion of the problems involved in historical writing and language, the problems around which all of the chapters in this book revolve. The power of the optical imagery of "focus" and "clarity" as a measure of sensible discourse and responsible thought is so great and generally unquestioned that the metaphorical status and implications of this imagery remain invisible. Sometimes we cannot see what is involved in "focusing" precisely because it is so well-focused a concept. In the summer of 1985, however, I heard an exchange that called the notion of focus into question for me.

It was the last morning of a conference in West Germany on narrative and history, sponsored by the journal *History and Theory,* a time when the conference participants sit around a vast table, having heard all the talk, read all the papers, and finally say to each other what is on their minds. An Australian philosopher of history trained in the Anglo-American school uttered at one point a phrase that, I have no doubt, he took to be innocent and self-evident, an article of faith for all who sincerely care about historical matters. To wit: "After all, what counts is to get the story straight." Across the huge table, a British historian-critic, whose historiographical work has emphasized the structural underpinnings of historical thought, shot back the retort: "Oh, but you see, the point is precisely to get the story *crooked.*" Around the table, the facial responses to Stephen Bann's remark seemed (in my view) to divide the international gathering in half: on the one hand were the smiles of those who had a sense that they had just heard something as true as it was clever, even if they were not quite in agreement as to how "getting the story crooked" was the point; on the other hand, the exasperated grimaces of those who, even if they could accept a fundamentally rhetorical description of the processes of historical representation, could not accept the playfulness of this response, its apparent abdication of epistemological responsiblity and perhaps of reality itself.

I thought about getting the story crooked for a long time. My problem was not deciding how to make sense of it; rather, it made sense in many different ways. I thought at once, for example, of Hayden White's assertion in *Metahistory* that it is the tension between modes of explanation, emplotment, ideology, and structure that do not "naturally" align themselves that causes a work to retain that special power found in the classics of historiography, as opposed to the shorter-lived consistencies of the doctrinaires. "Getting the story crooked" in that sense is what distinguishes Michelet from Guizot even more than their differences of politics and personality, although, to be sure, politics and personality are very much involved in the kind of story they chose to tell.

A second, more personal and trivial, event happened more recently, putting Bann's remark into the perspective that I want to present here. I had dropped my opera glasses several years ago, jolting them uselessly out of alignment. They would not focus. After shopping a bit for new ones, I decided to look again at the insides of my troubled glasses. The usual lenses, prisms, and eyepieces fell victim to the tiny screwdriver, but I could not improve on the situation. Reassembling the thing, I noticed some tiny sets of holes at each side of the prism chambers, lilliputian screws therein. Proceeding empirically, I was able to adjust the sprung prisms back into alignment. At last I could focus. Whereas before there had been two images, one above and to the side of the other, now there was one—magnified eight times. Before this accidental discovery, I was all too aware that the object in my hand was an instrument of calculated distortions, bending light, bouncing it about, delivering it to my eye (which does rather the same thing, I gather) for a precise purpose, such as getting a better view of Tannhäuser and Venus from the balcony in the opera house. After the adjustment, lenses and prisms were forgotten, the better to enjoy (or deplore) the matter at hand. My view was straight, not crooked. The glasses themselves disappeared, so to speak. Bann's point came to mind. To examine the historical text, we must see it "crooked," even if doing so makes it harder to attain the precise purpose of the text. To see the text straight is to see *through* it—that is, not to see it at all except as a device to facilitate knowledge of reality.

The case of my opera glasses is not so different, in fact, from the metaphor offered by Timothy Reiss in his book *The Discourse of Modernism*. Reiss claims that the *telescope* is the basic model for the modern "analytico-referential" way of knowing, and that such a model entails not only a semiotic (or rhetorical) shift, but also a special investment in a new notion of what reality is.

> The word, the very concept of sign, passed down the telescope with the image, so to speak, until it was conceived of as a simple mental creation, possessing a quite arbitrary relationship with the thing. The sign had been in all ways the equal of the thing. Now the word has become as it were a means of visualizing the object. It has become the mark of, but also a bridge over, a new space between the intellect and the world. It is now possible to turn an abstract system into a true knowledge of a real world, one taken as *not* ordered by man.[1]

That history and literature were once equally part of a "republic of letters," in which writers of both sorts revealed the world through mimetic language, and the poet could claim as strong a hold upon reality as the historian, is so well known that it hardly needs mention. Literature as a technique blended into history as a technique; books of rhetorical rules for the writing of history were composed as late as the seventeenth century in a form unthinkable at a later date.[2] Mimesis, the claim to represent a reality external to the representer, was the essence of letters, history included, within the classical frame. This bygone mimesis was the proper study of mankind, instilled and expressed through rhetoric, for the consideration of the reader. History in this mode (Voltaire, Montesquieu, Gibbon) presented itself as matter for active reflection and judgment, rather than as an image of a missing reality empirically proven by critical methodology. The historical narrator was as active and "visible" in his text as the fictional narrator of the eighteenth-century novel, perhaps because both narrators had a certain sort of reader in mind, a reader competent to ponder the problems and paradoxes of whatever material was at hand, a reader free from the self-incurred tutelage that Kant had warned against in his famous essay "What Is Enlightenment?"—in other words, a reader the equal of the author.[3]

---

1. Timothy Reiss, *The Discourse of Modernism* (Ithaca, 1982), 54.

2. Arnaldo Momigliano, *Studies in Historiography* (New York and London, 1966), 11.

3. Lionel Gossman, "History and Literature: Reproduction or Signification," in *The Writing of History: Literary Form and Historical Understanding*, ed. Robert Canary and Henry Kosicki (Madison, 1978), 23. In "Voltaire's *Charles XII:* History Into Art," *Studies in Voltaire and the Eighteenth Century* 25 (1963), 691–720, Gossman emphasizes the visual aspects of Enlightenment historiography: "The true heroes and conquerors are the intel-

6

The Other Sources: History and Language

The breakdown of the classical frame signaled the liberation of literature from standards of mimesis by thrusting into the foreground of literature the radical authenticity of the inner experience of romanticism, an experience that often demonstrated its authenticity by rejecting formal language, or even language altogether. As the poets cast off their mimetic heritage, historians, as though stunned by the sudden shift of ground, were forced to reclaim the terrain of realistic representation, but without the irony and self-assurance of an earlier fashion. While they did so, new techniques of realistic representation became increasingly virtuosic, but less evidently rhetorical: the silhouette, for example, or the historical diorama, or even the new science of taxidermy astonished people in the eighteenth and early nineteenth centuries with their "realism," putting the notion of mimesis, or realistic representation, on an entirely different level.[4] Mimesis, long the property of rhetoric and its tools, has left language for other parts. How could the historian compete on this new ground? For Prosper de Barante the answer was to place chunks of reality in his text as extensive quotation; for Augustin Thierry, to place numerous touches of "local color" in his work to create a multiple perspective. But neither of these relatively self-conscious responses won out.

Ranke's solution to the problem of the relation of the historical text to the documents from which it is fashioned was to separate the documentary chunks of reality from the image of reality, with the proviso that the image (the historical text "above" the gash on the page separating text from notes) is entirely verifiable below the line, showing but not presenting the past. Stephen Bann describes the process:

> The aim to 'show what actually happened' is breathtakingly free
> of the circumspection of *mimesis*. Indeed my references to the
> ideal of 'life-like' representation, in taxidermy, in the diorama and
> in the daguerreotype, have been largely devoted to establishing a
> representational space in which Ranke's claim could be seen to

lectuals, the spectators of the great comedy. What at first appears to be their humiliation—their impotence, their non-participation in history—turns out ot be their triumph. As pure see-ers they transcend both blind existence (history and the human condition) and arbitrary power (others). The reason of the intellectuals, unsullied by desire, untainted by will, becomes a pure seeing" (715). Yet because the Enlightenment historian possesses his text as an aesthetic object, he fails to "get it crooked," so that—in Gossman's words—"[i]ts inner dynamic is never perceived and all the figures in it remain masks" (716).

4. Cf. Stephen Bann, *The Clothing of Clio: A Study of the Representation of History in Nineteenth-Century Britain and France* (Cambridge, 1984), 30.

have meaning: a space in which new techniques were explicitly devoted to securing an overpowering illusion of presence. But I would wish to repeat my reservation about the 'novelty' of this aim, which can appropriately be seen as the intensification through technique, of the conditions of representation implicit in Renaissance perspective. In this light, the 'colourless' virtue of Ranke can be regarded as a disavowal of language, of the historical *signifier*, and Ranke's nineteenth-century reputation (which still persists) as the mythic perpetuation of this disavowal. By comparison, the relative undervaluation of Thierry, despite his strict contemporaneity with Ranke, should be understood in the light of his determination to assert simultaneously the claims of language and of science.[5]

The claim of language disappears in the straight, "colourless" (Lord Acton's description) Rankean *showing*; the transparency of his telescope becomes "visible" only when a crooked reading reasserts that claim and the reality it embodies.

Crooked readings of historical writing are beginning to abound; these studies unfocus the texts they examine in order to put into the foreground the constructed, rhetorical, nature of our knowledge of the past, and to bring out the purposes, often hidden and unrecognized, of our retrospective creations.[6] The ideology of focused representation itself is an important subject for reflection. The narratological problem of beginnings and endings, for instance, is a special issue in historiography because it demonstrates in an obvious way how the fundamental choices made by historians affect the stories they tell and reveal the nature of their historical understanding. To begin a history of the American people with the Plymouth landing entails a plot very different from one that starts with Columbus or with the Constitutional Convention. To end a history with the outbreak of war between the North and the South frames a kind of story quite different from one that leads to Reconstruction. Beginnings and endings are never "given" in our universe of life *in* time, yet without conventionalized temporal frames— historical periods—the landmarks that prevent events in time from

5. Ibid.
6. F. R. Ankersmit, Stephen Bann, Roland Barthes, Lionel Gossman, Dominick La-Capra, Linda Orr, Nancy Partner, Paul Ricoeur, and Hayden White are only a few of the many scholars involved in unfocusing historical and other forms of realistic nonfictional texts.

swirling meaninglessly would be gone. When beginnings and endings are not strongly marked by events, we find a notion of history in which discrete human events have a much reduced place; certainly, the *Annales* school exemplifies this. In Chapter 3, my discussion of historical beginnings describes some of the reasons why readers of history are never confused by always entering a story in the middle.[7]

This detour by way of beginnings and endings suggests only one of the strategies of crooked readings. The matter of metaphor, and figurative language in general, is a powerful tool for readers of history. I am not thinking primarily of the traditional praise given to "classic" historians for their vivid use of language, of "style in history." Far more important are the middle-level, regulative metaphors of history, which generate explanations rather than adorn them: the organic figures of growth, life-cycles, roots, seeds, and so on; the figures of time with their rises and falls, weather catastrophes, seasons, twilights; the figures of movement (flow of events, crossroads, wheels); the technical figures of construction, gears, chains; theatrical figures of stage, actors, contest.[8] Most of all, of course, the figure of History as pedagogue, ever "teaching" "lessons." On a more basic level than the study of middle-level metaphor is Hayden White's development of the theory of tropes (the four elementary figures of speech interpreted as fundamental modes of thinking) as "deep structural" principles that regulate historians at every step, and often appear themselves in disguise as stages of historical development. Part III of this book is devoted to these "deep" figural structures, their implications as generators of narratives, and the anxieties that such implications bring forth.

The issue of narrative has re-emerged lately in historical studies. Although the debate often sticks to the conventional question "Should historians tell stories?" the essence of the problem is better addressed in the terms of Paul Ricoeur, who suggests that all understanding of meaning in time is a narrative understanding, even if it is an understanding of a history of "long duration," within which occur those "quasi-events" that take centuries to transpire. If all historical understanding

7. In "Making Up Lost Time: Writing on the Writing of History," *Speculum* 61:1 (1986), Nancy Partner notes: "All past events, persons, and phenomena, however abstractly defined, emerge into identity only as part of a formal pattern which controls time. 'Tick' = origins, causes, predisposing factors, fundamental premises. 'Tock' = results, effects, achievements, recovered meanings. In the 'middle,' our plot enables us to identify manifestations, symptoms, developments, characteristics" (93).

8. Alexander Demandt's *Metaphern für Geschichte: Sprachbilder und Gleichnisse im historisch-politischen Denken* (Munich, 1978) offers a vast catalogue of middle-level metaphors.

is a narrative understanding, then, Ricoeur asserts, this understanding is entirely controlled and guided by the basic armature of narrative, what Aristotle called *muthos* or plot.[9] This emphasis on historical emplotment is an enormous advance over previous ways of reading history because it spotlights the innumerable choices that must be made at every turn; to emphasize the choices that must be made and rejected is to unfocus, to read crookedly, the historical text.[10]

Ultimately, however, discussions of the historical text must come down to the question of *sources*. From the beginnings of historical production down to the present maturity (or dotage) of the nineteenth-century Western professional historical consciousness, the notion that a historian is only as good as his or her sources has been an influential one. The eyewitness testimony of Thucydides gives way to the dreamed-of "discovery" of a trove of documents (whether by Poggio Bracciolini or Robert Darnton), but the surest professional rewards go to those whose sources are the freshest and most virginal. The historian's sources are, as we have been taught, those particles of reality from which an image of the past is made; while few historians object to the idea that histories are produced, most will assert that the guarantee of adequacy in the historical account is found in the sources. If the sources are available, scrupulously and comprehensively examined according to the rules of evidence, and compiled in good faith by a reasonably mature professional, the resulting work will more or less "image" reality. Rhetoric, poetics, even dialectics (in the medieval sense) are subsidiary issues here because of the primacy of the source.

The word "source," so central to historical methodology of all sorts, deserves historical scrutiny. The use of the word in English to signify the raw materials of historical research is a late and figural one, dating from the late eighteenth century, but the word itself may be traced five centuries before that. As "the fountain-head or origin of a river or stream; the spring or place from which a flow of water takes its beginning," the word "source" appears in the fourteenth century; this meaning is still a current one. It is not difficult to understand the metaphoric transformation from a hydraulic to a documentary "source," "a work, etc., supplying information or evidence (esp. of an original or primary character) as to some fact, event, or series of these."[11] The earliest trace-

9. Paul Ricoeur, *Time and Narrative*, vol. I, trans. Kathleen McLaughlin and David Pellauer (Chicago, 1984).

10. See Chapter 12, "Narrativity in History: Post-Structuralism and Since."

11. *Oxford English Dictionary* (Oxford, 1971), s.v.

The Other Sources: History and Language

able source of "source" is the Latin *surgere*, "to surge."[12] As water gives life, so sources give life to history; the hydraulic metaphor reveals itself when one speaks of sources drying up. In German, the language in which much of the modern historical method was first codified, the word for "source" is *Quelle*, which has precisely the same association with water, although it stems from an entirely different etymological root.[13]

Two polar points of view confront the issues of history, sources, and language. On the one hand there is the attitude that historical substance always rests upon the materials that make up its sources, and that any significant change in our vision of the past will result from an advance in research that unearths new facts. This approach sees the research operations as the infrastructure and the written historical text as the superstructure. Another position takes just the opposite tack. On this view, it is the mental protocols, always linguistic at base, that are infrastructural, while the facts are the superstructural materials used in creating some expression of this structural vision. Quite a different picture emerges if we are to maintain that rhetoric, or more generally mental and linguistic conventions, are primary, and that consequently *they* are the actual sources of historical work. This reading suggests that history is not "about" the past as such, but rather about our ways of creating meanings from the scattered, and profoundly meaning*less* debris we find around us. This view of the past asserts a chaos, potentially terrifying in its indifference to the needs of humanity, or, perhaps, sublime in its destructive course. Such a view is found in Schiller's historical lectures and in Nietzsche (Schiller-hater that he was), and seems more a throwback to the older historical understanding because it presents history as an object of active contemplation, feeling, even reverie; contemplating history in this manner is active and creative precisely because of the essentially meaningless face behind what is contemplated. There is no story *there* to be gotten straight; any story must arise from the act of contemplation. To understand history in this way is not to reject those works which make claims to realistic representation

12. Literally, *surgere* is "to lead straight up," and is composed from "*sub-*, up from below + *regere*, to lead, rule." The Indo-European root of *regere* is reg-[1], the sense of which, "to move in a straight line," leads to a host of words signifying rectitude and law, and regalism and regime, which direct in a straight line. See *The American Heritage Dictionary of the English Language* (Boston, 1976), s.v. source.

13. Goethe, in *Faust*, exploited the multiple implications of the word for history. See the discussion of *Quellen* in Goethe's *Faust*, in Chapter 6, "Figures in the *Rumpelkammer*: Goethe, Faust, Spengler."

based upon the authority of documentary sources; it is rather to read them in a way that reveals that their authority is a creation effected with other sources, essentially rhetorical in character. This, we may say, is the way of reading "crookedly."

The rhetoric of research and evidence is governed by principles of selection and patterning that seem to be hardly rhetorical at all; to read research operations as the practice of a rhetoric is to maintain that the "facts" of history (about which there is generally no dispute) are not the "givens," but rather the "takens," so to speak. These facts are "taken" in large part from the language and cultural understanding within which they must be expressed, and thus possess a literary dimension that invades the very act of research itself. The medievalist Nancy Partner notes: "Archives contain many interesting things, but Truth is not included among them."[14] What, then, is the truth of history?

In chapters 3 and 4 from Book V of Jules Michelet's *History of France*, Michelet raises questions that are in my opinion crucial to any current discussion of "literary language" and the "truth of history." In these two chapters, Michelet discusses the reign of King Philip the Fair of France, and in particular his destruction of the militant religious order of the Templars. The chapters that have preceded these have related Philip's catastrophic foreign losses, and his momentous conflict with Pope Boniface VIII. The period is the early fourteenth century. I shall concentrate here on these two chapters for two related purposes: first, to determine in what ways they demonstrate, even dramatize, certain notions about historical writing that pervade this book; and, second, to ask the pertinent but rarely posed question "Where should a historical *reading* stop?" Answers to this question, I think, will to a large extent shape the future direction of historical studies.

In a recent book on intellectual history, Dominick LaCapra has leveled a serious charge at his fellow historians:

> In a sense, historians are professionally trained not to read. Instead they are taught to use texts in rather narrow, utilitarian ways—to "strip mine" or "gut" them for documentary information. Indeed, historians tend to appreciate texts to the extent that they provide factual information about the given times and places.[15]

This statement does not say that historians are not professionally

14. Partner, "Making Up Lost Time," 111.
15. Dominick LaCapra, *Rethinking Intellectual History* (Ithaca, 1983), 339.

trained to read, but that they are precisely trained *not* to read. The sort of reading that is proper to historical work is a mitigated one, which slights not only most of the true complications inherent in written texts, but also the necessary dialogical interplay of reader and text and the conflict of voices within a text itself. For this reason, it is natural that historians should have all but abandoned study of the greatest works, since these works are by definition not merely or simply "representative" of any time or place. It is clear, after all, that the greatness of such works has little to do with the information or ideology found therein, but rather resides somewhere in the suspect realm of "art." Hence, even the classic historians wind up sooner or later as literature rather than as living historical thought; and historians who approach their sources from the perspectives of modern art (or modern philosophy or modern criticism) are rare. It seems that "reading" in the modern critical sense is not only deemed "not historical" per se, but is also something that a historian *ought* not to do, apparently on moral grounds, because questioning language also calls into question the nature of the "truth of history" that is constituted by language.[16]

It is not hard, then, to see what LaCapra means. Even the current discussion of the narrative revival in historical studies seems to focus on the storytelling aspect of narrative—that is to say, on narrative in its nineteenth-century sense, as though the realist novel of a certain literary period were the natural and proper form of the genre. Historiographers have paid little attention to any modernist developments in literary narratives, or to that branch of critical studies that is encompassed by the term "narratology." Nor, in spite of what some historians see as encroachment on their territories, have literary scholars, in fact, devoted nearly enough attention to nonfiction prose; the careers are still to be built studying Flaubert rather than Fustel de Coulanges, Dickens rather than Darwin.

Historians as a guild feel a corporate anxiety about language and about those who study language. Each academic tribe produces and harbors a system of anxieties that, perhaps more than anything else, identifies a scholar as a member of the group, as a philosopher, a historian, a critic, or a chemist. In general, the anxieties of historians as readers are the following. The first is a sense that the *totality*, however understood, is not a rhetorical construct (and thus an illusion of art), but

16. The professional anxieties brought forth by the confrontation with the textuality of historical writing are discussed in Chapter 11, "Triangular Anxieties: The Present State of European Intellectual History."

rather the essence of the nature of things (i.e., that there *is* a totality, rather than a *sense* of a totality). It is a corollary of this anxiety that the meaning of a part will be incomplete without at least some reference to the whole, because the whole is taken to be more secure in its meaning than the part. Second, there is a corresponding anxiety about the existence of a fundamental *unity* in written texts. This anxiety enables historians to carry out their customary rhetorical operations, which are paraphrase and summary, and to avoid detailed and prolonged meditation on small pieces of texts. Third, *coherence* is the goal (and assumption) of historical readers, who desire to create coherence from among the scattered relics of the past. From this, we tend to infer that while *this* or *that* coherent representation may fail, there is *in reality* some coherence to "what actually happened" that further thought and research may better approach. Even those historians who assert that the study of the past must serve the present—the past having no eternal coherence of its own—assume that the present has a coherence that authorizes it to make demands of the past. Finally, historians show anxiety about *closure*.

These anxieties are proper to historians as readers: to intellectual historians perhaps most self-consciously, but to all historians in practice. Currently, the broader professional anxieties felt by historians are triangular, dealing with the powerful pulls of marxism, psychoanalysis, and structuralism. However, it is the larger and more comprehensive issue of the allegorical nature of historical writing in general, as both a form of discourse and a form of logic, that will define the future problematics of historical theory, if I am correct. It is this matter that I would like to address here in a brief reading of Michelet, a reading intended only as a sort of self-reflexive experiment, with a second eye on the reader, for the purpose of articulating a few questions that might normally remain unvoiced.

The third chapter of Book V begins with an allegory so explicit that it can only be taken ironically:

> Gold, says Christopher Columbus, is an excellent thing. With gold, people form treasures. With gold people do all they want in this world. They can even get their souls into paradise. (430)[17]

Gold, Michelet tells us, is the "god of the new world we are entering."

17. All citations in the text are from Jules Michelet, *Le Moyen Age* (Paris, 1981); the translations are mine.

And, fittingly, in his text we find gold growing in linguistic stature in the next few paragraphs. Gold is initially so superior to other forms of wealth because of its smallness. ("A small thing, portable, exchangeable, divisible, easy to handle, easy to hide; it is already wealth made subtle—I almost say spiritualized.") It is the sudden creation of the bureaucratic royal government at the beginning of the fourteenth century that creates the infinite need for gold. The allegory grows as Michelet, in the next paragraph, turns gold into "the fisc, this monster, this giant." (Note the inflationary increase in size of this allegorical character.) It cries out at birth, "Give me food, give me drink," like Rabelais's Gargantua. It would, if need be, eat flesh and drink blood. A series of problematic transformations then takes place in the text—the fisc is a cyclops, an ogre, a gargoyle, with the Great Council for its head, the *Parlement* for its claws, and the *Chambre des Comptes* for its stomach. Michelet inflates his images by extending his allusion to an earlier age, and doubling its range. The "blind and inert Plutus" (the god of wealth) of Aristophanes is saluted by the other gods (including Jupiter and Mercury) as their master. Gold is enthroned in the place of God.

After this opening apostrophe to gold, Michelet sets out on his subject proper; the election of Pope Clement V, and the promises he made to Philip the Fair, promises that set in motion the steps toward the movement of the papacy to Avignon. The stage is now set for the drama that will "begin" modern times, at least for Michelet; Philip the Fair's unprecedented need for money will drive him to pillage the Jews, the bourgeoisie, and finally the Church. The great symbolic drama will be the conflict with Pope Boniface VIII and the destruction of the Templars.

Doubling plays an essential literary and psychological role in Michelet's story; in an almost structuralist sense, things come in mutually defining pairs. Ironically, the dangers, indeed the sinfulness, of this literary procedure had been pronounced for the Middle Ages in the bull *Unam sanctam,* in which Boniface VIII had written: "To recognize two powers and two principles . . . is to be a heretic and a manichaean." "But," adds Michelet, "the world of the Middle Ages is manichaean, it would die as such" (415).

The Rome of the Jubilee year of 1300 is described as the widow of two antiquities (Pagan and Christian). The chapters have two protagonists, Philip and Clement. Two trials are at the center of events: the posthumous proceeding against Boniface (which Philip had forced upon an unwilling Pope Clement), and the actions against the Templars. In this second matter, two courts are convened, one royal, one ecclesiastical. Two gods are in combat: "This anti-christ, this anti-god, will despoil God, that is to say the Church; the secular church, the priests, the pope; the regular church, the monks, the Templars" (432). The Templars are opposed by their rivals the Dominicans from *without*. They also find themselves divided *within* into ideal and real: *templiste* and *templier*. "The *templiste* remained in the poems, a cloudy and semi-divine figure; the *templier* drowned himself in brutality" (439).[18] Two ages meet in these events, the medieval age and the modern age, but the medieval age is also twinned with the ancient world.

> The Middle Ages is already a second Antiquity, which we must, with Dante, seek out among the dead. The last poet of the symbolic age lived long enough to be able to read the prosaic allegory of *The Romance of the Rose*. Allegory kills the symbol; prose kills poetry. (463)

The last sentence is rich in ambivalence, a doubled meaning for the doubled vision of the chapter. Michelet's intended point is clear: the Middle Ages was a world of poetry, in that it made sense of the world through an explicitly figural set of spiritual and intellectual protocols ultimately dependent upon the faith that God ordered the world in poetic ways (which is simply another way of saying that the world has some intrinsic order). The modern world, by contrast, is the age of prose; it is ordered, not by discarding the poetic (which Michelet, the great reader of Vico, knew to be impossible), but by deadening its figurality through allegory. The Templars, for all their alleged and real vices, remained fundamentally metaphoric and poetic in their vision and in their ritual, and it was this spirit of living symbolism that was, in Michelet's account, the great cause of their downfall, their weak spot. Not Philip the Fair, a mere representative of the new world emerging in the fourteenth century, but that world itself, in the (allegorical) "persons" of gold, the fisc, government, and bureaucracy, destroyed the Templars and their already dead world of the Crusading era. For this new world, at an explicitly poetic level, allegory and *The Romance of the Rose* may stand as symbols. In short, Michelet's gospel, here as elsewhere in his prodigious work, is: "The letter killeth, but the spirit giveth life."

18. Although the psychoanalytic protocols of this reading are not meant to describe the mental status of any past people, I cannot resist mentioning that the structures of doubling and fratricidal rivalry are characteristic of narcissism. The Templars, according to Michelet, scorned women, engaged in "dirty monkish loves," and worshiped the order itself as a god. The order loved nothing outside itself (439).

This incessant doubling (or displacement) in Michelet's text mirrors or thematizes *as a double* the stated conditions of the age. Birth and death are occurring here, but in a sense it is death (symbolized by gold, the fisc, the state, literal authority, the god of the modern world) that is being born. The double-faced events were a murder ("This execution, of which the judges were unaware, was obviously a murder" [462]), and a suicide ("this great suicide of the Church" [463]). Everything generates a rival, and a murderous paranoia results; events are mirrored in an indefinite series of repetitions in the text, which thus may be said to reenact performatively the events that it purports to represent.

Having suggested that the doubling in the text is a performative mirror (or double) of the age itself as conceived by Michelet, let us push this clue further in our own reading. The surface of Michelet's page also has a double, equivocal, voice. The recently published French edition of *Le Moyen Age* suppresses all notes, presumably in deference to the tastes and purses of the modern reader, but the nineteenth-century editions have a full set of footnotes, which often fill more of the page than the text itself. In these notes, as was customary before the era of impecunious presses and widely available published documents, we find documents, in Latin, Italian, English, old French, with which the text is in dialogue. The relationship of notes to text is quite complicated and almost totally ignored by historical readers in terms other than content. In Thierry, for example, the notes contain the documentary passages from which the text is derived. In structuralist terms, the notes contain the system or paradigm, while the text is the syntagm. Michelet, according to Stephen Bann (who alone, to my knowledge, has investigated the relation of notes and illustrations to historical texts), specifically resists this sort of simple double-voiced syntagm-system relationship, which is explicitly allegorical in its division of a living textual voice moving over a dead system of documents; he does this by injecting another living voice into the notes, filling them with comments, opinions, self-references, in the midst of documents and citations from which Michelet claimed his work wholly derived.[19] If this is but another way of saying that Michelet's anxiety as a professional historian was different from that of Thierry, it also denotes an era when professionalism had not standardized the anxieties proper to the guild. Some see this as the infancy of a profession, filled with childish follies; others see it as the

19. Stephen Bann, "A Cycle in Historical Discourse: Barante, Thierry, Michelet," in *Twentieth-Century Studies* 3 (1971), 110–30, reprinted in *The Clothing of Clio*; Michelet, "Preface of 1869" to the *History of France*, many editions.

Golden Age, when history was closer to the literature, philosophy, and criticism of its time, and ironically had a major impact on the world of events as well.

If we stop our reading at this point, we are left with a sense of Michelet's mastery of imagery, his stylistic and poetic drama, and of course his idiosyncracies, neuroses, and anxieties. We may feel uncomfortable with this, and with his bold general statements and open partisanship, but his art is beyond dispute, if we mean by art that detachable element in a created work such as a history that calls attention to the means of creation—in this case, language. "Monsieur Symbole," as his detractors called him during his lifetime, tells his tales very well.[20]

But if we look into his words a bit harder, we find some difficult and frankly puzzling notions. Michelet has used the devices of symbol and allegory not merely as descriptive tools for characterizing two ages; he is also suggesting that the intellectual procedures in symbol and allegory are somehow operative historical forces. If Foucault in *The Order of Things* turns tropological breaks into epistemological breaks, Michelet does the reverse, turning an epistemological break between the medieval and early modern world into a tropological break between symbol and allegory. Periodization is always in question. If, as *Annales*-oriented historians correctly suggest, the notion of the Renaissance (an invention of Michelet's, according to Lucien Febvre) has no relevance when applied to the price of grain, then why not use various means of drawing historical boundary lines? Michelet begins with an economic-political principle of periodization (the allegory of Gold that inaugurates the modern world), but he ends with the practice of literary language.

The problem is this: Michelet's hatred of allegory is expressed *historically,* that is to say, *as allegory.* He himself recognizes this problem when he writes: "Nothing is as cruel, as ungrateful, as prose, at the moment when it mistakes the old and venerable poetic forms within which it grew up." ("Rien n'est plus cruel, ingrat, comme la prose, au moment où elle méconnait les vieilles et vénérables formes poétiques, dans lesquelles elle a grandi.") Allegory, *allegoria,* despite all the variations of its definitions, remains that which says one thing and means another—in other words, a double voice. Michelet has attacked the double voice of allegory ("this means that") throughout his work; it is the method, he

20. Linda Orr, *Jules Michelet: Nature, History, Language* (Ithaca, 1976), 9.

believes, of literalism and death, the *voice of authority*.[21] He defends his text against it in his metaphoric style, his use of notes, and his, finally, literary judgments. This paranoid defense suggests Michelet's anxiety that the voices in his text are not the voices who speak to him from out of the tomblike archives, but rather versions of his own voice, the voice of the allegorical author.[22] At the beginning of the age of prose, Michelet saw another fall, a fall into explicit interpretation based on authority.

The expression "literary language," much discussed since the Russian Formalists brought the question to the foreground in their work, implies that there are two sorts of language, literary and nonliterary, and that you ought to try to distinguish between the two for various purposes. However, there is virtually no part of literary language that is not universal to all language—metaphor, narrative voice, genre forms, all may be found in any sort of writing. Even the charts and maps in Fernand Braudel's *The Mediterranean and the Mediterranean World in the Age of Philip II* have an important literary role in determining the narrative genre of the work.[23] Literary language is a product of *reading*, produced by the will of a reader (often following clues and conventions in the text itself). A lyric poem may be read without regard to its literariness (as a psychoanalytic symptom, or an example of word frequency, the first appearance of a historical idea, etc.), while a physics text may be read for its figural or narrative structures. Reading is an act of choice, an act of will, and it is done for a *purpose*. It is not simply, as Quentin Skinner has suggested, an innocent act of following the clues.[24]

This much said about "literary language," what of the "truth of history"? Michelet has something to say about this:

> The true cause of their [the Templars'] ruin, what set all the
> people against them, leaving them not one defender even among
> the noble families to which they belonged, was this monstrous

21. On the relationship of allegory to history as an emblem of death, see Walter Benjamin, *The Origin of German Tragic Drama*, trans. John Osborne (London, 1977), chap. 4; on authoritarian discourse in general, see Mikhail Bakhtin, *The Dialogic Imagination: Four Essays*, trans. C. Emerson and M. Holquist (Texas, 1982), and Hayden White, "The Authoritative Lie" (review of Bakhtin), *Partisan Review* 50 (1983), 307–12.

22. On the problem of allegory and the authorial voice, see Paul Smith, "The Will to Allegory in Postmodernism," *Dalhousie Review* 62 (1982), 105–22.

23. See Chapter 7, "Disorderly Conduct: Braudel's Mediterranean Satire."

24. Quentin Skinner, "Hermeneutics and the Role of History," *New Literary History* 7:1 (1975), 209–32.

accusation of denying and spitting on the cross. This accusation is precisely the one which was admitted by the greatest number. (462)

Michelet pulls no punches here; he is speaking of *truth*, "true cause," precisely the essential "truth of history." He has saved this "truth," foreshadowing it along the way; it is the lead-in to his conclusion about the misunderstood symbol. The true cause of the fall of the Templars, and the suicide of the Church (their double), and the end of the middle ages, is a change in the practice of *reading*, in the sense of interpretation. Their practice of denying and spitting on the cross was part of a mysterious symbolic ceremony in which the initiate underwent a total degradation and separation from the salvation of Christ, followed by a symbolic entry into Grace and the Order. The Templars, however appalling their mode of life to the morals of the day, however dangerous their wealth and power to the monarchy, retained, at least in the ceremony that was the "true cause" of their downfall, a medieval, symbolic, vision of the world and its meanings. The literal allegorism of modernity had not touched this ceremony, so they were betrayed, tortured, burned, and expropriated. "Allegory kills the symbol; prose kills poetry."

We could stop at any point in our reading of Michelet and give it unity, make it cohere, relate it to some larger totality. Michelet's problematic attitude about the "truth of history"—whether it is gold and the fisc or the mental structures of symbol and allegory—may be attributed to his personal ambivalences, his class status, the gloom of the July Monarchy, an attempt to position himself among the many histories appearing at the time, or a dozen other "causes."

On the one hand, allegory might be subsumed into the world of gold as its ideological form of self-expression, or, on the other, gold may be subsumed into a world of allegory as its degraded image of value. In the first case, a materialist reading, in the second an idealist reading; both are perfectly legitimate and traditional choices. And if all of this is taken as Michelet's attempt to redeem his own hated world of literalism and greed, then his attack on allegory from within an allegorical form of discourse, history, is "explained." But if we read the text with both positions upheld—economics is the truth, and allegory is the truth—then we are left with their interchangeability. Gold is allegory and allegory is gold; neither represents the other. Neither allegory nor symbol, they function more like the allegory of symbol or the symbol of allegory. This literary language refuses to be recuperated, unless we stop well short of

The Other Sources: History and Language

a thorough examination of what is involved in this text. Freud believed that anxiety had two aspects: one, the attack itself, is inexpedient; the other, the apprehension that leads to adjustment and preparedness, is useful. In the interests of contributing to a useful set of professional anxieties, I would like to pose the question again. Where should a historical reading stop?

Michelet, as is well known, presented himself as the personal embodiment of the voices that he heard calling to him from the archives. The Templars were clear examples of the tortured, forgotten souls lying lost in the dust of medieval documents; Michelet, in fact, published an edition in two volumes of the documents relating to the trial of the Templars. His proclaimed devotion to the sources was obsessive. Yet he also acknowledges in this text the other sources, the sources that unfocus his discussion of the Templars. Allegory and symbol are more than literary examples, his citation of *The Romance of the Rose* more than a gesture toward the "totality" of the culture. Michelet believed that the other sources of his history, literary and rhetorical as they were, were also the "true" causes of the action he described. By unfocusing the text as readers, getting the story crooked, we sense why Michelet has been the subject of so much interest of late.

A good way to unfocus any discussion is to ask the historian's question—"Why now?" That is, why is it possible, even unavoidable, to question the relationship of rhetoric and historical study at this moment, when it would have been eccentric a decade ago, and quite unsupported twenty years ago. Then, there was little work seriously probing the rhetorical basis of historical consciousness, little interest in nonfiction prose among literary scholars, and less interest in rhetorical understanding on the part of historians. Besides, the tropological and narratological tools provided by recent poetics were not yet in use. Historiographers and intellectual historians were content with the paraphrasing, summarizing, and, above all, sociopolitical focus of their work, which would place any thinker on a spectrum defined by other historians. In standard works like *France Reviews Her Revolutionary Origins, Napoleon—For and Against,* or *Beyond the Finland Station,* historiography became a political litmus: *events* traced the ideological blueprints within a nation, and historians used those blueprints to image events. What mattered about Michelet was his populism, about Treitschke his nationalism, about Macaulay his Whiggery, and so on. The undeniable crookedness of each historian's vision was attributed to a political bias, an ideological or partisan persuasion, or simple craziness.[25] Representation was taken for granted; that is, it was basically invisible to the historical reader.

Then, something happened. From scattered sources, essays began to appear labeling the historian's language an ideology in itself. The linguist Emile Benveniste and the critic Roland Barthes asked questions about the discourse of history with an aim to demystifying its claims to be the privileged representation of reality. Certainly, in the United States, the publication in 1973 of Hayden White's *Metahistory: The Historical Imagination in Nineteenth-Century Europe* was an important event, and other works followed. A journal like *History and Theory,* founded in the 1960s to bring together historical thought and the work of the then-reigning social sciences, began to show the turn in events. In 1979 a colloquium on *Metahistory* was held, and its proceedings published. A floodgate seemed to open. Lionel Gossman's work on Thierry and Linda Orr's reading of Michelet (following Barthes's early work on the same subject) found new and important reasons for examining these classic works. The old question of history and its relation to narrative returned, but in a new and much more sophisticated guise prompted by the response of critics and philosophers to the work of the French school of historians associated with the journal *Annales.*

What had happened? Why is it possible to read history now in a way that was not possible two decades ago? Why has history become a special focus of attention for a few literary scholars who might have found in lyric poetry the most promising road to a career? The simplest answer is, in a word, structuralism, which inaugurated a revival of rhetoric and an interest in semiotic cultural codes.[26] The structuralist poetics that developed in the 1960s was obsessed with a distrust of realism; it offered powerful tools of analysis for the suspicions of a generation confronted increasingly with the "expertise" of the specialist, an expertise deployed by ever-more-remote institutions of all sorts. In short, we may hypothesize that structuralism's appeal stemmed from its demythologizing power, as well as its analytical elegance. The discovery in the West of the forgotten Soviet critic Mikhail Bakhtin, whose work has been interpreted as meaning that any discourse that represses the divergent voices within its own languages (its "crookedness," we might say) is an authoritarian discourse, always deserving of the car-

25. When I was an undergraduate history major at Harvard in the early 1960s, I heard the word "crazy" used to describe both Vico and Michelet.

26. Stephen Bann, "Structuralism and the Revival of Rhetoric," *Sociological Review Monograph* 25 (1978), 68–84.

nivalized laughter of deconstructive strategies of interpretation in the interests of freedom, brought together the formalist analytic inherent in much structuralist work with the deconstructive philosophical play of Jacques Derrida.

Resistance to structuralism from critics and historians alike was rapid and anguished. The principal charge was a lack of "decorum," an ethical failing that stems from a misplaced sense of proportion. The sort of thing that I mean is to be found in many places, but in history, book reviews are a good place to start looking for genuine anxieties. The review is a far less formal exercise than the monograph. Thus, John Clive could write:

> All historians, whatever their outlook or ideology, must at some point put the results of their researches into a readable form. "Form" means, as battalions of formidable literary critics armed to the teeth with modes and tropes have recently been reminding us, a certain manner of literary construction and presentation.[27]

Now, Clive is not an archive-bound diplomatic historian, nor a computerized social historian. Not only is he an intellectual historian at Harvard, but in fact a historiographer, whose work on Thomas Macaulay—a nineteenth-century historian of literary fame—is now standard. Why such a comment from such a man?

I need not point out that the passage I have cited is loaded. It reaches a higher emotional level than the sentences that surround it, in spite of the fact that it is a throw-away, having nothing to do with the book review at hand. It is aimed at the converted, and offers neither an argumentative structure nor evidence. It is more ritual than rhetoric, a quick secret signal that will give members of the club a sense that they are not in questionable company, but rather in trustworthy hands. Two semantic registers are invoked in the second of the two sentences I have quoted; both are outside the general tone of Clive's prose, at the opposite extremes. On the one hand, the image of armed invading battalions sounds the chord of barbarism and an attendant destructiveness that thoughtlessly, almost playfully, sweeps away the delicate products of centuries of culture. The arms with which these literary swarms advance, however, are precisely the most learnedly technical and least playful devices of an aged literary culture—the fruits of an autumnal

27. John Clive, review of *A Liberal Descent* by J. W. Burrow, *New York Review of Books*, 24 June 1982, 41.

overripeness, so to speak. The tension between these opposing semi-otic paradigms is a productive one. The battalions are made ridiculous by their weaponry, which is not really dangerous at all, rather like the "weapons" of the Old Men in Aristophanes' *Lysistrata*, which are so mercilessly belittled by the Old Women (who should know those "weapons" best). The intellectual value of rhetorical study is defused by the ironic *topos* of the impotent "learned horde." Further, the message that Clive attributes to these battalions is of momentous banality in his description. Most important, Clive has cleared for himself and for the implied readership of this sentence (that is, those who will not look into *its* rhetorical form) a space, a middle ground for those with good sense who are neither armed barbarians nor pedants who use vaguely Greek-sounding words. This is the historian's space; and it is the historian's anxiety to defend it. The space cleared by Clive's remark is a tactical space. Historians have problems today defining what constitutes their subject matter, and even more trouble making coherent the theoretical relationship, if any, between the work of the historian of South American slave revolts, the historian of French reformation political theory, and the historian of pre–World War I diplomacy. Yet without such a defi-nition of what history *is*, prestige declines, departments erode, salaries, new positions, and job offers lag. Consequently, history has clung to a self-understanding based on the rhetorical decorum of the middle style, and of the social morality associated with it. The historian is neither the fool, with his uninformed (that is, undocumented) opinions, nor the egghead, with his or her uselessly overrefined ways of analyzing away the REAL. In effect, like the *honnête homme* of a Molière play, the histo-rian stands between the dupe and the duper, even if they happen to be identical, as in the case of the literary battalions.

Now, this appeal to the middle way, to the decorum of the middle style of ancient stylistics, is a profoundly moral position, couched in terms of value-free common sense. To appeal to it is to summon all that is connected with the most powerful ideology of the modern world, the ideology of truth. Perhaps the best summary of the ideology of truth that has pervaded our culture since its beginning is found in one of the few sayings attributed to Jesus that meets with nearly universal assent: "And ye shall know the truth, and the truth shall make you free" (John 8:32). Imputing liberating power to the knowledge of truth is the secu-larized dogma of the modern world. The tradition of Bacon, Bayle, Locke, Kant, Marx, Freud, needs little explanation or defense. To be sure, some have suggested that knowing truth is not enough, because it must be changed through political revolution or psychoanalytic trans-ference, but the principle of enlightenment remains. What could it mean to challenge truth?

Basically, to challenge the ideology of truth is not to champion lies, falsify documents, or suppress information; it is to assert the con-structed nature of the human world, to follow Vico in asserting that any meaning that can be gotten from the world is a meaning for some human purpose, and gotten with human tools. Historians do not "find" the truths of past events; they create events from a seamless flow, and invent meanings that produce patterns within that flow. Whether these patterns are, as Nietzsche asked, useful for human life or not is a moral question. It cannot be answered from history alone, but only as a part of a large cultural discourse of which historical understanding is a part, and not apart.

Defenders of "history" against its "enemies" tend to regret the "unhistorical" trend of much recent thought, with its emphasis on the synchronic, its suspicions of historically emplotted explanations, and its ruthless attacks on essentialized terms. But, as Hayden White has pointed out, it is advocating not a rejection of history, but rather *another way* of looking at history, a way that tries to call into question the authoritarian discourse of reality in the interests of some human pro-ject, with which we are free to disagree only after noting that our own opinions themselves may not be based upon *history* but rather on a *cer-tain vision of history.*[28] Every academic field must rest on the unshakable authority of some other discourse that will not be shaken by its own debates. History has served as a source of this bedrock for a long time in our culture; its facts purportedly belonged to an order different from and higher than the interpretations and disputes of literary critics or social scientists. Hence, the anxiety to save history from rhetorical read-ings and their sometimes crooked paths.[29]

This crooked introduction will conclude with a citation from a master rhetorician, Richard Lanham, and a cartoon from the *New Yorker* maga-zine. The cartoon I am thinking of shows two men at a cocktail party, in serious conversation. One says to the other: "My feeling is that while we

---

28. Hayden White, "Historical Pluralism," *Critical Inquiry* 12 (1986), 482.

29. Certainly the learned enemies of rhetoric are many. The distinguished historian of antiquity, M. I. Finley, has presented rhetoric as a *paideia* better done away with, funda-mentally elite in scope and rooted in a social structure controlled by a small minority. In his view, literature cannot deal with all of the human condition or with universal values. See "The Heritage of Isocrates," in *The Use and Abuse of History* (New York, 1975), 211.

should have the deepest respect for reality, we should not let it control our lives." The irony of this statement lies in its unconscious indication of the distance between "reality" and "our lives." This distance, the middle space of interpretation and rhetoric, is another "reality," a reality that calls into question the independence of either the shapeless, but allegedly positive, reality "out there" or the far less tangible reality of mind. For the irony inherent in rhetoric, neither of these realities is supreme.

Lanham believes that the rhetorical understanding of human minds and events is not only a historical phase, to be dated by historians of ideas, but also a " 'rhetorical' reality," which is an unchanging part of the human condition, eternally confronted by the "really real society really out there for realistic fictionists and tough-minded historians." What I have called the "ideology of truth," Lanham calls "Pastoral Humanism," a moral stance based upon the authenticity of the individual and the fear of the anarchy that might lie in a playful, creative approach to reality:

> In Pastoral Humanism, we really do have a central self to be true to, and we really do take part in a serious reality beyond participatory drama. And we do things for real purposes. Our behavior grounds itself in use. In this view, play and game are other names for human pride, at best frills, at worst decadent luxuries. As Pastoral Humanists we like to think of ourself as living a life of sensible use and usefulness. Our pastoralist may be urban and intellectual rather than bucolic and sheepish, but we still strive for a simpler if not a simple life, one that somehow stands closer to what is natural for the species. The historical and theoretical range for this kind of humanism has More's *Utopia* at one end and Veblen's *The Theory of the Leisure Class* at the other.[30]

To read history out of focus, then, in a crooked way that promotes human ways of knowing, at least provisionally, to the status of the "primary sources" of our understanding of the past is perhaps a sign of the "deepest respect for reality," a respect that playfully insists that even reality (the notion of which is always a construction for a purpose) should not control our lives, which must remain in the awkward crookedness of unending examination, re-emplotting, and re-interpretation. Getting the story straight, after all, is what we must do only in order to turn it about and see it another way.

30. Richard Lanham, "The Rhetorical Paideia: The Curriculum as a Work of Art," *College English* 48:2 (1986), 138.

2 TIME OUT

THE DISCONTINUITY OF

HISTORICAL CONSCIOUSNESS

I

In Orson Welles's classic film *Citizen Kane* (1941), a key problem of historical knowledge is dramatically posed. An enigmatic and controversial man, Charles Foster Kane, has died in the grandiose, gothic seclusion of his unfinished palace, Xanadu; his dying word is "Rosebud." A journalist, facing the inadequacy of the official facts of Kane's life, begins a rigorous quest for the key to the code of its meaning. He seeks to identify "Rosebud" through a series of interviews and investigations in unpublished sources, carrying out the kind of work familiar to most practicing historians. Yet the sources do not speak. Kane's wife, colleagues, servants, know nothing of "Rosebud," although they create an increasingly consistent picture of a man obsessed by a compulsion to manipulate the masses, to purchase or coerce affection, and to treat people as means rather than as ends. All the sources implicitly agree that Kane never revealed the seat of his power, the center of his mind. His enigma increased with the size of his pretensions; as his monuments to himself accumulate, as the documents of his life proliferate, the meaning becomes as spectral as Welles's photographic treatment of Xanadu.

The final scene of the film takes place amidst the vast collection of objects amassed by Kane, a collection of never-uncrated *objets d'art* and never-discarded personal possessions. The journalist-researcher, having exhausted these sources, retires from the scene in defeat, sealing Kane's mystery. Surveying the enormous expanse of objects from Kane's acquisitive life, the camera indifferently records the evidence, hovering closer and closer to the objects themselves. These objects, the sources, the texts of Kane's life, do not speak from the gloom. Soon we see workmen burning the worthless items; they toss a small, crude sled into the fire. With loving attention, Welles's camera documents the bubbly evaporation, then flaming consumption, of the insignia on the sled—the insignia that says "Rosebud."

The familiarity of *Citizen Kane* and the gimmicky aspect of its conclusion and "message" should not blind us to its abiding relevance for historians. The tragedy of Kane is subsumed in the Sisyphian dilemma of historical research. The meaning of Kane's life, which was as unrecoverable to him as the youth symbolized by his Rosebud sled, is lost also to the world. The historian—who, like the Greek tragedian, often performs the task of converting private catastrophe into triumph, or at least instruction, for humanity—is helpless when confronting Kane's life. Of course, this helplessness is not effective in stilling the voice of reporters or historians; this voice will continue to speak, but will elicit the response often expressed by readers of scholarly biographies: that the massive documentation does not present or suggest a full man, that the sum of the parts does not create a whole, that something (a Rosebud-like *je ne sais quoi*) is missing. Seen in this light, the import of *Citizen Kane* resembles that of Wittgenstein's *Tractatus Logico-Philosophicus* (1922): "that all that really matters in human life is precisely what, in his [Wittgenstein's] view, we must be silent about."[1] Historians, however, are not mystics, and usually fail to appreciate the eloquence of silence. Whether from traditionalism or from intellectual courage, the historian will agree with Bertrand Russell that this philosophy "seems to have grown tired of serious thinking and to have invented a doctrine which would make such an activity unnecessary. I do not for one moment believe that the doctrine which has these lazy consequences is true. . . ."[2]

Whether the "doctrine" is "true" or not, the problem posed is a serious one, perhaps the most serious one faced by history as a mode of thought. While the matter of available evidence, its types and uses, has often been discussed in the long series of historians' handbooks, the negative side of the issue, unavailable or nonexistent information, has been relatively ignored. John Lange has cited the difficulty of locating theoretical discussions of the argument from silence, the historical argument that *"does not rely* on evidence statements."[3] Yet without a

1. Allan Janik and Stephen Toulmin, *Wittgenstein's Vienna* (New York, 1973), 191.
2. Bertrand Russell, quoted in E. Gellner, *Words and Things* (London, 1968), 5.
3. John Lange, "The Argument from Silence," *History and Theory* 5 (1966), 288.

constant awareness of this issue, much historical literature resembles a lipogram, a piece of writing in which the author rejects all words containing a certain letter.[4] The psychological reaction of an *unwarned* reader encountering a lipogram is a vague uneasiness, the sense that something inexplicable is wrong; it is the same kind of feeling that Kafka's "K" had in *The Castle* and *The Trial*. Kafka creates a sense of a lipogrammatic absence at the center of events, which is systematically obscured from his protagonist; the hero's attempts to explain the mysterious happenings fail. His world, it seems, is not functioning according to expected rules, not playing with a full deck. The journalist in *Citizen Kane* at least knew that he lacked the mystery of "Rosebud"—he knew he was dealing with a sort of lipogram.

The problem of information, however, is rarely so simple or clear as in the movies. Historians often—one is tempted to say always—do not know exactly what they do not know. Remains of past phenomena do not present a continuous façade; at a most basic level, that of information, the appearance of the past is clearly discontinuous. The documentary *sources* from which history is written in no way imitate the lived, experienced, "real" form of the past itself, if we may speak of such a thing, for the form of the past depends on the text of written history, its continuity depends on the continuity of accounts, its substance depends on the linguistic substance embodied by the historical imagination.

Possible responses to the problem of lost information are four; they range from a pragmatic disregard for the problem to a specific study of unavailable evidence. Most historians evince, at one time or other, all of the following reactions in an unselfconscious way, and tend to shift attitudes as the situation demands. First, the most common attitude is to ignore the problem, to organize existing information into as seamless a web as possible, and to assume what a literary critic would call the role of "omniscient narrator." The advantages of this pose are several: the narrative flow is unbroken by assertions of ignorance, the pose of historian-as-storyteller is maintained, and the rhetorical force of the historian's account is boosted by this show of confidence. It has become a convention; and the reader questions the historian's ability to under-

---

4. The *Oxford English Dictionary* cites Tryphiodorus, who was said to have written a lipogrammatic *Odyssey*, in which the letter *sigma* did not appear. A more recent example is E. V. Wright's 1939 novel *Gadsby*, a full-length work using no word that contains the letter "e."

stand the minds and actions of his protagonists no more than he does that of the novelist. The novelist, however, has created his world, while the historian has not, or at least not in quite the same sense. When a fictional narrator expresses ignorance or confusion as to what motivates a character, we know that this ignorance too is knowledge in the text, and that nothing outside the text can remedy it; but for the historical narrator, there are other options.

Sooner or later, a point is reached in which the normal historical convention of eliding the unknown becomes excessively awkward, and a clear hiatus appears. The loss of a key cable during a period of sensitive diplomacy, an obscure uprising by unlettered peasants, a few unrecorded years in the life of a character, or some similar problem arises; and the historian, unable to ignore it, adopts a second stratagem—that of the irritated apology. In at least this one area, the historical narrator implies, one must proceed with caution. The path is here uncharted, the syntax broken. If enough of these hiatuses appear in the evidence, a third response may be required, that of skepticism. A historian's skepticism involves stepping outside the role of omniscient narrator in order to underline the hypothetical nature of a particular explanatory assertion. This new pose may not be long maintained, for there is the risk of implying that the whole work is a fabric of speculation. This "mitigated skepticism" is often coupled with a precise identification of the existing information, or with a hopeful prediction that future work in a given area will till the field where the needed knowledge lies. The irritated apology also adds rhetorical reinforcement to the structure of the total work by pointing, negatively, to the greater certainty of the whole; the gap in the documentation serves as a sort of enfolded margin that defines the outlines of what is there, an outside that creates the inside.

A fourth response to the problem of missing information remains: a study of the types of nonavailable information and the structure of its effective loss or destruction. This sort of study benefits historians in a number of ways by seeking to define the selective rules by which information is lost or destroyed and thus to discover the structure of available information. Because the more remote past offers a more fragmented image of itself than do later ages, those who deal with that farther past—archaeologists, ancient and medieval historians—have had to employ the latter response more frequently and more seriously than historians of modern times. The problem, in a theoretical sense, is common to all.

The Other Sources: History and Language

George Dennis O'Brien has pointed out that Hegel, while recognizing that great quantities of human events have been lost to our knowledge, refuses to recognize this loss as a loss of history. Thus Hegel writes: "The periods, whether we suppose them to be centuries or millennia, which peoples have passed before the writing of history, may have been filled with revolutions, migrations, the wildest transformations. Yet, they are without objective history because they lack subjective history, records of history. Such records are lacking not because they have accidentally disappeared through the long ages, but because they never could have existed."[5] Those events which have "histories" are historical; those that are not recorded are not historical events. History, in short, is a "designated subset of human actions."[6] But the subset, whose secure existence is clearly important to Hegel's system, proves itself unstable and variable. Hegel himself writes of Shi-hoang-ti, the Chinese emperor who built the Great Wall and who "made himself especially remarkable by his attacks on the old literature, especially on the historical books and historical studies generally."[7] The obscurantist attacks of Shi-hoang-ti represent an assault on the integrity of the stability of Hegel's "designated subset," but he cleverly saves the appearances. "This Book-burning is a very important circumstance, for in spite of it the strictly canonical books were saved, as is generally the case."[8] Within the previously designated subset, historical events, Hegel has created a new subset, *inessential* information, of which the books burned by Shi-hoang-ti are members. By the optimistic identification of essential information with what has been preserved, Hegel has protected the field of his philosophy of history.

Other philosophers, and more particularly historians themselves, have been a bit less optimistic. Marc Bloch tells of visits from local historians who wished to write village histories. His standard advice to them amounted to an experienced analysis of the structure of information. Because peasant communities rarely maintained archives, Bloch observed, the seigneuries were the best source of information. The fundamental question was therefore: "Who was the seigneur of the village in 1789?" The question admitted three answers: either the seigneur was

5. G. W. F. Hegel, *Reason in History,* trans. R. S. Hartman (Indianapolis, 1953), 75, cited in George Dennis O'Brien, "Does Hegel Have a Philosophy of History?" in *History and Theory* 10 (1971), 298.

6. O'Brien, "Hegel," 299.

7. G. W. F. Hegel *The Philosophy of History,* trans. J. Sibree (New York, 1956), 119.

8. Ibid.

a cleric, or a noble who emigrated, or a noble who did not emigrate. From these possibilities, Bloch pointed to the first as most favorable— the records of the Church were generally better kept—and the last as most problematic, since the documents may be "lost, eaten by rats, or scattered by the caprice of sale or inheritance through the attics of three or four houses on different estates. . . ."[9] Yet, he goes on, the goddess Catastrophe, who had destroyed so much in the guise of the Revolution, does not always take away: "Only the eruption of Vesuvius preserved Pompeii."[10]

W. H. Walsh gives special credit to the positivists of the last century for their influence in encouraging the scrupulous examination, ordering, and publication of historical records, although this conventional attribution slights the contributions of figures like Guizot and the professional records officers and antiquarians.[11] The French historians Langlois and Seignobos, whose *Introduction aux études historiques* is a good indicator of late nineteenth-century academic attitudes, give some attention to the problem of gathering documents. It would not be long, they predicted, before all historical documents would be where they belong, in a few centralized institutions.[12] This optimism is predicated on a narrow concept of historical data as old paper; it also presumes that no basic disagreement exists about what old paper is worth editing, cataloging, and publishing.

Critical and analytical philosophers of history have generally agreed on the documentary tyranny over the past. F. H. Bradley states that "recorded events" are all that exist for critical history. "Failing to be thus," he writes, "they have failed to be for history, and history can never be for them."[13] Croce elaborates the same idea: "A history without relation to the document would be unverifiable history; and since the reality of history lies in its verifiability, and the narrative in which it is given concrete form is historical narrative only in so far as it is a *critical exposition of the document* (intuition and reflection, consciousness and

9. Marc Bloch, *The Historian's Craft*, trans. Peter Putnam (New York, 1961), 72–73.
10. Ibid., 73.
11. W. H. Walsh, *The Philosophy of History* (New York, 1960), 157. On the development of the archival professions, and the marginalization of antiquarians and archivists by the new historical profession, see Philippa Levine, *The Amateur and the Professional: Antiquarians, Historians and Archaeologists in Victorian England, 1838–1886* (Cambridge, 1986).
12. Ch. V. Langlois and Ch. Seignobos, *Introduction aux études historiques*, 4th ed. (Paris, n.d.), 3–10.
13. F. H. Bradley, *The Presuppositions of Critical History*, ed. Lionel Rubinoff (Chicago, 1968), 89.

auto-consciousness, etc.), a history of that sort, being without meaning and without truth, would be inexistent as history."[14] Bloch adds to this line of thought: "Explorers of the past are never quite free. The past is their tyrant. It forbids them to know anything which it has not itself . . . yielded."[15] Yet Bloch also says that the past will not be changed in the future.[16] This creates a self-contradiction that tends to afflict this style of thought. If the past really exists only through documentation, and if documentation itself has a history, the real past must be assumed to change. The critical tradition of historiography stresses that the past exists only in its documentation, and that positive knowledge of the past must be positive knowledge of the sources. The idea of "a history without relation to the document" is metaphysical and hence objectionable. If, at date a, a past X amounts to a set of sources Y, then $Xa=[Y]$. At a later date b, the sources that make up X have changed; some sources p have been destroyed or lost, some sources q have been discovered or reconstituted. Thus, $Xb = [Y - p + q]$. Missing information constitutes a null set, which is a subset of every other set, although it has no members. And, as the mathematician Martin Gardner has pointed out, "The null set denotes, even though it does not denote anything."[17] My point in these simple formulas is that the past has become a variable, itself changing in time, although such a premise is not explicitly admitted. The problem may be one of semantics, the "past" may be different from "history"; but if history is our only knowledge of the past, it becomes difficult to grant the distinction.

Indeed, the analytic philosophy of history, dealing principally with history as narrative, manages to avoid the matter by design; its problems are simply different. Arthur Danto begins his book on the subject with the hypothetical supposition that all historical gaps are filled; his approach deals with the possibility of making true statements concerning *any* set of information, however complete, about the past.[18] Michael Oakeshott summarizes the attitude of this tradition: "It is a presupposition of history that every event is related and that every change is but a

14. Benedetto Croce, "History and Chronicle," in *The Philosophy of History in Our Time*, ed. Hans Meyerhoff (Garden City, N.Y., 1959), 47.

15. Bloch, *The Historian's Craft*, 59.

16. Ibid., 58.

17. Martin Gardner, "How the Absence of Anything Leads to Thoughts of Nothing," *Scientific American*, Feb. 1975, 98.

18. Arthur C. Danto, *Analytical Philosophy of History* (Cambridge, 1965), 2, 27.

moment in a world which contains no absolute *hiatus*."[19] However, the presupposition of a lack of hiatus is only a fictional convention, adopted to eliminate the disorderly nature of historical evidence. The situation of historical sources is clearly otherwise.

II

Before considering other aspects of what is nonexistent but essential, we must first confront the proposition that the problem is peculiar to historical knowledge and is a reflection of its fundamentally flawed character *as knowledge*. This argument states that because historians cannot generate their own information (unlike sociologists, historians cannot normally conduct polls or surveys) or strive for repeatability as an aid in verification like the laboratory scientist, they deal with a peculiarly intangible world governed by a peculiarly intangible form of explanatory logic.

A more forceful argument against the real integrity of historical consciousness would run somewhat as follows: history, which purportedly deals with all the phenomena of human consciousness in such a way as to lend them meaning and apparent direction, cannot in fact duplicate individual consciousness, which is continuous in its effective operation and rationally realistic in its depiction of the world of phenomena.[20] To put it in other words, this thesis states that the implicit governing metaphor of history must be that of individual consciousness itself and that by this standard, history reveals itself to be inadequate. The pane of consciousness cannot be imitated by the distorted and fragmented lens of history, or can it?

Much discussion of the nature of historical thought has centered, whether explicitly or implicitly, upon the proffered choices of art and science as models. This discussion is partly vitiated by the antiquated notions of both art and science held by the defenders of history, a problem that Hayden White has pinned to the nineteenth-century flowering of historical creativity. He writes: "In sum, when historians claim that history is a combination of science and art, they generally mean that it is

19. Michael Oakeshott, "Historical Continuity and Causal Analysis," in *Philosophical Analysis and History*, ed. W. H. Dray (New York, 1966), 209.

20. As Locke wrote of man's conscious powers: "God has not been so sparing to men to make them barely two-legged creatures, and left it to Aristotle to make them rational."

a combination of *late nineteenth-century* social science and *mid-nine-teenth-century* art."[21] Although White has exposed the vapidity of these disputes and their results, perhaps there is a deeper problem. Perhaps the problem is not whether history is best conceived of as an art, a science, or both, or neither, but whether art or science or something else is the most adequate representational model for historical consciousness. If individual human consciousness itself, especially in its cognitive aspects, were taken as the model rather than some epiphenomenal symbolic form like art or science, the art-or-science disputes might in fact be seen as hiding the central matter from scrutiny. I believe that this is the case. White's point that historians shrink from artistic or scientific innovations made since the age of Thackeray or Weber is thoroughly applicable to the deeper metaphor of consciousness. The image of individual consciousness, whether seen from the aspect of classical psychoanalysis, of behavioral psychology, or of physiology, has been radically altered since the mid-nineteenth century. With agreeable consistency these three sciences concur that consciousness itself shares with historical thought the problems of disjunctiveness, interference, and destruction of information, as well as simple forgetfulness and fatigue. A survey of three parallel models of consciousness follows.

In *Beyond the Pleasure Principle*, Freud develops the idea that organisms are more concerned to avoid stimuli than to receive them. The sense organs therefore

> consist essentially of apparatus for the reception of certain specific effects of stimulation, but . . . also include special arrangement for further protection against excessive amounts of stimulation and for excluding unsuitable kinds of stimuli. It is characteristic of them that they deal with only very small quantities of external stimulation and only take in *samples* of the external world. They may perhaps be compared with feelers which are all the time making tentative advances toward the external world and then drawing back from it.[22]

21. Hayden V. White, "The Burden of History," *History and Theory* 5:2 (1966), 127, collected in *Tropics of Discourse: Essays in Cultural Criticism* (Baltimore and London, 1978).

22. Sigmund Freud, *Beyond the Pleasure Principle*, trans. J. Strachey (New York, 1959), 53–54. Perhaps this passage was in R. D. Laing's mind when he wrote, on the subject of family histories: "It is naive to think one discovers a situation by taking a 'history' from one or two parties. But such a 'history' of the situation is a *sample of the situation*. What one does when 'taking a history' is not primarily to *discover history*. One uncovers a story, that is, one person's way of defining the situation; this way of defining the situation may

This passage implies that only "excessive amounts of stimulation" are excluded by the sense organs. If this were so, the sense organs could be described as a sort of potentiometer, which regulates, for example, sound volume without seriously altering the essential contours of the sound. Freud, however, uses the metaphors "feelers" and "samples" to describe something quite different from the image of a volume-regulator. One would not speak of listening to a musical recording, even at a level of volume different from that at which it was recorded, as taking a "sample" of the work.

Freud did not mean, however, that only "excessive amounts of stimulation" are prevented from passing through the sense organs. If his own metaphors cited above do not clarify his meaning, his article "A Note Upon the 'Mystic Writing Pad'" does. This brief article develops one of the boldest and most illuminating metaphors in modern literature—the detailed comparison of the human sensory and mnemonic systems to a child's toy. Amplifying what he had only hinted at in *Beyond the Pleasure Principle,* Freud expresses his idea more explicitly.

> My theory was that cathectic innervations are sent out and withdrawn in rapid periodic impulses from within into the completely pervious system Pcpt.-Cs. So long as that system is cathected in this manner, it receives perceptions (which are accompanied by consciousness) and passes the excitation on to the unconscious mnemonic systems; but as soon as the cathexis is withdrawn, consciousness is extinguished and the functions of the system come to a standstill. . . . I further had a suspicion that this discontinuous method of functioning of the system Pcpt.-Cs. lies at the bottom of the origin of the concept of time.[23]

In other words, Freud maintains, consciousness is not at all continuous, but seems to involve a pulsing activity; perhaps if he had been writing a few decades later, he might have used radar or sonar systems as metaphoric models.

---

an important part of the situation *we* are trying to discover. Nor do dates make history. Dates are discontinuous markers left behind by history: dates are made by history" (*Politics of the Family* [New York, 1971], 33–34). Laing, in maintaining that there exists a "situation" waiting to be "discovered" by the analyst-as-historian, shares Freud's anxieties about analytical control, discussed below in Chapter 10.

23. Sigmund Freud, "A Note Upon the 'Mystic Writing Pad,'" in *General Psychological Theory,* ed. P. Rieff (New York, 1963), 211–12. The abbreviation "Pcpt.-Cs." is Freud's usual symbol for the system of perception and consciousness.

The Other Sources: History and Language

The models of physical consciousness suggested by Freud in the 1920s are not canonical psychoanalysis; he himself wrote that his ideas were "speculation, often far-fetched speculation, which the reader will consider or dismiss according to his individual predilections."[24] I have discussed them here because they are not as well known as the more mentalistic Freud and because they have proven strikingly prescient of later physiological and psychological developments. The theme presented by these passages is the discontinuity of consciousness and the role of the sensory system in *defending* against the transmission of information. If these speculations about consciousness are not admitted into modern psychoanalytic theory except as marginal works of the master, the notion of defense against knowledge, especially against self-knowledge, certainly is. By 1894, in his article "The Defense of Neuro-Psychoses," Freud was developing his idea that disease, especially hysteria, was a mental defense against a mental stimulus, or memory. The distortion, condensation, overdetermination, displacement, and interruptions in dreams are the most widely known aspects of the mind's resistance to certain types of stimulation. Because they deal with information that has already passed through the sensory system, these types of dream-work are not directly applicable to the models of consciousness presented here; but the kinds of distortive, defensive mental work that they perform are as relevant as they are familiar. And Freud's idea that consciousness may be neither continuous nor comprehensive in its intake and recording of information has found recent support from physiology, support that attempts to comprehend systematically this loss of information.

Physiologists specializing in cellular communication have suggested that what we call "consciousness" consists as much in the destruction of information as in its transmission. In the case of neurons, nerve cells, in particular, the transmission of electrochemical impulses, which is not continuous but must wait until the requisite charge has built up, corresponds remarkably to Freud's intuitive suggestions. However, at each gap, or synapse, between the nerve cells, certain impulses fail to be transmitted, depending on the chemical content of the transmitting cell. Thus, the frequency with which impulses arise in a postsynaptic cell reflects an on-going summary of information rather than a continuous reporting.[25]

The nervous system may be divided into three parts: a sensor, or

24. Freud, *Beyond the Pleasure Principle*, 47.
25. G. S. Stent, "Cellular Communication," *Scientific American* 227 (Sept. 1972), 46–47.

input, subsystem; an effector, or output, subsystem; and an internuncial section known as the brain. In the higher mammals the brain dominates the production of consciousness; as is true of the sensory neurons
described above, much of the work of the brain consists of information
destruction. "The processing of data by the internuncial part consists in
the main in making an abstraction of the vast amount of data continuously gathered by the sensory part. This abstraction is the result of a
selective destruction of portions of the input data in order to transform
these data into manageable categories that are meaningful to the animal."[26]

An important example of this abstractive process and of its consequences is found in the visual pathway of the higher mammals. In the
eye itself a process of abstraction creates "meaningful relative contrast
data," which are transmitted to the brain; in the visual cortex of the
brain, the cortical neurons have their own system of responsiveness,
which eliminates light stimuli that do not correspond to a straight-line
perspective. As a result, we "see" in terms of Euclidean, straight-line
geometry. If evolution had given us a different mental program with
which to create consciousness, geometries of concave or convex sur-
faces might seem more "natural" than plane geometry.[27]

The notion that a program, a set of innate ideas, exists in the nervous
system of an organism contradicts the Lockean mainstream of psychological thought since the late seventeenth century. Yet we are told that
"each transformation step [in the mind] involves the selective destruction of information, according to a program that preexists in the
brain."[28] At this point, certain structuralist models of knowledge
become relevant, and the physiologist lends support to structuralism's
antipositivist attitudes. It is interesting to note, however, that the first
explicit attempt at a structural model of physiology is that of Ludwig
von Bertalanffy, whose work was inspired by the psychological theory
of *Gestalten* or perceptive structures defined in a cognitive, non-
physiological sense.[29] Fundamentally, what has happened is that physicochemical models have supplemented the "specific biological
notions" used in Bertalanffy's work.[30]

This coalescence of biological, physicochemical, and structuralist

26. Ibid., 45–46.
27. Ibid., 51.
28. Ibid., 50–51.
29. Jean Piaget, *Le Structuralisme* (Paris, 1968), 41.
30. Ludwig von Bertalanffy, *Modern Theories of Development*, trans. J. H. Woodger (New
York, 1962), 180.

ideas is experimentally supported by the work of behavioral psychologists, who furthermore have adopted a model from the area of technology to describe and direct their own work. Information theory, which describes a universal communication system, was proposed by Claude E. Shannon in his famous paper of 1948, "The Mathematical Theory of Communication."[31] That information theory has not been widely applied to the survival of historical evidence—and could be—is not my point here. It has, however, become a directing model for behaviorists studying human consciousness, especially in the area of hearing.

The crucial position of hearing in human development is often underrated by our visually oriented age. However, as D. E. Broadbent has pointed out: "Although a brain which can listen to speech can usually also read it, it is the ear which is primary in the development of language and written alphabets are secondary."[32] The fundamental problems of speech and auditory perception are selective listening, potential capabilities, the effects of noise interference and the ability to filter it, the nature of extinction of stimuli, and the possibility of performing two auditory tasks simultaneously—problems with relevance by analogy to the role of the historian as listener to the past. Like the physiologists, the psychologists have found that discarded information is not discarded altogether at random.[33] To cite only one aspect of the problem, that of auditory discrimination: "It may be desirable to think of the stimuli used in any experiment as having positions in an 'information space' made up of all the dimensions discriminable by the sense-organs. Discrimination takes a shorter time when they are farther apart as well as when they are fewer in number."[34] The problem of reaction time here becomes a limiting factor in the quantitative possibilities of perception; and the nature of the stimuli or their disposition in "information space" affects reaction-time and perception. The possibilities of knowing are thus partly shaped by the disposition of the objects of knowledge.

Not only factors external to the organism, such as position in "information space" (which is a mental construct itself), govern the destruction of auditory information. Selective attention serves the purpose of

31. *Bell System Technical Journal* (July–Oct. 1948). The link between information theory and structuralist thought was the problem of machine translation and its adaptability to syntax. Cf. Noam Chomsky, *Syntactic Structures* (The Hague, 1963).

32. D. E. Broadbent, *Perception and Communication* (London, 1958), 3.

33. Ibid., 35.

34. Ibid., 78.

filtering out information irrelevant to the task at hand, whether this information is noise or is related to some other task. Because time is often required to ascertain whether information is or is not relevant, two separate information storage systems are supposed to exist: a short-term store of limited time span and a long-term store, which is the "memory." At each step of the information system, stimuli are competing to pass further; novel stimuli, those which have not recently passed through a filter, are more likely to succeed; and the filter will also probably show a bias toward stimuli of great intensity and high frequency.[35] When two stimuli have been selected one after the other, the probability of the second signal following the first may remain in the long-term storage; this memory has been suggested as the origin of human induction.[36] As stimuli are repeatedly presented, their order of priority will tend to be reversed, since the previously favored novel stimulus will have lost its novel status. Confusion at this point may lead to the kind of error reported by Bruner and Postman in which experimental subjects identified anomalous playing cards (a red six of spades and a black four of hearts) as though they were normal.[37] Black must become red or spades hearts so that the structure of expectations can have its way, at least for a while.

Information theory and the structural models it has lent to psychology have enabled psychologists to analyze and estimate the probability of perceptual failures and information loss. Other models, such as the paradigmatic approach of Bruner and Postman or the classic stimulus-response analysis, may reveal the same results in different conceptual form. My point is that *consciousness involves information destruction as a primary characteristic and that this destruction can be analyzed.*

The purpose of this discussion of the psychoanalytical, physiological, and psychological views of consciousness has been to underline resemblances between individual human consciousness and historical knowledge. Both share the problems of loss of information,

35. F. R. Ankersmit has suggested that the reception and discrimination of historical works function in a similar manner. Repetition of information found in other works is ignored, while what is novel and unique is recognized as the defining quality of a history. Only the existence of competing views makes possible the perception of any view of the past at all. See F. R. Ankersmit, *Narrative Logic: A Semantic Analysis of the Historian's Language* (The Hague, 1983), esp. chap. 8.

36. Broadbent, *Perception and Communication*, 191, 194.

37. Jerome S. Bruner and Leo Postman, "On the Perception of Incongruity: A Paradigm," *Journal of Personality* 18 (1949), 206–23, cited in Thomas S. Kuhn, *The Structure of Scientific Revolutions* (Chicago, 1962).

whether from selective destruction, lack of perception, or some mechanical failure in the storage system. If we accept or at least consider the proposition made above, that consciousness rather than some symbolic form of it is the model for formal knowledge, then the very flaws in the fabric of historical consciousness might be the outward signs of some hitherto unperceived inward grace. Realization of the "all-too-human" character of historical thought must not be confused, however, with the contention that history is only "common sense"; for it is precisely this common sense that has given to consciousness the aura of pure receptivity that I have tried to explode. Larry Shiner has appealed for "a phenomenological approach to historical knowledge," which in his view "is not simply the description of the way consciousness grasps a certain structure of the world but is at the same time the way in which this structure grasps consciousness."[38] The models presented above may help to further this project.

One vital distinction must be made between the sciences of consciousness discussed above and history viewed metaphorically as a kind of perceptual study of the consciousness; that distinction is the systematic, structural nature of the analysis of information loss and destruction. Yet who would deny that historians exhibit "selective attention," that novel stimuli attract attention that repeated ones do not, or that certain information may be masked by noise—a plethora of intense but irrelevant stimuli? This kind of structured filtering of available stimuli is the essence of historical thought. Unavailable information seems to be a separate problem, but an attempt at a description of this kind of information may reveal that it too has a structure.

III

There is no history without sources. Yet the traditional definition of sources as the documents and monuments surviving from the past, often conventionally compared to human memory, evokes a distinct problem, a problem that also appears when we examine various descriptions of human consciousness. In each case, destruction of information is an essential part of the process. For the most part, this mental suppression of information enables the subject to make a cer-

---

38. Larry Shiner, "A Phenomenological Approach to Historical Knowledge," *History and Theory* 8 (1969), 268.

tain kind of sense of experience—human sense. Sometimes destruction of historical information has the same effect, or so it would seem.

Methodologically, we might look upon the "past" (that is to say, all signs that remain from the past) pragmatically, as a complex of evidence whose goal is survival. Like organisms, the culture can hope for survival only through descendants, so it must transmit its cultural genes to the future through germ cells; and the germ cells of a culture are precisely what historians consider evidence. To rephrase the proposition, cultures exist for the purpose of leaving documents of one sort or another for historians; every datum then faces a Darwinian struggle. Effectively, the very assumption by some historians that the past can be reconstructed through the use of surviving documents implies a tacit assumption of the "survival of the fittest," at least in the same sense that the cognitive information that survives the structured destruction in our sensory systems seems to be the information fittest to survive.

Before a structural exploration of information availability is possible, some kind of phenomenology must be devised. What follows is an attempt at such a phenomenology of unavailable, unrecovered, and unimagined information; it presumes a pure, "vanilla" type of information (not discriminating between texts, ruins, crop patterns, etc.) and does not attempt to categorize factors of availability determined by the nature of the information itself. For example, a document in *Die grosse Politik* or the Vatican archives exists and is available, but must be found; information from published trade statistics exists and is available, but must be gathered and abstracted; the works of Nietzsche exist and are available, but discerning their meaning is no mechanical procedure. Surely, different types of information are involved in these three examples. Information theory, however, has dealt with disparity in the types of information by reducing all information to "bits"—simple, mathematical dualisms. While this permits the bulk processing of information by efficient processors such as computers, it also severely limits the kind of thing that may be said. This is the reverse of my goal.

My purpose is bifocal. First, I would like to point out the kind of knowledge and observation that could create structural principles about the survival of historical information; the following outline is intended as a guide, however primitive. In addition to this aim, the following discussion attempts to integrate and categorize a particular kind of historical creation that cannot be fitted within the categories of critical, positivist history, but that poses useful questions about such history.

The Other Sources: History and Language

By far the greatest amount of information about the past was *unrecorded*. Some will agree with Hegel that it is pragmatically inapt even to grant existence to such events. However, because we experience the loss of such unrecorded information in our own consciousness, because we often deduce the existence of such information from such commonplace working presuppositions as the continuity of space and time, and because we intuit that there was more to the past than what we know, this category must be taken seriously. Berkeley himself would not suggest that Shakespeare ceased to exist during the undocumented years of his life. Within this category, two kinds of information exist: nonverbal information, the sort of thing that an observer would have seen (an obscure death, a blighted harvest, a canal or road long vanished); and verbal information, which an observer would have heard. In the latter type, unrecorded conversations and speeches are customarily of special interest to historians.

A second category of historical information is that which is *recorded but destroyed*. In other words, this information has succumbed to a secondary historical event besides the one of which it is itself a record; the secondary event destroyed either part or all of the record. Some documents are destroyed by nature, without human agency. Disintegration, earthquakes, floods, and the depredations of time in general account for an enormous loss. The quality of the recording vehicle is also a factor here, as is the quality of human maintenance, if any. Men have also destroyed much information by design. Some of this destruction is simply the destruction of no-longer-useful information such as old business files, personal letters, and waste paper. However, information is often destroyed by design to protect the agent of its destruction. Not all such destruction is as sinister as the alleged erasures of the Watergate tapes; Johannes Brahms had a custom each New Year's Day of burning all of his work from the past year that he considered unworthy of him. Still other information has been destroyed without design. The "Rosebud" sled mentioned at the beginning of the chapter, for example, was destroyed by design as a worthless relic; it was destroyed without design as a piece of historical information. The Hôtel de Ville in Paris, which was destroyed in 1871, held considerable quantities of public documents and private papers; the building was destroyed by human agency during the fall of the Commune, but without the necessary design of destroying its contents as information.

Information that exists but is *unfound* constitutes a third category of historical information. Unworked archives provide a clear example of information sources whose existence as available information is known but unrecovered as such. Another kind of information is that which is known but unlocated. This type is particularly tenuous, because a given item may in fact have been destroyed. Information that is known but unrecovered has an established location, but the unlocated variety is assumed to be lost. Literary periodicals regularly feature requests from biographers seeking the scattered correspondence of a certain individual—what they are seeking is known in a general way (for example, letters written by Somerset Maugham), but unlocated. Yet another sort of information under this third rubric is that which is unknown and unlocated. Effectively, this information resembles the unrecorded and destroyed information of the first two categories; it differs, however, in the important aspect of its potential recoverability. Although popular wisdom has it that "what you don't know won't hurt you," one of history's traditional tasks has been to eradicate this unlocated and unrecovered information as such.

The fourth category, information *nonexistent in time and space,* may appear puzzling to both the historian and the analytic philosopher of history. However, if new and creative treatments of the past are to be conceivable, speculative information must be granted existence and must be subjected to analysis and use. This category would include an imaginary encounter between Tamerlane and Joan of Arc, an event made impossible by *spatial* separation. A dialogue between Giambattista Vico and James Joyce, which is a temporal impossibility, has recently been created and will be discussed below. Although such creations have a faintly humorous ring to them because of their incongruity with conventional notions of linear space and time, they are authentic creations of one type of historical imagination; to exclude them from any consideration as products of valid historical thought is to limit and perhaps to desiccate future thought about the past. I shall return to this matter, for it involves important considerations regarding the relation of historical literatures to other literatures.

The fifth category, information *not imaginable,* may seem frivolous or even absurd, but this is not the case. Although it is difficult to speak of this sort of information, one is obligated to consider it if one accepts the discontinuity of our consciousness of the past. Since future events will provide information about a past that has not yet happened, we may suppose that there will be at least some unimaginable aspect to this information. If we do not admit this possibility, then we shall be guilty of presuming that the future will essentially resemble the past; this pre-

44

The Other Sources: History and Language

sumption of historical thought has been fiercely attacked since Nietzsche as fundamentally antilife.

Bloch's advice to the local historians about the *probability* of locating sources in various places is the kind of knowledge that could define the structure of historical information. If, for example, a period of violent revolutionary activity has half-destroyed, half-fossilized the historical records of a comparatively peaceful century preceding, then a future is effectively altering a past in a way more fundamental than mere reinterpretation. Not only what exists, but why and how it exists, must be asked. This approach, which is already familiar to historians, would strive to map the first three categories of unavailable knowledge.

Another more speculative approach to the structure of missing information involves the description and analysis of possibilities.[39] Alternative constructions with quite different consequences may be formulated from alternative possible pieces of information. An example from the area of cultural history may illustrate the situation. The Canadian pianist Glenn Gould identified a particularly interesting consequence of the loss of certain information in what he calls the "van Meegeren syndrome." Han van Meegeren was the remarkable Dutch art forger who produced "Vermeers" with such aesthetic skill and scientific awareness that his paintings were consistently authenticated by experts up to the time they landed their creator in prison. The van Meegeren syndrome concerns the problem of evaluating works of art on the basis of available information. To illustrate this problem, Gould asks that we imagine the discovery of a Haydnesque piece of music (forged). As long as the fraud was maintained, the piece would be accepted at par value, "at Haydn's value." If, however, one alleged that it was the work of the young Felix Mendelssohn, the value of the piece would decline. Conversely, attribute it to Vivaldi, living over a generation before the stylistic date of the piece, and you have a "landmark in musical composition"—unless the fraud is somehow discovered, in which case the work is worthless and its creator indictable or at least ridiculous.[40]

The consequences of the van Meegeren syndrome need not apply only to forgeries. If a work of art bearing no signature was found in some archive, monastery, or castle, the vagaries of reputation described above are equally conceivable, as scholars, using their various modes of

39. Cf. Lange, "Argument from Silence."
40. Glenn Gould, "The Prospects of Recording," *High Fidelity,* April 1966, 54–55.

analysis, compete to defend differing attributions of the piece; with each new study the value of the piece could soar or sink. In none of this process has the information in the text itself changed at all, nor has there been a shift in the taste of the audience. Yet the entire valuation of the work depends upon one piece of information—in this case, its accurate position in time.

IV

The rhetorical force of historical prose usually depends upon the single solution, the *true* presentation of the past, rather than a presentation of a number of competing versions within a single historical account. Because historical rhetoric is based on an argument from authority in which the evidence broadly construed is supposed to be the authority, the tendency of such rhetoric is to eliminate rather than entertain possibilities. Insofar as creations of a *possible* past have been accomplished, they have been, as a rule, modest attempts to reconstruct familiar, documented situations, using familiar but undocumented details. But a glance at the reconstruction of historical dialogue, to focus on but one example, shows that one can go beyond even the possible past to an impossible one and that the step may not be as large as it seems.

> "If it please you go into your privy chamber," said Wolsey, "we will show you the cause of our coming."
>
> "My lord," she answered, instantly on her guard, "If you have anything to say, speak it openly before all those folks: for I fear nothing ye can say or allege against me, but that I would all the world should both see and hear it."
>
> Wolsey, with a glance at the surrounding women, began to speak in Latin.
>
> "Nay, my lord," she cut him off, "speak to me in English, I beseech you. Although, "—with gentle irony,—" *I* understand Latin."[41]

This confrontation, between Cardinal Wolsey and Catherine of Aragon, took place in July 1529. The dialogue above was written by Garrett Mattingly, whose book *Catherine of Aragon* represents a well-known

---

41. Garrett Mattingly, *Catherine of Aragon* (Boston, 1942), 240.

attempt in English by a professional historian to create history of academic standards and nevertheless to compete with the romantic biographies in a more popular marketplace. In this regard Mattingly himself comments only, "I have tried to restore her figure to something like what her contemporaries saw."[42] To this end he has invented some dialogue (but not much), produced some palpable prose ("Wolsey lay tumbling in his naked bed at York House after a sweaty session at Blackfriars"), organized his story with an eye to dramatic force, and hidden his documentation at the end. As a novelist, Sterne was bolder; so was Dickens. Novelistically, *Catherine of Aragon* is not very novel, but it is a good book.

The author, however, wished to create a Catherine of approximately contemporary stature. That this is not precisely possible no one would dispute, nor that it is the goal of most historical writing. To do so Mattingly must enter into personal discussion with his sources—to face them with his own perceptions and to interpret them in a way that speaks to his readers. "Time," we read, "has spared a little bundle of yellowing letters from Henry to Anne, . . . not very different, either, from the embarrassing revelations so often read out in divorce courts, and breach of promise cases."[43] Accepting the conventions of the form, we do not ask who "Time" is, or why "it" spared the letters; we do not question Mattingly's assumption that a sixteenth-century lady of spirit would speak with "gentle irony" to a political enemy, nor do we evince much surprise that the love letters of men in apparently similar situations should resemble each other across a barrier of four centuries. Mattingly enters his story in order to comment, and the literary conventions he has selected permit it.

Creating historical dialogues has a long past. Thucydides could claim to have heard some of the speeches he reconstructed; the New Testament gospellers, too, probably got some of their evidence at first hand. Boswell's nights were spent getting down what Dr. Johnson had just said. Pepys and Saint-Simon wrote down what everybody said; every room they were in was bugged. The creation of dialogue, whether by Boswell or Mattingly, is judged by standards of verisimilitude. The question is not "Were these words spoken?" but "Could these words have been spoken?" Yet we do not question Mattingly's *own* dialogue with the sources, either; anachronistic dialogue, seen as an explicit or

42. Ibid., not paginated.
43. Ibid., 247.

implicit dialectic between the historian and his texts, is a characteristic convention of historical narrative, and the characteristic conventions of historical narrative, related as they are to the nineteenth-century novel, Mattingly does not violate.

These literary conventions have, however, been violated in the twentieth century, and some historical thought has followed.

"Two books get on top of each other and become sexual."
Two books on top of each other—
John Cage told me that this is geometrically impossible.
But let us try it.
    The book of Doublends Jined.   FW, 20
At least we can try to stuff *Finnegans Wake* into Vico's *New Science.*
    One world burrowing on another.   FW, 275
To make a farce.[44]

Norman O. Brown's *Closing Time,* the aim of which is to try the impossible and to make a farce, is only an extension, although a considerable one, of the dialogue-creating technique essential to historical discourse. But the primary dialogue in *Closing Time* is not between Cardinal Wolsey and Catherine of Aragon, nor even between the historian and his documents, but between Giambattista Vico and James Joyce, or rather between personifications of *The New Science* (1725) and *Finnegans Wake* (1939); it is truly an intercourse of books.

Murray Krieger, in his discussion of poetic and historical creation, has granted the contention that historical forms follow the same literary patterns as other genres.[45] He has, however, refused to grant a total continuity between history and poetry, since he insists on the "difference of materiality." In short, "the very notion of 'evidence'—the notion that such a term is relevant even if difficult to agree upon—suggests a criterion, a need for support, for empirical relevance, that is foreign to the poet in his freer creativity."[46] Nevertheless, the freer creativity attributed to the poet has been infused into historical thought by economists in the form of "counterfactual statements." Such statements, cast in the form of the "if . . . then . . . " proposition, but with

44. N. O. Brown, *Closing Time* (New York, 1973), not paginated.

45. Murray Krieger, "Fiction, History, and Empirical Reality," *Critical Inquiry* 1 (1974), 339. A fuller treatment of the poetic prefiguration of historical writing is Hayden White's *Metahistory: The Historical Imagination in Nineteenth-Century Europe* (Baltimore and London, 1973).

46. Krieger, "Fiction, History, and Empirical Reality," 340.

48

an antecedent that is known to be false, have been defended by George
Murphy on the grounds of heuristic value. Without the use of counterfactuals, he writes, "we shall deprive ourselves of asking some of the
really important questions in economic history."[47] Thus, Robert Fogel
may ask what an American economy without railroads would have produced in 1890 and may construct a model of such a hypothetical economy.[48] The evidence is not "freely created," but the counterfactual
nature of its assemblage is. The result of his model "is not a product of
free imagination," as Murphy puts it; it is, however, a piece of information of the fourth category described above, "nonexistent in time and
space." There were, after all, railroads in 1890.

Michel Foucault has called for precisely this kind of freeing of statements from the "unities of discourse" that seem to enclose them. His
goal, as presented in *The Archaeology of Knowledge,* is "to be able to grasp
other forms of regularity, other types of relations."

> Relations between statements (even if the author is unaware of
> them; even if the statements do not have the same author; even if
> the authors were unaware of each other's existence); relations
> between groups of statements thus established (even if these
> groups do not concern the same, or even adjacent, fields; even if
> they do not possess the same formal level; even if they are not the
> focus of assignable exchanges); relations between statements and
> groups of statements and events of a quite different kind (tech-
> nical, economic, social, political). To reveal in all its purity the
> space in which discursive events are deployed is not to undertake
> to re-establish it in an isolation that nothing could overcome; it is
> not to close it upon itself; it is to leave oneself free to describe the
> interplay of relations within it and outside it.[49]

Although opinion is as divided about Foucault's archaeology as it is
about Fogel's counterfactuals, it would be unwise to dismiss them as
"fictions," or worse.[50] If the traditional dialogue of the historian and his

47. G. G. S. Murphy, "On Counterfactual Propositions," *History and Theory, Beiheft 9:
Studies in Quantitative History and the Logic of the Social Sciences* (1969), 17–18.

48. Cf. Robert Fogel, *Railroads and American Economic Growth: Essays in Econometric
History* (Baltimore, 1964), cited in Murphy, "On Counterfactual Propositions."

49. Michel Foucault, *The Archaeology of Knowledge,* trans. A. S. Smith (New York, 1972),
29.

50. The literature on Foucault as historian is already vast. A good guide is Allan Megill's
"The Reception of Foucault by Historians," *Journal of the History of Ideas* 48:1 (1987), 117–41.
The debate on Foucault is represented by Hayden White, "Foucault Decoded: Notes

sources is a permissible anachronism, we must make theoretical room for other varieties of mismatches and prepare to deal with the results.

In *Closing Time* Vico and Joyce do not converse; their books, in a sense, do. This involves not only a violation of time and space, but also a metonymic personification. The work stands for the man and speaks, but the breath of life has been donated by Brown as reader. *Closing Time* is thus a book created by a reader, not a writer. Lucien Febvre used to quote Fustel de Coulanges: "L'histoire se fait avec les textes,"[51] which may be interpreted as saying that history makes itself from the texts. However, at least since Dilthey and Croce, the notion attributed to Ranke that texts speak for themselves and that the historian is a mere reporter of textual evidence has been rarely defended. In fact, Brown's treatment of his texts is quite respectful of their "materiality"; his obsessive need, expressed in a previous book, *Love's Body,* to acknowledge "indebtedness to a very great company, both living and dead: my authorities, my authors" has led him to permit them to speak in their own words. This style of juxtaposed quotations makes *Closing Time* different from the dialogue-of-the-dead tradition of manufactured conversations as practiced by Lucian, Fontenelle, Santayana, or Peter Gay, although not necessarily more or less "real."

The historical imagination of *Closing Time* uses concepts that at least attempt to escape from time and space; it is only in the imagination that this attempt can be made, but history has always been a kind of imaginary work. Another comment by Lucien Febvre, that "a good book is written in the margins of others," seems to reveal that Brown's thought as reader is orthodox history in at least one sense. If one kind of historical imagination may create an anachronistic dialogue between the historian and his sources, why may not another historical imagination create a dialogue between the sources themselves, striving as Brown does to ensure a maximum autonomy and integrity for the evidence by displaying the reference instead of hiding it, and by rejecting a syntactic style in favor of a paratactic, discontinuous style of juxtaposition? The

---

from Underground," *History and Theory* 12 (1973), 23–54; and George Huppert, "*Divinatio et Eruditio:* Thoughts on Foucault," *History and Theory* 13 (1974), 191–207. It is interesting to note that these two essays differ not so much about Foucault as about what constitute the essential *sources* of history. For White, Foucault's originality and strength come from his use of the *rhetorical* sources, the tropes. (On this, see below, Chapters 8, 9, and 10.) For Huppert, Foucault has failed largely because he has perversely chosen to use the "wrong" *documentary* sources.

51. Cited in Charles Morazé, "Lucien Febvre et l'histoire vivante," *Revue historique* 217 (1956), 5.

structure of the category of historical consciousness that violates time and space is largely unmapped; but when it is more thoroughly charted, if that is possible, works like *Closing Time* may seem a modest attempt to make the sources speak to each other. The dialogue of Joyce and Vico is as genuine as a van Meegeren Vermeer, but establishing the value of either is a problem. If they are seen as expressions of imaginatively recoverable historical knowledge, perhaps the problem and the nineteenth-century Puritanism that created the problem will dissolve.

V

In 1681 a Maurist Benedictine monk named Jean Mabillon published *De re diplomatica,* a work that established the method of criticism and verification of archival documents. Diplomatics, the study of textual criticism, soon became an essential pillar of critical historical method, and Mabillon is consequently recognized as one of the great contributors to modern scientific history. The publication of *On Diplomatics* came in the midst of an important conflict over the veracity of many documents of the early middle ages. The Bollandist Jesuits had begun their mammoth undertaking of publishing the lives of the saints in the Church calendar, and their work was highly critical of the records pertaining to materials of the past. One Bollandist in particular, Daniel Papebroch, had gone so far as to suggest that most of the documents in the archives were spurious or interpolated with anachronistic entries. To counter this extreme skepticism, and to defend the charters on which the wealth and power of the venerable Benedictine order were based, Mabillon, an expert in Merovingian and Carolingian documents, undertook his examination of the archives of France and his exposition of the proper methods of verification of documents.

Mabillon made it clear that, in his opinion, the truthfulness of Merovingian documents was of the highest current import, and that those who would impugn their veracity were involved in dangerous work.

> Therefore, one cannot help seeing how important the treatment of this subject is, for it concerns not only literature and antiquities, but also churches, monasteries, and noblemen as well; in short, the status of one and all is at stake. Consequently, those who strive to diminish, either in whole or in large part the trustworthiness and authority of ancient documents of that kind on

very slight grounds or because of minor difficulties do great harm and damage to the entire commonwealth.[52]

Belief in the historical past, properly construed by critical study, is presented by Mabillon as a moral imperative; history, represented by the documents in archives like the one at Saint Denis, is the foundational origin of institutional power, authority, and property. Mabillon contrasted the "moral" demonstration of authenticity, dependent upon probability and resemblance to previously verified archetypes, with "metaphysical" proofs offering an unattainable certainty.

> Therefore, the only reason I should be required to give for considering genuine the documents and records which I used as examples is that the type of script, the style, and everything else about them clearly indicate that they belong to the ages whose dates they bear. This was not my opinion alone, but also the opinion of those who are most expert in this field. To put it briefly, for deciding questions of this kind one should not require a metaphysical reason or demonstration, but rather a moral one of the kind which can be applied in these matters, and which is no less certain in its own right than a metaphysical demonstration. For these matters, just as in moral matters, we deal with falsehood and error as well as truth. Beyond a doubt moral certitude cannot be acquired without long and constant observation of all the coincidences and circumstances which can lead to attaining the truth. In exactly this way the authenticity or spuriousness of ancient documents can be demonstrated. It is specified by law, and all intelligent judges of these documents agree that a document which cannot be proved spurious by any certain and invincible arguments can be considered authentic and genuine. Many fines have been imposed on those who for no good reason accused an ancient document of spuriousness. Let those who capriciously deny the authenticity of all ancient documents see what others receive as their punishment. No one ever attempted to do this unless he was a complete novice who had no experience at all in antiquities, and who did not understand how useful and necessary such documents are not only to the study of literature but also to the commonwealth.

52. Jean Mabillon, *On Diplomatics (1681): Supplement of 1704*, trans, R. Wertis, in *Historians at Work*, vol. II, ed. P. Gay and V. Wexler (New York, 1972), 165.

IV. Therefore, those who wish to learn the art of criticising ancient documents must consider themselves experts only after careful and thorough preparation. For if it is difficult for someone without experience in this field to give an authoritative judgment about one single document, how much more arduous and dangerous will it be for him to judge all kinds of documents if he does not have as his guide that experience which cannot be acquired without long familiarity with documents of this kind? The liberal arts, the study of finished oratory, and the constant reading of the classical authors are not enough to produce this ability to judge documents; rather, these studies are a great obstacle if the same elegance or purity of diction is expected in those ancient documents. For in rejecting and disputing those documents the student would be guided by his own fancy because he is so familiar with those polished authors. The stylistic niceties of these authors must in some way be unlearned so that the mind may become more accustomed to the vulgar Latin of these documents. And yet those who are so familiar with the classical authors arrogantly claim expertise in judging ancient documents, and they ridicule those who disagree with their judgments. Therefore, the same must be required of those who wish to call themselves experts in diplomatics as Quintilian demanded of children's tutors: "Either they should be completely educated or they should realize their deficiencies."[53]

The argument of this appeal is forensic from the start: the document is, as it were, innocent until proven guilty. "Experts" support this position of pragmatic rather than perfect certitude; indeed, moral certitude may be described only as the product of expertise ("long and constant observation"), although this formula is modified by the subsequent assertion that Mabillon's expert allies are also "intelligent." After this indirect slur on the mental powers of those who question documents irresponsibly, Mabillon strikes a practical note; fines may be levied as well. The historical skeptics are both inexperienced in archival studies and unaware of the great social, political, and personal dangers of questioning the genuineness of documents. Although he has pointed out that the dangers are aesthetic as well as political, because the documents are necessary to the study of literature as well as to the maintenance of the commonwealth, Mabillon proceeds to attack the study of literature as detrimen-

53. Ibid., 170–71.

tal to mastery in his field of diplomatics. The student of rhetoric and the classics must come down to earth, forgetting the excellence of the school models, and facing the vulgar imperfections of historical reality. Mabillon cannot resist ending this argument with a tag from the arch-rhetorician of antiquity, Quintilian.

Mabillon stands here as the philosopher of the *source;* he defends the genuineness of archival documents against skeptics with threats about the collapse of institutions. Anxiety pervades his text, although he never mentions what is not there. What historians in later centuries will call the sources of history, Mabillon, living before the French Revolution, sees as the sources of society, religion, and culture itself. Other sources of historical understanding, sources derived from linguistic studies and rhetoric, are rejected out of hand, although Mabillon's forensic case makes use of them with great skill. These other sources may have their place, but not in the direct apprehension of the document, which he sees as foundational. Mabillon, of course, does not consider what is absent from the archives. If his quest admits that forged documents undermine the authority of institutions of power, he does not note that the presence of a verified document may mask the absence of others that call its claims into question. What is missing is as dangerous as rhetoric is. The point is to defend what is there.

My proposition here has been that historical research resembles the model of human consciousness in that the destruction of information, rather than its transmission, constitutes the major activity of both systems. In the area of consciousness, as elaborated above, certain structures, both known and yet-to-be-described, oversee the destruction of information and shape our conscious perceptions, our "common sense" world. Escaping the pressure of these structures is quite difficult, but the example of nonlinear geometries suggests that the mind can escape its "natural" conceptions and entertain others. It is clear that without this selective destruction of information, consciousness is impossible.

Although it is not normally viewed as such, our knowledge of the past, even at the level of the material sources, is as structured as our knowledge of the phenomenal world. Without falling into a Hegelian optimism about the availability of essential knowledge, we can see that certain descriptive statements about the information from the past can be made; both specific descriptions of material in a small field (e.g., French villages) and general sketches of the history of heuristic serve to illustrate, in a very limited way, this kind of work. The categorization of types of unavailable information attempted here is designed not only to facilitate analysis of the structure of information in various fields, but also to suggest kinds of historical thought that violate the common sense of historical consciousness. The van Meegeren syndrome, counterfactual statements, the archaeology of knowledge, and the work of N. O. Brown are attempts to escape the one-true-solution, space-and-time-bound common sense of history and to hint at a different reality that has been structured out of historical consciousness.

We have, however, no guarantee of our position in the universe, nor of any privileged ability to know it in any ultimately adequate way. Hegel's optimism seems unwarranted in our century; the lines of Ezra Pound ring truer:

> And even I can remember
> A day when the historians left blanks in their writings,
> I mean for things they didn't know.

Historians cannot leave such gaps in normal historical prose. Giving indications of missing evidence of whatever description is by no means the same as representing the essentially fragmented and even arbitrary nature of historical *sources*, defined as the texts from which history is fashioned. In the fashioning, other sources take over, sources derived, not from the evidence, but from the language that purportedly represents the evidence. In fact, it does not represent the evidence at all, scattered, fragmented, contradictory. The language of the historical text must represent a mental image that will always strive for coherence. If consciousness is discontinuous, and the historical record is equally discontinuous, we nevertheless use our narrative abilities to make that record appear seamless.

3

BOUNDARIES OF THE TEXT

HISTORY AS PASSAGE

Narrative exists to make continuous what is discontinuous; it covers the gaps in time, in action, in documentation, even when it points to them. One problem, however, lies both inside and outside the historical text, or, one might say, it exists in a space of its own. This is the problem of *boundaries*. Because historical works are caught in certain ambiguities entailed by their position in language, distinctive and instinctive ploys are regularly used, not merely to deny that the problem exists, but to exploit it and thus to make writing human history possible. The creation of textual space through beginnings and endings is a matter of particular interest; not only the old matter of historical periodization, but also the very shape of the historical text itself, is a function of decisions made about the "boundaries" of the text. Byron's lines, "Nothing so difficult as a beginning / In poesy, except perhaps the end," apply to almost all ventures. I shall begin by looking at some words.

In almost any discussion of texts, one word appears, almost inevitably, unnoticed, quite innocently, despite the ambiguity, inappropriateness, and paradoxes of its usage. The word is "passage," used as Boswell, for example, does when he cites a college tutor who advises his pupils, "Read over your compositions, and wherever you meet with a passage which you think is particularly fine, strike it out." Critics, or anyone who discusses written works, generally suggest that we look at a certain "passage." The word is familiar and the usage seems unproblematical. It is not such an innocent word, however, for it masks a troublesome paradox about writing.

The *Oxford English Dictionary* lists sixteen numbered definitions for "passage"; some of these are archaic ("9. an evacuation of the bowels"). However, the main thrust of the nonliterary definitions of "passage" concerns action or *motion* in phrases like "the action of passing," "movement from one place or point to another," "transition from one state or condition to another," "a voyage across the sea." The second class of definitions is constituted by a metonymy of means for actions—- "that by which a person or thing passes or may pass; a way, road, path, route, channel," "a lobby or hall." At last in the fourteenth definition we find the one we are seeking: "An indefinite portion of a discourse or writing, usually of small or moderate length, taken by itself, a part of a speech or literary work relating to some particular matter." The relation of this definition and usage, so familiar to all of us, to the rest of the meanings of the word, is peculiar. The figural extension of language has taken a word of motion, extended this word to mean the place where the motion may occur, and finally (I use this adverb in terms of poetic logic, not etymological history) embraced the concept of a place, a *locus* of a certain sort, without regard to motion in it at all. For, make no mistake, when we speak of a passage in a text, we are precisely denying its function as passage-way. The very strategy of plucking the passage from the text eliminates what came before and what came after; the scrutiny is turned within. To put it otherwise, a passage-way is, *as passage-way*, a means of getting from one locus to another one; if the passage-way itself is regarded as a locus on its own, that is, as a "passage," it ceases to be a passage-way. If I am correct, then, a passage ought to be a place that is a nonplace, connecting two places, but not a place itself, *in the same sense*. Consequently, our familiar use of the word "passage" to describe a portion of discourse is a sort of hidden catechresis, or logical abuse, although the abuse is embedded within the perfectly authorized lexical procedures of language.

The word itself is a sort of logical abuse, so I shall abuse it a bit further. The definition states: "An indefinite portion of a discourse or writing, usually of small or moderate length . . ." In practice, there are *no rules* for selecting passages; one may choose as one pleases—a phrase, a few sentences, even a number of pages. May we not under certain conditions even consider the entire text itself as a "passage"? At this point some critics may rise up and cry, "No!" To consider the whole literary text as a passage is to imply, through the ambiguities built into the word, that it stands in relation to something outside itself, whether an influence, a set of antecedent circumstances, or at least the intention of an author. These relationships much recent criticism is not ready to acknowledge as useful. The literary text for them is a locus, not a passage to or from anything. As literature, the text makes no claims outside itself, and lives within its own textual space, generating itself in language. A locus, not a passage; or, if a passage, a kind of absurd passage that leads nowhere, a dead-end.

"Passage" is thus like those "primal words" discussed by Freud, whose "antithetical meanings" not only correspond to the dream-work but also reveal the "regressive, archaic character of thought-expression in dreams."[1] If the term shows regressive qualities, if its polysemous ambiguity is potentially subversive, shall we then strike this usage from the word, replacing it with a phrase like "textual segment" that seems more safely univocal? Yet it is precisely the tensions both within the word and within the process that the word describes—that is, the creation of passages in the broadest sense—that figure forth a number of illuminating consequences.

To create a passage is to quote. To quote is to create new beginnings and ends within middles, to remove something from one context and to place it in a different one in order to make one's own words out of another's. Like passage, both the word and the process of quotation are familiar but harbor a hidden hazard. Let me quote from a book on the poetics of quotation:

> In the technical language of literary criticism and also in popular usage, the word "quotation" is used in two senses. In the broader sense, "quoting" can mean that one alludes to or cites not the literal words, but the content of specific literary passages or even of entire literary works. Reference, allusion, pastiche, parody, plagiarism—these are all related somehow to the quotation proper or have at least manifold and often compelling points of contact with it. Precisely because the transitions are so fluid and the boundaries sometimes so uncertain, we consider it practicable to limit ourselves in general to quotations in the narrower sense of the word. Otherwise the danger arises that we will get lost in a limitless mass of material.[2]

The "limitless mass of material" is all of language, perhaps even all information. To push the definition of quotation toward the extreme of all language may be as dangerous as Mayer suggests, or at least cumbersome, but as with "passage" it is a point to press. Just as "passage" becomes problematic when we notice its double nature as place and motion (like the famous rabbit/duck drawing of Jastrow, cited by Wittgenstein and Gombrich), the process by which "passages" are cre-

1. Sigmund Freud, "The Antithetical Sense of Primal Words," in *Standard Edition*, vol. XI, ed. John Strachey (London, 1953), 155–61.

2. Herman Mayer, *The Poetics of Quotation in the European Novel*, trans. Theodore and Y. Ziolkowski (Princeton, 1968), 9.

ated—that is, quotation—also faces a contradiction in which part of language threatens by extension to become limitless.

What happens in quotation? To select a passage from a text, or to create a passage that is the text itself, acts that are essentially similar, is to commit an act of violence. The charge of quoting out of context seems absurd; to quote *is* to remove from context. If a "passage" is an "indefinite portion," then what rules exist for selecting a passage? No definite rules exist. When we quote, thus creating a passage, we often feel that it would have been better, time or space permitting, to have started quoting a paragraph earlier or to have extended the passage a bit further, all in the interest of amplification, context. The more text quoted, the more honest the quotation seems to be. At the same time, the quotation also appears bloated to us, more than *we* need, overloaded with surplus meaning implied by the looming context that we have maimed by creating the "passage." No rules exist; if they did, our anxieties about these matters would disappear. Of course, there are conventions, such as not violating syntax, or not reversing meanings; but these conventions are badly enforced. When the musicologist Donald Francis Tovey deplored the "bleeding chunks" torn from Richard Wagner's *Ring of the Nibelung* to be played in the concert hall, he was reacting to a kind of syntactic atrocity; and the creation of publicity blurbs from critical reviews often disregards the conventions of veracity. The existence of these conventions serves to deny the creative authority of one who quotes by implying that the text already contains a finite number of predefined "passages." Syntax, as priest, says to us reader-communicants, "This is my text, broken for you. This do in remembrance of me." We may then take, or quote, a piece of the host, but not break the bread ourselves.

Nevertheless, despite the sacerdotal claims of syntax and semantics, I return to my contention that there are no rules. All citation is out of context, every passage a "bleeding chunk." This is no neat surgical slice; it is a fracture. The term "fracture" has in fact been used in one way or another by the French critic-philosophers. Foucault speaks of *diffraction*, Derrida of *effraction;* we are told by the latter that Freud accords a privilege to pain because "fraying fractures," and by Barthes that dystaxy fractures the sign. A fracture may be understood as a break without separation. The interruption of continuity that defines a break is made, yet the gap or opening is missing or denied. Clearly, a fracture (in the orthopedic sense) is not an amputation. In a typical etymological development, "fracture," from the Latin *frangere,* has a subtle, reparable tone to it that "break," with its series of Old Teutonic roots, lacks.

"Break" is a harsh, barbaric word—"to sever into distinct parts by sudden application of force, to part by violence." This is more or less how I have described the creating of passages and the act of quotation in general. Perhaps "break," with its violent emphasis on separation and dispersion, is a better word to use. Perhaps the text is "broken" out of language so forcibly as to constitute its own world.

Not all texts are equally Mallarméan, however, although all may be surveyed poetically. What I am driving at is that different kinds of texts make different kinds of claims, and that one of these claims has to do with the violence of separation from the whole of language acts. Some texts, the lyric poem being the conventional example, are irrevocably broken out of language, and do not claim responsibility to any world outside themselves. But other kinds of texts, while they are made from and in language, do claim responsibility beyond themselves. These works (and the historical texts I shall discuss below are among them) regret the break and would like to deny their status as mere language. In other words, their hidden structural metaphor, their scandal, is *fracture*; and it is an important consequence of that scandal that the texts themselves seek, through a number of rhetorical devices, to *set* the fracture in the hope that it will heal and, by healing, deny that there ever was a fracture, let alone a break, at all. The historical text is typically structured as a fractured passage, inevitably caught up in the ambiguities of position and proportion that situate people in both history and language. To quote, as I mentioned before, is to create new beginnings and endings from middles; and this is what historians generally do. So before we get to our texts, we shall look briefly at some theories of beginning. Certain structuralist theorists of narrative have pointed out that narratives do not (to quote the King of Hearts in *Alice in Wonderland*) "begin at the beginning, . . . and go on til [they] come to the end; then stop." Instead, they begin with an "initiating event" that "established a state of affairs."[3] The "initiating event" need not be situated at the start of a text, although it traditionally is near that point.

Modern literatures, of course, with their desire to alter in all possible permutations the conventions and conditions of narrative, have sometimes placed the initiating event at the end (as when the murderer in a mystery reveals his hidden motive), or hidden the event itself. Since, as Nancy Partner has suggested, our sense of living in the *middle* of a

3. John Holloway, "Supposition and Supersession: A Model of Analysis for Narrative Structure," *Critical Inquiry* 3 (1976), 43.

meaningful story is the sign of a highly developed (and thus conventionalized and internalized) view of ourselves, the ability to play with these conventions by violating them is an important function of art; the conventions are thereby strengthened, not weakened.[4] Histories usually do not trifle with the placement of the initiating event, but there are some characteristic displacements that have become commonplaces. Readers of political histories of nineteenth-century Europe regularly discover that the events of the nineteenth century did not really begin on the first day of January 1801 throughout the continent; but perhaps in the summer of 1815 in Vienna. The century ended, according to this conventional scheme, in the summer of 1914, in Bosnia, of all places. Similarly, the death of Louis XIV in 1715 ends the seventeenth century (or begins the eighteenth); the assassination of Henry IV in 1610 ends the sixteenth (at least for French history); and so forth. We see that historians have long grasped the significance of initiating and terminating events. But already arguments crop up around the problem of periodization, which is really the rhetorical problem of naming and identity. A well-known example concerns the renaissance of humanism and classical learning: Haskins in his classic *The Renaissance of the Twelfth Century* suggests that this rebirth (and the freedom of spirit occasioned by it) was effectively over by 1200; Burckhardt, in his *Civilization of the Renaissance in Italy*, regards it as a *Quattrocento* and *Cinquecento* phenomenon, when he bothers with dates at all. Rather than reject either of these two admirable historians, one might compromise: the renaissance may have begun about 1400 and ended around 1200. In any case, such arguments about naming, which occupy a traditional role in historical debates, seem far less critical to the interpretation of historical texts than is the mode of generating historical discourse, or setting it in motion, by creating the *sense* of a beginning.

In generating their histories, historians customarily use a process similar to a hypothetical model used by certain physicists to account for the generation of information in the universe. This notion is the "big bang," an untested, probably untestable, principle of philosophical interest, used to explain many different things. Let me quote a very brief definition of the "big bang": "If the motions of the galaxies are extrapolated into the past as far as possible, a state is eventually reached in which all the galaxies were crushed together at infinite density. This

4. Nancy F. Partner, "Making Up Lost Time: Writing on the Writing of History," *Speculum* 61:1 (1986), 90.

state represents the big bang, and it marks the origin of the universe and of everything in it."[5] Note that the theory is obtained by reasoning backward on the basis of the existing data of motion, that the theory is then presumed to create the initial conditions necessary to generate the data, and that by further extrapolation, the theory may be used to address such questions as "will the universe expand forever?" and "is time (whether historical, thermodynamic, or cosmological) reversible?" and "are macroscopic and microscopic information different in kind?"

What is the historian's big bang? It is, quite simply, a description or indication of the state of events that generates the later events he will describe. Examining a variety of historians, we find, for example, Fustel de Coulanges's section "Ancient Beliefs" in *The Ancient City*, Tacitus' "The Character of Augustan Rule" in his *Annals* (This subtitle was added by an editor, but the substance of the section stands nevertheless), Thomas Macaulay's "The State of England in 1685" in the *History of England*, and, as will be discussed later, Georges Lefebvre's chapter "The Crisis of the Monarchy" in *The Coming of the French Revolution*. In each case, a state of affairs, set of beliefs, social system, or political crisis is represented in such a way as to appear to generate a series of events, once a series of constraints is imposed. If "big bang" seems an excessively dramatic term for the whiggish gentility of a Macaulay, we are assured by astrophysics that it may well have been "an exceedingly gentle process."[6] What is important to the comparison is the creation of constraints, initial conditions, *boundary* conditions, posed by the hypothetical models. That, after all, is the purpose of the models in both cases.

However, the big bang of astrophysics and that of historical practice quickly part ways. The astrophysicists write: "It is not meaningful to ask what happened before the 'big bang'; it is like asking what is north of the North Pole."[7] In other words, since the cosmological "big bang" generated all existing information, it is without meaning to ask what came before it. Such information objectively does not exist. Since the historian's "big bang" is a rhetorical generator, however, it acts to repress the all too meaningful, and dangerous, question of what came before. Differing according to the range and scope of each work, the

5. J. Richard Gott III, James E. Gunn, David N. Schramm, and Beatrice M. Tinsley, "Will the Universe Expand Forever?" *Scientific American*, March 1976, 64.

6. David Layzer, "The Arrow of Time," *Scientific American*, Dec. 1975, 68.

7. Gott et al., "Will the Universe Expand Forever?" 65.

strands of argument (events, evidence) are pursued no further back, but are instead gathered into a ball ("Ancient Beliefs," "The Character of Augustan Rule," "The State of England in 1685," "The Crisis of the Monarchy") and detonated, however gently. This is the historical "big bang"; its purpose, when well done, is to frustrate the question of "what came before." Let us look at a typical case of the "big bang" at work.

The Coming of the French Revolution by Georges Lefebvre, for example, focuses the issue of passage in a highly concentrated way.[8] It is a book that has a beginning, and claims to represent a beginning. The French title, *Quatre-vingt-neuf,* posits the presuppositions. It is merely the name of a year, the one after *quatre-vingt-huit* and before *quatre-vingt-dix*. But the title is only the nickname for the year; the century is omitted. Not 1489, not 1889—no need to state the obvious, it is 1789. To a Frenchman, there could be no mistake. For non-French readers, apparently, "Eighty-nine" won't do, because it is a strategy for marshaling presuppositions—presuppositions that we may or may not have. Obviously, '89 is not a number in a series, equal in status to other numbers in the series; if it were, say, only the passage from '88 to '90, the title would not do. Rather, '89 is a locus in French history, a place or landscape with a spirit of its own. The spirit of 1789 is that of beginning; the beginning of the Revolution, of European liberty, of modern times, of all the ideological formulas that have crystallized around the Revolution.

No year, of course, views itself as a beginning, and Lefebvre recognizes this:

> No one dreamed that the Revolution was barely beginning. And after all, the popular feeling was not entirely mistaken, for the days of October, by securing ratification of the decrees of August, had consecrated the demise of the Old Regime beyond hope of renewal, and at least the Revolution of 1789 was over.[9]

At this point, Lefebvre foreshadows the remark Churchill would make three years later: "This is not the end. It is not even the beginning of the end. But it is, perhaps, the end of the beginning." If beginnings have ends, they must also have beginnings.

Edward Said's *Beginnings: Intention and Method* points out that "to

---

8. Georges Lefebvre, *The Coming of the French Revolution*, trans. R. R. Palmer (Princeton, 1947); first ed., *Quatre-vingt-neuf* (Paris, 1939). All citations are from the English edition.

9. Ibid., 205.

identify a point as a beginning is to classify it after the fact . . . ," as we have just noted. He further writes that "beginning is a creature with its own special life. . . ."[10] The nature of this "special life" mandates that the historian "set" the fracture in time of his text by various methods, such as the pre-echoing initiating event that Lefebvre uses in *The Coming of the French Revolution.* In this way he wins a certain space within which to generate his text; this is a successful beginning.

We normally think of space as a visual quality, as something we *see,* but we may speak of hearing space as well. For example, the orchestral recordings made in NBC's broadcast studio 8-H in the 1940s and 1950s with Arturo Toscanini and the NBC Orchestra are notoriously claustrophobic and cramped in a way that the orchestra's recordings in Carnegie Hall are not. The key to the difference is reverberation; reverberation is the acoustical generator of a sense of space. A "fractured text" that wishes to set, or to resist, its fracture from language and from time will try to win itself some space by reverberating somehow. Yet there is a major difference between true acoustical reverberation and its figurative use in writing. In a hall, sound coming from its source can reverberate only after it has been produced; recordings, however, sometimes have an irritating thing called pre-echo, a faint presentation of the sound before it is actually heard directly.

Pre-echo is one important device that historians conventionally use to set their fracture in time. Georges Lefebvre's *The Coming of the French Revolution* offers us an unmistakable example of the pre-echoing initiating event. The opening line of the book resounds indefinitely backward. "The ultimate cause of the French Revolution of 1789 goes deep into the history of France and of the western world."[11] At the level of causation, we are gestured back to the *ultimate* cause (but only gestured, because it cannot be named); at the level of diachrony, we are sent "deep" into history; in the scheme of space, we are directed outward from one nation into the entire western world. Each of these gestures is an attempt to begin by denying beginning. But as yet there is no *narrative* beginning, no initiating event. This appears only at the end of the second chapter ("The Crisis of the Monarchy"), after a series of pre-echoing repetitions. We read there:

> Should the Third Estate have contented itself, respectfully and
> submissively, with what the great majority of the aristocracy was

10. Edward Said, *Beginnings: Intention and Method* (New York, 1975), 29, 18.
11. Lefebvre, *Coming of the French Revolution,* 1.

willing to offer it? In any case, it did not think so, and loudly demanded equality before the law. At this point, strictly speaking, the Revolution of 1789 began. [12]

Yet there have already been a series of events in the text, progressively intensifying: Calonne's reform plan, the King's vacillation, the Assembly of Notables, the resistance of the Parlements, the calling of the Estates-General. What do these have to do with a story that has not yet, "strictly speaking," begun? Obviously, a great deal, if we accept the notion of diachronic, cause-effect related events. Where do the pre-echoes end (or begin)? Logically, they do not end, and the nightmare of infinite regress haunts the scene. But practically, there is a point of pre-echoic entropy, beyond which the pre-echoes are not related recognizably to the initiating event of the selected story, in this case the Revolution of 1789. The first sentence of the book made a gesture toward a vast, if not infinite, space; but the opening sentence of the second chapter assures us that Lefebvre's true sympathies lie with human scale and proportion. He writes:

> The government crisis went back to the American War. The revolt of the English colonies may in fact be considered the direct cause of the French Revolution, both because in invoking the rights of man it stirred up great excitement in France, and because Louis XVI in supporting it got his finances into very bad condition. [13]

Lefebvre has opted here for a human scale of explanation; the size of his gestures are well within the scope and span of a single life (about a decade's elapsed time), a single culture (seen in the traditional eighteenth-century Franco-English rivalry), and a single sphere of activity (that is, political events like wars and revolutions). Contrast, for instance, the French historian who wrote not too long ago that the cause of the peasant revolts of the seventeenth century was original sin; this is not what I would call a human scale of explanation.

The original ending of *Quatre-vingt-neuf*, in the edition of July 1939, was a call to defend the principles of the Revolution, and to resist the enemies of liberty with the same spirit of *la patrie en danger* shown by the men of '92. In the English edition this final paragraph, which caused eighty thousand copies of the book to be destroyed by the Vichy government, was eliminated, presumably because it seemed inappropriate

12. Ibid., 36–37.
13. Ibid., 21.

in a postwar world. We recognize, however, a familiar echoing tactic, the conventional appropriation of time and space through gestures that reach beyond the text, beyond the passage, and suggest that there is a *con*text that focuses the meaning of the segment that is the text itself. In the case of *Quatre-vingt-neuf,* this is done allegorically by making certain principles into actors and then sending them out into the world as immortals to do battle. "Liberty, Equality, and Fraternity" were not born with the Revolution; we recall Lefebvre's pre-echoes from the American Revolution, etc. Yet for Lefebvre's story, and for France, they are nevertheless "the principles of '89."

This process of transforming history into nature, by projecting historical moments in such a way as to deny their historicity, is the modern creation of myth with ideological intent, particular norms presented as "evident laws of the natural order," as Roland Barthes put it. More than this, however, it is also one historical attempt to secure and defend the borders of the historical text by reaching out in both directions to heal the broken nature of historical telling. To appeal to an audience's shared traditions, to allegorize abstract principles, to generate the story with a "bang" while "setting" (and softening) the fracture involved with pre-echoes, are the commonplaces, almost the enabling conditions, of human history. There are other possibilities, however. Quite different from Lefebvre's conventional history is Fernand Braudel's monumental *The Mediterranean and the Mediterranean World in the Age of Philip II.*[14] This work, published in 1949, has elicited a considerable amount of attention and commentary since its publication, primarily because it seemed (and claimed) to be "a new kind of history" (1238), descended from Lucien Febvre and Marc Bloch, and characterized by a methodological and conceptual boldness not attempted before. This venture Braudel calls an attempt at "total history," combining geography, demography, economics, sociology, politics, and a host of other disciplines into something new in deep and significant ways, particularly with regard to quantification. Far more original and significant, however, are the structure and rhetoric of the work, for these categories not only control the enormous quantity of material in the book, but also offer a resolu-

14. Fernand Braudel, *The Mediterranean and the Mediterranean World in the Age of Philip II,* trans. Siân Reynolds (New York, 1972); first ed., *La Méditerranée et le monde méditerranéen à l'époque de Philippe II* (Paris, 1949). All citations are from the English translation of the second edition.

This work is discussed below at greater length in Chapter 7, "Disorderly Conduct: Braudel's Mediterranean Satire."

tion of the problem of fracture so powerful and so extreme as to undermine the entire venture of human history.

The Mediterranean is a sea surrounded by land; men live and die on
land, despite their ties to the sea. Inevitably, the Mediterranean world
will take the form of a circle, and so does Braudel's book. The principal
dynamic image of the book, however, is the *wave;* repeated, renamed,
displaced, disguised, the waves rule Braudel's world. From the "slow-
furling waves" (102) of the deep structures, with their "extremely slow
pattern of oscillation" (101), the book progresses with increased pace
until "history becomes many-stranded once more, bewilderingly complex and, who knows, in seeking to grasp all the different vibrations,
waves of past time which ought ideally to accumulate like the divisions
in the mechanisms of a watch, the seconds, minutes, hours, and days—
perhaps we shall find the whole fabric slipping away between our fingers" (893). Sometimes the waves become "electrical currents" determined by "differing voltages" (137). Elsewhere, contacts between
nomads are "like electrical charges, violent and without continuity"
(161). At one point, Braudel rejects the image of waves, saying that
"southern influence did not spread through the North in waves," but
rather "along narrow channels" (223). The preoccupation remains, even
in denial. What is the effect of these waves, currents, oscillations, that
lap and overlap the Mediterraneans, the Saharas, the Atlantics, the
Europes? It is light, "that even light which shines at the heart of the
Mediterranean" (231). Braudel's vision and his rhetoric are clearly not
modest, and seem suitable to the enormous structures and institutions
he depicts in the first two-thirds of his work. But what of the last part,
the *histoire événementielle,* which Braudel hesitated to publish at all? We
must accept his own highly equivocal answer, that the people who took
part in the events of the sixteenth century "felt, rightly or wrongly, that
they were participating in a mighty drama," and that "this illusion . . .
helped to give meaning to their lives" (901). He adds that he is "by no
means a sworn enemy of the event."

Even after we have accounted for the descent into the "drum and
trumpet" world of the third section of Braudel's *Mediterranean,* the bat-
tle-by-battle, year-by-year report of the second half of the sixteenth century, the closure of the text, the sense of an ending (for it is only a sense,
not an ending) is a surprise, hardly in keeping. Braudel ends part three
of *The Mediterranean and the Mediterranean World in the Age of Philip II,* the
section on politics, diplomacy, and human-scale events, with the death
of Philip II, a piece of great news that traveled quickly throughout the

Mediterranean world in September 1598. The author tells us that he has withheld Philip's death until the end, out of its proper place in the chronology, but he adds in his own defense that this omission is trivial, as the mood of Spanish Mediterranean policy was one of continuity. Typically, Braudel assures us that this human death had little real significance, changing Spanish foreign and even domestic policy but little. He apologizes for recounting the well-known details of the death (as he had apologized for the last 350 pages of events in general), but he includes them because they are revealing of this enigmatic man, and because it is "moving," human. Then he turns to the dying king. "But what of the sovereign, the force of history symbolized by his name? This is a very different matter from the solitary and secretive man himself. To historians he is an enigma: he receives us as he did his ambassadors, with the outward courtesy, listening to us, replying in a low and often unintelligible voice, never speaking of himself at all" (1236). That is to say, the documentary sources are silent about Philip the man. Other sources will come to the foreground.

Philip, Braudel tells us, died in dignified certainty of his role and his fate; it was the death of a Christian and of a king, a public, pious, and prolonged death of fifty-three days. But as the description of the death goes on, it becomes evident that Braudel, far from retelling a familiar, "touching," story, is in fact crafting an entirely new one. In Braudel's version, Philip is erased, bit by bit, sense by sense, from the text; his leaving the world of history is almost incidental. The Philip most accessible to us is the king, whom Braudel describes as an "intersection of the endless reports that combine to weave the great web of the Spanish Empire and the world." His presence was always to be doubted, in a sense: "This is the man who sits silently reading at his desk, annotating reports in his hasty handwriting, far from other men, distant and pensive, linked by the threads of information to that living history which makes its way towards him from every corner of the world." He alone sees the whole picture, the balance sheet; he is the conductor whose silence marks his sole possession of the full score.

In short, Philip was the one man on the world stage who made no sound, did not speak himself; his words were unintelligible. The king is mute, shrinking, but still visible. We read on, nearing the end: "He was not a man of vision: he saw his task as an unending succession of small details." Philip is now mute and blind before us, and receding rapidly from our view. In the next sentence he all but disappears: "Every one of his annotations is a small precise point, whether an order, a remark or the correction of a spelling mistake or geographical error. Never do we find general notions or grand strategies under his pen. I do not believe that the word Mediterranean itself ever floated in his consciousness with the meaning we now give it . . ." (1236). Into this small precise point, the great Philip II has disappeared, as into the pit of a whirlpool. No general understanding is his. Philip was already distant from us; when his "voice" and his "vision" disappear in the text, the man is dead. But these traits are all characteristic of his life, and have nothing to do with his final illness. Braudel is allegorizing here.

> Geography in the true sense was not part of a prince's education. These are all sufficient reasons why the long agony which ended in September, 1598 was not a great event in Mediterranean history; good reasons for us to reflect once more on the distance separating biographical history from the history of structures, and even more from the history of geographical areas.

Philip's death, then, is not physiological, but existential. It is man as significant actor who has been swept away. Freud speaks in *The Interpretation of Dreams* of a navel, the point of a dream that resists interpretation and remains always dark. Philip is such a navel, mute, blind, rapidly receding into a "small precise point," infinitely small. (1237) Philip's death is clearly the point at which the inward reverberations of the book disappear, but what about the outward gestures?

The expanse of the book, its size, is a structural gesture, mirroring "the Mediterranean of historical dimensions . . . extending well beyond the shores of the sea in all directions," in fact, "a global Mediterranean" (168). Using an image closely related to the waves mentioned above, Braudel calls the sea "a radiant center whose light grows less as one moves away from it, without one's being able to define the exact boundary between light and shade" (168). The full Mediterranean is the cosmos: no boundaries. And the rhetoric of no boundaries is *apologia*: "This sketch of the mountain ranges is necessarily incomplete. Life cannot be reduced to a simple outline" (53); or: "the list could be easily extended . . ." (28), after an already extensive list; or: "this is not the place for discussion of this controversial issue" (26). This last decision is presented regretfully, as an act of will. The radiant waves move outward and inward indefinitely; the historian who follows them cannot tell when they cease to have form. After all, their apparent entropy may reflect only the limitations of the historian's oscilloscope. A second figure of rhetorical expansion, the so-called rhetorical question, is a turn that resonates in the absence of reply. To be sure, this gesture is, to my knowledge, more widely used by French writers than by those who write in English or German; nevertheless, an illuminating index of Braudel's use of this tactic is found in the nineteen question marks that reside in the normally secure world of the table of contents. Braudel presents the Mediterranean as a sort of mean between everything and nothing, to use Pascal's terms, whose very name and identity relate only to the arbitrary size and shape of human comprehension. There are no proper boundaries in time, in space. The text radiates outward in suggestion of a global Mediterranean, and inward into the black hole, the blind, mute navel that was the death of Philip II. At nearly 1,400 pages, the book is large, but we perceive that the space it claims is far more vast.

There is another sort of hypothetical model for the kind of universe we think we live in, an explanation without a "big bang" from total concentration. This so-called "steady state" theory involves simply an alternating expansion and contraction of the universe. This model, though out of fashion with scientists at the moment, suggests Braudel's generating principle. As he puts it, "The rule has been that the Mediterranean spreads far beyond its shores in waves that are balanced by continual returns. What leaves the sea departs and then comes back once more" (170). The oscillations are unbounded; the moments of reversal, unclear; the resonance, infinite. If we suppose, however, that at least his *subject* is privileged, that the Mediterranean in the age of Philip II is special and concentrates in itself meaning that it radiates out as a beacon, we again underestimate the span of Braudel's gesture. For when, in the conclusion to the second edition of *The Mediterranean and the Mediterranean World in the Age of Philip II*, he cites Croce's comment that "any single event . . . contains in embryo the whole history of mankind" (1243), even the status of the Mediterranean collapses. There can be no "big bang," because every monad of time and space is a universe. It is the language, the gestures, the rhetoric of this book, not its statistics, maps, or descriptions, that create a Mediterranean *world*, and this world is that of a mystic.

The biggest recorded bang in our culture comes at the beginning of the book of Genesis. Historians only rarely venture back so far, to the point beyond which there can be no pre-echo. One who did, however, was Jacques-Bénigne Bossuet, the French orator, preacher, and bishop of Meaux, who wrote a classic *Discourse on Universal History* in the later 1670s for the edification of the dauphin and perhaps also for the father of

the dauphin, King Louis XIV.[15] The *Discourse* is a late example of pro-
vidential history and offers some suggestive indications of another kind
of history without, as it were, man. It begins, predictably, with "God
creating heaven and earth through his word and making man in his
image (1 A.M. 4004 B.C.)." These lines describe the start of the "First
Epoch: Adam, or the Creation," and the first part of the *Discourse* traces
twelve such epochs, the last being "Charlemagne, or the Establishment
of the New Empire." Part two is called the "Continuity of Religion," and
*re*begins with "The Creation and the Early Ages." In the final section,
entitled "The Empires," Bossuet is unable to trace his subject quite back
to the Creation, but he goes as far as he can, to "the Scythians, the Ethi-
opians, and the Egyptians." The book, in short, consists of three sections: respectively chronological, religious, and political. As in Braudel,
these three sections may be seen concentrically, the epochs of chronology delineating the structures (or areas closest to God's time), while
the part describing the continuity of religion through its rising and falling fortunes resembles Braudel's conjunctures, passing the great glacial
motions of the structures on into the innermost ring. That ring, I hasten
to add, is the ring of human events; neither Bossuet nor Braudel thinks
much of it, but both tolerate it.

At the beginning of the Sixth Epoch, Bossuet positions the completion of the Temple in Jerusalem by Solomon in a characteristic way:

> It was about the year 3000 of the world, in the 488th year after the
> Exodus from Egypt and, to adjust the dates of sacred history with
> those of secular history, 180 years after the Fall of Troy, 250 years
> before the founding of Rome, and 1000 years before Jesus Christ,
> that Solomon completed that marvellous edifice. (20)

This is a peculiar style of placement, rigid because it does not reverberate, does not create a space in which the event may occur. In fact, there
is almost no sense of space in Bossuet, because events do not echo
within the system; their meaning comes from without. The outcome is
not known to man; but it *is* known. Intentions and power are deceptive
both in the short and in the long run.

> That is why all rulers feel they are subject to a higher power. They
> achieve either more or less than they plan, and their intentions

15. Jacques-Bénigne Bossuet, *Discourse on Universal History,* trans. E. Forster, ed. O.
Ranum (Chicago and London, 1976); French consulted: Bossuet, *Oeuvres*, Bibliothèque de
la Pléiade (Paris, 1961). All citations are from the English edition.

have always led to unforeseen consequences. They neither control the configuration of circumstances that was bequeathed to them by past centuries, nor can they foresee the course of the future, much less control that course. All this is in the hands of him who can name what is and what is yet to be, who presides over all the ages, and who knows in advance what will come to pass. . . . In a word, there is no human power which does not unintentionally serve other ends than its own. (375)

These considerations, coming near the end of the *Discourse*, mark its final tenor. There are no echoes at all; men act in illusion, according to a plan that they cannot know, and cannot perceive, since, as Karl Löwith has pointed out, Bossuet refuses to grant that "there is any visible mark of providence in the history of the world."[16] Meaning in this history is an act of faith, not a modulated system of echoes and pre-echoes. Rhetorically, Bossuet has, in the terms described here, quoted the whole text of history, leaving himself no space to gesture in the fracture-setting sense. But it would not really have mattered much if he had fractured for himself a passage out of language and history, because, as we saw in his placement of the completion of the Temple, human events have no resonance at all, only position.

Both Bossuet and Braudel cast their historical circuses in three rings, but the bishop's rings do not vibrate, are anechoic, while Braudel's reverberate infinitely. Bossuet thus takes universal history and makes it a prison; Braudel takes a few decades and makes them a universe. Both of them, however, deny the privileged status of human history, and I have tried to show how both the denial and the affirmation of human history are accomplished in language and time. Both No Space and Infinite Space create the same result—No Man.

Up to now I have discussed three texts of no great difficulty, several familiar words, and much oversimplified versions of some scientific speculations. There is in my subject, however, something larger than the textual tactics that I have presented thus far. In the masterwork of Braudel, now forty years old, we sense a phenomenon that may be described in terms of subject matter, methodology, or rhetorical structure, but that is present in any case. This has been called the "death of man." It is Michel Foucault who has most articulately offered us the prospect of a world that is no longer centered on a certain idea of humanity, so I shall quote him here at some length.

16. Karl Löwith, *Meaning in History* (Chicago and London, 1949), 143.

The Other Sources: History and Language

> Since man was constituted at a time when language was doomed
> to dispersion, will he not be dispersed when language regains its
> unity? . . . Ought we not rather give up thinking of man, or to be
> more strict, to think of this disappearance of man—as closely as
> possible in correlation with our concern with language? Ought
> we not to admit, since language is there once more, man will
> return to that serene non-existence in which he was formerly
> maintained by the unity of Discourse? Man had been a figure
> existing between two modes of language; or, rather, he was con-
> stituted only when language, having been situated only within
> representation and, as it were dissolved in it, freed itself from that
> situation at the cost of its own fragmentation; man composed his
> own figure in the interstices of that fragmented language. Of
> course, these are not affirmations; they are at most questions to
> which it is not possible to reply; they must be left in suspense,
> where they pose themselves, only with the knowledge that the
> possibility of posing them may well open the way to a future
> thought.[17]

If we read "history," understood in the sense described here as an
attempt to quote from the fullness of words and time, into Foucault's
"language," we sense how in his view a certain moment of human history came, and went. History on a human scale was composed, to paraphrase Foucault, in the interstices of that fragmented language; history
is "a figure occurring between two modes of languages," acknowledging, yet inevitably resisting, "the unity of Discourse." The fruitful ambiguity of "passage," that "indefinite portion" of a text, which has served
Lefebvre quite well in his conventional structure of controlled echoing,
appears to be giving way. Just as Bossuet, writing before the construction of "man" in history, refused to place his text within human time,
so the enormous gestures of Braudel's book suggest that to him, man
is lost in the atopia of non-proportion described by Pascal as "an all in
relation to the nothing, a nothing in relation to the all"—neither an
actor in God's drama as Bossuet would have it, nor an actor in his own
drama as Lefebvre suggests. When Foucault writes, in the last, echoing lines of *The Order of Things*, "that man would be erased, like a face
drawn in sand at the edge of the sea," we know what will erase his

17. Michel Foucault, *The Order of Things: An Archaeology of the Human Sciences* (New
York, 1970), 386, a translation of *Les mots et les choses* [Paris, 1966].

image.[18] Waves will do it, and Mediterranean waves at that, from a "sea in the middle" that can no longer be defined.

Every history must somehow define its subject by setting boundaries, yet these boundaries always entail a recognition of the gaps created by definitions. The gaps in documentary evidence provoke anxieties that can be smoothed over by narrative. Because it is narrative itself, however, that generates the anxiety before boundaries, the solutions are more complex. No further research will solve the problem of passage; it stems from the "other" sources of history.

18. Ibid., 387.

PART TWO

THE LANGUAGE OF HISTORIANS

FOUR SHIPWRECKS

Although "totality" as a concept has been claimed most particularly by marxism in both its scientific-mechanical and Hegelian-organicist modes, it is hard to find any significant historical venture that does not strive for some vision of totality. "Only connect" might serve as the ideal historical slogan. Hegel had stated that "the truth is the whole," but that observation hardly solved the problem of what the whole might include. His further clarification, that "the whole is only the essence perfecting itself through its development," has had a tremendous impact, but brings the question back to the problem of essences, and how to name and describe them. A historical text inevitably gives a vision of a whole, as F. R. Ankersmit might put it, and that whole is the text itself, or rather the image it embodies. The kind of historical thinking described in Martin Jay's *Marxism and Totality* and Alvin Gouldner's *Against Fragmentation*—marxist holistic historicism—strives for a totalized vision of the past in the interests of totalizing the future, to create a healthy, unified community. Lionel Gossman has described Augustin Thierry's bourgeois historical goal as identical.

Whatever wholeness a history will have or lack, it will have or lack *as a text*, as a product of language. This means simply that the limits and contradictions of language, the fundamental mediator of parts and wholes, will apply. Each of the four historians discussed in this section is striving for a particular form of totality, some form of integration in the interest of meaning. Each fails in some way, falling into a contradictory position regarding the linguistic structures in his text.

François Guizot's goal from the start is to demonstrate the unity of the elements of a culture and society without acknowledging that this unity is a conceptual creation. This leads him to read both literature and society as a mass of "facts," such as classes, institutions, ideas, which can be shown to have a coherent relationship to one another. When a "fact" appears that cannot be accounted for by its appearance in the series, Guizot's social history founders. Guizot, to his credit, refuses to reduce Shakespeare to a historical example, to fit him into the totality of civilization. If Shakespeare is too "high" to be totalized, the "lower" bounds of the human world, the environment, present problems as well. Jules Michelet dramatically (yes, melodramatically) wrestles with the inert life—if we may coin a Micheletan oxymoron—of French geography with the intention of grasping France whole, forging the perfect national integrity that is eternally the object of his desire. That he cannot do so by geo-history is an allegorical sign of the call to recite, the demand to narrate the whole story to the present. And that tragic demand, in turn, is an allegory of the terrible necessity of the historical process itself, with all its pain and waste of life.

Oswald Spengler's version of totality is monistic; Fernand Braudel's is cosmic. Spengler presupposes a fundamental discontinuity between cultures; they have nothing to tell each other, so to speak. However, the culture itself is virtually a perfect totality, evincing a personality as integral as Spengler supposes human identity to be. Yet his own culture (ours, that is—historical culture), the culture that has allowed him to make his momentous discoveries, has a peculiar personality. Called "Faustian," this culture that discovers the essence of other cultures has no essence itself except its desire to change, to differ eternally *from* itself in a process that produces ironies fatal to Spengler's vision. It is Braudel who used the term "shipwreck" as a metaphor for the conceptual experiment in history. Let us note at the start that for him the moment of shipwreck is the purpose of the exercise and the guarantee of its value. The point at which the historical model, the reach for meaning or totality or vision, founders is the moment at which the "other" sources reveal themselves and the artfulness of the history appears. Like Braudel, I feel that this is the "most significant moment," for it gives us a notion of a reality always in tension with the means of representing it. Claude Lévi-Strauss has noted the compromises faced by any attempt at a total history that desires to unite "low-powered" history, which is lived and experienced by human beings, and the "high-powered" history beyond our experience.

> For any gain on one side is offset by a loss on the other. Biographical and anecdotal history is the least explanatory; but it is the

richest in point of information, for it considers individuals in their particularity and details for each of them the shades of character, the twists and turns of their motives, the phases of their deliberations. This information is schematized, put in the background and finally done away with as one passes to histories of progressively greater "power." Consequently, depending on the level on which he places himself, the historian loses in information what he gains in comprehension or vice versa, as if the logic of the concrete wished to remind us of its logical nature by modelling a confused outline of Gödel's theorem in the clay of "becoming." The historian's relative choice, with respect to each domain of history he gives up, is always confined to history which teaches us more and explains less, and history which explains more and teaches less.[1]

This, of course, is also Braudel's most important discovery.

In each of the following chapters, the historian we read has boldly selected a method of work that makes his accomplishment possible, while establishing limits to it; in each case, he has boldly pushed his thought to that limit and felt its presence. Michelet and Braudel self-consciously display the limit, and make their inevitable frustration in language a theme of their work, while Guizot and Spengler merely confront the limit as exception or paradox. The four shipwrecks described here suggest that the limits to "totality" of comprehension always reside within the means of representation.

1. Claude Lévi-Strauss, *The Savage Mind* (Chicago and London, 1966), 261–62.

4   GUIZOT AND THE POETS

"A Puritan born in France by mistake" was Walter Bagehot's summary of François Guizot. Since the nineteenth century, Guizot's political unpopularity has not abated. His views were far too complicated and qualified for an age when division lines were clearly drawn, often at barricades. He appears as a philistine, a political calculating machine whose calculations ultimately erred. He left no school, no followers, no party, to defend him. He never understood the cause of his downfall. But if Guizot the politician has lacked defenders, Guizot the historian has not. Contemporaries from Mill to Marx read and learned from Guizot, and it is primarily as a *philosophe*-historian that he is best know today. Yet there is more to Guizot than his political career and his prolific efforts as historian. Guizot was also a distinguished man of letters early in life; and this literary work has been quite overshadowed by his later work. In his *Etudes sur les beaux-arts en générale, Corneille et son temps*, and *Shakspear et son temps*, another Guizot emerges.[1] In a period of great literary turmoil, when reputations and

1. Guizot's major writings on art and literature each began as part of collaborative ventures. Later, after his political career was over, the works were republished in expanded versions with new titles. The later editions appeared almost simultaneously in English translations.
   The work on Corneille began as a volume of *Vies des poètes français du siècle de Louis XIV*, vol. I (Paris, 1813); the later version was *Corneille et son temps, étude littéraire* (Paris, 1852); the English version, *Corneille and His Times*, trans. anon. (New York, 1852). Quotations in the text are from this English edition.
   The essay on Shakespeare first appeared as an introduction to a French translation of the complete works, *Oeuvres complètes . . . traduites par Letourneur: Nouvelle édition . . . précédée d'une notice biographique et littéraire sur Shakespeare* (Paris, 1821); Guizot's contribution reappeared as *Shakspeare et son temps, étude littéraire* (Paris, 1852); and as *Shakspeare and His Times*, trans. anon. (New York, 1852). Quotations are from this edition.
   The discourse on the arts first appeared anonymously as part of two huge volumes containing engravings of works in the Louvre, *Le Musée royal publiée par Henri Laurent, . . . ou Receuil de gravures d'après les plus beaux tableaux, statues et bas-reliefs de la Collection royal, avec description des sujets, notices littéraires, et discours sur les arts . . .* [by E.-Q. Visconti, F. Guizot, and Comte C.-O.-F.-J.-B.-de Clarac] (Paris, 1816–18); Guizot extracted his own introduction and other contributions as *Etudes sur les beaux-arts en générale* (Paris, 1852); translated by G. Greve into English as *The Fine Arts: Their Nature and Relations* (London, 1853). Quotations are from the 1852 edition.

styles rose and fell like regimes, Guizot showed a principled flexibility, breadth of sympathy, and considerable insight, even ingenuity. One cannot accept a caricature of Guizot after reading his writings on literature.

Guizot's "puritanism" was also in a sense the very image of historical puritanism. This accounts, perhaps, for the higher regard in which he has been held as a historian, while Michelet's reputation, for example, has suffered. To be sure, Guizot's work abounds with judgments, but they are balanced, sober judgments, based upon a scrupulous attention to circumstances, "human nature," and the documents. More to the point, Guizot's historical puritanism is a linguistic puritanism. His lectures on the history of civilization, delivered in the last years of the Restoration, have none of the Rabelaisian linguistic overflow of Michelet's lectures on the history of France, delivered in the opening years of the July Monarchy. Compared with Michelet's treatment of the suppression of the Templars (discussed in Chapter 1), Guizot's treatment is pale and judicious indeed. The symbols, images, flights of reference, ambivalence, literary doubling, and so on are missing; what remains is narrative of events and analysis. This is typical of Guizot and of the doctrinaire historians in general. His prose is relatively unfigured, lacking in literary metaphor. It does not call attention to itself, while his literary judgments criticize any language that *does* call attention to itself for insincerity. Not language, but facts are what count for Guizot; the opening lecture of his course in the history of civilization in Europe is a paean to the "facts," which flow into the great ocean, the great "fact," civilization. "Facts are to the mind what rules of morality are to the will," Guizot remarked in the Twelfth Lecture.

Facts, however, come in many varieties for Guizot: individual facts, social facts, general facts, and civilization itself.

> You will easily comprehend the difficulty of reducing facts so various, so important, and so closely united, to a true historical unity. It is, however, necessary to do this. When events are once consummated, when they have become history, what are most important, and what man seeks above all things, are general facts, the connexion of causes and effects. These, so to speak, are the immortal part of history, that to which all generations must refer in order to understand the past, and to understand themselves.[2]

2. F. Guizot, *The History of Civilization from the Fall of the Roman Empire to the French Revolution*, vol. I, trans. William Hazlett (London, 1902), 218.

When Guizot began his lectures on the history of civilization in France, he prefaced the Second Lecture with the advice to his audience that they first read a good political narrative history. (He recommends that of Sismondi.) His analysis, he says, will be higher than the "primitive" narrative synthesis, but nevertheless dependent upon it. This is not to say that Guizot is in any way a philistine historian, nor that he is interested only in sociopolitical analysis. His histories are, if anything, even more concerned with literature than Michelet's. The literary history that he undertook during the late Napoleonic years forms the basis for many chapters of his later general histories.

Guizot's history depends upon allegory, like all analytic history. When he describes styles, institutions, and above all classes, Guizot is creating allegorical characters that he can compare, place in conflict, and unify into still larger allegories. Michelet, as noted in Chapter 1, recognizes allegory as the way in which prose, the language of the modern world, imprisons representation; to write history is to write allegory, but Michelet will resist it in a language that battles the embalmed "facts." Allegory fixes its subject by essentializing what it represents, by systematizing it, making it available for analysis. Guizot the literary puritan denounces *literary* allegory for its failure to capture "reality." Guizot the historical puritan will not recognize that his history is equally allegorical; he calls his allegories "facts." Contextualization proceeds by the comparison and interconnection of essentialized entities.

Guizot's literary writings have remained largely unexamined for a long while.[3] The critics Sainte-Beuve, Taine, Pelissier, Babbitt, all wrote

---

3. The literature on Guizot is extensive and distinguished, although limited almost entirely to his political life, and to a lesser extent to his work as a historian. Douglas Johnson's *Guizot: Aspects of French History 1787–1874* (London, 1963) is the best English biography, although the work of Charles Pouthas, especially *Guizot pendant la Restauration* (Paris, 1923), remains unsurpassed for his early political career. Pierre Rosanvallon's *Le moment Guizot* (Paris, 1985) describes the attempt of the "generation of 1814" to build a new France by assimilating the Revolution in order to bring it to a conclusive end. The "doctrinaire" political stance represented by Guizot is analyzed in Vincent Starzinger's *Middlingness: "Juste Milieu" Political Theory in France and England, 1815–48* (Charlottesville, Va., 1965) and in E. L. Woodward's *Three Studies in European Conservatism: Metternich, Guizot, the Catholic Church in the Nineteenth Century* (Hampden, Conn., 1963).

Guizot's influential philosophy of history is discussed in Karl Weintraub's *Visions of Culture* (Chicago, 1966); Stanley Mellon's *The Political Uses of History* (Stanford, 1958); G. P. Gooch's *History and Historians in the Nineteenth Century* (rev. ed., Baltimore, 1955); Friedrich Engel-Janosi's *Four Studies in Romantic Historical Writing* (Baltimore, 1955); Mary Consolata O'Connor's *The Historical Thought of François Guizot* (Washington, D.C., 1955); Shirley Gruner's "Political Historiography in Restoration France," *History and Theory* 8

of his work as historian; Wellek, in his more recent study, mentions Guizot's books on Corneille and Shakespeare, and quotes from them, but the extent of this notice amounts to one paragraph in the midst of five volumes.[4] Among historians of criticism, it is C. M. Haines, in his study *Shakespeare in France*, who forcefully asserts the importance of Guizot's work on Shakespeare, calling it "the only French work until recent times of which no student of Shakespeare can afford to be ignorant."[5] Guizot, writes Haines, was the first in France to judge Shakespeare historically and to specify that Shakespeare had created his own art and order, distinct from that of classical tragedy. The battle of classicists and romantics may have been finished by Stendhal and Hugo, but Guizot was a leader of the vanguard, "the most powerful force in the struggle."[6] In short, "although the conflict continued until [Hugo's Preface to *Cromwell* in] 1827, the blow which actually decided it was dealt by Guizot six years earlier."[7]

Before examining Guizot's discussions of literature, we should first examine where he placed literature in relation to "the fine arts." Guizot saw the arts, taken as a whole, as spreading across a spectrum. The "beaux-arts," painting and sculpture, exist at the end of the spectrum that consists of pure form; study of these media is "absolutely foreign to the affairs and combats of life" (*Beaux-Arts*, Preface, v). Sculpture represents the extreme case, dealing primarily with "situations" and sacrificing even truth to beauty when necessary (*Beaux-Arts*, 13). The painter, especially the historical painter, having more means at his disposal than form alone, may not escape his obligations to truth, for his subject is

---

(1969), 346–65; and Dietrich Gerhard's "Guizot, Augustin Thierry und die Rolle des Tiers Etat in Französischer Geschichte," *Historische Zeitschrift* 190 (1960), 290–310.

A fine brief introduction to Guizot's thought is found in Stanley Mellon's introduction to his edition of Guizot's *Historical Essays and Lectures* (Chicago, 1972). This collection, which contains a section from *Shakespeare and his Times*, is the only Guizot readily available in any language, and it is therefore indispensable.

4. Among nineteenth-century opinions of Guizot, those of John Stuart Mill, *Dissertations and Discussions*, vol. III (Boston, 1864); Ch.-A. Sainte-Beuve, *Nouveaux Lundis*, vols. 6 and 9 (Paris, 1863, 1867); Hippolyte Taine, *Essais de critique et d'histoire* (Paris, 1896); and George Pelissier, *The Literary Movement in France During the Nineteenth Century,* trans. A. G. Brinton (New York, 1897) retain their interest. All of these works, as well as Irving Babbitt's *Masters of Modern French,* deal primarily with Guizot's historical writings.

In René Wellek's *History of Modern Criticism,* 6 vols. to date (New Haven, 1955–86); see especially vol. III, 2–3.

5. C. M. Haines, *Shakespeare in France* (London, 1925), 111.

6. Ibid., 126.

7. Ibid., 123.

"action," not situation. His role is different from that of the sculptor. Sculpture creates a synchronic image, while painting's task is diachronic (*Beaux-Arts*, 15–20). "Truth" and "Beauty" are absolutes in sculpture and painting because of the sensory bases of the fine arts. The realm of painting is "everything in these objects which belongs to the sense of sight"; if visual cognition is assumed to be absolute, then visual truth will be theoretically absolute. Yet it is the relation to time that guarantees the truth of visual representations for Guizot. Because sculpture depicts situation, and has Beauty as its principle, Truth must often be sacrificed to Beauty by the sculptor. Painting, on the other hand, represents action and motion, wherein Guizot places Truth. The diachronic scope of the history painting is a higher and more truthful form than the synchronic sculpture because it has a wider vision.

Guizot's characteristic need to systematize emerges in an ironic comment on the vulgarity of the enormous busts that David had made popular. "It is the system of quantity!" wrote Guizot of the sculptures.[8] Without a relativistic paradigm of perception, theorists of the visual arts in the early nineteenth century were bound to a mimetic model of visual representation, although it was less absolute in the field of literature, whose relative nature had been illuminated both psychologically and historically. In this situation we find Guizot, whose literary writings seem in consequence more rewarding than his essay on the fine arts.

Guizot saw dramatic poetry as existing diametrically opposite the fine arts of painting and sculpture. The absolute truth that is the goal of the latter, and the absolute rules that direct the quest for that goal, obtain to a certain extent in the drama because a part of human nature is as unchanging and absolute as is sensory information. But in addition to these absolute rules, dramatic art possesses nonabsolute, relative rules—rules that set it apart from the fine arts. The relative rules of dramatic art "flow from the changeful state of society" (*Shakspeare*, 143). What changes in art "flows from" a changing society: the base/superstructure model later taken over by Marx presents itself. Here is a major joint at which Guizot was forced to mediate between apparently irreconcilable positions. Is a man a creature with a "nature," consequently demanding an absolute form of representation; or is he a creature with a "history," describable only through relative means? Although

8. François Guizot, *Lettres de François Guizot et de la Princesse de Lieven*, vol. I: *1836–39* (Paris, 1963), 244.

Guizot's implicit reply to the question was that man had both a nature and a history, his talents were better adapted to describing the changes of human history than the eternal aspects of human nature. Nevertheless, Guizot was not only theoretically aware of the need to integrate poetry and history; he was also specifically critical of those who would keep them apart as separate realms of fact.

In his lectures on the history of France, Guizot, who is conventionally judged a most unpoetical historian, cited the verse of Voltaire on the tales and superstitions of the Middle ages:

> Oh! l'heureux temps que celui de ces fables,
> Des bons démons, des esprits familiers,
> Des farfadets, aux mortels, secourables!
> On écoutait tous ces faits admirables
> Dans son château, près d'un large foyer.
> Le père et l'oncle, et la mère et la fille,
> Et les voisins, et toute la famille,
> Ouvraient l'oreille à monsieur l'aumônier,
> Qui leur faisait des contes de sorcier.
> On a banni les démons et les fées;
> Sous la raison les grâces étouffées
> Livrent nos coeurs à l'insipidité;
> La raisonner tristement s'accrédite;
> On court, hélas! après la vérité:
> Ah! croyez-moi, l'erreur a son mérite.[9]

Guizot noted that these lines counter, in both tone and intent, the description of that same age presented by Voltaire in his *Essais sur les moeurs et l'esprit des nations*, in which all that was "gross, absurd, odious, and calamitous in this epoch" was thoroughly excoriated. The judgments of the Enlightenment *philosophe* differed as he changed hats from cultural historian to poet; and Guizot regretted Voltaire's divided outlook.

> Voltaire was wrong to call *error* the poetic side of those olden
> times; undoubtedly the poetry associated with those days had
> many errors; but in itself it was true, although true in a very
> different way from philosophic truth, and it answered to the very
> legitimate needs of human nature. Besides, this incidental obser-

9. *Histoire de la civilization en France depuis la chute de l'empire romaine* (Paris, 1840), III, 230–31.

vation [of Voltaire's] is of little importance; what is important to note is the singular contrast between Voltaire the poet and Voltaire the critic: the poet feels vividly impressions of the middle ages to which the critic is completely foreign; and the former deplores the loss of these impressions which the latter works at destroying. Nothing better demonstrates the lack of political impartiality and of poetic sympathy of the eighteenth century, of which I earlier spoke.[10]

Voltaire here literally lacks integrity, oneness. He is a two-faced *philosophe*. Identity in the historian is as important as identity in history. The relation of the charming ghosts and fables to the odious age must be specified. For Guizot himself, "political impartiality" was the goal of the historical task, but to achieve a total view of a culture, "poetic sympathy" must be integrated. In fact, in a socially vigorous and intellectually active community, historical narrative itself may evoke as strong a personal response as poetry—Guizot remarks that the narratives of Herodotus delighted the Greeks as much as did the songs of Homer.[11] He renders an implicit verdict against the eighteenth century for separating history and poetry so widely. All in all, the *philosophes* were "men of parts." They lacked the grasp of totality that Guizot (and the generation of "the Guizot moment") sought.

Although it seemed unlikely to Guizot that the modern age could reproduce the Golden Age of Athens, he often pondered the question of what combination of factors provided the necessary ingredients for a vital literary culture in modern times. Why, he asked, had great ages in both French and English literatures occurred under absolute monarchs, Louis XIV and Elizabeth I? In 1813 Guizot wrote of Louis XIV: "The protection of a King is less enthralling than the familiarity of nobles: his laws may be more severe, but his constraint is less habitual; and poetry has perhaps less need of liberty than of leisure" (*Corneille*, 65–66). Four decades later, in exile after the Revolution of 1848 ended his political career, Guizot wrote a new preface to his work on Corneille, sketching the literary scene when the work was first written, in the later years of the Empire. In effect, he treats his own text as if it were an artifact, a literary document in need of historicization. In so doing he creates a social history of literature under Napoleon, an allegorical tale in which factions represent the essences of moments of French history.

10. Ibid., 231.
11. *Histoire des origines du gouvernement représentatif en Europe* (Paris, 1851), II, 4–5.

Three elements stood forth in that age: the *Journal des débats*, which championed the grandeur of the seventeenth century; Mme. de Staël, with her steadfast devotion to Enlightenment standards; and M. de Chateaubriand, who, for good or ill, contained within himself the characteristic passions and pieties of the young nineteenth century. All three groups opposed Napoleon (*Corneille*, iii–iv). Yet, Guizot recalls nostalgically, "literature was carefully cultivated and truly loved at that time, which left it so little space for its manifestation" (*Corneille*, v). Bonaparte lacked both legitimacy and the flexible humor that secure absolutism sometimes brings. He feared writers and censored them, because he himself was seen as only a temporary necessity. It was not the degree of power that affected the creative potentialities of a people, but rather the extent to which it had to be exercised.

> No periods are perhaps more favorable to the fertility and origi-
> nality of mental productions than those times at which a nation
> already free, but still ignorant of its own position, ingenuously
> enjoys what it possesses without perceiving in what it is deficient:
> times full of ardour, but very easy to please, before rights have
> been narrowly defined, powers discussed, or restrictions agreed
> upon. The government and the public, proceeding in their course
> undisturbed by fears or scruples, exist together without any dis-
> trustful observance of each other, and even come into communica-
> tion but rarely. If, on the one side, power is unlimited, on the
> other, liberty will be great; for both parties will be ignorant of
> those general forms, those innumerable and minute duties to
> which actions and minds are more or less subjected by a scien-
> tifically constructed despotism, and even by a well-regulated
> liberty. Thus it was that the age of Richelieu and Louis XIV con-
> sciously possessed that amount of liberty which has furnished us
> with a literature and a drama. (*Shakspeare*, 16)

And so, according to Guizot, did the age of Elizabeth. Despite the adulatory phrases of the courtier, the arrogance of the monarch, and the glory of her state, the reality of Elizabeth's power was limited by the very existence of Commons and sanctioned by an extraordinary popular loyalty. If the queen overruled Parliament, it had nevertheless still met and spoken; her power to decide had not stilled their right to speak.

> Poetic ardour and religious asperity, literary quarrels and the-
> ological controversies, taste for festivities and fanaticism for
> austerities, philosophy and criticism, sermons, pamphlets, and

epigrams, appeared simultaneously and jostled each other in
admired confusion. Amid this natural and fantastic conflict of
opposite elements, the power of opinion, the feeling and habit of
liberty were silently in the process of formation: two forces, brilliant at their first appearance and imposing in their progress, the
first-fruits of which belong to any skilful government that is able
to use them, but the maturity of which is terrible to any impru-
dent government that may attempt to reduce them to servitude.
(*Shakspeare*, 19–20)

It was otherwise with Napoleon, whose reign was sanctioned by
silence. The principal problem for Guizot's criticism was to discover the
relation between a society and its literature; this issue was a natural
response to Napoleonic censorship.

The most interesting and fully developed of the connections Guizot
reveals is found in his sketch of the series of genres that made up the
history of French poetry until the late seventeenth century. In this narrative, a close correspondence is posited between social facts—the
entry of various classes into the world of poetic discourse, changes of
power relationships, conflicts of groups—and the various forms
assumed by literary art. He prefaces his discussion with a question that
reveals his quest for principles: why do apparently similar conditions
produce quite different literatures in different nations?

We shall look for the secret of the different effects which have
resulted in the different literatures, in the special nature of the
governments, in the manners of the peoples, in the particular
character of the troubles which agitated them, and in the personal
position in which the authors and actors of these troubles were
placed; and we shall thus be led to acknowledge the influence of
those innumerable secondary causes, whose nature or power it is
impossible accurately to define, and whose reality it is sometimes
even impossible to affirm. (*Corneille*, 27–28)

This passage acknowledges the problem of constructing great allegorical images ("the different literatures," "the nature of the governments," "the manners of the peoples") from the finely sifted stuff of the
"innumerable secondary causes," which may even not exist as causes at
all.

The first product of the French poetic genius is the poetry of love, in
the Provençal style. In Guizot's opinion, this style too often departed
from the sincerity suitable to both love and poetry into that fantastic

and fanciful form which has since afflicted the French. Thus he cites the song of Raimbault de Vaqueiras, who protested against the refusal of his mistress to receive his attentions after her marriage by composing six couplets—the first in Provençal, the successive ones in Tuscan, French, Gascon, and Spanish, and finally a couplet mixing all five languages, indicating her fickleness (*Corneille*, 29–30). The responsibility for such macaronic frivolity and for the domination of poetry by amorous subjects lay in the class of its authors; love "had become the principal business of an idle nobility" (*Corneille*, 29).

The next genre discussed, satire, appears in Guizot's account to develop logically from the Provençal love lyric and the social conditions of its age; love, being both a social and a combative matter, created conflicts that could not be resolved under "that semi-despotic, semi-aristocratic form of monarchy, which leaves the victims of abuses no other resource than complaint or ridicule" (*Corneille*, 33). Thus the concept of class struggle appears in the literary work of Guizot before he uses it in his historical lectures. Guizot attributes the growth of satire alongside the poetry of love to the diffusion of poetry among the lower classes, who inject a vitality, "a satirical and sportive character, more natural to subjects than to princes" (*Corneille*, 34).

Guizot's hostility to the development of Provençal love poetry is a moral one, but the precise focus of his disapproval is the moment when language assumes center stage and indicates its status as a conventional device. What is wrong with Raimbault de Vaqueiras is not so much his sentiments as the form of their expression. *To indicate the substantiality of language is to signal insincerity.* Satire remedies this failure. Its sentiments are very real, based on oppression; Guizot sees in satire the potential power that Mikhail Bakhtin associates with "carnival." However, satire has a flaw that frustrates its grasp of truth; and this flaw is also linguistic. "Satire pre-supposes the existence of determinate moral ideas; and thus morality abounds in the satirical works of this period; but it is less the morality which follows as a natural consequence from the narrative of human actions, than that which is the result of reflection, and which instructs the mind without animating it with any elevated and powerful sentiments" (*Corneille*, 35). Morality is a consequence of genre, of *narrative*, to be exact. A nonnarrative form must fail as a moral stimulus, just as sculpture, another nonnarrative form, failed as a representation of truth. Truth is found in action; action belongs to narrative.

Love and satire represented only feelings and ideas, not action. They came naturally to classes either lazy or impotent. More was necessary to capture the substance and reality of life, and to discourse on human nature. One solution that appeared as the middle ages waned was merely to personify the sentiments and ideas of the older styles. In allegory, Guizot astutely remarks, action and characters appeared, but reality did not. At the wedding of Henry II's sister to the Duke of Savoy, a play depicted "Paris" as the father of three marriageable daughters, "University," "Town," and "City," the three sections of the medieval city; the blatant artificiality of this style made it obviously inadequate for an ever-broadening audience. Other models, superior to allegory, already existed in France; these were the romances of chivalry, which "as pictures of manners, are as faithful as could be permitted by the system upon which they were founded" (*Corneille*, 36–37). The cause of this realism, Guizot leaves no doubt, was popular opinion, the spreading of the literature from court to a somewhat larger, noncourtly, audience. In the verses of Marot, "the true type of the old French style" emerges, combining contraries, "a mixture of grace and archness, of elegance and simplicity, of familiarity and propriety" (*Corneille*, 37). In his description of Marot and the "true" French style—compounded from aristocratic and popular influences—Guizot prefigures literarily Montlosier's *De la monarchie française* of 1814, in which the mixture of Franks and Gauls is presented as the dynamic force in French development.[12]

Up to this point in his discussion, Guizot has remained vague about both genres and societies. The totality of life has appeared chaotic, undefined, and in flux; from this chaos styles emerge and vanish. The next great turning point after the birth of Provençal literature comes with the establishment of a distinct court society in the sixteenth century. The lively confusion of late medieval and early renaissance life had finally created a "middle" style, a blend of courtly and noncourtly ingredients. Because this style, represented by the verse of Marot, mediated between court and people, Guizot found in it truth and universality.

The political tone of Guizot's literary history increases as he approaches the poets of the later sixteenth century, whose effect he pointedly calls a revolution, sudden and unforeseen.

> Let us not be astonished at the names of Ronsard, Dubartas, Jodelle, Baïf, and others: revolutions in taste, like those of

---

12. Gerhard, "Guizot, Thierry, und die Rolle des Tiers Etat," 301.

empires, exert no influence upon the duration assigned to the course of human life; and events sometimes occur with such rapidity, that one single generation may witness an entire change in the aspect of the world. (*Corneille*, 39)

In this process, Ronsard becomes a rejected hero (foreshadowing, albeit as farce, Mirabeau): "The men who effect revolutions are always scorned by those who profit from them" (*Corneille*, 47). The imitators of Ronsard took his brilliant style, so distant from the simplicity of Marot, and pushed it to an extreme of pedantry, creating a new poetic disorder demanding reform. This reform is portrayed as a counter-revolution: "The revolution which had taken place in reaction upon that attempted by Ronsard, appeared complete; but the movements of the human mind always result in progress, and never in any but apparent retrogression" (*Corneille*, 54). The inward preciosity of Ronsard, resulting from the removal of the poet from popular influence, gives way to the mere verse-smithing of Malherbe, whose model convinced far too many hacks that they, too, were poets.

Louis XIV put an end to this welter of literary revolution and counter-revolution—Guizot is nearing the Golden Age. The protection of an absolute ruler replaced the tyranny of the nobility, and eliminated the need to survive in a petty world of fashion, "une société encore peu éclairée"; literature must be freed from society. Before Louis XIV, the fashion was to write without effort, "sans ce qu'on appellait pédanterie." Seriousness vanished; no object was seen as it really was. Scarron, "the hero of burlesque," dominated. A poet of this age is quoted by Guizot: "I write verses, it is true, but it is to kill time; and then they are only little gallant epistles which I compose while my hair is being dressed" (*Corneille*, 92).

The poetic activity of the seventeenth century was at first without direction. Aware of the richness of their materials, the poets first set about the task of reducing it to order. Guizot perceived that their project was to create "regularity" and "correctness." "The principal object of their labors," Guizot adds, "was the purification of the language" (*Corneille*, 94). The early development of the French Academy, beginning as a private coterie, later protected by Cardinal Richelieu, and finally dominating the letters of the nation itself, signaled an important power shift within French society; it marked, in fact, the creation of a new aristocracy of letters, whose prestige grew as the prestige of the aristocracy of birth waned.

In proportion as, during the reign of Louis XIV., court distinctions became less honorable, distinctions of mind were more sought after, and these it was in the power of men of letters to bestow. At the beginning of the seventeenth century, they had been obliged to waste their talents in pandering to the frivolous pastimes of society: when the eighteenth century arrives, society was desirous to understand those serious ideas which formed the subject of their mediations. This revolution in manners was destined soon to become an intellectual revolution, and finally to operate a political revolution, and to change the face of the world, after having at first only changed the social relations of men of letters to men of the world. But I pause before the immense horizon and the fathomless abyss which simultaneously open before me. (*Corneille*, 109)

As a literary historian, Guizot led his readers imaginatively to the edge of "le profond âbime"; as a historical being himself, he was aware that he stood on the other side of the abyss, living within a world quite removed from that of Corneille and his predecessors.

It is interesting to search in *Corneille et son temps* for a hidden philosophy of history. This social history of literature functions by positing two essentialized series, unified by a series of primarily verbal resemblances. A frivolous aristocracy produces a frivolous love poetry. The frustration of the oppressed under despotism produces satire, the embodiment of subterranean class struggle. The artificiality of allegory mirrors the motion without movement of sixteenth-century court life, and so forth. The apparent connections of cause and effect are basically mimetic: a social situation gives rise to a literary form that resembles its description.

With the creation of the French Academy, however, Guizot's tactics change. By giving French literature the bureaucratic regularity of an institution, whose very creation and prestige lent to all men of letters a new power, the Academy appears to have cut literature free from society and this play of verbal resemblance. Actually, however, Guizot simply reverses the series of resemblances: the "revolution" in manners inspired by the literati became a political revolution, then a world revolution. Yet the revolutionary aspect of the literary series of events depends entirely upon its resemblance to the political series of which it is ostensibly the cause. The hierarchy of the two series becomes interchangeable and interdependent. This is the fathomless abyss that stops Guizot. The base/superstructure model that has served him well for the earlier years of French vernacular literature, and that is based on resemblances of allegorized forms, cannot account for a literature that challenges the dominant order, so literature itself is allegorized as a primary phenomenon rather than an epiphenomenon. The logic of this move may be questionable, but it permits Guizot to maintain his causal "link" with social reality, and to avoid the notion that both the social forms and the styles are linguistic constructs, linked metaphorically.

Despite the time and space separating Corneille and Shakespeare, each man stood at the center of a glorious literary age. Ages like theirs mark watersheds. They force critics to define both what went before and what came after in reference to the peaks. Yet the age of Corneille and the age of Shakespeare left quite different legacies to their respective cultures. When Guizot turned to this second literary study, *Shakspeare et son temps,* he found in it an opportunity to contrast French and English development. In doing so, he stood in the middle of a line of French critics stretching from Voltaire to Taine. Why, Guizot asked, do different nations produce different literatures? The factors of climate and history were familiar to the critic-historians of the late eighteenth and early nineteenth centuries, and Guizot did not slight them. His basic premise, however, had to do with comparative social structures and their reflections in literary form. These speculations sound very much like an embryonic literary sociology. In his *Pour une sociologie du roman,* Lucien Goldmann describes one fundamental concern of the sociological critic as follows:

> For the very first problem that a sociology of the novel will have to confront is that of the relation between the *form of the novel* itself and the *structure* of the social environment within which it developed—that is to say, of the novel as literary genre and modern individualist society.[13]

It is precisely this relationship with which Guizot sought on his own terms to grapple. In France's classic age, the styles of comedy and tragedy were scrupulously separated; in Elizabethan England they were not: the question is thus posed. His conclusions—that a mixed style corresponds to a mixed society, and that a pure separation of styles corresponds to a highly stratified social structure—again demonstrate the linguistic and allegorical structure of social literary history.

In Guizot's own words:

> We may therefore affirm that, in France, comedy, in an imperfect,

13. Lucien Goldmann, *Pour une sociologie du roman* (Paris, 1964), 34–35.

but distinct form, was created before tragedy. At a later period, the rigorous separation of classes, the absence of popular institutions, the regular action of the supreme power, the establishment of a more exact and uniform system of public order than existed in any other country, the habits and influences of the Court, and a variety of other causes, disposed the popular mind to maintain that strict distinction between the two styles which was ordained by the classical authorities, who held undisputed sway over the drama. (*Shakspeare*, 82–83)

The separation of French classes and the various forces that effected and sustained this separation thus populate a paradigm of "distinctions," of the strict sense of decorum and otherness that is the essence of the classical style and mind. No such paradigm existed in England, "asylum of German manners, as well as of German liberties" (*Shakspeare*, 84). In England, the mixed society dictated the mixed style of English comedy, a style that was at once fantastic and romantic (*Shakspeare*, 84–85). At this point Guizot's argument takes on its own romantic aspect as he describes the origins of England's semipermeable class structure. English feudalism, according to Guizot, created a relationship of lord and vassal so close that a social bond emerged from the economic relationship of agriculture, and a cultural tie from the social tie. By analogy, Guizot argues that "men who are accustomed to meet together for business, will meet together for pleasure also; and when the serious life of the landowner is spent among his fields, he does not remain a stranger to the joys of the people who cultivate or surround them" (*Shakspeare*, 45). In the mixed society of medieval England originated the peculiar uniqueness of Shakespearean comedy, so troubling to the mind of France in its classical age because of what appeared to be a serious lack of self-cohesion.

Guizot himself cannot hide his discomfort with some of the comedies; for him, although they encompass everything, create an entire world, they nevertheless lack at times the principle of ensemble. It is this totality that constitutes "reality" for Guizot. The tragedies evidence law, cause, and effect; but the comedies at their most fantastic are always flashing, changing. These represent for Guizot the anarchic potentialities of a mixed society; even chaos can be totalized and related to the whole of an allegorized social whole. It is inconceivable for Guizot that an image of reality might be unstable and chaotic.

The best of Shakespeare's comedies, however, escape the mercurial fantasy of what Guizot calls "le goût romantesque." _The Tempest_, for example, although "peopled with sylphs and sprites" and ruled by fairy power, unfolds in perfectly consistent and uncomplicated fashion once its world is granted and set in motion. _A Midsummer Night's Dream_, another fairy drama, lacks the logic of _The Tempest_, and Guizot can defend "this amazing and brilliant extravaganza" only by a bold rhetorical appeal to the pleasure principle. "Are originality, simplicity, gaity, and gracefulness so common that we shall treat them severely because they are lavished on a slight foundation of but little value?" (_Shakspeare_, 93). The crucial difference, Guizot implies, between _The Tempest_ and _A Midsummer Night's Dream_ lies in the social configuration of each. In the latter, we are presented with three separate societies— nobles, rustics, and fairies; and the "hackneyed incident" of the noble lovers are redeemed only by the grotesque confusion and elfin fantasies of the others. The groups pass and touch each other in the ignorance of night, but they cannot mix, having no common problem in life. With the day, they are again themselves, and without memory. In _The Tempest_, on the contrary, a real mixed society is created, unified for the span of the drama by a shared situation. Even the language of the play reflects its univocality, for in no other play has Shakespeare, Guizot observes, used so few plays on words. The unity, _ensemble_, of _The Tempest_ models the unity, however transitory, of its inhabitants.

> We must probably ascribe this fact partly to the singularity of the position, and to the necessity for bringing into harmony so many different conditions, feelings, and interests, which, for a few hours, are involved in a common fate, and surrounded by the same supernatural atmosphere. (_Shakspeare_, 420)

The virtues of _The Tempest_, then, are at least in part sociopolitical, in Guizot's view; but the other sources of this judgment are linguistic. _The Tempest_ excels because it reinforces the totalizing process that produces unified allegorical characters upon which his social history depends. Characters become classes; the play becomes society itself. Without this principle of ensemble, history becomes chaos.

One of Guizot's most unorthodox judgments concerned Shakespeare's _Timon of Athens_, which he esteemed highly _as a comedy_, even as an example of "that scientific style in which the ridiculous is made to flow from the serious, and which constitutes _la grande comédie_." Timon, in effect, joins the company of Molière's misanthropes, learned ladies, hypochondriacs, ridiculous pedants, and the rest. The effect, Timon's misanthropy, is absurdly disproportionate to its cause, the inconstancy of his friends, which in itself is lacking "neither in truthfulness nor effect." Seen as comedy, Timon parodies the extreme, focuses on the gap between norm and exception, and leaves a clearly implied latent image of what a reasonable world *ought* to be—hence, the connection to *la grande comédie.*

At their best, however, Shakespeare's plays eradicate the distinction between comedy and tragedy—in these works Guizot found not tragedy leavened by comedy nor comedy deepened by tragedy, not tragicomedy, nor comi-tragedy, but rather life. In *The Merchant of Venice*, the plot of which is "entirely romantic" and thus ostensibly comic, Shakespeare "entered into the real world in which the comic and the tragic are commingled, and, when depicted with equal truthfulness, concur by their combination to increase the power of the effect produced" (*Shakspeare,* 96). At the moment of Portia's judgment, and Shylock's disastrous triumph, comedy and tragedy emerge together simultaneously from a story of early origin and romantic tenor. From a virtual farce, Shakespeare has created reality.

Guizot suggested that *The Tempest, Timon of Athens,* and *The Merchant of Venice* occupy, each in its own way, the central ground of Shakespearean drama; the essence of each is mixture. *The Tempest* mixes plausible cause with absurd effect; and *The Merchant of Venice,* at its climactic moment, presents comedy and tragedy so indissolubly fused in one character as to obliterate their distinction entirely. The privileged position of these three plays consists in precisely their central location, not within the temporal span of Shakespeare's dramas, but rather in the logical space plotted in his works. In other words, if the works of William Shakespeare may be viewed as a society, the plays discussed above constitute *a middle class.* We perceive quickly that the plays contain in Guizot's description the basic structural elements and virtues of the social class. The mixed form, which exists in all of Shakespeare's work to some extent, and is epitomized by the three plays mentioned, challenges the concepts of style entirely, just as the middle class is the class that strives to deny the existence of classes.[14]

It is utterly futile to attempt to base any classification of Shakespeare's works on the distinction between the comic and the tragic elements; they cannot possibly be divided into these two styles,

14. For a discussion of the bourgeoisie as mythmaker, see Roland Barthes, *Mythologies* (Paris, 1957), 224ff.

but must be separated into the fantastic and the real, the romance and the world. The first class contains most of his comedies; the second comprehends all his tragedies,—immense and living stages, on which all things are represented, as it were, in their solid form, and in the place which they occupied in a stormy and complicated state of civilization. (*Shakspeare*, 97–98)

But Guizot did not merely rename comedy and tragedy; indeed, he fashioned an opposition between a dramatic form in which events pursue their course, and one in which a character dominates events. Since Guizot's criterion of criticism was obviously fundamentally mimetic, the question of judgment dissolved into philosophy of history, which asked whether determinism or the sovereign individual is the central focus of change. Guizot, characteristically, granted neither side. The fantastic, artificial manipulations of *A Midsummer Night's Dream* represent a virtual parody of determinism; the characters are led through their maze without awareness, learning nothing, and concluding as before the first-act curtain. Basically the action is not comedic at all, but absurdist—Puck's comment on the mental powers of mortals is reflected in the structure of the play. On the other hand, to attribute the propellent and unifying force of history to individual wills would not only be to deny the existence of supra-individual forces, but would also deny the meaning of tragedy itself. So Guizot's fundament in the Shakespearean edifice is the middle class of plays, those whose structures mix the necessity of event with the shaping force of human intent—situation and response.

Having located Shakespearean drama within the fluid space of a mixed society, and having described a particularly mixed group of plays as the most potently real of the opus, Guizot clearly identified the playwright's social status. "Shakspeare's family," we are told, "belonged to that *bourgeoisie* which early acquired so much influence in England" (*Shakspeare*, 21). Class considerations were inferred by Guizot as the cause of Shakespeare's retirement from the theater. Giving an account of the social history of the English theater and of the social composition of the audiences of Elizabethan England, Guizot concluded that the difference between the audiences at bear-baitings and at Blackfriars was not great, nor was the social difference great between a strolling player and an actor in an established theater. Given the opportunity, Shakespeare rejected the coarse public and the common colleagues, and left "in oblivion an existence which had given him but little satisfaction"

(*Shakspeare*, 118). With the purchase of a house and land in Stratford, Shakespeare attained the respectability of order and security.

Guizot's defense of the mixed style of Shakespeare, and his description of its connection with the mixed society of Elizabethan England, was anything but an attack on the separation of styles. His historicism was too thoroughgoing to ignore both the power and the decorum of classicism, in which comedy and tragedy divide an ordered world between them, each showing, with a precision bred of specialization, a separate part of reality.

> Thus every art and every style received its free and isolated development, within the limits of its proper mission. Thus tragedy and comedy shared man and the world between them, each taking a different domain in the region of realities, and coming by turns to offer to the serious or mirthful consideration of a people who invariably insisted upon simplicity and harmony, the poetic effects which their skill could derive from the materials placed in their hands.
>
> In our modern world, all things have borne another character. Order, regularity, natural and easy development, seem to have been banished from it. (*Shakspeare*, 79–80)

A simple, well-defined world requires a clear division of labor; and the ancient world in which comedy and tragedy were born could be adequately described in these styles. Guizot's image of the birth of comedy and tragedy was sketched in his work on Corneille, and shaded, but not redrawn, in the work on Shakespeare. The simplicity of the ancients permitted "the free and harmonious development of the human mind"; the origin of literature, then, is but "spontaneous expansion" of their nature (*Corneille*, 22). In Homer's age neither letters nor coinage were known, but the simplicity of that age was gone. The enormous complexity of modern history has made the precise roots of the literatures of modern nations virtually impossible to discover. Guizot wrote of these literatures:

> They came into being in the midst of a crowd of obscure and discordant circumstances which it would be necessary to distinguish and connect, in order properly to link together the chain of facts, and to discern their progressive influence. Do we believe that we have discovered some of these decisive indications which serve to explain the character and conduct of peoples? We soon perceive that even these indications do not disclose the secret of

the causes which have determined the genius of literatures; for the great events of history have acted upon letters only by unknown and indirect affinities, which it is almost impossible to apprehend. (*Corneille*, 26)

If the origins of literature were ultimately obscured by history, the critic nevertheless had his own task as a participant in the literary battles of his own day.

All criticism in the early nineteenth century focused in one way or another on the question of romanticism. Yet there seemed to be as many romanticisms as there were self-styled romantics; the word "romantic" then had no accepted definition, hardly even a set of consistent "family resemblances." Shakespeare, however, was at the center of the romantic debate, as Schlegel pointed out in 1800. To justify Shakespeare's ways to the modern man of the nineteenth century was to strike a blow for romanticism—whatever it was. One thing was clear to the critic: Shakespeare was no classicist.

The classical system had its origin in the life of its time; that time has passed; its image subsists in brilliant colours in its works, but can no more be reproduced. Near the monuments of past ages, the monuments of another age are now beginning to arise. What will be their form? I cannot tell; but the ground upon which their foundations may rest are already perceptible. This ground is not the ground of Corneille and Racine, nor is it that of Shakspeare; it is our own, but Shakspeare's system, as it appears to me, may furnish the plans according to which genius ought now to work. This system alone includes all those social conditions and all those general and diverse feelings, the simultaneous conjunction and activity of which constitutes for us, at the present day, the spectacle of human things. Witnesses, during thirty years, of the greatest revolutions of society, we shall no longer willingly confine the movement of our mind within the narrow space of some family event, or the agitations of a purely individual passion. The nature and destiny of man have appeared to us under their most striking and their simplest aspect, in all their extent and in all their variableness. (*Shakspeare*, 181–182)

In this passage we may hear either resonances of Schlegel and Novalis or foreshadowings of Stendhal and Hugo; but the voice is uniquely Guizot's. He historicized aesthetic norms and rejected classicism as the voice of a bygone age, an age whose brilliance may be admired but not recovered. This much will become conventional romantic criticism.

Shakespeare was also historicized, but for a different purpose. Guizot the social historian has created verbal images of the essence of Elizabethan society and the Elizabethan audience: both are mixtures, dominated not by either extreme, but by the middle segments. Shakespeare's age was his own, his audience unique; yet his "system" served as a model for the modern artist of Guizot's day. To demonstrate this, Guizot had first to demonstrate that Shakespeare had a "system." A verbal image of the Shakespearean essence, already hinted at in Guizot's implied description of his opus as a social spectrum, was necessary.

> Italy alone and France, the fatherlands of modern classicism, are not yet recovered from their astonishment at the first shock given to those opinions which they have established with the rigor of necessity, and maintained with the pride of faith. Doubt presents itself to us as yet only as an enemy whose attacks we are beginning to fear; it seems as though discussion bears a threatening aspect, and that examination cannot probe without undermining and overturning. In this position, we hesitate, as if about to destroy that which will never be replaced; we are afraid of finding ourselves without law, and of discovering nothing but the insufficiency or illegitimacy of those principles upon which we were formerly wont to rely without disquietude.
>
> This disturbance of mind cannot cease so long as the question remains undecided between science and barbarism, the beauties of order and the effects of disorder; so long as men persist in seeing, in that system of which the first outlines were traced by Shakspeare, nothing but an allowance of unrestrained liberty and undefined latitude to the flights of the imagination, as well as to the course of genius. If the romantic system has beauties, it necessarily has its art and rules. Nothing is beautiful, in the eyes of man, which does not derive its effects from certain combinations, the secret of which can always be supplied by our judgment when our emotions have attested its power. The knowledge or enjoyment of these combinations constitutes art. Shakspeare had his own art. (*Shakspeare*, 142)

What is at stake here, Guizot is quite aware, is not merely the aesthetic question of Shakespeare's place in the history of western literature, nor the course that a future literature ought to take. Rather, it is faith in our human ability to represent the historical universe in consistent, orderly terms while at the same time guaranteeing a proper degree of human freedom. The political background is clear: the chaos that the classical rules dreaded was realized in the Revolution, the order that those rules maintained has no place (and deserves none) in the new post-Revolutionary world. The tyranny of Bonaparte is a temporary makeshift in Guizot's view. Yet the Shakespearean accomplishment that is the model for romantic art seems to be a return to chaos. Doubts, fears, illegitimacy, disquietude, follow. Is it to be science or barbarism?

The purpose of Guizot's social history of literature was to find an order to the flux of styles and tastes in European art. This he hypothesized by suggesting that style "flows from" the changing state of society, and is a thoroughly historical phenomenon, no more arbitrary or fanciful than the course of history itself. His notion of "flowing from," however, depends upon formal analogy—that is, similarity of verbal descriptions, essentialization. As we have seen, when problems arise, when characterizations of literary style do not easily match descriptions of social institutions, the relations may be reversed. Literature becomes the institution, as in the founding of the French *Académie*, and social change may "flow from" literature. Encoded in this way, social determinism and historical idealism become interchangeable.

The Shakespeare problem is quite a different one for Guizot, but he attempts a similar tactic. Although there is no institution in England like the Academy that Guizot can use as an allegorized actor in the narrative, turning on its creators and assuming an independent status, Shakespeare can be rescued from the status of the historically meaningless, which is identical with the indescribable, that which cannot be essentialized. Although his plays, even the best of them, which capture "reality" and "life" in its totality, appear to defy genre and essentialization, they must have a "secret" order, or else they could not affect our emotions. The horror of what lacks rules proves the existence of order in apparent chaos. Disorder is the enemy of art, and beauty the result of rules, but rules that are hidden, "secret," and revealed only from within. In one sense, Guizot had classicized romanticism by insisting on order in art. Seen from another angle, he had sublimated apparent disorder into a deeper order in an almost Hegelian fashion. What began as an understanding and judgment based on descriptions of the social "order" and its literary productions circles around to become a justifica-

tion of a new social order based upon the literary effects of its metaphoric representatives, Shakespeare's plays, or a few of them. What is
not thinkable in Guizot's social history is a disorderly, unsystematic
vision of reality. Even more than a *partial* vision of reality, a chaotic reality that cannot be captured in language and its rules is morally
unacceptable. The same linguistic puritanism that led Guizot to dismiss
the frivolity of Provençal poetry or any art for its own sake demands that
the historian salvage order even when his linguistic strategies break
down.

5

NARRATING THE "TABLEAU"

QUESTIONS OF NARRATIVITY

IN MICHELET

I

*We may distinguish two major kinds of arrangements of
these thematic elements: (1) that in which causal-temporal
relationships exist between the thematic elements, and
(2) that in which the thematic elements are contempo-
raneous, or in which there is some shift of theme without
internal exposition of the causal connections. The former are
stories (tales, novels, epics); the latter have no "story,"
they are "descriptive" (e.g., descriptive and didactic poems,
lyrics, and travel books such as Karamzin's* Letters of a
Russian Traveller *or Goncharov's* The Frigate Pellas.
Boris Tomashevsky[1]*

Historical and literary theorists have just begun, halt-
ingly and grudgingly, to accept the proposition that, as Paul Ricoeur put
it, history and fiction together form a "grand narratology," a narratology that stands, for better or worse, as the basis of our culture and
its unique way of defining, describing, and dominating human reality.[2]
Storytelling may indeed be universal, but formal narratives of the sort
to be found in the novel or the history are certainly not, requiring as
they do a certain notion of time, of mind, and of power to produce that

1. The epigraphs of the four sections of this essay are from Boris Tomashevsky's "Thematics," in *Russian Formalist Criticism: Four Essays,* trans. Lee T. Lemon and Marion J.
Reis (Lincoln, Nebr., 1965), 61–98.
2. Paul Ricoeur, *Temps et récit* (Paris, 1984), II, 230.

vision of human reality which a certain culture finds plausible at a certain time.[3] If narrative is the reflection *par excellence* of the Western mentality in its broadest sense, it is because of its perceived formal truthfulness, the implicit feeling that we experience the world in the same form as we report those experiences, as stories. Thus, although narrative may at any moment be an invitation to falsehood, it remains the dominant *mode* of truth about human affairs, the "natural" form of *mimesis*.[4]

One could give up this narratology—that is, deny its sway over history or fiction. In the first case one would assert that historical reality is discovered or reconstructed, rather than made or constructed, and that therefore the inescapable narrative aspects of history are derived from reality rather than from art, which is itself merely mimetic insofar as it is narrative in form; in the second, one would deny to the representation of causal events in time the central place in prose, and elevate a systematic algebra of parts and types as the essential formal model of literature. But to do so would seem to herald a radical dehumanization, which will divorce people not only from their community, but also from the forms of their own experience and thus their own identity. No stories, no people.

Because the primary debates over historiography forty years ago were about explanation, the terms of that debate rarely included narrative per se. Between the developmentalism of the historicists, the empirical falsificationism of the Popperites, and the strict reductionism of the covering-law adherents, the linguistic status of history was excluded as a given; histories manifestly were mainly narratives, so the arena of argument was the nature of proper explanation within historical narratives rather than inquiry into the nature of historical narratives as such.

We should keep in mind the fundamental forms that the attitude toward narrative in history has taken in the last three decades.[5] The

3. On this, see Roland Barthes, "Introduction to the Structural Analysis of Narrative," in *Image-Music-Text*, trans. Stephen Heath (New York, 1972); and Hayden White, "The Value of Narrativity in the Representation of Reality," in *Critical Inquiry*, 7:1 (1980).

4. Erich Auerbach's *Mimesis: The Representation of Reality in Western Literature* (Princeton, 1968) is for the most part a study of narratives; the few exceptions, plays such as *Adam and Eve* or *Henry IV*, Part I, are discussed from the point of view of narrative categories, plot and character, as though they were proper narratives.

5. The discussion that follows is broadly taken from Hayden White's "The Question of Narrative in Contemporary Historical Theory," *History and Theory* 23:1 (1984), 1-33, an indispensable survey of the subject.

The Language of Historians: Four Shipwrecks

Anglo-American tradition of analytic philosophy has maintained that narrative is *the* proper form of historical procedure not merely because it represents a mode of discourse that bears the facts and explanations that history requires, but rather because it is itself the mode of historical explanation in that it provides meaning and causation in, and only in, the telling of a story. This attitude quite naturally corresponds to the historical practice that emphasizes the "found" rather than "created" nature of events, and stresses above all the importance of "getting the story straight."[6] Against this notion of narrative as a reputable means of explanation (and of all other means as disreputable), we find the stance of the structuralists of the 1950s and 1960s, such as Lévi-Strauss and the early Barthes, who held that narrative was a purely ideological device, not the relatively innocent carrier of myths, but basically mythic itself, intent on projecting its own form onto the world, which is thereby held to consist in reality of stories and their baggage, including subjects, beginnings, middles, and, perhaps above all, ends. This point of view seems obviously related to the attitude of the historians of the French *Annales* school, who for a time attacked and, more to the point, rejected narrative in their own work, not because its form was an essentially ideological coding, but because its available contents, the kinds of things that they felt that narratives privileged (such as human events, wars, politics, and so forth), were of increasingly less interest to the historian in the age of mass movements, the modern social sciences, and the computerization of information. Against this view, however, was the position of hermeneutic philosophers, who noted the importance of inner time-consciousness in human understandings of all human life, and who maintained that textual narrative, related as it is to the narrativity of human understanding itself, is the necessary and inescapable form of temporality itself—human fate, as it were.[7]

The high level of this debate, and the advanced and timely nature of most of the positions espoused in it, have not carried over into discussions of narrative by historians themselves. Lawrence Stone, in a widely discussed article of 1979 on the "revival" of narrative, manages to miss almost all of the substance of the literature on history and narrative and to maintain that a recent turn to narrative on the part of certain French historians who had attacked it from the *Annales* position a

6. The work of J. H. Hexter and that of Geoffrey Elton serve as examples.

7. These issues are further discussed in Chapter 12, "Narrativity in History: Post-Structuralism and Since."

decade before was the result of "a belated recognition" of things like power, chance, politics, and so forth. He further suggests that the new narrative historians have at last become "relevant," and offers a long list of "burning issues at the moment," things like death and sex, which were apparently far from people's minds in the more quantitative 1950s and 1960s. Even when purportedly discussing the formal side of the "new narrative," Stone resolutely finds contents. "Under the influence of the modern novel and of Freudian ideas, [the new narrative historians] gingerly explore the subconscious rather than sticking to the plain facts. And under the influence of the anthropologists, they try to use behavior to reveal symbolic meaning."[8] This is far from the notion that narrative constitutes an artificial coding that distorts reality in the same way that all representational modes do, or that the least deceptive form of representation is the one that points most self-consciously to its status as a system of effects. By treating narrative as the natural carrier of certain kinds of content (whether the old, outmoded ones of kings and armies, or the new, relevant ones of disease and concubines) and ignoring any sense that narrative or nonnarrative forms may in themselves bear ideological and semiotic implications, Stone and the many who entered into debate with him seem to be model "straight readers," for whom the formal and textual properties of narrative discourse are as unnoticed as the lenses of a telescope, described by Timothy Reiss as the essential metaphor of modernism.

In his work of the last ten years, Paul Ricoeur has considered the question of narrative and history more comprehensively than anyone else. Narrative is for him almost a sacred scripture in that it alone represents and works out the human relationship to temporality and eternity. Further, he presents this argument from within a view of history deeply influenced by and sympathetic to recent French nonnarrative history. Ricoeur accepts the elevation of plot as the center of historical writing put forth by Paul Veyne, Hayden White, and others, but he feels that this does not explain how narrative remains the essence of history when history ceases to be about events.[9] This is the key problem for all "narrativist" understandings of history, particularly in the face of the French historical accomplishment, about which Ricoeur has written in

8. Lawrence Stone, "The Revival of Narrative: Reflections on a New Old History," *Past and Present* 85 (1979) 3–24.

9. Paul Ricoeur, *Time and Narrative*, trans. Kathleen McLaughlin and David Pellauer (Chicago, 1984), I, 174.

The Language of Historians: Four Shipwrecks

The Contribution of French Historiography to the Theory of History. "This question today must be addressed to all holders of a 'narrativist' theory of history. English-speaking authors have been able to avoid it because their examples usually are naive and do not surpass the history of events."[10]

The key ambiguity haunting the debate on historical narrative is a quite basic one. The historian's notion of narrative, as we have seen, is considerably narrower than that which reigns in narratology in its broadest sense, foregrounding as history does the function of representation of events, which is neither a necessary nor a sufficient condition for narrative in its literary sense. The strictness of construction in historical narrative definitions might seem an advantage but, given the muddied nature of the debate over historical narrative, is evidently not.

The problem, I think, has to do with the idea of the event. The idea that "all change enters the field of history as a quasi-event" does, indeed, admit the great *Annales* accomplishment to the favored side of narrative history, but it does not account for further "analogies." That is, by remaining true to the historian's concentration on represented time in the past, the extension of the notion of event does not address Ricoeur's own stated basis of concern, the narrativity of human understanding, and the inherent narrativity of writing itself.

I would like to examine one particular case here: a famous, lengthy, "nonnarrative" *tour de force* within a much longer history, the "Tableau de la France," or "Picture of France," which makes up all of Book III of Jules Michelet's *History of France*. In the "Tableau," Michelet reveals the same anxieties displayed by Ricoeur and others that the absence of narrative entails the absence of human history, while at the same time facing the realization that the personal subject necessary for a narrative of French history adequate to his vision could only be fashioned by a traumatic break in his story.

10. Quotation: ibid.; *The Contribution of French Historiography to the Theory of History* was published by Oxford University Press in 1980. See also my discussion of Ricoeur and narrative in Chapter 12.

II

The development of a work is a process of diversification
unified by a single theme.
Boris Tomashevsky

Book II of the *History* traces the Merovingian and Carolingian eras already recorded by Augustin Thierry; indeed, long passages of Thierry are inserted directly in Michelet's text, since, as
Stephen Bann has noted, the moral strictures against this procedure in
historical practice were not yet in place.[11] With the accession to the
throne of Hugh Capet near the end of the tenth century (987), Michelet's
own voice reappears in its most characteristic form. After first noting
the irony that this most momentous occasion in the history of France
went almost unnoticed in the distant provinces, so unconcerned were
the lords of Gascony, Languedoc, and Provence with the affairs on the
distant Seine, Michelet calls a halt to the forward course of his narrative.
The year 1000 signified the expected end of the world for the millenarian
vision, and Michelet notes that their world did end. He proposes, first,
a pause for a look backward.

The rise of this third age of French history, that of the modern monarchy, after the earlier ages of Rome and Charlemagne, suggests inevitably the question of the failure of either of the two empires to
accomplish the same work of establishing a lasting order and unity.
Michelet considers the unity attained in earlier times deceitful, a mask
that, however magnificent, hid the differences and hostilities of race,
language, feeling, and much else; it was only a "material and external"
unity. At this point Michelet begins the play of analogies and substitutions that is a pillar of his style.

Matter tends to dispersion; spirit to unity. Matter, essentially
divisible, seeks disunion and discord. Material unity is a contradiction in terms, and, in policy, is tyranny. Spirit alone has the
right to effect union. It alone comprehends, embraces, and, to say
all in one word—loves. As has been so well put by the meta-

11. Stephen Bann, *The Clothing of Clio: A Study of the Representation of History in Nineteenth-Century Britain and France* (Cambridge, 1984); 33.

physics of Christianity—Unity implies Power, Love, and Spirit. (148)[12]

Thus construed, the course of French history up to the year 1000 can be figured as a series of exercises in futility, while the future beyond that pivotal year will be an agony of spiritual birth.

A new set of metamorphoses follows. Under feudalism, man becomes land, and "jurisprudence becomes a matter of mere geography." Nature takes charge of the affairs of men, breeding division and war, resulting in each point of space asserting itself independently. History must follow this dispersion, writes Michelet, and describe the rise of each feudal dynasty on each point of space.

> In its historical development, each was clearly modified by the different influence of its respective soil and climate. Liberty is potent in civilized ages; nature in barbarous ones. In these the accidents of locality are all-powerful as the laws of fate; and mere geography becomes a history. (148)

Thus ends Book II.

Book III is the "Tableau de la France," which has become a landmark in nineteenth-century historiography. It stands among the most often-cited forerunners of the *Annales* school's preference for nonnarrative forms. If one indicator of narrative is the way in which each part implies the others within the causal constraints of plot, the "Tableau" deviated so far from its narrative environment as to be totally separable, so that it could be published and republished throughout the nineteenth and twentieth centuries, first as a patriotic panorama entitled *Notre France,* and later as a totem for the new social history in France, which sought to move from the "knowns" of geography to the "unknowns" of social and political life. For the *Annaliste,* the intrinsically suspect endeavor of political history needed the bedrock of a nonnarrative tableau.[13]

Michelet is a "solitary peak" in the nineteenth century, writes Jacques

---

12. Citations from Michelet's *History* are, unless otherwise noted, from Jules Michelet, *History of France,* trans. G. H. Smith (New York, 1857).

13. According to François Furet, political history is of questionable value because it must follow the "this before that" procedures characteristic of narrative. Cf. Hayden White, "The Question of Narrative," 8–9.

In a standard work on *Annales* historiography, Traian Stoianovich cites Michelet as model, adding that *Annales* historians "aspire to a history like Paul Bois' study of the rural folk of western France; it opens with a tableau of the twentieth century—thus with the contemporary knowns—and proceeds to the unknowns of the French Revolution and eighteenth century. . . ." *French Historical Method: The Annales Paradigm* (Ithaca, 1976), 165–66.

Le Goff, noting the distaste of the *Annaliste* for the trio of political history, narrative history, and history of events.[14] Michelet's priority in the field of historical geography is secure, and the "Tableau" is often cited as his masterpiece.[15]

We have just noted, however, that Michelet's "Picture of France" was not inserted into his vast text with the same arbitrariness as those early historical illustrations which were beginning to enter history books in this period.[16] The "Tableau" was carefully framed by an announced pause in the narrative of events, an analeptic meditation on the history of France to the year 1000, which leads to the announcement of the thematic of matter versus spirit, contrasts that quickly change into hate versus love, and nature versus liberty. These metamorphoses lead to an implied catechresis ("mere geography becomes a history"), which reinforces the initial irony that the great commencement of the history of modern France went largely unnoticed in much of the country.

The "Tableau de la France" itself, which runs about eighty pages in the most recent French edition, is a series of vignettes, province by province; in each of these, Michelet displays his powers of characterization by grasping each province in its turn, bringing its natural setting to life, sketching the character of its people through anecdotes and the recognition of its famous men and women. He does not, in any way, relate the history of any province, nor is there any *temporal* movement in his journey around his country.

French history begins with the language, which is found first in the Oath of Strasbourg of 843. That this statement begins Book III of a work titled *History of France* is typical of Michelet, whose history is full of beginnings and rebeginnings. Contradiction is the first and second note in the "Tableau" because, Michelet asserts, beneath the dispersion, multiplicity, and variety of the feudal world he will describe, France

14. Jacques Le Goff, "Is Politics Still the Backbone of History?" in *Historical Studies Today,* ed. Felix Gilbert and Stephen R. Graubard (New York, 1972), 340.

15. "At the head of the second volume of his *History of France,* he placed a tableau of France, the first ever written to base the history of France on geography, and one of his undeniable masterworks." Georges Lefebvre, *La Naissance de l'historiographie moderne* (Paris, 1971), 195.

Harry Elmer Barnes calls the "Tableau" "the best summary ever written by a historian until very recent times" (*A History of Historical Writing* [New York, 1962], 188); G. P. Gooch, "a signal achievement of the historian's greatness" (*History and Historians in the Nineteenth-Century* [London, 1913], 179); James Westfall Thompson, "magnificent" (*A History of Historical Writing,* vol. II [Gloucester, 1967], 236). And so forth.

16. Cf. Stephen Bann's discussion in *The Clothing of Clio,* 43–47.

nevertheless manifests herself as an identity. The third paragraph begins French history for the second time on one page, and from a different point.

> The true starting point of our history is a political division of France, founded on its natural and physical division. At first, history is altogether geography. It is impossible to describe the feudal or the *provincial period,* (the latter epithet is equally characteristic,) without first tracing the peculiarities of the provinces. Nor is it sufficient to define the geographic form of these different countries. They are to be thoroughly illustrated by their fruits alone—I mean by men and the events of their history. From the point of view where we are about to place ourselves, we shall predict what each of them will do and produce; we shall indicate to them their destiny, and dower them in the cradle.(149)

The point of view mentioned we may call the "belvedere," because Michelet proposes in the next sentence to gain a view of France as a whole by ascending a mountain, either the Vosges or the Jura as you prefer, with one's back to the Alps.[17] Thus situated, his gaze (and that of his interlocutor, since he usually speaks of "we" and often addresses his narratee-companion on this survey) quickly begins to describe things as they are not. His figures are again ironic misuses: Brittany and Auvergne are "two continental islands"; England and France form one valley between them, of which the straits are the bottom. The opposition England/France is further complicated by noting that England faces France with her German side, keeping her Celtic side to the rear, while France faces England with her Celtic side, keeping her German side to the rear—a geographic figure of rhetoric, so to speak. By contrast, the other faces of France seem peaceful, German France peacefully parallel to Germany (so much for Michelet's clairvoyance), Roman and Iberian France facing the sea and Africa.

Michelet needs a beginning once again, and he finds it in another linguistic abuse: "It has been said, *Paris, Rouen, and Havre are one city, of which the Seine is the high street*" (150). It is at the mouth of the Seine, facing west toward Brittany, that he chooses to begin, for *chronological,* rather than geographic, reasons.

It is here, however, that we wish to begin our study of France.

---

17. On the "belvedere," see F. R. Ankersmit's *Narrative Logic: A Semantic Analysis of the Historian's Language* (The Hague, 1983).

> The Celtic province, the eldest born of the monarchy, claims our
> first glance. Hence we will pass on to the old rivals of the Celts,
> the Basques and the Iberians, not less obstinate in their moun-
> tains than the Celts in their heaths and marshes. Then we may
> proceed to the countries blended and confounded by the Roman
> and German conquests. We shall thus have studied geography in
> chronological order, and have travelled at once in space and time.
> (150)

Here is yet another beginning. Celtic Brittany is the least French part of
France, being at its extremes toward Finisterre a *Bretagne bretonnante*,
which retains the character of ancient Gaul and lacks the French language. The rhetorical figures of self-difference or linguistic otherness
found in the ironic tropes are joined by tautologies (Bretonnizing Brittany, the true France, the center of the center), which have the same
effect, doubling identities that undo themselves by suggesting a non-
Breton Brittany, a France that is not truly France, a center that is not
central.

Broadly described, Michelet's course is a large circle, beginning to the
west of the mouth of the Seine, proceeding west, then south to the
Pyrenees, then turning east across Provence and up along the German
borders, until at last Paris is reached. The figures and descriptions continue on the paradoxical course signaled earlier in the text, when men
became land, jurisprudence became geography, geography became
history—all heralded by the irony of the unnoticed Great Event.

Poitou, to cite one example, is a compound of opposites, like the
Melusina of song. The province is the battleground of South and North,
contributing lawyers to the North and troubadours to the South.

> This mixed and contradictory character has hindered Poitou
> from ever bringing any thing to a conclusion; but it began every-
> thing. (156)

Among the famous figures of Poitou is Elinor, whose sons Henry, John,
and Richard the Lion Hearted never solved the internal contradictions
of their natures ("Poitevin or English, Angevin or Norman"). The
Poitevin character, however, was hidden, and "knew not itself," until
the revelation of the Vendée rebellion, in which the peasants, "children
of the night," arose spontaneously to fight the revolution and the centralization it represented (157). When Michelet reaches the Pyrenees, he
refuses to deal with pure geology. That is another history, but in contrast to the history of France, Michelet was not personally present.

> We must look to the science of Cuvier and of Elie de Beaumont,
> for the narrative of this ante-historic history. They were present—
> not I—when nature suddenly produced her amazing geologic
> epopee. . . . (160)

Although Michelet himself wrote four nature books years later (including *La Montagne*), he rejects pure nature here. Yet the people of pure race
like the Celts, Basques, Brettons, and Navarrais are themselves nature
for him; when they give way to mixed races, on Michelet's course, "the
frontiers had to give way to the centre, nature to civilization" (162).

As Michelet considers the German-speaking provinces, an extraordinary scene takes place in which the narrator draws back from Alsace as
if a Medusa head were shown to him. After describing the "wandering
and indeterminate race" that had grown up in the middle ages in the
forests and valleys of Lorraine, a Babel that has always resisted reduction to a common system, Michelet refuses to go on.

> The French tongue ceases in Lorraine, and I will not go beyond
> it. I refrain from crossing the mountain-chain, and gazing on
> Alsace. The German world is a dangerous ground for me—for it
> has a lotos-tree, all-powerful to induce oblivion of one's native
> land. Were I once to look on thee, divine spire of Strasburg—were
> I to descry my heroic Rhine, I might be tempted to follow its
> current charmed by its legends. . . . (170)

Michelet relates half a dozen legends in a footnote, but that danger does
not invade his text proper.

The goal of the "Tableau," Paris, the center of the center, the sen-
sorium, is textualized as the one-word summary of Michelet's entire
work.

> To say Paris, is to sum up the whole monarchy. How happens one
> city to have become the perfect symbol of the entire country? It
> requires a whole history of the country to explain it, and Paris
> would be its last chapter. (181)

Certainly Michelet's enormous *History*, leading as it does toward the
apotheosis of France in the Parisian-dominated Revolution, is that story
signaled so early here.

The victory of Paris over the provinces, of centralization over diversity, of identity over disunity, is finally *the victory of narrative over
analysis.*

Society and liberty have subdued nature, and history has effaced geography. In this marvellous transformation spirit has triumphed over matter, the general over the particular, and the ideal over the real. Individual man is a materialist, and spontaneously attaches himself to local and private interests. Human society is a spiritualist; it tends unceasingly to free itself from the miseries of local existence, in order to obtain the lofty and abstract unity of— a country.

The beauty of this centralization, which, by the way, Alexis de Tocqueville, the great nonnarrative historian, found tragic and incomprehensible, is the beauty of prose and of personality. The "Tableau" ostensibly has ended with the triumph of good over evil, history over geography, identity over chaos. But the text, Book III of Michelet's *History,* ends on a note of real sadness. To plunge into the past is to go deep into darkness. Far from the light of modern times, how much pain and blood remains for France, as she bears that "child of sorrow," the middle ages, which will itself die with no conclusion, leaving behind a memory for which "all the joys and greatness of modern times will fail to console us" (183).

The "Tableau" began by citing the "language" as the start of French history; Book IV, which follows it, begins with a Fall. Each province described in the "Tableau" has acquired its own "voice." This is a world of voices, instead of a world of language. Narrative must take up its task again, because what had passed before had been a sort of illusion. The personality, the beautiful centralization, was a mirage because it had not occurred *in time.* Like Poitou, or the middle age itself, the "Tableau" could not bring anything to a real conclusion because like them it had no inner coherence. Its narrativity was false because it reflected textual, not temporal, events.

III

> *A story may be thought of as a journey from one situation to another.*
> Boris Tomashevsky

Thus, the "Tableau de la France" is a sort of recoding of the full *History of France* itself, in that the course that it signals without narrative events is identical with the narrative of the coming-into-being of Michelet's France. The geographic survey is recoded as a temporal survey, leading to the creation of a historical subject, the French people, without which a true historical narrative could not be said to exist. The "Picture of France" is not a narrative history because it contains no represented events that pertain to the story interrupted at the accession of Hugh Capet and resuming in the year 1000. Each of the many anecdotes and tales found in the "Tableau" and its notes serves a nonnarrative function such as illustration of character types or proleptic glimpses into the future of the province because the geographic tour of France has no proper time in which events can take place. What transpires in the "Tableau" must be otherwise described, and is generally otherwise described, as description, geo-history, a portrait, and so forth, but not as historical narrative.

At the same time, it is quite clear that there are many aspects of narrative in the "Tableau." Events are related throughout, but with no causal relation to one another, nor to the position in the *History* that the "Tableau" occupies. They are illustrations of provincial character for the most part, or occasionally revelations of the prodigies of nature in certain areas. Such events constitute neither history, nor chronicle, nor annals, because they lack a temporal component that implicates them with one another in a process of change.

If we accept the common literary definition that the presence of a narrator is the certain sign of narrative, then the "Tableau" is certainly a narrative, although not necessarily a historical narrative. The narrative voice is not only continuous (as it is not in, say, drama) and communicative (as it is not, say, in lyric), but it employs deictics of every variety to personalize the narrative voice as the voice of Jules Michelet. The narratee is likewise personalized, addressed as a character in the "Tableau," and thus given a textual position between the agents of the *History of France,* on the one hand, and the implied reader on the other. However, these clear narrative signs are traditionally discounted in discussing historical narratives because of the foregrounding of the event; the presence of a narrator and even a textualized narratee, which is adequate for at least a minimum level of narrativity in literature, does not qualify a historical text as narrative if it lacks a story. Plot, as Ricoeur notes, is the key.

The position of the "Tableau de la France" in Michelet's *History* is of course open to question. Why there, or why then? Nothing in the "Tableau" relates directly to events that may have transpired between 987 and 1000. Michelet, as we have noted, provides reasons, perhaps too many, for his pause at this point, but the intention to narrate events is not one of them. Rather, the "Tableau" is responsible for establishing Michelet's personal authority to narrate, and provides the possibility of such a narration. To establish his own authority requires a narrative subject; and for Michelet, a personal identification with that subject is the only acceptable form of narrative authority.[18] Without the consciousness of a social center, history proper is impossible, and only *annals* can be produced.

Michelet has transferred his dominant plot structure, that of *romance*, from the realm of *narrated* events (narrative proper) to the realm of *narrative* events (the peculiar transactions that occur between the narrator and the implied reader) in the "Tableau." The romantic plot offers the historian a particularly close focus on his moral theme because it enables him to recast each episode as an ever-renewed and ever-renewable conflict between the positive and negative forces that drive the narrative forward.[19] Hence, the repeated beginnings of Michelet's work. The romantic restaging of episodic confrontations renders history as an essentially binary system; it will seek, and find, these opposing forces in virtually any field of events, figure it into an *agon*, and narrate the combat as triumph or pathos. Naturally, this choice of narrative emplotment offers the reader precisely the spectacle that Roland Barthes claimed was the function of narrative per se.[20] Neither the tragic law-governed analyses of Tocqueville or Marx, nor the developmentally comic narratives of Ranke or Hegel, can match this romantic history for pure spectacle. Ironic histories, such as those of Burckhardt or Huizinga, also "fail" in this regard because their stories, when they choose to tell them, pointedly lack points, and thus elicit the dreaded response cited by the sociolinguists: "So what?"—which is their point, to some extent.

The peculiarity of the romantic plot, however, is its diffuseness, its

18. Hayden White describes the need for authority to narrate in "The Value of Narrativity," 5–27, also in *The Content of the Form: Narrative Discourse and Historical Representation* (Baltimore, 1987), 1–25.

19. The way in which plot structures guide historical arguments is described in Northrop Frye's essay "New Directions from Old," in *Fables of Identity* (New York, 1963). Frye's work on plot in *Anatomy of Criticism: Four Essays* (Princeton, 1957), 158–238, forms the basis of Hayden White's extensive discussion of modes of emplotment in *Metahistory: The Historical Imagination in Nineteenth-Century Europe* (Baltimore and London, 1973).

20. Barthes, "Introduction to the Structural Analysis of Narrative," *Image, Music, Text* (New York, 1977), 115.

tendency to become a potentially endless chain of episodes with no real center. This can be remedied only by placing a hero at the center of things in order to hold the episodes together. This is rather obviously the narratological function of the "Tableau de la France" within the *Histoire de France*. It will establish once and for all that the text has a center, and that the long series of events that will follow in thousands of pages has a subject-hero. If any doubt lingers as to the identity of the hero, the integrity of the narrative is undermined, and the unity of the text destroyed. The unity of the text, then, depends upon the unity of the diachronic narrative of French history that it embodies, and that in turn depends on the geo-historical synchronic identity constituted by the "Tableau." The stakes are high. In the most famous single sentence from the "Tableau," Michelet states: "England is an empire; Germany, a country—a race; France is a person" (182).

Michelet's reflective play of analogies (the essence of romantic narrative procedures) leads him circularly into his own text and his own person. But in order to establish the unity of his text, he must break it in two, by the insertion of a foreign voice that will validate what follows, even as it invalidates what precedes it. Michelet's fear of disunity is quite consistent because each of the levels of his vision flows into the others: his text, history, subject, and life are presented as utterly permeable. Without a unified subject, his discourse will be incoherent and without motivation, and that discursive incoherence will be a version of the incoherence of French history itself; but since France (unlike other nations) is a *person*, it is human identity that is at stake in the "Tableau." The danger was personal. Michelet wrote in his "Preface of 1869": "My life was in this book, it passed in it. It was my only event. But does not this identity of the book and the author have a danger?" This helps to explain the fear of Germany and the Rhineland, with its dreamy legends, its music that gives life and death, and its diffuse poetic spirit.

The "ideology of unity" in Michelet has been linked by Linda Orr to Michelet's according to language "a space and identity of its own," within which Michelet "reinvestigates his personal and professional concerns."[21] Indeed, as we have seen in Chapter 1, Michelet often mentions in his *History* literary forms and styles that appear and play a part in whatever age he is narrating; these references often reveal his writerly plight as historian. At the end of his account of the destruction of the Order of the Templars by Philip the Fair, Michelet writes with clear

21. Linda Orr, *Jules Michelet: Nature, History, Language* (Ithaca, 1976), 24.

disgust of the death of the symbolic and of poetry, and the triumph of allegory and prose. Yet despite the agony of the Templars episode, and Michelet's disapproval of the modern age begun (yet again) with Philip the Fair and the fourteenth century, he nevertheless champions the very prose that makes his work and his life possible. Roland Barthes notes in *Michelet par lui-même:*

> One element sums up all the qualities of the insignificant—
> Prose. The king of France is prosaic, centralized France is prosaic,
> that is to say that in it a general form unifies the particularity of
> the movements and of the origins. . . . For Michelet, prose is a
> sign of homogeneity, and because of this it is a value, the fruit of
> grace or of conquest. He perceived himself as threatened by
> Poetry as by a natal hell, and aspiring to Prose was a decisive
> liberation.[22]

Prose is presented by Michelet as the highest, most abstract, generalized form of thought; France is the land of prose.[23] By "prose" here Michelet means narrative. All nonnarrative forms, whether poetry or geography, are concrete, analytical, and material. Only narrative admits of a plot, which Ricoeur, in terms Michelet would obviously accept, describes as comprehending reality into an intelligible whole, synthesizing the heterogeneous.[24]

In the "Tableau," while discussing the land of Champagne, Michelet refers to the Menippean satire, which he attributes to some lawyers of Troyes, and which he calls "the most pungent pamphlet in our language" (175). This reference is accompanied by a long footnote establishing the "jeering spirit of the North" as shown in their popular celebrations, the sort of thing we today call the spirit of carnival. Here is a clue, in my opinion, to Michelet's puzzling relation to his nonnarrative text. Mikhail Bakhtin and Northrop Frye have brought the Menippean satire into our critical consciousness by allegorizing it as the existential projection of the multivoiced nature of certain forms of discourse. Bakhtin speaks of heteroglossia, dialogism, and carnivalization, in which the inner voices of a discourse reveal themselves in a sort of discursive play of the marketplace, a play that undermines the authoritative pretensions of single-voiced, ideological discourses.

22. Roland Barthes, *Michelet par lui-même*, (Paris, 1954), 27–28.

23. Jules Michelet, "Introduction à l'histoire universelle" (1831), cited in Barthes, *Michelet par lui-même*, 37.

24. Ricoeur, *Time and Narrative*, I, 142.

Michelet wants a holy writ, pure narrative, pure prose, pure spirit. His hope (a false one) at the beginning of the "Tableau" was based on a single language. "L'histoire de France commence avec la langue française." This book of his history is vital to establishing the authority to narrate, to speak with one voice for France; but by the end of Book III, all of the "voices" have returned again in a heteroglossic carnival that destroys Michelet's subject, and with it his narrative authority and personal identity. The gloom with which Michelet ends the "Tableau," looking forward to the middle ages as "a child of sorrow" that was born in tears, reared in prayer and in visions, and in anguish of heart, and that died without having brought anything to a conclusion," seems to suit the book that is ending as well as the age yet to be narrated. The nonnarrative "Tableau de la France" is to be the guarantee of a perfect narrative history, the one constructively intrusive voice into the prose of Michelet-France. That one intrusion, however, fails by certifying instead the "voices" within time itself, which ultimately cannot be stopped, even in geo-history. The unified France, which Michelet so desperately needed to produce his narrative, disappears at her first appearance, and with it the subject for his *Histoire*. More beginnings will be needed, endlessly.

IV

> *If all the parts of the work are badly suited to one another, the work is* incoherent. *That is why the introduction of each separate motif or complex of motifs must be* motivated.
> Boris Tomashevsky

Although Michelet's belief in the importance of geography to history dates back into the 1820s, it was the publication of Victor Hugo's *Notre-Dame de Paris* that gave him the formal apparatus he needed to create his "Tableau." Hugo's chapter "A Bird's-Eye View of Paris" (in 1482) appeared (to vast acclaim) in 1831, the year before Michelet prepared the lectures that were to become the famous "Tableau de la France." In many ways, Hugo's work left its mark in Michelet's *Histoire*. The "Tableau" inverts Hugo's methods to some extent: the spiral (an important trope in Hugo's mythology), found in both the ascent to the towers of Notre-Dame and the visual itinerary of Paris, is repeated in Michelet, but going from outside to inside, reversing Hugo's plan. Hugo works from the whole (the still-walled medieval Paris) to the parts (City, University, Town), soon to be lost in the growth and decline of the modern Paris of 1831, a tragic image of dispersal; Michelet works from the parts, provinces and regions, to the whole, a yet unborn France soon to arise with the centralizing late medieval monarchs.

As noted earlier, Fernand Braudel's *The Mediterranean and the Mediterranean World in the Age of Philip II* (1949) begins with a three-hundred-page section, "The Role of the Environment," cast in the same spiral movement around the concentric rings of the sea's geography; the book also uses characteristic Micheletan figures and themes. The work as a whole has a distinct narrative movement that ironically comments upon and undercuts the elements of its (verbal) construction: from the geographic world, where meaning is most secure, but names are most misleading, to the world of human events, where names and language are most adequate, but meaning is ephemeral.[25]

The irony of tracing the quantitative antinarrativist trends of *la nouvelle histoire* back to Braudel, and beyond to Marc Bloch and Lucien Febvre, and beyond them to Michelet, and beyond him to Hugo is like the irony of any quest for origins.[26] Social scientific history has an important ancestor in the romantic novel, just as narrative history does. This ironic genealogy of *Annales*-school anti-narrativism does not close the debate on narrative historiography, but it does reformulate certain questions. Since it is not the geo-historical, but precisely the literary (formal, rhetorical, and phenomenological) aspects of Michelet's "Tableau"—the parts Michelet might have gotten from Hugo—that Braudel employs, perhaps it is there that historians must look for the sources of meaning and reality in their texts? And since this nonnarrative interruption of a narrative text (at least for Michelet and Hugo) proves in fact to be narrative on a number of different levels, perhaps the historiographic debates might be a bit more subtle in their definitions (and rejection) of narrative events?

25. Braudel's version of the problems of language in the representation of historical meaning is discussed below in Chapter 7, "Disorderly Conduct: Braudel's Mediterranean Satire."

26. The standard version of this genealogy is sketched in the essay "Annales" by Jacques Revel and Roger Chartier, in *La Nouvelle Histoire*, ed. Jacques Le Goff, Roger Chartier, and Jacques Revel (Paris, 1978).

The Language of Historians: Four Shipwrecks

The example of Michelet's "Tableau" is imperfect, like all examples, but it has certain virtues as an allegory. Not only is this nonnarrative "other" that separates the death of one world (the Carolingian) from the birth of another (for Michelet, modern France) saturated, as we have seen, with narrativity once we focus on the narrator and reader rather than on any "characters" to be found in the chapter; it also serves a narrative purpose within the structure of the entire *Histoire*. One might say that its insertion into a "Realm of Conversation" between the narrator and reader frames its own narrativity, while its position in the "Storyrealm" of the whole *History* lends it a quasi narrativity (as a sequentially functional part of a narrative whole), although its referentiality conjures up a "Taleworld" for the "Tableau" itself that does not present an imitation of human actions.[27] This simple, but I think plausible, scheme is useful if we consider the publication of the "Tableau" in 1875 as a separate patriotic work. As *Tableau de la France: géographie physique, politique et morale*, the piece has been wrenched from one "Storyrealm" and made into a complete "Storyrealm" of its own, without a narrative "Taleworld" surrounding it. Yet it has also entered into a new "Realm of Conversation" that is less constrained by historical narration, but equally fated to be subsumed into one or another historical understanding. In short, cutting this chapter loose does not eliminate its narrative ties; it repositions them.

As an allegory, this example offers us a bit more. Because certain French historians have taken this work and its author, and inserted them into a narrative of the genealogy of their approach to a certain form of history (in this case, the less event-oriented historiography of the *Annales* school), the relevance of Michelet's "Tableau" to twentieth-century historical writing is not trivial. As I have already noted, Braudel's *Méditerranée* is formally similar to Michelet's mixed genre, except that the proportions have been reversed. When Braudel ironically states that the form of his book may be seen as that of an hourglass, infinitely reversible, he has explicitly recognized what is implicitly recognized throughout the rest of the book: that language and its formal constraints cannot be overcome. The double, and contrary, movement in Braudel's book—from order to chaos at the level of

27. This narrative scheme, about the simplest imaginable, is drawn from Katharine Young, "Ontological Puzzles About Narrative," in *Poetics* 13 (1984), 239–59. Note that "Storyrealm" and "Taleworld" correspond roughly to the more usual terms *discourse* and *story*, and that neither should be seen as some sort of "reality."

meaning, and from chaos to order at the level of names and referent (epistemological tragedy superimposed upon linguistic comedy)— would be quite different if the order of the parts were reversed.

The debate over narrative and history is usually conducted with mistaken premises. Twenty years after Hayden White noted that historians defined their trade using a nineteenth-century vision of both science and art (with a particularly aged notion of narrative modeled on the nineteenth-century novel) and Louis Mink began his work in delineating narrative as a "cognitive instrument," the debate over narrative is still talking about *stories*, as though that were the essence of narrative rather than simply one of its many modes.[28] The refusal to recognize narrativity takes many forms. For example, Jürgen Kocka, in an essay intended to stress the interdependence of quantification and "theory" in history, sets both of them against "just descriptive, merely narrative" history, although he denies that there is a strict dichotomy between the two. However, his working definition of theory ("an explicit and consistent set of related concepts that can be used to structure and explain historical data but cannot be derived from the study of the source materials alone") fits fully the rhetorical and literary structures that, in fact, define human understandings. The six tasks that are set forth for "theory" (spelling out criteria for selecting data, offering hypotheses for linking factors, offering hypotheses for explanation of change, determining units of comparison, deciding issues of periodization, and formulating "interesting questions") are precisely the domain of rhetoric. To be sure, Kocka recognizes the complexity of historical arguments, but his assertion that "frequently, theories become just the backbone of an argument that itself contains nontheoretical, descriptive, and narrative dimensions as well" slights the theoretical dimensions of both description and narrative, as well as the rhetorical dimensions of theory per se.[29]

28. Hayden White, "The Burden of History," *History and Theory* 5:2 (1966) 111–34; collected in *Tropics of Discourse: Essays in Cultural Criticism* (Baltimore and London, 1978); Louis O. Mink, "The Autonomy of Historical Understanding," *History and Theory* 5:1 (1966), 24–47; collected in *Philosophical Analysis and History*, ed. William Dray (New York, 1966), 160–92. See also Mink, "Narrative Form as a Cognitive Instrument," in *The Writing of History*, ed. Robert Canary and Henry Kosicki (Madison, 1978), 120–49.

On the varieties of narrative, see Robert Scholes and Robert Kellogg, *The Nature of Narrative* (London and Oxford, 1966), chap. 1.

29. The word "theory" comes from a Greek word describing a procession of *theors*, religious ambassadors or observers. In the word "theater," the spectatorial aspect is

The reasons for these misunderstandings are easy to see. The debate is not really over narrative and "science." It is about power and legitimation within the profession, not how best to present or conduct research. As Dominick LaCapra has pointed out, the recent surge of social history to leadership in historical studies has brought with it a devaluation of, even scorn for, other types of historical pursuits. LaCapra laments the anti-intellectualism of social history, which would see all sources as documents and devalue the master-texts of a culture as ideological, elite cultural products.[30] His most radical charge, that "in a sense, historians are professionally trained not to read," points up the problem of social history's attempts to assume the role of "the mother hen of historiography in general."[31] When Lawrence Stone, for example, describes "the collapse of traditional intellectual history treated as a kind of paper-chase of ideas back through the ages (which usually ends up with either Aristotle or Plato)," he refers to an intellectual history that had been superseded already in the mid-1950s (although it has still not "collapsed" to this day).[32] Stone writes: " 'Great books' were studied in a historical vacuum, with little or no attempt to set the authors themselves or their linguistic vocabulary in their true historical setting." The assumption that the "true historical setting" is known prior to reading texts and that certain kinds of readings generate "historical vacuums" while others do not, as well as the priority of "the authors themselves," demonstrates many of LaCapra's complaints about the simplistic use of context, essentialized view of history, and reductive attitude to reading. "Historical vacuums" are frequently used for sweeping condemnations of certain forms of inquiry; I have never seen any historians attacked for working in a "rhetorical vacuum." Stone's assumption that the "new historians" are asking questions "which preoccupy us all today" and which are concerned "with the masses rather than the elite" certainly

---

stressed; in "theory," the processional. Thus, the modern, conceptual use of the word "theory" would seem to involve a processional, narrative sort of apprehension. Ironically, the etymology of "narrative" leads to a Proto-Indo-European root /gno/, relating "narrative" to *gnosis*, and knowledge as such, with no processional or configural reference.

30. Dominick LaCapra, "Rethinking Intellectual History and Reading Texts," *History and Theory* 19 (1980), 245–76; collected in *Rethinking Intellectual History: Texts, Contexts, Language* (Ithaca, 1983). See also the preface to LaCapra's *History and Criticism* (Ithaca and London, 1985).

31. "Not to read" in LaCapra, *Rethinking Intellectual History,* 339; "mother hen" in *History and Criticism,* 10.

32. Stone, "The Revival of Narrative," 14.

presumes that "we" are quite uninterested in texts.[33] The present-mindedness and moral tone of this example of modern historical pastoralism, which I have chosen only because it is likely to be familiar and not because it is either typical or atypical (although I would suspect that it is the former), are based on a large number of material assumptions that preclude examination of discourses of power underlying the descriptions of what "we" might all be interested in, and why.

It is worth considering whether there are not moral, as well as practical, reasons for getting beyond the discussions of storytelling that mask internecine power struggles within the historical profession, and seeking the relation of narrativity itself to historical reason and writing, and its function in making possible the imaging of reality in time that history, more than any of the other arts or sciences, claims to perform. The advantages of emphasizing narrativity rather than a certain traditional sort of narrative are significant. More important, it helps to unite historians who, really, do not wish to banish their opponents from the profession, regardless of the short-term advantages of assuming fundamentalist postures. It might also help solve that most vexing problem of historiography, the consignment of great historical works of the past to the storage room of outgrown ideologies or "mere" literature.

33. Ibid., 15.

6

FIGURES IN THE

RUMPELKAMMER

GOETHE, FAUST, SPENGLER

Neither Goethe nor his creature Faust displays a high regard for history, at least insofar as history is the product of specially trained men and women called historians. Their plaint was not that history failed to mirror its subject, but rather that it had two subjects and mirrored only one of these all too faithfully. The faithfully mirrored subject was the historian, whose subjectivity won out over the other "subject" of historical reflection, the past. The texts and sources of history, already vast by that period we call the *Goethezeit* and about to undergo an explosive expansion that continues relentlessly, could assume one of two forms, in Goethe's view. On the one hand, history was a detritus, a meaningless mass of ruins; on the other, an allegory in which the characters parrot or re-enact the sentiments or events of the present. That these poles are utterly interdependent is figured for us (if not for Goethe) by Gibbon, who mused among the ruins until the ruins became his muse, at least on his own account of the genesis of *The Decline and Fall of the Roman Empire*. This late Enlightenment quickening of historical spirit seems quite foreign to Faust.

> WAGNER: Verzeiht! es ist ein gross Ergetzen,
> Sich in den Geist der Zeiten zu versetzen;
> Zu schauen, wie vor uns ein weiser Mann gedacht,
> Und wie wir's dann zuletzt so herrlich weit gebracht.

> FAUST: O ja, bis an die Stern weit!
> Mein Freund, die Zeiten der Vergangenheit
> Sind uns ein Buch mit sieben Siegeln.
> Was ihr den Geist der Zeiten heisst,
> Das ist im Grund der Herren eigner Geist,
> In dem die Zeiten sich bespiegeln.
> Da ist's denn wahrlich oft ein Jammer!

Figures in the Rumpelkammer: *Goethe, Faust, Spengler*

Man läuft euch bei dem ersten
Blick davon: Ein Kehrichtfass und eine Rumpelkammer
Und höchstens eine Haupt- und Staatsaktion
Mit trefflichen pragmatischen Maximen
Wie sie den Puppen wohl im Munde ziemen!

WAGNER: Your pardon! yet the joy is unsurpassed
Of insight into eras long ago,
To see how wise men then thought thus and so,
And how we reached our splendid heights at last.

FAUST: Oh, starry heights indeed!
To us the times of yore, it is decreed,
Are like a book by seven seals protected;
The so-called spirit of the age, you'll find,
In truth is but the gentleman's own mind
In which the ages are reflected.
And there you're apt to face a scene of gloom!
One glance is quite enough to make you stagger:
A refuse barrel or a lumber-room,
At best a stiff bombastic masque aswagger
With such sagaciously pragmatic saws
As might come fitly from a puppet's jaws. (*Faust* I, 570–85)[1]

Faust's metaphors are harsh. The "book by seven seals protected," we recall from the fifth book of Revelation, can be opened only by the Lamb of God. The pain of human historical revelation, in Faust's view, would be the realization of the randomness of the past as "Kehrichtfass" or "Rumpelkammer," and of the banality of the moral lessons "drawn" from the past. The "times of yore" are hermetically sealed; the "so-called spirit of the age" is a human fiction. Faust mocks Wagner for believing that he can remedy the brevity of life, and assume the longevity of art, by drinking from a holy fount of parchment (*Faust* I, 558–67). Life, as usual for Faust, is elsewhere.

Goethe's own comments on history are more diverse than Faust's, but they suggest that his character was voicing an important part of his own

1. Citations from Goethe's *Faust* are identified in the text by part and lines (e.g., *Faust* I, 570–85); citations from Spengler's *The Decline of the West*, by volume and page (e.g., *DW*, I, 13). The edition of *Faust* is that of Erich Trunz (Hamburg, 1966); the English translation is by Walter Arndt (New York, 1976). *The Decline of the West* is translated by C. F. Atkinson (New York, 1934).

sentiment. In particular he objected to a history that impoverished a vital tradition. His conversation with Eckermann (15 October 1825) expresses this view, which in turn presents problems of its own.

> "Deficiency of character in individual investigators and writers is", he said, "the source of all the evils of our newest literature.
>
> "In criticism, especially, this defect produces mischief to the world, for it either diffuses the false instead of the true, or by a pitiful truth deprives us of something great, that would be better.
>
> "Till lately, the world believed in the heroism of a Lucretia,—of a Mucius Scaevola,—and suffered itself, by this belief, to be warmed and inspired. But now comes your historical criticism, and says that those persons never lived, but are to be regarded as fables and fictions, divined by the great mind of the Romans. What are we to do with so pitiful a truth? If the Romans were great enough to invent such stories, we should at least be great enough to believe them."

Like Faust, Goethe here focuses first upon history as a human creation, which reflects the spirit and failings of historians. In both poem and conversation, Goethe plays with *Quellen*, "sources." Faust has mocked Wagner's hope that scholarly work would lead him upward to the "source" ("Durch die man zu den Quellen steigt!" ["By which the primal sources may be breached"], *Faust* I, 563), by naming parchment as the "sacred spring" ("Das Pergament, ist das der heil'ge Bronnen, / Woraus ein Truck den Durst auf ewig stillt?" ["Of parchment then is made the sacred spring, / A draught of which forever slakes all thirst?"], *Faust* I, 566–67). Goethe cites character as the source ("Quelle") of difficulty in his remarks to Eckermann. Where there is discussion of history, discussion of sources will not be far away. Goethe's enemy (in 1825) was modern historiography, which then found itself involved, particularly in ancient history, in the preliminary ground-clearing known as *Quellenkritik*, the criticism of sources. Yet his strategy of attack, both early in Faust's exchange with Wagner, and later in his own words to Eckermann, is itself an explicit *Quellenkritik*. Faust noted the irony, well known to him, of a thirst-quenching parchment. Parchment is a figure for the whole process of historical scholarship; history is dry and random, "unless from your own inmost soul it burst" ("Wenn sie dir nicht aus eigner Seele quillt," *Faust* I, 569). Goethe's *Quellenkritik* cited above is somewhat different from Faust's. His interest is precisely to defend the valuable components of tradition from the "character" of researchers, who eagerly replaced rich truths with meager facts, and whose image of the past seemed shapeless and banal. Their impersonal search for truth reflects the impoverishment of their personality. Yet despite Goethe's decidedly mixed feelings about history, Friedrich Meinecke has placed him at the culmination of the development of modern historical thought. Meinecke suggests that all of Goethe's thinking on history is a comment on the notion, presented in *Dichtung und Wahrheit*, that the past and the present were one. Regardless of Goethe's specific attacks on certain forms of historical thought, in the end his scientific research had become "essentially historical."[2]

Oswald Spengler, like Goethe, found much historical writing lacking in the source of living insights. In *The Decline of the West* (*Der Untergang des Abendlandes*, Vol. I [Munich, 1918]; Vol. II [Munich, 1922]), he sketches a vast portrait gallery of human cultures in which he believed he had solved the "problems of history." "The means whereby to identify dead laws is Mathematical Law. The means whereby to understand living forms is Analogy" (*DW*, I, 4). Spengler's major analogy is between Western culture and Goethe's *Faust.* There was something about Faust that made him the figure Spengler chose; to understand the source of Faustian man is to understand the source of Spengler's vision.[3]

A clue to one source of the magic of the Faust of legend, the Faust of Goethe, and the Faustian man described (and embodied) by Oswald Spengler is found in the *Faustbuch* of 1587. This Faust is the captive of language in its capacity as a tool of the Devil.

> For he accompanied himself with Divers that were seen in those Devilish Arts, and that had the Chaldean, Persian, Hebrew, Arabian, and Greek tongues, using Figures, Characters,

2. Friedrich Meinecke, *Historism: The Rise of a New Historical Outlook*, trans. J. E. Anderson (London, 1972), 388, 494.

3. Meinecke did not treat Oswald Spengler, his junior by eighteen years, with much respect in an essay of 1924, when the so-called *Streit um Spengler* was in full swing. Like other German scholars, Meinecke accuses Spengler of amateurism, conservatism, and *Geschichtsklitterung.* Cf. "Über Spenglers Geschichtsbetrachtung," reprinted in *Zur Theorie und Philosophie der Geschichte* (Stuttgart, 1959). In this essay, Meinecke makes no significant references to Goethe and ignores Spengler's explicit claim to have followed Goethe at every step. When Meinecke notes that "what is good and fruitful" in Spengler is his further advancement of "the principle of individual formation," the model invoked is Ranke, not Goethe. This technique of "saving" Goethe from Spengler by refusing to notice that which links them is characteristic of the large polemical literature against Spengler.

> Conjuration, Incantations, with many other ceremonies belong-
> ing to these infernal Arts [66] as Necromancy, Charms,
> Soothsaying, Witchcraft, Enchantment, being delighted with
> their books, words, and names so well, that he studied day and
> night therein: in so much that he could not abide to be called a
> Doctor of Divinity, but waxed a worldly man, and named himself
> an Astrologian, and a Mathematician: and for a shadow some-
> times a Physician, and did great cures, namely, with herbs, roots,
> water, drinks, receipts, and clysters.[4]

The overwhelmingly literary vehicle of the magical arts that brought
Faust to his damnation (at least in the sixteenth-century versions)
stands opposed to the holy scriptures ("Göttlichen Schrifft"), which
Faust has failed to obey, despite his "excellent perfect" ("Redsprechig")
knowledge. The "Weltmensch," or worldly man, which Faust has
become, is the result of *a certain sort of language*, which is infernal not
because of its foreignness or unsacred nature (Hebrew and Greek, after
all, are the languages of holy scripture), but because of their figurality.
Faust's desire, whether the bumptious adventurousness of the 1587
Faustbuch or the "ever not quite" of Goethe, is not the full measure of his
sin, which lies rather in the "books, words, and names" that he culti-
vates as the route to power. The *figure* of power is what Faust is after; and
even as it fails him time and time again, Faust falls once more into a
passion for the word, inflated into a figure of thought that will bind up
and hold fast the wholeness of things.

The great Faust monologues of part I delineate a figurality that
informs the whole text. The power that Faust seeks is the power of a
figure, but he wants at the same time to go beyond words. This is the
cause of the dilemma described in his first speech:

> Drum hab' ich mich der Magie ergeben,
> Ob mir durch Geistes Kraft und Mund
> Nicht manch Geheimnis würde kund;
> Dass ich nicht mehr mit sauerm Schweiss
> Zu sagen brauche, was ich nicht weiss;
> Dass ich erkenne, was die Welt
> im Innersten zusammenhält,
> Schau' alle Wirkenskraft und Samen,
> Und tu' nicht mehr in Worten kramen.

4. Johann Spies, "The Faustbuch," in *Faust: Sources, Works, Criticism,* ed. P. A. Bates
(New York, 1969), 9.

So I resorted to Magic's art,
To see if by spirit mouth and might
Many a secret may come to light;
So I need toil no longer so,
Propounding what I do not know;
So I perceive the inmost force
That bonds the very universe,
View all enchantment's seed and spring,
And quit my verbiage-mongering. (*Faust* I, 377–85)

What it is that holds the world together in its innermost being is a synecdoche, that trope which represents the whole by a part that embodies
some quality deemed to be the essence of the whole. This trope, in its
purest form, stands in relation to the whole as a microcosm to the macrocosm.[5] Faust's venture into his volume of Nostradamus illustrates his
synecdochic desire and its failure. He ponders the sign of the macrocosm ("das Zeichen des Makrokosmos"), is filled with the "power of
nature," which makes his "dry intellect" seem reductive and pale by
comparison. However, because the symbol of the macrocosm is only a
symbol, Faust rejects his experience as merely a play ("ein Schauspiel
nur"). In so doing, he indulges in more *Quellenkritik:*

Euch Brüste, wo? Ihr Quellen alles Lebens,
An denen Himmel und Erde hängt,
Dahin die welke Brust sich drängt—
Ihr quellt, ihr tränkt, und schmacht' ich so vergebens?

You breasts where, all life's sources twain,
Both heaven and earth are pressed,
Where thrusts itself my shriveled breast,
You brim, you quench, yet must I thirst in vain? (*Faust* I, 456–59)

This process of approach toward and falling away from a synecdochic
symbolization of the whole defines Faust's progress before Mephi-

5. A good discussion of the microcosm/macrocosm relationship implicit in synecdoche
is found in Kenneth Burke's essay "Four Master Tropes," in *A Grammar of Motives* (Berkeley and Los Angeles, 1969), 503–17. The use of tropes as structural principles in historical
writing is demonstrated in Hayden White's *Metahistory: The Historical Imagination in
Nineteenth-Century Europe* (Baltimore and London, 1973).

stopheles enters. Faust twice calls himself an "image of the godhead" (*Faust* I, 516, 614), with "image" ("Ebenbild") serving as the synecdoche that seems to create a microcosm/macrocosm relationship, but he comes to recognize the frailty of the figure.

It is in the translation scene that Faust's desire moves beyond the word most decisively. His progressive rendering of "Logos" as "das Wort," "der Sinn," "die Kraft," and "die Tat" recapitulates the processes of the four master tropes, metaphor, metonymy, synecdoche, and irony. Faust's rejection of "word" and "mind" is easily understood; he has already decried them as mere play and "dry" respectively. "Force" is another matter, but the potentiality of this synecdochic process had already contrasted with the active nature of both the macrocosm and the earth spirit.[6]

At last, when Mephistopheles appears, he identifies himself, not by name, for a simple word betrays reality in Faust's view, but rather as the eloquent master of complicated part/whole relationships and of the reversals that these relationships entail. This is a riddle to Faust ("Was ist mit diesem Rätselwort gemeint?" ["And that conundrum of a word implies?"], *Faust* I, 1337), but Mephistopheles goes on to jest at man for thinking himself whole. As a "part of a part" ("ein Teil des Teils," *Faust* I 1349), Mephisto recognizes the nature of the whole, and the inability of any part to grasp it, except illusively. Hence, his status as the "spirit that always negates" (*Faust* I, 1338). Mephistopheles' consciousness of the "created" nature of representations—the ordering of parts and wholes—renders him ironic; his irony is the counterpart of Faust's despair. At a tropological level, the drama of Faust is a working through of the conflict of Faust's desire to grasp the world whole and Mephistopheles' awareness that all such comprehensions are only human representations. The final Chorus Mysticus grants Mephisto's insight,

> Alles Vergängliche
> Ist nur ein Gleichnis

> All in transition
> Is but reflection

6. For a discussion of the tropological narrative of comprehension implicit in this scene, see Chapter 8, "A Bedrock of Order: Hayden White's Linguistic Humanism." Spengler states that the mythical notice of Force is unique to the Faustian nature-concept. "Western physics is by its inward form dogmatic and not ritualistic [*kultisch*]. Its content is the *dogma of Force* [*Kraft*] as identical with space and distance, the theory of the mechanical *Act* [*Tat*] (as against the mechanical Posture) in Space" (*DW*, I, 412).

but further asserts an over-world of the "un-vergänglich," the unchanging whole, unrepresentable.

Spengler believed that all comprehension was morphological, which meant to him a pattern of relationships of developing forms rather than numbers, organic physiognomy rather than mechanical system. The morphology of history amounts to a universal symbolism, effective at all levels of existence. "This is the idea of *the Macrocosm, actuality as the sum total of all symbols in relation to one soul*" (*DW*, I, 165). This "truly Goethean method" finds its true source in its dominant trope, synecdoche. It is this figure that regulates the figurality—that is to say, the intellectual content—of Spengler's work. Metaphor, like synecdoche an integrative trope, is sanctioned, but only within the larger synecdochic framework. By this I mean that the innumerable analogies (such as Alexander/Napoleon, Pythagoras/Descartes) are not free or decorative, but obtain their status only from the inner coherences of the cultures, which are defined synecdochically. Analogies that are merely ornamental or suggestive (Ranke's are cited by Spengler as examples) have no role in *The Decline of the West*.

For Spengler, the trope of synecdoche serves as the heart of his vast construction. He chooses a part of each of the cultures he discusses, and uses that part not merely to name or to represent the whole, but rather to embody in some sense the most vital quality of the whole. In *Faust*, for example, as cited above, "das Pergament," used synecdochically for "scholarly research," was not simply a part of scholarly research that could be used to stand for the whole (in the way that "pen" is used in the expression "the pen is mightier than the sword")—this would be metonymy, quite a different figure. Instead, "parchment" serves to evoke the quality that for Faust symbolizes this activity, that is to say, dryness and perishability. Synecdoche unifies the concept of the whole by attributing to it some essence found in the part.

In dubbing Western culture "Faustian," Spengler uses one quality, "pure and limitless space," in the sense of a desire for the infinite, to characterize all of the strivings of Western man (or, put in another way, he characterizes all of Western humanity as striving). Faust the historical and literary figure actually becomes overwhelmed by Faust the tropological figure, which is at once part and whole. Although Spengler grasps other cultures synecdochically, in naming Classical culture "Apollinian," for instance, or Arabian culture "Magian," it is clear that these figures do not function in quite the same way as Faust. Spengler writes:

> From Homer to the tragedies of Seneca, a full thousand years, the
> same handful of myth-figures (Thyestes, Clytemnestra, Heracles
> and the like) appear time after time without alteration, whereas in
> the poetry of the West, Faustian Man figures, first as Parzeval or
> Tristan, then (modified always into harmony with the epoch) as
> Hamlet, Don Quixote, Don Juan, and eventually into Faust or
> Werther, and now as the hero of the modern world-city romance,
> but is always presented in the atmosphere and under the condi-
> tions of a particular century. (*DW*, I, 13, n. 1)

Faust, we notice, is only an example, a member of a set that he himself
names and embodies. He is a part of a whole, which is figured synecdochically by a part. The Faustian appears in its own changing form,
yet remains an essence in the sense that it can be identified as Faustian
in its very adaptability. However, this essence differs from others such
as the Apollinian precisely because of its mutability.

Spengler, in defense of his vision of our culture, a vision that is saturated by the synecdochic and consequently by the symbolic, characterizes even physical knowledge of the mathematical sort inaugurated
by the scientific revolution (the phrase is mine, not Spengler's) as symbolic. This tactic is unusual because most visions of the world that base
themselves on either synecdochic or metaphoric strategy regularly consign the physical, mathematical sciences to the figure of metonymy,
usually for the purpose of tarring the natural sciences with the supposed "flaw" of metonymy, its reductiveness, so that these natural sciences may be rejected as guides to knowledge of the world, or at least
set aside in favor of other, more comprehensive or more "human," ways
of knowing. In other words, the famous statement by Galileo that the
book of nature is written in mathematical language and cannot be read
except by those conversant with the language of number is interpreted
as an explicit part/whole reduction, in which the variety of phenomena
is reduced to mere quantity, which then stands for the phenomena for
scientific purposes without ever claiming to represent them except in a
reductive, manipulative form conducive to the creation of "laws." This
approach to science, epitomized by Newton, was particularly repug-
nant to Goethe, who sought in so many ways to create a synecdochic
science that would "liberate the phenomena once and for all from the
gloom of the empirico-mechanico-dogmatic torture chamber."[7]

---

7. Goethe, cited in Erich Heller, *The Disinherited Mind* (New York, 1959), 22. Heller's
essay, "Goethe and the Idea of Scientific Truth," gives a good description of the search for
a synecdochic science.

Spengler takes a different course. Instead of posing a manichaean dualism of science and feeling, quantity and quality, or primary and secondary characteristics, Spengler *absorbs* physical knowledge into the mythic and symbolic field of history and culture, while granting that it is metonymic in relation to nature. First, he reduces "all Western mechanics" to "an intellectual *conquest by measurement*" that finds "the essence of the phenomenon" in a system characterized in Helmholtz's view by *motion* (*DW*, I, 377). Thus, motion serves the physicist as a metonymy for mechanics. Spengler cannot admit the power of this figure, for to do so would divide and disrupt his image of the culture-soul, would partially displace his own synecdoche, and would explode his vision of discrete culture knowledge by presenting a universal rather than a culture-bound reality. The status of mechanics must be unmasked as mere appearance, as figure: "Alles Vergängliche ist nur ein Gleichnis."

> It is self-evident that no *practical* results and discoveries can prove anything as to the "truth" of the *theory*, the *picture*. For most people, indeed, "mechanics" appears as the self-evident synthesis of Nature-impressions. But it merely appears to be so. For what is motion? Is not the postulate that everything qualitative is reducible to the motion of unalterably-alike mass-points, essentially Faustian and not common to humanity? (*DW*, I, 377)

Spengler's strategy reveals the linguistic basis of modern physics as a mystifying figure. In noting this aspect of science, Spengler is of course writing ironically, because he is noting the arbitrary relationship of sign and referent. However, the tropological irony leveled at physical science is in the service of his own figure, the synecdoche of Faustian man. In saying that "the form-language of mechanics" is "a vessel of the myth like the root-words," Spengler clearly arranges the hierarchies of figures, and the dominance of representation over reduction.

> Modern physics, as a science, is an immense system of *indices* in the form of names and numbers whereby we are enabled to work with Nature as with a machine. As such, it may have an exactly definable end. But as a piece of *history*, all made up of destinies and incidents in the lives of the men who have worked in it and in the course of research itself, physics is, in point of object, methods and results alike an expression and actualization of a Culture, an organic and evolving element in the essence of that Culture, and every one of its results is a symbol. (*DW*, I, 378)

This assertion of the universal symbolism affirms the dominance of the synecdochic integration. Number, systems, mechanics, laws, and causality are Spengler's foes because of their tropological status. He calls the active man "whole" (microcosmically), while the contemplative is dominated by mind, a part (*DW*, II, 16). Like Faust, who rejected "Sinn" as a metonymic translation of "Logos" for the same reason, Spengler attacks those who have attempted to make of history a positive science. "The more historically men tried to think, the more they forgot that in this domain they ought *not* to think" (*DW*, I, 151). Sentences like this are easy to attack as long as one ignores their source, which is a certain logic of the symbolic. Faust's line about history flowing from one's own soul differs little in spirit.

In this morphological repetition of whole in part that Spengler designates as universal symbolism, the book itself, *The Decline of the West*, assumes a form that is Faustian. Once we have ventured into the text and learned that the symbol of Faustian man is "infinite space," we notice that the extravagant compass of the enterprise, the span of all recorded history, the variety of cultures, the spectrum of human thought and activity from pure mathematics to money and machines, all re-enact Faust's desire. Like Goethe's *Faust*, *The Decline of the West* seeks the "thundering word," the symbol that will unlock secrets. It is Spengler's goal to delineate the separation of the Western and the Classical, and by so doing to bring them into a common morphological form, as it was Faust's wish to experience a classical love and a classical "Walpurgisnacht" in order to unite ancient and modern in himself.[8]

The Decline of the West, like Goethe's *Faust*, has two parts—the first psychological and artistic, concerned with the inner life of cultures; the second social and political, more concerned with public forms and events, cities, states, money, machines. Spengler's Introduction, which is clearly set apart from the first chapter by the inserted fold-out charts in the German edition, hovers over the text like Goethe's "Prologue in Heaven," while the "Prefaces" in contrast situate the work quite locally, like Goethe's "Prelude in the Theater." (The "Preface" to the first edition, dated 1917, goes so far as to cite the "German military achievements"— the English edition drops this sentence.) Goethe's "Dedication" is certainly paralleled by Spengler's epigraphical citation of Goethe's poem "Wenn im Unendlichen," a sort of dedication to Goethe. Thus, in a general way, *The Decline of the West* morphologically mimics *Faust*.

8. H. Stuart Hughes is essentially correct when he notes that the core of the book is discussion of only two cultures, "ancient" and "modern." *Oswald Spengler: A Critical Estimate* (New York, 1952), 7.

Figures in the Rumpelkammer: *Goethe, Faust, Spengler*

Both Spengler and Goethe begin with a sort of ground-clearing. Faust's famous recital of the many studies that he had exhausted in his unsuccessful pursuit of the essence of things leads him to despair; Spengler similarly lists a series of errors that have led to the prevailing misunderstanding of history and nature. Historians, Spengler charged, while scrupulous and effective in research, become careless at the moment when interpretation begins, at least when "judged by the standards of the physicist and mathematician" (*DW*, I, 7, n. 1). Ranke, Kant, and Schopenhauer come under respectful fire for, respectively, superficial analogies, static categories, and contempt for history. The major divisions of space (and the term "Europe" itself) should be "struck out of history"; the major divisions of historical time, "Ancient," "Medieval," and "Modern," are likewise misleading and doomed (*DW*, I, 16). This sort of history, upon which the superstructure of Western historical study still stands, Spengler consigns to the "Rumpelkammer" of dead ideas described by Faust. History has become for him merely historical.

Spengler states most explicitly: "The philosophy of this book I owe to the philosophy of Goethe, which is practically unknown today, and also (but in a far less degree) to that of Nietzsche" (*DW*, I, 49, n. 1). It is hard to imagine a more Goethe-saturated book than *The Decline of the West*. From the smallest matters, such as Goethe's attitude in *Wilhelm Meister* toward double-entry bookkeeping, to the great "method" of the book, Spengler relies on Goethe constantly. The organicism, which speaks of "the living Nature of Goethe, and not to the dead Nature of Newton" (*DW*, I, 21), the idea of morphology (*DW*, I, 104, n. 2), the universal symbolism, the concept of styles (*DW*, I, 205), the vision of the world-as-history (*DW*, I, 25), all are taken from Goethe. Goethe's nature-studies are, for Spengler, the best illustration of "what historical investigation *really* is, namely pure Physiognomic" (*DW*, I, 157). Often in *The Decline of the West*, a striking phrase will recall a Goethean source to the reader's mind; when Spengler writes: "*Finally, speech and truth exclude one another*" (*DW*, II, 137), we hear Goethe's line "Sobald man spricht, beginnt man schon zu irren." Or when Spengler calls writing "*the grand symbol of the Far,*" we recall Faust's "Das verfluchte Hier! / Das eben, leidig lastet's mir" ("That blasted *here!* You see? / That's just what sorely weighs on me," *Faust* II, 11,233–34). Spengler even attributes the foundation of his charts to Goethe in an obscure footnote in the second volume: "Goethe, in his little essay '*Geistesepochen,*' has characterized the four parts of a Culture—its preliminary, early, late, and civilized stages—with such a depth of insight that even today there is nothing to add. See the tables at the end of Vol. i, which agree with this exactly" (*DW*, II, 37, n. 1). This three-page reflection of Goethe's also uses the Spenglerian term "Weltschicksal."[9] Goethe's work also stresses a cyclical rhythm in science, art, and nations. Friedrich Meinecke writes:

> The cycle, in his [Goethe's] view, was the exterior form of histor-
> ical life, within which all the valuable inner primal forms, with
> their rich metamorphoses, could have free play and development.
> Further, it was seen by him as a guarantee of a palingenesis for all
> living forms, a pledge that death can never have the last word.[10]

The Goethean idea of polarity, συγκρίνειν and διακρίνειν, recomposition and decomposition, was also incorporated into Spengler's vision as the sequence of culture and civilization.

But the crucial Goethean idea used by Spengler in the *Decline* is the choice of the Culture as his *Urphänomen*. It is at this point that non-ideological critics have usually assaulted Spengler. R. G. Collingwood, for instance, articulates quite clearly an opinion of synecdoche seen from an ironic stance.

> The fallacy lies in the attempt to characterize a culture by means
> of a single idea or tendency or feature, to deduce everything from
> this one central idea without recognizing that a single idea,
> asserted in this way, calls up its own opposite in order to have
> something to assert itself against, and henceforth proceeds, not
> by merely repeating itself, but by playing a game of statement and
> counter-statement with this opposite.[11]

Wilhelm Düren made a similar point from an allegedly Goethean perspective.

> Oswald Spengler teaches that culture is an *Urphänomen*. That is a
> mistake, for it is only a phenomenon like the plant, like all exter-
> nal phenomena. *The Urphänomen must remain pure according to its
> own idea*, it may not be applied here and there or articulated at
> will, that is to say mistakenly, where it contradicts its own true
> idea. [12]

9. J. W. von Goethe, *Werke*, vol. XII (Hamburg, 1958), 300.

10. Meinecke, *Historism*, 479.

11. R. G. Collingwood, "Spengler's Theory of Historical Cycles" (1927), reprinted in *Ideas of History*, ed. R. H. Nash, vol. I (New York, 1969), 163.

12. It is indicative of the ephemeral nature of ideological criticism that Wilhelm Düren used Goethe *against* Spengler. "People speak too quickly of the decline of the West: *We want to speak of its rising!*" The year was 1934. *Goethe Widerlegt Spengler* (Bonn, 1934), 23.

Figures in the Rumpelkammer: *Goethe, Faust, Spengler*

Ludwig van Bertalanffy, on the other hand, appreciated the conceptualization of culture as a model, and states quite correctly that theoretical history of Spengler's sort is "not empty speculation, but rather an expansion of ordinary ways of thinking."[13] Each of these men recognized that the source of Spengler's history, for better or worse, is the figural scaffolding.

Quellenkritik, the "criticism of sources," is much the same for Goethe and for Spengler. Unlike the critical historians, who locate, sort, and evaluate the written documents of the past, labeling and enshrining these as sources (and, if they are "contemporary" in a chronological sense with the events they describe, as primary sources), Goethe and Spengler find their sources in the principles upon which a vision of the world is based. As Faust had noted the irony of a flowing, *quellen,* from dry parchment, so Spengler remarks that the fragmentary, arbitrary analogies of prior historical thought had hit upon truth ("in the essential sense of the word that remains to be determined") mainly by luck. As Faust said that history must flow from one's own soul ("aus eigner Seele quillt"), so Spengler writes for readers who can "live themselves into his words" (*DW,* I, xiv). Historical study for both Goethe and Spengler was soft at its core because its sources were not the true sources of insight.

The special status of Faust as figure is reinforced when Spengler compares him with rival possibilities. Clearly, Faust has some *Ur*-quality in him that other figures lack. (For example, "Don Quixote, Werther, Julian Sorel, are portraits of an epoch, Faust the portrait of a whole Culture," *DW,* I, 101.) Further, it is not merely the Faust of legend and literature whom Spengler has in mind; it is Goethe's Faust as he develops and "becomes" *in a book.* When Goethe wrote *Werther,* he had reached the "spring time" of Petrarch and Minnesingers; by *Urfaust* he was Parzival; the author of *Faust I* was Hamlet, and that of *Faust II* a man of the nineteenth century "who could understand Byron" (*DW,* I, 110). Spengler reads Goethe's work as in some way prefiguring his own, even in prophetic matters:

> Thus the Faust of the First Part of the tragedy, the passionate
> student of solitary midnights, is logically the progenitor of the
> Faust of the Second Part and the new century, the type of a purely
> practical, far-seeing, outward-directed activity. In him Goethe

13. Ludwig von Bertalanffy, "Cultures as Systems: Toward a Critique of Historical Reason," in *Phenomenology, Structuralism, Semiology,* ed. H. R. Garvin, *Bucknell Review* (Lewisburg and London, 1976), 54.

presaged, psychologically, the whole future of West Europe. (*DW,* I, 354)

If Faust represents the history of Western culture, he also reflects its future.

Historical epochs find themselves judged against Faust's character, with analogy dissolving any sense of cause/effect. The renaissance, for example, for which Spengler has little use, is only a *countermovement*, "a *revolt against the spirit of Faustian forest-music* of counter-point." "The inwardly recalcitrant forces—*Faust's second soul that would separate itself from the other*—are striving to deflect the sense of the Culture, to repudiate, to get rid of or to evade its inexorable necessity; it stands anxious in the presence of the call to accomplish fate in Ionic and Baroque" (*DW,* I, 233–34). The culture is reflected in Faust, and Faust is reflected in the culture. The microcosm/macrocosm relationship implicit in synecdochically organized world-views has its pure form in the term "Faustian culture." The world of evidence is similarly organized in Spengler's view, with "nothing, however small, that does not embody in itself the sum of fundamental tendencies" (*DW,* I, 47). This statement also defines the style of *The Decline of the West;* each page seems to contain the essence of the total vision. Epigrams and axioms abound, making Spengler tremendously quotable. The case is not built step by step. It is asserted again and again, always the same through a series of virtuoso variations and a vast itinerary of subjects, like the "Labyrinth / Der wundersamen aus vielen einsgewordnen Burg" ("this citadel's / Moot labyrinth which fuses muchness into one," *Faust* II, 9145–46). Mephistopheles' ironic words to the student reflect much of Spengler's style of thought—negatively, of course. He sketches the ordinary steps—one, two, three—of the philosophers and their ways of forcing causes from effects.

> Das Erst' wär so, das Zweite so,
> Und drum das Dritt' und Vierte so,
> Und wenn das Erst' und Zweit' nicht wär',
> Das Dritt und Viert' wär' nimmermehr.
> Das preisen die Schüler aller Orten,
> Sind aber keine Weber geworden.
>
> The first being thus, the second thus,
> The third and fourth must needs be thus,
> And were it not for one and two,

> The three and four could not be true.
> His pupils laud him, busy as beavers,
> And somehow never turn into weavers. (*Faust* I, 1930–35)

Spengler is rather a weaver, and his text rarely has a "one, two, three" succession of ideas. At one point, in discussing the historian's ideas of intercultural "influences," he writes: "This is pure nineteenth-century. What is sought is just a chain of causes and effects. Everything follows and nothing is prime" ("Alles 'folgt', nichts ist ursprünglich," *DW,* II, 55).

The Decline of the West was not intended simply to be a panoramic view of human history, edifying, informative, and endlessly suggestive. It places itself as an important event in history because it introduced the last and crowning achievement of Faustian culture:

> Herein, then, I see the *last* great task of Western philosophy, the only one which still remains in store for the aged wisdom of Faustian Culture, the preordained issue, it seems, of our centuries of spiritual evolution. No Culture is at liberty to *choose* the path and conduct of its thought, but here for the first time a Culture can foresee the way that destiny has chosen for it.
>
> Before my eyes there seems to emerge, as a vision, a hitherto unimagined mode of superlative historical research that is truly Western, necessarily alien to the Classical and to every other soul but ours—a comprehensive Physiognomic of all existence, a morphology of becoming for *all* humanity that drives onward to the highest and last ideas; a duty of penetrating the world-feeling not only of our proper soul but of all souls whatsoever that have contained grand possibilities and have expressed them in the field of actuality as grand Cultures. This philosophic view—to which we and we alone are entitled in virtue of our analytical mathematic, our contrapuntal music, and our perspective painting—in that its scope far transcends the scheme of the systematist, presupposes the eye of an artist, and of an artist who can feel the whole sensible and apprehensible environment dissolve into a deep infinity of mysterious relationships. So Dante felt, and so Goethe felt. (*DW,* I, 159)

This sweeping proclamation, invoking as it does the "Faustian" Olympians Dante and Goethe, situates itself very absolutely in cultural history: its possible vision is unique to itself, alien to all others, never possible before, a matter of duty, and extended to all existence! This image of the last great Faustian task evokes the aged Faust of Goethe. *His* vision is of a world of millions, living in constant danger of destruction by nature. This is his "paradiesisch Land" (*Faust* II, 11,569), because the danger has made one of many, given them a "common urgency" ("Gemeindrang") toward practical labor, a will that makes them "free people on free ground"—in Faust's opinion. This vision is pure illusion for the blind Faust, but it elicits his famous saying:

> Ja! diesem Sinne bin ich ganz ergeben,
> Das ist der Weisheit letzter Schluss:
> Nur der verdient sich Freiheit wie das Leben,
> Der täglich sie erobern muss.

> Yes—this I hold to with devout insistence,
> Wisdom's last verdict goes to say:
> He only earns both freedom and existence
> Who must reconquer them each day. (*Faust* II, 11,573–76)

The idea that freedom consists of choosing necessity with a single will is not foreign to German thought; with this vision, Faust expires. The words remain in the subjunctive ("Zum Augenblicke durft' ich sagen: / Verweile doch, du bist so schön!"); Mephistopheles loses his wager for Faust's soul.

Spengler's vision, as that of spokesman for an aged Faustian culture, resembles Faust's, or so it would appear. Practical labor is what Spengler encourages his contemporaries to take up. Roman times call for Romans, not belated Hellenists; good roads, not bad poems. Faust dies in ecstasy, and Spengler also becomes lyrical in sketching the project that the *Decline* heralds:

> Poems and battles, Isis and Cybele, festivals and Roman catholic masses, blast furnaces and gladiatorial games, dervishes and Darwinians, railways and Roman roads, "Progress" and Nirvana, newspapers, mass-slavery, money, machinery—all of these are equally signs and symbols in the world-picture of the past that the soul presents to itself and would interpret. "*Alles Vergängliche ist nur ein Gleichnis.*" (*DW*, I, 160)

Yet there is a quality here that makes us look further, a quality of *lastness*. "The physiognomic of world-happening will become the *last Faustian philosophy.*" Although Faust's vision was his end, he had no sense of an ending, but rather of a beginning, an accomplishment that time could not efface ("Es kann die Spur von meinen Erdetagen / Nicht in Aönen untergehn—" ["My path on earth, the trace I leave within it / Eons untold cannot impair"], *Faust* II, 11,583–84). Faust's vision of free men bound together in struggle against a constant peril, Nature, was an inner vision, the fruit of his Care-inflicted blindness. It is Faust who *desires* "Caesarism" ("Das sich das grösste Werk Vollende, / Genügt ein Geist für tausend Hände" ["To bring to fruit the most exalted plans, / One mind is ample for a thousand hands"], *Faust*, II, 11,509–10); Spengler who *predicts* it as destiny.[14]

Spengler, however, has no illusory vision of an open future, perhaps because he has registered Mephistopheles' comment on Faust's demise:

> Die Zeit wird Herr, der greis hier liegt im Sand.
> Die Uhr steht still—
>
> Time triumphs—stranded lies, a whitened shell.
> The clock is muted— (*Faust* II, 11,592–93)

Faust's blindness and vision were caused by Care ("Sorge"), although he refused to acknowledge her power. The great project of land reclamation and social engineering of *Faust* II, book v is precisely the sort of thing Spengler sees as paternal care, of which the state is the symbol. Spengler's comment upon this Care is striking:

> So once more, the imaging-power that is the efficient in dynamics conjures up the old great symbol of Faustian man's historical passion, Care—the outlook into the farthest far of past and future, the back-looking study of history, the foreseeing state, the confessions and introspections, the bells that sounded over all our country-sides and measured the passing of Life. The ethos of the word Time, as we alone feel it, as instrumental music alone and no statue-plastic can carry it, is directed upon an *aim*. This aim has been figured in every life-image that the West has conceived—as the Third Kingdom, as the New Age, as the task of mankind, as the issue of evolution. And it is figured, as the destined end-state of all Faustian "Nature," in Entropy. (*DW*, I, 422)

14. Spengler's prediction of a coming Caesarism is quite specific. In a footnote near the end of the second volume of the *Decline*, he writes that the German constitution of 1919, the most up-to-date of constitutions because the one closest to "the verge of the decline of democracy," grants "a Caesarism of organizations" to the political parties. He adds: "A few quite small alterations and it confers unrestricted power upon individuals" (*DW*, II, 457, n. 3).

Entropy is the modern, irreligious form of *Götterdämmerung,* the Gothic legend that is equally Faustian. Faust dies when his goal has been reached, and Faustian culture approaches entropy—*"world's end as completion of an inwardly necessary evolution"* (*DW,* I, 424)

Entropy, however, has its own evolution. The term was chosen by Rudolf Clausius in the mid-nineteenth century from the Greek τροπή, "a transformation," the same word used for the figures of language, the tropes. Entropy is the "mathematical measure of the disorganization of a system"; and maximum entropy, the state that Spengler clearly has in mind, is "a state of stable thermodynamic equilibrium." Movement does not cease, but effective directionality, the ability to do work, ends; Space, Spengler might say, exists, but Time has stopped: *"Die Uhr steht still—."* This entropy is to be found not only in the arts, literature, philosophy; even the sciences have passed their moment. "Our great century has been the nineteenth. Savants of the calibre of Gauss and Humboldt were already no more by 1900" (*DW,* I, 424). Only the factual side of life, "politics, technics, and economics," remains for development.

The entropy of a culture is its tendency toward the awareness that all of its expressions are symbolic, transient moments of something else that is apparently the whole. For Spengler, *"Alles Vergängliche ist nur ein Gleichnis"* is the classic entropic-prophetic statement. It is a call into the future, a call for *The Decline of the West* and the project that it heralds, the last Faustian task. In addition to his morphology of cultures, Spengler calls for a morphology of the exact sciences and the rendering of all knowledge into a vast system of relationships. This relational spirit is the basis of Faustian mathematics, quite opposed in spirit to the mathematics of the classical world, which is based on "pure magnitude." The Faustian sees numbers as *"pure relation,"* making the symbol of the West "the idea of *Function"* (*DW,* I, 75).[15] One imagines that if *The Decline of the West* were written today, it would be full of advanced computer theory, for the computer seems a classic late Faustian device, with an infinitely large grasp based upon the simplest principle of binary selection. In the computer, all is relationship.

Entropy is a figure of Irony, insofar as Irony represents self-consciousness in matters of language and the ways in which it enables us to order the world. Spengler presents the entropy theory as "the beginning of the destruction of that masterpiece of Western intelligence, the

---

15. Again Goethe is guide. Spengler cites in a footnote Goethe's definition: "Function, rightly understood, is existence considered as an activity" (*DW,* I, 86, n. 2).

old dynamic physics" (*DW,* I, 421). Because the opposition of theory and actuality became a part of theory itself (dealing with the theoretical reversibility and actual irreversibility of processes), this vision of entropy calls to mind the ironic figure oxymoron, in which two opposing semantic elements are joined, as in "cold fire" or "darkness visible." The term Entropy, which is inwardly meaningful like Force and Will, is defined differently by each authority. "Here again, the intellect breaks down where the world-feeling demands expression" (*DW,* I, 420).

If Spengler is beginning the last Faustian task in writing "the philosophy of our time," a "material philosophy" to some extent, then surely he must be only a modest, impersonal formulator of ideas that have crystallized for all to see. Stephen C. Pepper, whose chapter "Organicism" in *World Hypotheses* is quite illuminating when applied to Spengler, notes that "to the organicist, facts are not organised from without; they organise themselves."[16] Spengler writes that the relations and connections "presented themselves," "linked themselves," "were revealed," "appeared," and "open[ed] out for us the true style of history" (*DW,* I, 47). This Faustian history will see the present as if from a great distance, with no personal ideas, origins, hopes, or fears (*DW,* I, 93). Although Spengler credits the vision of this detachment to Nietzsche, it will be, he says, far from the "innocent relativism of Nietzsche and his generation" (*DW,* I, 25). Nor does he claim to be blessed with a unique perspective afforded him by his position in space and time, for his history is Copernican in that "it admits no sort of privileged position to the Classical or Western Culture" against the other cultures of world history (*DW,* I, 18). The language of these assertions has a positivist ring of impartiality. Spengler, however, contradicts this midwifely historical pose; he points out that even positivist history is not "pure becoming," but "a world-form radiating from the waking consciousness of the historian . . . " (*DW,* I, 95). All history is philosophy, and all philosophy expresses only its own time (*DW,* I, 41); consequently, the world-history that Spengler opposed so strongly (progress-oriented, beginning with the Greeks, composed of "ancient, medieval, and modern"—all fallacies in Spengler's eyes) is "*our* world-picture and not all mankind's" (*DW,* I, 15).

Since everything sees history in relation to itself, every member of Faustian culture has an individual picture of history. Criticism, *Kritik,* has only a limited role:

16. Stephen C. Pepper, *World Hypotheses: A Study in Evidence* (Berkeley, 1966), 291.

> Thus Nature and History are distinguishable like pure and
> impure criticism—meaning by "criticism" the opposite of lived
> experience. Natural science *is* criticism and nothing else. But in
> History, criticism can do no more than scientifically prepare the
> field over which the historian's eye is to sweep. *History is that
> ranging glance itself,* whatever the direction in which it ranges.
> (*DW*, II, 24)

"Geschichte ist dieser Blick selbst. . . ." The Faustian historian claims to
possess such a glance, but the reader of *Faust* will surely recall that it
was in order to attain a view of what would prove the last Faustian task
that Faust caused the destruction of Philemon and Baucis.

> Dem Blick eröffnen weite Bahn,
> Zu sehn, was alles ich getan,
> Zu überschaun mit einem Blick
> Des Menschengeistes Meisterstück . . .
>
> From branch to branch, for vistas deep
> Of my achievement's fullest sweep,
> With all-embracing gaze to scan
> The masterpiece of sapient man . . . (*Faust* II, 11,245–48)

These masterpieces of the human mind are the foci of Spengler's *Blick* in
The Decline of the West, but he warns us against regarding the book and
the vision as a chance event made possible by Goethe's existence, nor is
the course of Western culture dependent on one man. If Goethe had
died young, his "ideas" would have lived. "Faust and Tasso would not
have been written, but they would have 'been' in a deeply mysterious
sense, even though they lacked the poet's elucidation" (*DW*, I, 145). The
clue to this mysterious sense is the synecdoche that makes a symbol out
of a part, makes it represent the whole. Insofar as Faust (or Goethe or
Spengler) represents the whole in a microcosmic sense, then it *is* the
whole in a figural sense and would be implicit in it even if it, the part,
did not happen to exist. The "fact" of its absence would not efface the
"truth" of its presence.[17]

At this point, Spengler re-enacts Faust's fundamental gesture, the
endless desire that by its very definition ensures its own frustration. Yet
Spengler, standing above Faust in the realm of the Faustian, which is
quite a different thing, has solved the problem of the frustration of

17. "Facts and truths differ as time and space, destiny and causality" (*DW*, II, 12).

desire by making desire itself (or its symbol, infinite space) into the focus of desire. Thus, desire could function as desire in the Lacanian sense without the loss and failure implicit therein, because what was desired was in fact the arena of further desire rather than some illusory partial object. Space is the locus of this special displacement, and it is space with which Spengler associates Faustian man. Kant erred in dealing with space and time in a single critique: space is a conception; time, only a word. Primitive man instinctively knows space, and indeed *has* time, but does not know it. Time is a discovery made by thinking, a creation of man that only later leads to the suspicion "that *we ourselves are time,* inasmuch as we live: (*DW,* I, 122). Time, thus, is Destiny, a most important Spenglerian notion; it is experienced by man, but not really comprehended.

> The female, on the contrary, *is herself* Destiny and Time and the organic logic of the Becoming, and for that very reason the principle of Causality is forever alien to her. Whenever Man has tried to give Destiny any tangible form, he has felt it as of feminine form, and he has called it Moirai, Parcae, Norns. (*DW,* II, 327)

Time, whether seen as Destiny, woman, or the "organic logic of the Becoming," represents the limit of Desire, even divine desire. Just as Man represents or controls Woman, the bachelor Spengler tells us, so the supreme deity only represents Destiny. Woman, the seeress, does not know, but rather is, the future. "The man *makes* History, the woman *is* History" (*DW,* II, 327). This synedochic equation of a part, woman, with a whole, History, is based upon woman's embodiment of Destiny. The figure becomes reversible, making History "heavy with fate [*schicksalsschwer*] but free of laws" (*DW,* I, 118). A series of analogies is strung from this basic dualism. "*Time is a counter-conception* [*Gegenbegriff*] *to Space,* arising out of Space, just as the notion (as distinct from the fact) of life arises only in opposition to thought, and the notion (as distinct from the fact) of birth and generation only in opposition to death" (*DW,* I, 126–27). Time is both the enemy of Faustian *man* and the siren that lures him forward. Caught in this paradox, Spengler seeks to obey Destiny (rather a paradoxical idea itself) by in effect spatializing history, making Time (Woman, Destiny, Becoming) subservient to Space, the arena of a desire that is always slipping elsewhere. The Spenglerian charts, the whole morphological apparatus of *The Decline of the West,* privilege Space over time; Spengler is Faustian man, striving in and for "endless space," hostile to time. But in carrying out the "last

Faustian task," Spengler also knows and names himself, his culture, and its goals. Consequently, his recognition of the hegemony of time, Destiny, "the organic logic of Becoming," woman, and the other rather mystical embodiments of this notion places him with Destiny in an ironic awareness of the limits of even the boundless. Seen from this Spenglerian perspective, the last task of Faustian man is to become woman, the seeress. This Spengler has tried to do. As the logic of the Faustian trope leads to irony, as Faustian culture runs to entropy, so Faustian desire can only remain itself by becoming something else.

> Das Unbeschreibliche,
> Hier ist's getan;
> Das Ewig-weibliche
> Zieht uns hinan.
>
> Human discernment
> Here is passed by;
> Woman Eternal
> Draws us on high. (*Faust* II, 12,108–11)

For Spengler, this awareness of the inadequacies of language in all forms is never missing. He devotes considerable space to the role of language in the development of cultures, the origin of language, forms of language (*"talk [Sprechen] belongs to the castle, and speech [Sprach] to the cathedral,"* DW, II, 153), and the history of grammar. Naturally, the familial development traced by the nineteenth-century linguists is illusory for Spengler:

> Instead of *sum*, Gothic *im*, we say *ich bin, I am, je suis*; instead of *fecisti*, we say *tu habes factum, tu as fait, du habes qîtan*; and again, *daz wîp, un homme, man hat*. This has hitherto been a riddle because families of languages were considered as beings, but the mystery is solved when we discover in the idiom the reflection of a soul. The Faustian soul is here beginning to remould for its own use grammatical material of the most varied provenance. (*DW*, I, 262)

Faustian languages possess the notion of Will; the first person towers up in the Culture in many forms. From the Gothic spire and buttress, in Aquinas and Kant, in ethics and the concept of personal immortality, the "I" is supreme (*DW*, I, 302, 308–9).

With Goethe, who wrote, "All forms, even those that are most felt, contain an element of untruth," Spengler believes that "speech and truth exclude one another" (*DW*, II, 137). Because no signs (*Zeichen*) can replace actuality (*Wirklichkeit*), true systems of thought cannot exist (*DW*, II, 144). The signs of script refer only to other signs; yet writing represents a new kind of language, a liberation from the present that satisfies the Faustian hatred of the foreground (*DW*, II, 149). Spengler writes with the apprehension that the age of the book, flanked by those of the sermon and the newspaper, is drawing to a close; this apprehension calls to mind Martin Heidegger's hostility to the empty *Gerede* of common language. Spengler: "Books are a personal expression, sermon and newspaper obey an impersonal *purpose*" (*DW*, II, 463).

At many points Spengler's problematics resemble Heidegger's. The beginning chapter of the second volume of *The Decline of the West*, on "the cosmic and the microcosm," is drawn from a "book of metaphysics" that Spengler hoped would soon appear, but that never did so. From the following paragraph we surmise the extent of Spengler's concern with ontology and its modes.

> And with this there emerges in all clarity yet another distinction, which is normally obscured by the use of the ambiguous word "consciousness" [*Bewusstsein*]. I distinguish *being* or "being there" [*Dasein*] from waking-being or waking-consciousness [*Wachsein*]. Being possesses beat and direction, while waking-consciousness is tension and extension. In being a destiny rules, while waking-consciousness distinguishes cause and effects. The prime question is for the one "when and wherefore?" for the other "where and how?" (*DW*, II, 7)

Heidegger, who himself never published a promised second half of *Sein und Zeit* (1927), would certainly recognize the concerns discussed here. While it is not clear what Heidegger has explicitly learned from Spengler, it is quite clear that both have learned from Goethe. *Both* Heidegger and Spengler make Care *(Sorge)* a key factor in their image of being. Heidegger writes: "The Being of Human-Being is Care" ("Das Sein des Daseins ist die Sorge"). This sentence immediately follows his statement about the guilt of human being as such. *"Being guilty does not result only from becoming guilty, but it is the other way around: the latter becomes possible only 'on the basis of' an original Being guilty."*[18] Spengler did

18. Cited in Walter Kaufmann, *Discovering the Mind*, vol. II: *Nietzsche, Heidegger, Buber* (New York, 1980), 209.

not share Heidegger's concept of original guilt. (Heidegger had claimed in 1921 to be "a Christian theologian" in a letter to Karl Löwith.) Spengler writes: "Culture is the being [*Dasein*] of nations in State-form" (*DW*, II, 362). The counterpart of the State is the Family, *res publica* and *res privata*. "And both, moreover, are symbols of care: ("Symbole der Sorge"). The maternal care in the family has its complement in the paternal care of the state, which is the "Care for the preservation of the whole" ("Sorge um die Erhaltung des Ganzen," *DW*, II, 362).

Care comes to Faust with three companions, Want, Debt, and Need (*Mangel, Schuld, Not*), but Faust's wealth keeps the others away. Care can slip through any keyhole. Faust muses on a desire to be done with magic—that is, with the *words* of magic—and to return to the path of mere humanity.

> Könnt' ich Magie von meinem Pfad entfernen,
> Die Zaubersprüche ganz und gar verlernen,
> Stünd' ich, Natur, vor dir ein Mann allein,
> Da wär's der Mühe wert, ein Mensch zu sein.

> Could I but clear my path at every turning
> Of spells, all magic utterly unlearning;
> Were I but Man, with Nature for my frame,
> The name of human would be worth the claim. (*Faust* II, 11,404–7)

When Care appears and asserts her power, Faust refuses to acknowledge it, so she makes him blind, saying "Die Menschen sind im ganzen Leben blind, / Nun, Fauste, werde du's am Ende" ("Man commonly is blind throughout his life, / My Faust, be blind then as you end it," *Faust* II, 11,497–98). It is this blindness that grants Faust his final vision into what Heidegger might call "das Sein des Daseins." Spengler notes that the "impoverishment of the sensual" gives an "immeasurable deepening" to "human waking-consciousness" ("menschliches Wachsein"). "It is now life *in* a self-centered light-world" (*DW*, II, 8). Care describes her effect to Faust as anxiety about the *future* (*Faust* II, 11,465), and the possibility of not finishing tasks. For Spengler, Heidegger, and perhaps the aged Goethe finishing his great task one hundred and fifty years ago, Care is the fear of Time.[19] Of the three, only Goethe finished the announced task.

Any study of Spengler must confront the question of what is vital and

19. "In every work that displays the *whole* man and the *whole* meaning of existence, fear and longing lie close together, but they are and remain different" (*DW*, I, 127).

what moribund in the work of this once prominent, now "dated" figure. Few today come forward to take his part; cultural critics as disparate as Erich Heller and Theodor Adorno, conservative and marxist, inveigh against the wickedness of Spengler's mind, the crudity of his brilliance, the waste of his erudition. Yet they also agree that in his predictions, precisely the area in which scholarship and humanism of all varieties have explicitly faulted him, Oswald Spengler was essentially right. Adorno notes that "the course of world history vindicated his immediate prognoses to an extent that would astonish if they were still remembered. Forgotten, Spengler takes his revenge by threatening to be right."[20]

If Spengler's predictions were correct, and if one has no *a priori* objections to his metahistorical ambition (as neither Adorno nor Heller does—both mock the German historical establishment of the 1920s and its outraged impotence in the *Streit um Spengler)*, then their rejection seems to be occasioned exactly by Spengler's rightness. Not that either one blames Spengler for causing the Caesarism, the barbarism, the bankruptcy of art, the decay of humanism. It is his fatalistic acceptance of these things that they reject and find wicked. For them, so to speak, a Faust that does not resist even destiny is not Faustian.

We are led by these observations on the response to Spengler by two representative moralist-critics of our time to a more troubling and, I think, more important question: what is left of Faust after one hundred and fifty years? And what is left of Goethe? By asking these questions, I do not intend merely to repeat the plaints of humanists that the classic works and authors are forgotten today, although this is probably the case. Young Americans have little notion of who Goethe was; young Germans, surveys tell us, know only a little more. The generation of Germans that routinely memorized a dozen *Sprichwörte* from *Faust* is passing (and this ability seems to have given them no special wisdom). Goethe, enshrined as the "greatest German poet," is no longer becoming, but rather has become—for Spengler, following Goethe himself, this signifies death.

20. Erich Heller, "Oswald Spengler and the Predicament of the Historical Imagination," in *The Disinherited Mind*; Theodor W. Adorno, "Spengler After the Decline," in *Prisms*, trans. S. and S. Weber (London, 1967), 54. Typical of much writing about Spengler, Adorno's essay contains no references and few citations from *The Decline of the West*. His summaries of Spengler's ideas are tendentious, to say the least; they almost invariably ignore the subtlety and interweaving of Spengler's thumping, apparently apodictic pronouncements. Heller cites Spengler's thousand-page work ten times in his essay; all citations are from the first volume, nine from the introduction.

Yet these matters seem trivial compared with a deeper and related change in Goethe's status. Spengler considered Goethe a philosopher, and called his own work, *The Decline of the West*, "a German philosophy" (*DW*, I, xiv). Goethe was analogous to Plato in Spengler's morphology; to invoke his name was a philosophical, even more than a literary, act. Goethe, the rival of Kant (that is, Plato versus Aristotle) in the minds of so many German thinkers, has in effect been demoted to the status of "mere" literature. That a philosopher today is far more likely to know Kant than Goethe and would be unlikely in any case to find serious philosophic interest in Goethe is again symptomatic of the change in Goethe's status—or of the change in the pertinence of philosophy, as Spenger might suggest.[21]

The name Goethe no longer designates a philosophy; but is not Faust nevertheless the accepted archetype of Western man, reaching for absolutes, destroying all roots? Perhaps not. The historian John Lukacs suggests that "the Germanic and bourgeois and essentially sentimental" story of Faust, inflated into a "fake heroic symbol" by Spengler, has far less meaning for the West than does the *Sorcerer's Apprentice*.[22] The considerations that might lead one to this conclusion are technological, military, ecological, and demographic, the sort of matters that are today routinely predicted by computer projections, and not from a morphological grasp of "destiny." If the Sorcerer's Apprentice has become the model for Western man (if there ever was such a thing as Western man), with no *Hexenmeister* to save the day, then Faustian man can be consigned to the *Rumpelkammer* of history, a fate Goethe's Faust feared. And although Goethe himself is the author of the *Sorcerer's Apprentice* as *Der Zauberlehrling*, its theme of respect for the limits of knowledge is as little heeded as ever—for Goethe, after all, is a poet, not a philosopher.

If fact, Spengler foresaw this as part of the end of Faustian man. At the end of the second volume, in his discussion of the machine, the image of the creature turning upon and dominating the creator becomes manifest. The machine is truly Faustian (just as the steam engine is contemporary with Goethe's Faust), with its "upward-straining life-feeling," weaving a web of forces over the earth, ever less mate-

21. In his last work, the three-volume study called *Discovering the Mind* (New York, 1979, 1980), Walter Kaufmann takes up the traditional German contraposition of Goethe and Kant, and uses it as a basis for evaluating Hegel, Nietzsche, Heidegger, Freud, and others. Few other philosophers have shown such awareness of Goethe's influence.

22. John Lukacs, in Alexis de Tocqueville, *The European Revolution and Correspondence with Gobineau*, trans. and ed. John Lukacs (Garden City, N.Y., 1959), 187.

rial, more silent and interior. With it, Faustian man deposed God and "sacred Causality."

> Never save here has a microcosm felt itself superior to a mac-rocosm, but here the little life-units have by the sheer force of their intellect made the unliving dependent upon themselves. It is a triumph, so far as we can see, unparalleled. Only this our Culture has achieved it, and perhaps only for a few centuries.
>
> But for that very reason Faustian man has become *the slave of his creation*. (*DW*, II, 504)

The magic synecdoche of microcosm/macrocosm, in which the part represents the whole as its equivalent—the figure that Faust calls "Eben-bild"—here reveals its inherent impossibility by becoming explicitly ironic: the part becomes *greater* than the whole. This is illusion, but it is also for Spengler the actuality of Faustian man in the twentieth century. The machine is devilish, its economy is Satanism; yet they differ from Goethe's canny Mephistopheles, the master of figurative relationships. He knew that he was "Ein Teil von jener Kraft, / Die stets das Böse will und stets das Gute schafft" ("Part of that force which would / Do ever evil, and does ever good," *Faust* I, 1335–36), and even "ein Teil des Teils . . . ." This insight, which we call ironic, into the subtleties of part/whole relationships, is given late to Faustian man—indeed, only at the *end* of *The Decline of the West*.

We have finally reached the point on which, in my opinion, Spengler and Goethe distinctly part company. Spengler's Cultures are monads in Leibniz's sense, self-specular mirrors reflecting a pre-established ("Ur") harmony that has somehow ordained their destiny. What a culture wills to express is in it *a priori*. "Influences" are myriad, but the only effective ones (the ones that historians trace) are inherent in the soul of a culture (*DW*, II, 55–58). For Leibniz, whom Spengler calls "without doubt the greatest intellect in Western philosophy" (*DW*, I, 42), the monad reflects the mind of God; in *Faust*, "Der Herr" stands apart from and above the drama. Spengler rarely suggests whose mind *his* monads reflect. We infer at times from his words that he considered his vision true *for himself*, rather than true *in itself* (*DW*, I, xiv)—that is to say, an interpretation or allegory, rather than a vision of reality. But at other times the microcosmic Spengler seem to *be* the story he is telling. He is within the bounded culture, like all creatures a part of it, yet also not a part, but rather a representation (and representer) of the whole, at once the contained and the container. Because "the Faustian man is an 'I' that in the last resort draws its own conclusions about the Infinite" (*DW*, II, 235), to be more than a part of Faustian culture is the true sign of being a part of it. The irony that springs from the paradox of perfect synecdoche, the part that stands for the whole without loss, as microcosm to macrocosm, is lost upon Spengler, despite his frequent explicit indications of the nature of these ironies. He will not decide whether his lived reality—*The Decline of the West*—is the work of a "destiny-Man" or of a "thinker," a man of books. He writes: "The thinker could discuss destiny if he liked: it was enough for these men [Alexander, Scipio, Caesar, Napoleon] to be destiny" (*DW*, II, 18). Goethe had recognized the daemonism of Napoleon, but denied that he himself had such power. Spengler *wills* himself to be a man of action, whose relationship to his age might carry the stamp of destiny, but we know (and he knew, after all) that he was really a thinker, a man of books, not a "destiny" by his standards.

Faustian man is not merely a character in Spengler's *magnum opus*, not an inflated trope glibly chosen to support the superstructure of Western culture. As I have attempted to show here, Spengler's text is woven throughout with materials and ideas found in Goethe and especially in *Faust*. The Faustian becomes a figure of desire for the infinite, and this desire can only be satisfied by a trope, synecdoche. The monadic enclosure beomes a field of infinite substitution. But since the whole requires an escape from words, from "mere" figures of speech, the yearning for action, and the self-consciousness regarding the figurality of language, turns the whole process into an ironic apprehension.

It is not Spengler's vast historical desire and daring that consign him to a forgotten corner of modern historiography; modern masters like Fernand Braudel have reached for a sort of "total history," but in an ironic mode. It is the governing trope that dates Spengler's work, its symbolism, its analogies, and its philosophy, just as it has dated Goethe's philosophy, but not his art. The *figure* in the storeroom, the *Rumpelkammer* of history, is synecdoche.

7 DISORDERLY CONDUCT

BRAUDEL'S MEDITERRANEAN SATIRE

I

> *To the extent that the divisions between the sections are effective, a comprehension of the organic totality of Mediterranean life is blocked. There are fine pages that illuminate their subject; but they do so, not because of these lines of demarcation so carefully laid out, but in spite of them.*
>
> Bernard Bailyn

> *After all, order matters rather little.*
>
> Lucien Febvre

Two things have been clear about Fernand Braudel's *La Méditerranée et le monde méditerranéen à l'époque de Philippe II* since its publication in 1949; first, that it is a remarkable work of historical scholarship and imagination, destined to become a landmark of twentieth-century historiography; and second, that the work is cast in a form that is both instructive and deeply troubling.[1] Lucien Febvre's review sig-

---

1. Because the purpose of this essay is to deal with formal issues and to sketch the response to Braudel's book with regard to them, I have not attempted to survey the large literature dealing with particular aspects of the work. Summaries of this material may be found in Ruggiero Romano, "A Propos de l'edition italienne de livre de F. Braudel, 'Civilta e imperi del Mediterraneo nell'eta di Filippo II,'" *Cahiers Vilfredo Pareto: Revue européene d'histoire des sciences sociales* 15 (1968), 97–108 (translation of Romano's review in *Rivista storica italiana* 67 [1955], 233–43); this issue of the *Cahiers Vilfredo Pareto* is devoted to Braudel's work. Of similar interest is an issue of the *Journal of Modern History* 44 (1972), which contains relevant articles by Braudel, H. R. Trevor-Roper, and J. H. Hexter. Chapter 2 of George Iggers' *New Directions in European Historiography* (Middletown, Conn., 1975) discusses "the *Annales* tradition"; and Traian Stoianovich's *French Historical Method: The Annales Paradigm* (Ithaca, 1976) is heavy with useful references.

naled the entry of *La Méditerranée et le monde méditerranéen* into the pantheon of historical classics, an entry that was virtually prenatal, since the reputation of the work and its author, at least to the readers of the journal *Annales*, was established two years before publication, at the time of Braudel's defense of his thesis in the Sorbonne. Febvre, to whom the book is dedicated, used Braudel's text repeatedly to promote the work of the *Annales* school of historians; it is not surprising to read in his review the terms "une révolution," "un bouleversement," "une mutation historique," "un livre qui grandit." The review was published not in *Annales*, but in the *Revue historique*, and its missionary fervor was intense.

And yet, in the midst of this political panegyric (which often seems to refer to some book other than Braudel's), Febvre revealed in oddly contradictory comments his own uneasiness with the work and with its implications for the role of history as a humanistic endeavor. Noting that the Mediterranean, "a complex of seas," was promoted for the first time "to the dignity of a historical personage," as its space was accorded the same elevation,[2] Febvre seems delighted that both the geographic concept (the Mediterranean Sea) and the mental category that considers its dimensions (Space) were granted by Braudel a status analogous to that of human and institutional agents—that is, the "dignity" at the very least of their recognition as identifiable forces in determining the course of events, forces that may be considered as *having an identity*. But Febvre at the same time signaled an opposite movement in Braudel's text, precisely away from privileging the dignity of the historical personage. Febvre proposed that "Man, subject of History," might be substituted for the abstract term "History" itself—"it is the logical and necessary outcome of the decomposition of Man, in his abstract unity, into a 'cortege of personages,' as Fernand Braudel says."[3] Man's *loss of a unified historical identity* in turn makes it possible for this now-fragmented Man to serve as the unifier in the three levels of this "new conception of History."

For it is man who answers the demands of the geographical milieu.

And man who lives in groups and participates by his nature in his groups. And man finally who lives his life as an individual—that

2. Lucien Febvre, "Un Livre qui grandit: *La Méditerranée et le monde méditerranéen à l'époque de Philippe II*," *Revue historique* 203 (1950), 218, 222.

3. Ibid., 223.

life of which the chronicle, ancestor of the newspaper, registers the random manifestations.[4]

So Man, the now-disunified, reunifies History at the moment of its apparent fragmentation. Seen from this angle, Febvre's elevation of the Sea (geography, or physical space) and Space (which, in fact, refers in Braudel almost invariably to time, the human experience of distance-as-duration) to the status of personages was undone by his tacit recognition of the ambiguous position of *personnage* as such in Braudel's text.

This problem is more than merely a matter of Febvre's rhapsodic prose; he had taken up his dissatisfaction with History, "this worn-out word which has no real meaning," in another article of 1949, published in the *Revue de métaphysique et de morale* and advertising Braudel's book as a "new kind of history."

> But what word would we use to replace [History] to contain at one and the same time the ideas of man, change, and duration? "Archaeology" has already been used up, and leads us back to that quite inept definition of history, "science of the past"; it does not contain any suggestion of humanity or of duration. Anthropochronology, ethnochronology—philistine inventions which would need explaining before anybody would understand them.[5]

Febvre wanted "a new kind of history" (hence his discomfort with the word itself), but had to retain an old kind of man (hence his rejection of proffered alternatives). He realized implicitly that the logical alternative to History was an Archaeology and that this Archaeology would accord no privilege to Man or to duration. This new kind of history, an "archaeology of knowledge" as it would be elaborated later by Michel Foucault, was glimpsed and rejected by Febvre. Defense against its demands shaped his reading of a fundamental issue in Braudel's text: the relation between its parts.

Febvre saw that the major problem of "a new kind of history" was formal: not the amassing of geographic, socioeconomic, and political materials, but rather the creation of an entity that would be adequate to

4. Ibid.
5. Lucien Febvre, "A New Kind of History," trans. K. Folca, in *A New Kind of History and Other Essays*, ed. Peter Burke (London, 1973), 43, n. 9; from *Revue de métaphysique et de morale* 58 (1949).

their wholeness. He characterized the three parts of Braudel's *Méditer-ranée* as "a series of tiered planes," "perpetually communicating—but distinct"; they form a "hierarchy," extending from "the most profound and constant to the most superficial and ephemeral." But Febvre, as we have seen, did not point out that the classical humanistic Man resided only in the ephemera. Febvre needed Man—a capitalized nominative—for reasons that are metaphysical as well as formal. Without the fiction of man, even interpreted as a "cortege of personages," Febvre cannot read Braudel's text as a unified whole, an order, as he puts it, "that separates nothing that should be united, but which permits, at each moment of passing time, illumination of the diverse planes on which the action takes place by the others."[6] To save History from fragmentation, man is needed, like Berkeley's God. But to perform the task, Man must be fragmented.

Febvre's reading of Braudel turned upon his sense of the *hierarchy* of stages and his consequent need to posit some whole that can mediate between the parts; this metaphysically necessary Man must be one and many, a theological construct. If we accept Febvre's reading of Braudel as a movement through a hierarchy from a relatively eternal world of order, through a world of conjunctive systems mediating between permanence and chaos, to a world of random and surely self-deceptive events, then its form as text is clearly tragic, like Dante's *Commedia* in reverse. And as Dante the Pilgrim serves to unite the three levels described by Dante the Poet, so Man (both sixteenth-century man and humanity itself) must exist to unite Braudel's "plans étagés."

Febvre's insistence upon the formal hierarchy of Braudel's plan, its unity-in-density, makes much of his review seem defensive. After pointing out Braudel's repeated use of personifications (not "the role of mountains" but "the role of the Mountain") and oxymorons ("liquid plains")—figures reminiscent of Michelet—Febvre hastened to note Braudel's great need for "unequivocal clarity" and "the obsession with the date that distinguishes the born historian from his brother and sometime enemy the sociologist." Defending against formal objections to Braudel's text, he added, "After all, order matters rather little."[7]

Lacking Febvre's concept of Man, J. A. van Houtte, writing in the *Bibliothèque d'humanisme et renaissance,* could not find in *La Méditerranée et le monde méditerranéen à l'époque de Philippe II* the formal balance and unity

6. Febvre, "Un Livre," 223–24.
7. Ibid., 222.

presented by Febvre. He recognized the magisterial nature of the book, its prodigious richness, fine pages, and vast sources. However, he read it as a socioeconomic study, with a perfunctory political history appended.[8] Braudel's goal of a human "geo-history" that would take time into account seemed unrealized to van Houtte. The disequilibrium between the first and second parts of the history together (both of which van Houtte considered the domain of the social historian) and the third were explained, but not excused, by Braudel's own disclaimer that he had found the last section "a little boring to write." While Febvre's defense of Braudel had stressed the relations between the levels of analysis, van Houtte found them unbalanced and inadequately connected. The "formal vice" that van Houtte saw in Braudel's book led him to suggest that the third section be sacrificed altogether, leaving behind a strong "social history pure and simple." If this advice seems extraordinary enough in the light of Febvre's insistence upon the work's formal integrity, van Houtte went further, suggesting that most readers of scholarly works do not read, but rather consult, and that Braudel has done little to aid the consulting reader, leaving the campaigns and negotiations of the third section as vain and sterile as in *l'histoire historisante*. In France the issue was thus posed from the beginning: was the work an enormous heap of diverse materials or a truly revolutionary step in historical methodology?

The historical response to the book in Germany and the United States was respectful but rather routine. Werner Conze's review in the *Historische Zeitschrift* described the work, recited its "revolutionary" claims, and blandly accepted them.[9] Garrett Mattingly, writing in the *American Historical Review,* was considerably more critical, suggesting (like van Houtte) that the book became less rewarding as it progressed and that certain of Braudel's "revolutionary" conclusions were about issues never in doubt. Mattingly writes that "the massive and exciting *decor* built up in the first seven-hundred-odd pages does little, after all, to enliven or illuminate the familiar drama," in large part because "the sea itself is slighted."[10] The future historian of *The Armada* points out the flaws in Braudel's knowledge of "ships and their uses" before concluding that "this is a brilliant, exciting, and profoundly stimulating book, a creditable labor of scholarship and historical imagination." Respect, even enthusiasm, were clearly present, but with the exception

8. J. A. van Houtte, review in *Bibliothèque d'humanisme et renaissance* 12 (1950), 428.
9. Werner Conze, review in *Historische Zeitschrift* 172 (1951), 358–62.
10. Garrett Mattingly, review in *American Historical Review* 55 (1950), 350, 352.

of Febvre, early reviewers quite understandably had no sense of an "event," and the hyperbole of two decades later was absent.

By 1951, though, "reconsideration" of Braudel's work was deemed necessary by Bernard Bailyn, whose essay remains the most succinct and direct statement of objections to the form of the book. Citing Febvre's essay on Braudel, Bailyn sweepingly denied any claims that the book may have had to unity or organic coherence. Bailyn recognized that the book's methodological innovation was organizational, yet he described it as "an exhausting treadmill."[11] The levels of structures, conjunctures, and events frustrate any grasp of a "world"; in Bailyn's view Braudel's "world" lay strewn about in "inert, unrelated, discrete" pieces. Foreshadowing J. H. Hexter's comments of twenty years later, Bailyn identified Braudel's problem as having "mistaken a poetic response to the past for a historical problem." With such a problem properly formulated, Braudel could have organized his material so as to create "a satisfactory and hence complex and subtle answer." Braudel's great sin is pride and *La Méditerranée* was his fall. "Sources will yield historical answers only to historical questions, and Braudel started by wanting to know not the wherefores of a movement or condition in the Mediterranean world but rather *everything* about it."[12]

Equally incisive, although less sharply critical, was Claude Lefort's essay of 1952, "Histoire et sociologie dans l'oeuvre de Fernand Braudel." Lefort did not question the larger form of the work so much as he did "the intention of the author." "The important thing is not that M. Braudel has added to the study of politics that of economics, geography, culture, etc., to establish history, but rather that he attain a privileged perspective, which confers on these approaches their historicity." However, rather than grasp the great issue of historicity itself, Braudel repeatedly rejects it as "too ambitious no doubt, nor suited to philosophical vanity."[13] Thus, Braudel's frequent assertions of the modest empiricism of historical artisanship contradicted the spirit of his enterprise as perceived by Lefort. Where Bailyn saw hubris, Lefort found a frustrating humility; its major expression is "the fear of causality." "The condemnation of the causal relationships leads him into a pointillism that seems contrary to the sociological inspiration of

11. Bernard Bailyn, "Braudel's Geohistory—A Reconsideration," *Journal of Economic History* 11 (1951), 279.

12. Ibid., 280, 281.

13. Claude Lefort, "Histoire et sociologie dans l'oeuvre de Fernand Braudel," *Cahiers internationaux de sociologie* 13 (1952), 122.

the work."[14] Regretting that Braudel too often offered "a mosaic of analyses," Lefort's essay nevertheless grants that the form of the book may be in some way homeomorphic with the form of its subject when it states that Braudel's history of banditry offers a "single symbolic expression of the incapacity of the Mediterranean world to organize its space and to establish firmly its structure."[15]

The second French edition of *La Méditerranée* ironically bore witness to Febvre's prediction that it was "un livre qui grandit," "a book that will grow." Eric J. Hobsbawm's brief sketch of the differences between the two editions notes, among other things, the new research, the changes in perspective, the addition of apparatus; he did not point out how evenly it had been augmented, as though each small part could have been expanded indefinitely. With the publication of Siân Reynolds' English translation of the second edition, English-speaking writers have described Braudel's work as more than a mere classic. "It would be tempting to call it the first historical work of our time, if such praise did not sound rather meaningless," wrote a reviewer in the *Times Literary Supplement*.[16] Meaninglessly or not, others called it "probably the most significant historical work to appear since World War II," and even "probably the best history book ever written."[17] At the same time, the tenor of many pieces changed from exclusive consideration of Braudel's major work to extended discussions of the "*Annales* school" of historical study, and its relation to structuralism.[18]

Disagreements about the influence of *The Mediterranean and the Mediterranean World in the Age of Philip II* are hardly surprising. In the *New York Times Book Review* alone, opinions polarized. Richard Mowery Andrews wrote that "Braudel revises all customary notions of early modern history" by his Mediterranean emphasis (a claim that Mattingly had specifically denied twenty years before), and that Braudel's school of history excels "because it conveys fewer illusions than the others—including the Marxian ones that focus only on relations between human beings (technology is not nature, nor is alienation), that are suf-

14. Ibid., 124.

15. Ibid., 131.

16. Review in *Times Literary Supplement*, 15 Feb. 1968, 156.

17. Quotations: "since World War II . . . ," Richard M. Andrews, *New York Times Book Review*, 18 May 1975, 1; "ever . . . ," John Bossy, *Encounter* 40 (April 1973), 70.

18. Thus, the theme of the Inaugural Conference of the Fernand Braudel Center for the Study of Economies, Historical Systems, and Civilizations, held in May 1977 at the State University of New York, Binghamton, was "Impact of the *Annales* School on the Social Sciences."

The Language of Historians: Four Shipwrecks

fused with voluntarism, and that offer the characteristically nineteenth-century and imperial mirage of a teleology that will one day resolve intellectual and moral consideration."[19] Andrews shares the "post-voluntarist" and "post-imperial" attitude that he finds in Braudel and his followers, and applauds the master's "acute sense of the mysteriousness and complexity of life."[20] Neither post-voluntarist nor post-imperial, J. H. Plumb regretted the influence of "Braudel's great work," and the "aridity" of recent *Annales* scholarship, which has "put history in grave danger—more so in Europe than in America."[21] And if scholars quite naturally clashed over the French influence in historiographical politics, they also differed over basic characterizations of *The Mediterranean:* for one, the work "verges dangerously on the mystical"; for another, its "bias is . . . materialist."[22] Where Bailyn had found "an exhausting treadmill," J. H. Hexter found literary relish, suggesting that it is a book best not read from the beginning, but rather sampled at random, drifting from one subsection to another *a piacere.* Yet although Hexter's denial of the tyrannical domination of directionality in the text saves it (for him at least) as a literary event (the stuff from which "classics" emerge), he joined Bailyn quite explicitly in criticizing the organization of the vast materials.

In sum, the commentary of three decades has not accepted *The Mediterranean and the Mediterranean World in the Age of Philip II* as a formal success. Widely viewed as a classic, the book seems nevertheless different from the classics of other centuries, from Gibbon or Macaulay, because it "isn't complete and unified in itself"—this attitude has become standard.[23] At best we find a reservation of doubt, as when H. R. Trevor-Roper wrote: "The work was at once recognized as a historical classic, although, as with many classics, it is difficult to define its peculiar quality."[24] Ever since Febvre's initial uneasiness with "its peculiar quality," Braudel's *Mediterranean* has struck readers as difficult—not conceptually or syntactically difficult, but formally and generically difficult. Although the language of the work has often been noted and described, in one way or another, this aspect has invariably been treated

19. Andrews, review, 45.

20. Ibid., 1.

21. J. H. Plumb, review in *New York Times Book Review,* 31 Dec. 1972, 14.

22. Quotations: "mystical . . . ," H. G. Koenigsberger, review in *Listener,* 3 Jan. 1974, 11; "materialist . . . ," Dan Stanislawski, review in *Geographical Review* 64 (1974), 598.

23. Koenigsberger, review, 12.

24. H. R. Trevor-Roper, "Fernand Braudel, the *Annales,* and the Mediterranean," *Journal of Modern History* 44 (1972), 472.

as ornamental, indicative perhaps of Braudel's poetic sensibility or of his commitment to *la grand histoire,* but not inextricably constituent of the work itself.

II

> *ANATOMY (G[reek] cutting up, dissection). The analysis of an issue into its constituent parts, for ease of discussion or clarity of exegesis; the term is not a traditional one, but has been increasingly used as a generic term for a technique that includes a number of the traditional dividing and particularizing figures.*
> Richard Lanham, *A Handlist of Rhetorical Terms*

> *It is anatomy in particular that has baffled critics, and there is hardly any fiction writer deeply influenced by it who has not been accused of disorderly conduct.*
> Northrop Frye

Historical discourse does not escape servitude to the forms of language that make it possible; these forms exact a certain payment from all linguistic acts in return for granting them existence. Yet few historians question in a serious way the linguistic forms of the texts that they study, feeling apparently that such an examination would reveal a merely ornamental dimension of language, divorced from its more essential role, which they presume to be semantic, communicative of meaning. Although Braudel has been written about and analyzed from many points of view, fundamental questions remain unasked. What is the genre of this text? Why is it cast in its present form? What does the form itself say? This, I believe, is the precise issue on which attempts to grasp the book have foundered, and the area that best reveals the nature of the work. Northrop Frye notes that in every period certain works are misunderstood because their genre is unrecognized or is unfamiliar to the age. Such works are judged in terms of the genre that they *seem* to resemble, and the "carelessness" with which they are often charged is really that of the reader who has come too quickly to conclusions and expectations.

The Language of Historians: Four Shipwrecks

The form of Braudel's *The Mediterranean and the Mediterranean World in the Age of Philip II* is that of the *anatomy*, or Menippean satire, an unusual genre at any time and quite rare in a history. Of late Roman origin, the Menippean satire began as an alternation of verse and prose, aimed particularly at satirizing mental attitudes rather than specific people, occupational approaches rather than individual foibles.[25] A sub-category of satire proper, the anatomy resembles satire in that it too is a *satura* (a medley or concoction of mixed fruits), and it too is saturated, sated, stuffed full. The encyclopedic nature of anatomy is an essential component—and here we have the clue that Hexter unearthed in his comparison of Braudel's cataloging with that of Rabelais. To quote Northrop Frye, "The Menippean satirist . . . shows his exuberance in intellectual ways, by piling up an enormous mass of erudition about his theme or in overwhelming his targets with an avalanche of their own jargon."[26] The term "anatomy," from an Indo-European root meaning "to cut," signifies a dissection. The theory and history of this genre have been little studied, but any consideration must take into account its origin as a mixture of verse and prose (although prose tends to absorb verse in modern anatomies), its ability to satirize abstract ideas and attitudes (making it the most intellectual of satirical forms), its encyclopedic thrust (encyclopedism being inherently satirical because of its stuffed, mixed, and saturated nature), and its narrative progression by means of division, digression, and detail. Frye adds: "It is anatomy in particular that has baffled critics, and there is hardly any fiction writer deeply influenced by it who has not been accused of disorderly conduct."[27] The statement holds true for writers of nonfiction anatomies; it is certainly true of Braudel.

The rhetorical figure of *divisio*, so essential to the learned farrago of the Menippean satire, includes many categories of description that sound strange to modern ears and that seem to prove the assertion that the art of rhetoric had an expression for everything: *anemographia*, the description of the wind; *prosopographia*, the physical description of a person; *topographia*, the description of places; *chorographia*, the description of nations or peoples; *chronographia*, the description of time; *geographia*, the description of the earth; *hydrographia*, the description of

25. In this essay I shall use the terms "anatomy" and "Menippean satire" interchangeably, following the practice of Northrop Frye: the description of the genre is drawn from Frye's *Anatomy of Criticism: Four Essays* (Princeton, 1971), 308–14.

26. Ibid., 311.

27. Ibid., 313.

waters; or *dendrographia*, the description of trees.[28] Since this list is itself a *divisio*, I presume that it is indefinitely extendible. Braudel, who is either praised for his love of the concrete or condemned for his obsession with nonincremental detail, follows these divisive and encyclopedic figures of renaissance rhetoric. For example, Braudel as anemographer does not merely cite or evaluate the effects of the wind upon the climate and navigation of the Mediterranean; he must name and chart the *mistral*, *levante*, north wind, *noroît*, monsoon, and *bora*. His index, under "Winds," cites a meager two references, but adds "see also under names of winds"—without mentioning the names of the winds. This is *extraordinary*, as though these winds were as unrelated and individual as human beings, simply because they possess their own *names*. Here is *divisio* with a vengeance, and a demonstration of Saussure's dictum that in languages both the signifier and the signified are arbitrary. Braudel's dendrography similarly exults in its mulberry, olive, fig, chestnut, plane yew, sandalwood, palm, walnut, orange, lemon, elm, eucalyptus, brazilwood—even this list of trees is not complete. The other figures of description find a greater or lesser place in Braudel's anatomy. The title and subject of the book suggest that it will be a *hydrographia*, while its structure and rhetoric are instead chronographic; one of the ironies of the text is the relative absence of the subject, the Mediterranean *as sea*, from its pages. Garrett Mattingly complained that "the sea itself is slighted"; and it is hard to disagree that this is the case, even in the second edition, where Braudel speaks hesitantly of "peaceful waters—at least we imagine them to be peaceful" (I, 352; all page citations refer to the English translation by Siân Reynolds). Mattingly's objection serves to underscore the digressive character of the book, and the paradox that Braudel's sea can only be grasped indirectly, by detailed consideration of all that it is not. The book is hydrographic only by indirection; but it is explicitly chronographic, discoursing often on the personified forms of time and describing the dialogue between them.

Explicit dialogue was a frequent characteristic of early Menippean satire, either a direct confrontation of representative positions or, in later forms, a confrontation of books as in such anatomies as Burton's *Anatomy of Melancholy* or Isaak Walton's *Compleat Angler*. Braudel also uses the *image* of dialogue often and at all levels of his text; but at least in

28. Richard A. Lanham, *A Handlist of Rhetorical Terms* (Berkeley and Los Angeles, 1969), 8.

the most important examples, he presents a dialogue of the deaf, an absurd dialogue. On the one hand, for example, we see the troubled but essentially real dialogues among Christian, Moslem, and Jew (II, 802, 808), despite the war and persecution of the age. Yet these dialogues, while they are cited and discussed in the text, do not take place there; the dialogue of *The Mediterranean and the Mediterranean World of the Age of Philip II* is the fundamental dialogue (again three-way) between structure, conjuncture, and event; these are the principal divisions of Braudelian *chronographia*, and their dialogic relationship is crucial to the book. This is a matter that Braudel rarely deals with directly, but when he does, the results are systematically ambiguous. The relationship of event to conjuncture is the clearest: Braudel strongly implies that there is none. Events are precisely what are not rooted in deeper patterns; and Braudel takes great pains to establish his view of their ultimate contingency, even against some of the younger *Annales* historians. The illusionary "chain of events" that made men believe that they were involved in matters of great import is paralleled by a second chain, the chain of economic events and conjunctures. "For us," he writes, "there will always be two chains—not one" (II, 902). In a footnote to the second edition, Braudel adds that the pursuit of links between conjuncture and political events seems to him "la chasse aux papillons"—a wild-goose chase (II, 899, n. 33).

If there is no real dialogue between event and conjuncture, what about the two "higher" forms of historical perception, conjuncture and structure? While there is a "dialogue between structure and conjuncture, the moment in time and the long or very long term" (II, 757), the outcome of such dialogue is a continuous series of oxymorons, the rhetorical figure that is "pointedly foolish" in its use of condensed paradox. Shakespeare writes of "bright smoke," "cold fire," "sick health"; oxymoron is the figure par excellence of the baroque age.[29]

> No sooner does the historian think he has isolated the particular quality of a civilization than it gives proof of the exact opposite. Civilizations may be fraternal and liberal, yet at the same time exclusive and unwelcoming; they receive visits and return them; they can be pacific yet militant; in many ways astonishingly sta-

29. Braudel refers to the renaissance and baroque cultures as the "morbid product" of economic recession (II, 899–900). The baroque heralded the end of the great sixteenth-century empires, and Braudel's rhetorical and generic choices are generally drawn from that period.

ble, they are nevertheless constantly shifting and straying, their surface disturbed by a thousand eddies and whirlpools, the tiny particles of their daily life subject to random [*absurdes*] Brownian movements. (II, 757)

This is a *topos* descended from Horace's phrase "concordia discors rerum," "the discordant harmony of things." Like the anatomy form itself, which is its existential projection (to borrow a phrase from Northrop Frye once more), oxymoron controls the sensibility of the baroque age, which is, after all, Braudel's subject. His stress on the mere appearance of change in civilizations, masking their basic stability, and the consequent relevance of even protohistory for a scholar of the sixteenth century (II, 775–76) grows from this baroque oxymoronic sensibility: if each thing is inherently also what it is not, then *all* things must be invoked to explain *each*. This is quite logical, and quite impossible, but, Braudel insists, quite necessary. This foregrounding of paradox, which is one of the essential devices of Braudel's satire, not only casts the dialogue between the three forms of time into question; it is also the principal technique *within* each of the sections of the text.

Braudel repeatedly tells his reader that the deep structure and long durations of history are the security, the "bedrock" of reality, while events are dust ("poussière," "lueurs brèves"). However, when we enter the "secure" first section of the text, we are confronted with a quicksand at the surface of the page. The Russian formalist Victor Shklovsky has written that "the technique of art is to make objects 'unfamiliar,' to make forms difficult, to increase the difficulty and length of perception because the process of perception is an aesthetic end in itself and must be prolonged. *Art is a way of perceiving the artfulness of an object; the object is not important.*"[30] With this in mind, the reader notes that Braudel has spared no opportunity to make the "natural" part of his book highly "unnatural," an orgy of defamiliarization. There is virtually nothing in part I, "The Role of the Environment," that does not escape our grasp through the most calculated defamiliarization of words and things. Displacements abound, making the Sahara "the second face of the Mediterranean" (I, 171), while the Baltic and North seas become "the Mediterraneans of the North" (I, 224). Unities multiply and turn upon themselves, as when Braudel points out that "Mediterranean was confronted, not with one Europe but with several

30. Victor Shklovsky, "Art as Technique" in *Russian Formalist Criticism; Four Essays*, trans. Lee T. Lemon and Marion J. Reis (Lincoln, Nebr. 1965), 12.

Europes, faces of the continent . . ." (I, 223). Germany is also called a land of "many faces" (I, 308–9), and the repetition of the image hammers home the message—language-reality is duplicitous. "Several Atlantics" (I, 224) address Europe to the West, but even this seems "too schematic" for Braudel, who must further identify land and sea, since "Europe also meant the northern seas, the Atlantic Ocean, and after the Great Discoveries, an all-conquering Atlantic, linked by Magellan to the Pacific and by Vasco da Gama to the Indian Ocean" (I, 224). This multiplication of entities is complemented by their division. There were two Mediterranean worlds, he writes at one point, separated as though by a "finely meshed filter" (I, 134); Europe is "a twofold or even threefold world" (I, 188). Yet shortly after, Braudel decides to treat Europe as four separate areas (I, 191). The two Mediterranean worlds are elsewhere redistributed as "a succession of small seas, . . . each with its own character, types of boat [a defamiliarizing detail], and its own laws of history" (I, 108–9).

Here Lévi-Strauss's comment that a mythographer can never get a clear view of the subject in his microscope, but can only choose between enlargements, is pertinent.[31] This structuralist strategy is seen by Braudel as the very structure of the sea itself. Speaking of the size of the Mediterranean, he writes: "Of all the commonplaces about the Mediterranean, in which literature abounds, that it is a 'sea within the measure of man' is one of the most deceptive—as if the measure of man could be taken once and for all" (I, 335). "Even when supported by documents, how can average speeds mean very much when we know that the length of any one voyage could vary from twice to three, four, even seven or ten times the shortest time recorded? The essential point to note here is this very variety, the wide range of times taken to travel the same journey: it is a *structural* feature of the century" (I, 360). Braudel has mocked definitions and to some extent shown the impossibility of definition; it remains for him to suggest the arbitrariness of things themselves through the words that sort them out. The most ironic figure of speech is catachresis, the abuse of language. Braudel is a master of the figure, and speaks with no self-consciousness of "liquid plains," "watery Saharas," "islands that the sea does not surround." "It would hardly be an exaggeration to say that Portugal, Andalusia, Valencia, and Catalonia were a series of peripheral islands attached to the Iberian

31. Claude Lévi-Strauss, "Overture" to *Le Cru et le cuit*, trans. Joseph H. McMahon, in *Structuralism*, ed. Jacques Ehrmann (Garden City, N.Y., 1966), 35.

mass through Castile" (I, 161). But the most striking of Braudel's many strategies of defamiliarization is visual—the map named "The Mediterranean and the rest of the world" presented with the South Pole at the top and dominated by an enormous, looming Africa. Here the familiar base, Africa, easily ignored in its conventional cartographic position, becomes, in Shklovsky's word, "difficult," and worthy of long contemplation. It has been supremely "defamiliarized."

What is the status of all this? Rather obviously, it is first of all a satire on the claims of geographers, cartographers, demographers, and a host of other special fields; Braudel says repeatedly that the "historian's Mediterranean" is not that of the specialist, and is always more complex. Hayden White writes that the historical satirist has lost faith in "essences"; his work turns upon wordplay, "a language about language," "suspicious of all formulas," and "delight[ing] in exposing the paradoxes contained in every attempt to capture experience in language."[32] This certainly characterizes Braudel's work. In saussurean terms, he satirizes the arbitrariness of both parts of the historical sign— the signifiers (or names, which he multiplies, divides, denies, replaces) as well as the signifieds (those places and things whose identities he consistently questions).

Although the notion that satire is necessarily a comic form is unfounded, it is traditional that humor act as the lubricant to prevent satire from falling into diatribe. On the face of it, Braudel's book is not very funny; few books, in fact, have a more earnest tone, make fewer *bons mots*, or strive less for surface wit. The humor, however, is present in the form of an erudite slapstick that theorists of comedy call nonincremental repetition. Nonincremental repetition is the absurd humor of a repeated event that should register an effect but does not—these may be the bricks that fall over and over on Oliver Hardy's head without knocking him out, or it may be Braudel's discussion of the battle of Lepanto, citing Voltaire, "A victory that led nowhere?" and the following capture of Tunis, "another victory that led nowhere." The effect of such humor, of course, is to underscore the absurdity of those whom it touches—that is to say, those for whom time (repeated events) does not bring change.

This satirical device is explicitly pronounced in the third section of the book, the section dealing with human events. The first two sections are

---

32. Hayden White, *Metahistory: The Historical Imagination in Nineteenth-Century Europe* (Baltimore and London, 1973), 233.

much more serious on the surface. But a remark by Braudel added to the second edition offers us a key to its entire form. A friend had written Braudel after the first edition was published suggesting that he could have written the work the other way around, beginning with the "spectacular and often misleading pageant [of events]" and proceeding to the "bedrock of history." Characteristically, Braudel makes no attempt at all to defend his choice of order—which was, after all, a crucial decision. Instead, he says that the work may perhaps be seen as an "hourglass, eternally reversible" (II, 903). To a formalist, this is a remarkable comment, since the hourglass, more than any other image except the Chinese water-torture, is a topos of nonincremental repetition. Time passes; the glass is turned, and is always the same in either direction. The implication is that the absurdly tragic form of the book (tragic because it moves from order and stability to chaos and illusion, and absurd because, being a synchronic description, it has in fact shown no movement *in time* at all) could be reversed and made comic, in the sense that Dante's masterpiece is comic in its movement from the pain and illusion of hell to the order and timelessness of paradise. It is all one in Braudel, tragedy and comedy, reversible.

This notion of reversibility leads us to a consideration of the dominant formal image of the text—that of roundness, in the form of a ring, wave, or wheel. When Karl Jaspers wrote: "Jedes Dasein scheint in sich rund" ("Every being seems in itself round"), he signaled the phenomenological perception that "roundness is a victory over accidents of form and the capricious events of mobility."[33] The evident fact that the Mediterranean world is round suggests the use of some references to round things, but the extent of roundness as Braudel's controlling image is extraordinary. In part I, "The Role of the Environment," for example, the entire progress of the text is doubly circular. The syntagmic text follows the concentricities of the geography. "Mountains Come First," reads the first subheading of chapter 1, and from the mountains the reader proceeds through plateaus, hills, plains, coasts, and islands, down to the sea, with the towns and societies that lead us to part II. At each level of descent, Braudel makes a full circle, as best he can; regarding his famous upside-down map, he suggests that we rotate the map as we trace "the different world horizons of the Mediterranean" (I, 169).

The second part of *The Mediterranean and the Mediterranean World in the Age of Philip II* is as phenomenologically round as the first, but in a more

33. Gaston Bachelard, *The Poetics of Space,* trans. Maria Jolas (Boston, 1969), 240.

subtle and intriguing way; the first part, on the environment, was geo-graphically round; the second, dealing with large-scale human activities, is thematically round. We find here the same syntagmic movement from outer to inner—that is, from larger to smaller. The start of the section deals with size itself in the form of "Distance, the First Enemy" ("L'espace—ennemi numéro un"). From this section, which emphasizes that in the sixteenth century there was too much space (an advantage and an obstacle), we move on to the vehicle of economic movement (money and specie), then to the movement itself (trade and transport), and to the participants in that movement, the Empires. The next two chapters, devoted to Societies and Civilizations, form the vir-tual center of the entire text. If we are to believe Braudel's odd claim that the book may be seen as an hourglass, this should be the narrow waist, the point at which reversibility matters least. Again, the book does not fail analysis. In the first edition, the order of chapters runs from Civi-lizations to Societies; the second edition reverses the order, in what is the major formal change of the work. (Within the Societies chapter, the order of class analysis is altered, with the bourgeoisie preceding the nobility in the first edition, the reverse in the second.) In Braudel's table of contents, the term "civilization" is a bit misleading, since it refers to culture; and it seems clear, at least to me, that he had a change of heart about the magnitude of these circles in his book. Of social change, he writes that it "is like all change, tending first in one direction then in another. In the long run, change may be neutralized and development may be difficult to discern at all" (II, 704). His comments on Civiliza-tions, as noted above, liken them to "random Brownian movements" (II, 757). The choice between undiscernible change and random move-ment is difficult, but must be made, and Braudel has it both ways. (Nei-ther of the comments cited just now is in the first edition.) The final chapter of the second section deals with the smallest form of "Collective Destiny," the most intimate of relationships between groups, "The Forms of War." Thus, the second part of the book has followed a course from the largest theme, distance itself ("the first enemy"), down to the smallest, War. At the end of this five-hundred-page section, however, Braudel, in an ironic turn, throws the entire order into a chaos. "*Bellum omnium pater,* the old adage was familiar to the men of the sixteenth century. War, the begetter of all things, the creature [*fils*] of all things, the river with a thousand sources, the sea without a shore; begetter of all things except peace, so ardently longed for, so rarely attained" (II, 891). War is the last and the first, just as distance had been what divided and brought together. This sort of calculated disruption of directionality within the circular forms of the work adds to their insecure nature, throwing meaning into an abyss of undecidability that pervades the text. When Braudel writes: "The sea is everything it is said to be . . ." (I, 276), it becomes saturated with meaning, everything that it *may* be said to be.

The multiple orders of concentric rings in the first two parts of Braudel's text are not static; they move in particular ways that carry on the paradoxical discourse. The principal image of dynamism is the wave, an image that is repeated often in many forms. The deep structures are "slow-furling waves" (I, 102) with an "extremely slow pattern of oscillation" (I, 101), but by the conclusion of this discussion of conjunctures, the wave image gets out of hand. "History becomes many-stranded once more, bewilderingly complex and, who knows, in seeking to grasp all the different vibrations, waves of past time which ought ideally to accumulate like the divisions in the mechanism of a watch, the seconds, minutes, hours and days—perhaps we shall find the whole fabric slipping away between our fingers" (II, 893). The very phenomenon of roundness studied by Jaspers and Bachelard is violated, undone, disseminated, by the wave image, which removes the perfect self-sufficiency of roundness and replaces it with erratic change of all sorts. Men and goods circulate around the sea in "concentric rings" (I, 170), while the "Mediterranean civilization spreads far beyond its shores in great waves that are balanced by continual returns" (I, 170). The steadiness of the wave image is sometimes contrasted to "electric charges, violent and without continuity" (I, 161). The electrical metaphor is quite developed at one point. In discussing the differences of living standards between East and West, he notes that this made necessary their unity, as "differences in voltage determine electrical currents; the greater the difference, the greater the need for currents" (I, 137). At times the image of roundness is reduced to its most trivial level in being applied to merely short-term changes—here the "wheel" or "cycle" is invoked (II, 702, 814, 899). On the other hand, the grandest tonality of roundness is the "even light which shines at the heart of the Mediterranean" (I, 231), "a radiant center whose light grows less as one moves away from it" (I, 168).

By undoing the stable roundness of the Mediterranean basin in his text, Braudel sets in motion an oscillation that ironically violates its own directionality and is thus the Braudelian movement par excellence: the Mediterranean flows away and returns (I, 170), and so does almost every moving thing in the book. Even in the first edition, Braudel shows his digressive delight with the speculations of Ugolini that Mediterranean civilization may have begun in the West and proceeded to Italy and to the East, from which it then returned to its source (I, 166–67). He says that, even if untrue, "it is pleasant to imagine this relay race."

We must imagine an oscillating wave if we are to grasp the form of the whole book, with its subject flowing outward, crossing all boundaries, denying all definitions, and with its point of view moving ever inward, from the outermost ring of the mountains ("fabriques des hommes"), downward and inward, geographically, then thematically, into the third section of the work, "Events, Politics, and People." This section has been criticized as a conventional finish for an unconventional book, as unnecessary as it is tedious. Such an objection totally ignores the formal coherence of the text, which in this last part oscillates inward to a vanishing point. Here Braudel is free to satirize man in more than merely sublimated ways, such as violating the language of geography, reversing the meaning of statements, or suggesting that his text be turned on its head like an hourglass. Events are "fireflies," whose total light creates "a particular kind of history." Braudel seems to add this section so as not to disappoint Philip II's contemporaries, who lived under the illusion "that they were participating in a mighty drama." However illusory, this thought "helped to give meaning to their lives" (II, 901).

The climax to this narrative, the nonincremental nature of which I have mentioned above, is the death of Philip II. Philip's death on 13 September 1598 is not the chronological end to the book; it is the *formal* end. Braudel apologizes for putting it at the end of his text, but he does not reveal his reasons. They become clear as we read on. Braudel does *not* repeat the mere details of human death; he removes historical man from the scene sense by sense. As I noted in Chapter 3, the death of Philip II is an allegory of the disappearance of human understanding *in* history. With Philip dead—that is, with the sensory limitations of man systematically removed from the stage—the subject quite naturally disappears, entirely anatomized. Philip's annihilation completes Braudel's task of deconstruction.[34]

Man is simultaneously present and absent in the text, both that which gives and that which lacks meaning; the sensitivity of Febvre and others

34. Reynolds' rather free translation of this passage serves to highlight physical aspects of disappearance; the French text is less graphic, but the formal disappearance is no less complete.

on this point from the inception of the book has often led to an avoidance of denial of the systematic paradox in the book. However, the discursive medium of the work itself, its language, clues us to the formal
satire it contains. Initially, the Menippean satire alternated verse and
prose in a true *satura* of mixed genres. Decorum later prescribed that
"subjective mythological epic" belonged to verse, and "objective historical narrative" to prose; or, to put it otherwise, that myth, the servant
of culture and its demands, was poetic, and that history, the disin-
terested, "natural" report of events, was prosaic. The verse/prose alternation of Menippean satire thus may be seen as a form of the culture/
nature polarity essential, according to Lévi-Strauss, to human self-defi-
nition. Braudel, of course, writes no verse. Although his writing is full
of the richness of figuration called "poetic" by some, his work shows the
tendency of "realistic" prose satire to reabsorb poetry.

However, as the work has reabsorbed the verse component of its
genetic inheritance, it has substituted for it something else, a *new non-
prose*. Maps, charts, tables, graphs, paintings, serial and satellite
images, photographs, and other non-prose signifiers populate the second edition, and their absence in the first, due to the economic strictures
of the late forties, was sorely lamented by the author. That these hun-
dred-odd eruptions into a prose text create the same *texture* as a verse/
prose pattern is in itself a minor analogy. However, as I pointed out
above, the verse/prose opposition corresponded to a culture/nature
relationship presumed to exist between myth and history. In Braudel's
text, this same relationship has been displaced and reversed. The charts
and graphs in Braudel's book serve a displaced mythic purpose, giving
the illusion of having no author and thus being privileged by their very
form. The correctness, presentation, or interpretation of any given
graph (or of any given myth) is open to question, but the status of
number as a privileged voice in the text is secure.

The alternation between prose and verse in the classical anatomy
focuses generically the impulse to overcome or reconcile the divisive
demands of the culture/nature paradigm. This opposition, which
appears as a rather elementary structure of mind in its various displacements as Cooked/Raw, Myth/Ritual, or Processed/Unprocessed, held
poetry (which affirms and asserts its figuration) as the voice of a deified
Nature, and prose (which denies its figured status) as the voice of
"mere" human culture until the birth of Greek philosophy objectified
Nature and culminated in the Platonic reversal: after Plato, "father of
the Logos" in Derrida's phrase, the deanimated Nature of Philosophy is

described by a deanimated (unfigured) prose, while poetry, a language of magical transformation (figuration), served a spirit world that rational men knew to be a cultural product. The de-naturalizing of figured language that was the precondition of Greek rationalism dominated Western thought (despite such important rebellions as Vico's conflation of *verum* and *factum*) until the "Romantic crisis" occasioned a powerful counter-reversal.[35] As Roman Jakobson has pointed out, the romantic urge to re-establish figured language as the language of Nature led them to the Metaphoric pole of language, while their "Realist" opponents continued the tradition of Metonymic realism, the denial of language's intrinsic figuration that makes *mimesis* thinkable. In the twentieth century, however, philosophies of language, whether neo-Kantian, Heideggerian, or structuralist, have tended to dissolve the distinction between poetry and prose, asserting the fundamentally figured—that is to say, poetic—nature of all language. At the same time, as prose has disappeared from its side of the Prose/Poetry displacement of the Nature/Culture paradigm, its position has been taken by a new pretender to an "unfigured language," quantification (ironically, the language of figures). Quantification thus becomes the "natural" language that prose had been, while all verbal language retreats into an accepting recognition of its ultimately poetic status (thus according to the quantifier in this genre a much greater freedom of imagery and expression in his prose).

Braudel inserts into historical discourse a voice that has no supernatural pretensions, but that shares with myth important differences from prose. The linguistic shifter "I" that begins the text ("I have loved the Mediterranean with passion . . .") signals that his voice will be the self-conscious voice of culture, always aware of its existence within language. The quantitative voices of geography, demography, economics, and so forth divide the text and recreate the illusion of a "natural" voice that is not imprisoned by its codes. In other words, the quantification/prose pattern replaces the verse/prose pattern; but the meaning of the latter, found in the culture/nature relationship, has changed. Prose history, the "natural" truth of traditional humanist thought, has crossed the barrier into the realm of the "cultural," man-made, "impressionistic," and self-deceived. Replacing it as the "natural," raw, unprocessed side of the balance is quantification. So "history" has replaced myth on the culturally relative side of the model, and its place is taken in

---

35. Cf. Tzvetan Todorov, *Théories du symbole* (Paris, 1977).

turn by a new non-prose, a language that is anti-language, an utterance that appears to have no utterer—the chart, the graph, the analytical map.[36]

Braudel self-consciously invoked Michelet and Ranke in *The Mediterranean and the Mediterranean World in the Age of Philip II*; Michelet, writing in a metaphoric (explicitly figured) mode, stands as the patron of geo-historical study; while Ranke, whose language is far less "poetic," though by no means totally unfigured, represents the tradition of *l'histoire événementielle*. Michelet/Ranke and Geo-history/History of events fill the Poetry/Prose paradigm of nineteenth-century historical discourse. Michelet's geo-history was the voice of a poetic subject, while Ranke attempted an objective report of events. In Braudel this traditional perspective is reversed. J. H. Hexter parodies Braudelian quantification in the first section of his essay "Fernand Braudel and the *Monde Braudellien*," using graphs and maps that are quite superfluous, yet mimic the texture of Braudel's pages very well. He clearly senses that the quantification is used as an ironic "other" to mere prose. To suggest, however, as J. H. Plumb has, that the quantification is "decorative" is to fail to sense the importance of Braudel's genre. H. Stuart Hughes describes this texture, with less good humor, as "romantic flights of rich prose alternating with long stretches of merciless quantification. . . ."[37] From a formal standpoint, what matters most is the *alternation*, and the powerful contrast between voices that is the mark of the Menippean satirist.

36. "Myths have no Author; from the moment when they are perceived as myths, and despite their real origin, they exist only as they are incarnated in a tradition" (Lévi-Strauss, "Overture," 54). "At the level of discourse, objectivity, the absence of any clues to the narrator, turns out to be a particular form of fiction, the result of which might be called the referential illusion, where the historian tries to give the impression that the referent is speaking for itself" (Roland Barthes, "Historical Discourse," trans. Peter Wexler, in *Introduction to Structuralism*, ed. Michael Lane [New York, 1970], 149).

Barthes further notes that the language of traditional historical practice follows linguistic strategies designed to underscore the "natural" quality of the utterance: the historian of this genre avoids the first person singular, uses special tenses, and in general tries to produce a "reality effect" in his discourse, to create a self-referential narrative that has no "I" in it. The current, hesitant but noticeable, re-emergence of the linguistic shifter "I" into the discourse of the human sciences corresponds closely with the displacement of the "natural" element of the discourse onto the quantifiable, the new rhetoric of "anti-I."

37. H. Stuart Hughes, *The Obstructed Path: French Social Thought in the Years of Desperation, 1930–1960* (New York, 1968), 59.

III

> *If I cannot get further, this is because I have bumped my*
> *head into the wall of language. Then, with my head*
> *bleeding, I withdraw, and want to go on.*
> Karl Kraus

> *Heterogeneity and the absolute exteriority of "seed," semi-*
> nal *differance, constitutes itself into a program, although*
> *a nonformulizable program. For formulizable reasons. The*
> *infinity of the code, and its rupture, so to speak, therefore do*
> *not have the same sort of form saturated with the presence*
> *that in its circular form, the encyclopedia does. . . .*
> Jacques Derrida

The proto-Indo-European root of "structure" is ster-2, "to spread," and related terms include "to strew" and that which is strewn, "straw." The Latin *struere,* from which come "construct," "destroy," "structure," and others, refers to the piling up of what may be strewn. Thus, etymologically, structure is made of straw; the act of piling up and the act of strewing are one. To put it another way, the claim of the structuralists—Lévi-Strauss in particular—to have created a universal science of culture is always already denied by their repeated insistence on the uniqueness of the forms of meaning conferred on the world of man.[38] The glorious futility of this aspect of the structuralists' venture, and the fetishization of this futility in the work of the post-structuralists (Barthes, Derrida, and Foucault), have been potentially apparent for a long while. We find it in Braudel's *Mediterranean,* if we look at the form and language of the text, rather than listening exclusively to its ideology (as the semioticians today like to call "the content"). Rarely has a text cried out more desperately to be noticed and understood formally, and the lack of formal study and penetration among reviewers and commentators (about which I can say little here) itself bespeaks an ongoing historical resistance to "reading" in the

---

38. Hayden White, "The Absurdist Moment in Contemporary Literary Theory," in *Directions for Criticism,* ed. Murray Krieger and L. S. Dembo (Madison, 1977), 104; reprinted in *Tropics of Discourse: Essays in Cultural Criticism* (Baltimore and London, 1978).

modern critical sense. Historical readers have seen language as transparent, and rhetoric as ornamental; even in Braudel's case the language
and form of the text have been ignored, patronized, or viewed as a
questionable and potentially dangerous national quirk.

Professional critics, on the other hand, are only beginning to overcome their longstanding lack of interest in nonfiction prose, largely
because of the influence of structuralism's tendency to conflate literature and language. The structuralists/post-structuralists themselves,
French ones at least, have a theoretical aversion to history as a form of
thought, and have yet to confront the *Annales* school adequately.[39] So
Braudel's text has gotten only half a reading from historians and critics.
Still, it retains an authority and interest for many whose knowledge of
the *Annales* school is slight. The continuing interest in Braudel's *Mediterranean* does not derive simply from its subject, nor from its congeries of
techniques, apparatuses, and information, nor even from the metahistorical nature of its claims and project, although all these factors
remain of the first importance. This work, history of the most uncom-
promisingly professional sort, has retained an authority after almost
thirty years, despite professional onslaughts on its parts. The cause of
this power is the fundamental ambivalence, the undecidability, at the
heart of it. It shares with the "master-texts" of Western humanistic
thought the *aporia,* or systematic self-reflective doubt, that draws readers to them without any specific interest in the subject matter, and without any necessary confidence that the works themselves are a definitive
treatment of anything. It is the very anti-definitiveness of the master-
text that outlines its authority. For works of this sort provide strategies
of interpretation for cultural artifacts in general, themselves included.
Thus, "global" history reveals and is aware of itself as a partial, culture-
bound view; and this awareness forms the formal essence of the *aporia*
in Braudel's text.[40] To this extent, all such texts are somehow ironic, and
reveal themselves to be so.

To suggest that the master-text possesses a sense of its own status as
an interpretation of interpretation, and a consequent willingness, even
demand, to be creatively misunderstood, does not imply that such
works are all alike, authorizing anything in their name. Braudel's dif-

39. This matter is discussed below in Chapter 12, "Narrativity in History: Post-Structuralism and Since."

40. For a discussion of *aporia* and the master-text, see Hayden White, Review Essay:
Leon Pompa, *Vico: A Study of the "New Science,"* History and Theory 15:2 (1976), 186–202.

ference lies in the anatomical variety of satire that his text fully assumes and that I have described above. It is this that sets his text apart from other products of the *Annales* school, and even opposes it to them, in my opinion. It is also the *form* that differentiates the text *from* itself, creating the ambiguity that is the work's great quality. Of course, just because *The Mediterranean and the Mediterranean World in the Age of Philip II* exhibits the *aporia* characteristic of the master-texts of Vico, Hegel, Nietzsche, and Freud does not guarantee for it entrance into the Western pantheon they inhabit. I feel, however, that Braudel's *Mediterranean* can lay claim to being a masterpiece of structuralist activity; and I should like to offer a few suggestions as to why this may be so.

Structuralism, born in the lectures of Saussure and raised to a great movement by the work of Jakobson and Lévi-Strauss, has remained tightly bound to its enabling premises: the separation of *langue* (language) and *parole* (speech), the assertion that there can be no science of *parole*—of the individual, and the separation of synchrony and diachrony, with the conviction that only synchronic systems may yield other than random meaning. The goal of structural anthropology, according to Lévi-Strauss's "Overture to *The Raw and the Cooked*," is to reveal oppositions that serve as conceptual tools with which groups think and form propositions. Departing from a single myth, selected intuitively, not for its centrality or representativeness, but rather for "its irregular position" within the group, the mythologist clusters around this "reference myth" a whole series of twining nebulae, amorphously suggesting a certain order beneath the chaos. This work is infinite, the myths are interminable, and their themes may be subdivided endlessly; but just as a linguist can and must create a grammar from an absurdly small sampling of the actual spoken performances of a group, the structuralist, avoiding preconceived classifications, will find a structure of meaning, albeit one whose unity is only "an imaginary phenomenon implicit in the effort of interpretation."[41] Braudel's "reference myth"— the late sixteenth-century Mediterranean world—was an intuitive choice made, as he tells us, by a man of the North whose passion for that sea was generated by its strangeness to him, his difference from it, its "irregular position" in his life. The substance of the book, like the substance of Lévi-Strauss's four-volume *Mythologiques*, is an elaboration and dissection around the germinal molecule of the reference myth.

41. Lévi-Strauss, "Overture," 37.

The infinity of the task, the endless challenge of subdivision, can be suggested only by the most sophisticated rhetorical turns, and Braudel, like Lévi-Strauss, is a master of them.

Braudel's rhetoric of indefinite expansion and contraction constantly denies the boundaries of the text, as I observed in Chapter 3, and projects beyond it onto "the idea of perfect history." Braudel writes at the end of the second edition: "But the historian's 'structuralism' has nothing to do with the approach which under the same name is at present causing some confusion in the other human sciences. It does not tend towards the mathematical abstraction of relations expressed as functions, but instead towards the very sources of life in its most concrete, everyday, indestructible, and anonymously human expression" (II, 1244). Here Braudel expresses the paradox not only of his own text but of the entire structuralist activity. Saussurean structuralism begins by separating a language from the utterances it authorizes, and states that there can be no science of the concrete utterance, only of the language. Braudel wants a "total history" ("l'histoire globale," II, 1238), but such a history may likewise be envisioned in one of two ways: *either* as a discussion of the systems of meaning by which past phenomena present themselves to us (that is, the *language* that creates the categories of "the historical"), *or* as a sum of the historical actions or situations at all levels in their concrete uniqueness (the *speech* of history). These approaches are mutually exclusive; in fact, the latter is precisely the nightmare of the linguist, the prospect that he must study all speech-acts before describing a language. But Braudel (like Lévi-Strauss) will not relinquish the concrete, the unique; this is the "born historian" in Braudel, as Lucien Febvre put it.[42] So "totality" may be *langue* or *parole*, but not both; and if not both, wherein can it claim totality? The term disintegrates into contradiction.

Braudel has written a book that is built upon its own contradiction at every level. The claims of structuralism to be a science of rules are swamped by a flood of anatomical details that serve to parody the structuralist activity itself, as though a linguist were to give an enormous catalogue of examples in place of a linguistic rule—an absurd situation. For it is language itself that makes "totality" impossible, even as it makes many other things possible. Braudel's inspiration was to turn his book into an implicit satire on the very aim of the project, which I like to call "the *idea* of perfect history," borrowing the term from George Hup-

42. Febvre, "Un Livre," 220.

pert. The work is a satire on its own claims; it tells us everywhere that "perfect history" can exist only in a linguistic utopia, in which words really *do* correspond to things (and things really correspond to themselves), and without the arbitrariness of signifier and signified. Although "total history," or "global history," or "perfect history" are structured out of our grasp, the "idea" of these things is not—language presents us with traditional forms, figures, and techniques that celebrate the paradox, contradiction, and elusiveness of language. Braudel, as I hope I have shown, has used these resources: satire, irony, catechresis, oxymoron, *digressio*, *distinguo*, among others. There can be no mistaking his moves. The text painstakingly deconstructs itself as it goes along. An abyss opens up at each step of the way, but the abyss is "infinitely saturated with its own representation."[43] Satire *(satura)* is etymologically saturation, and Braudel ironically saturates his abyss with the following comment. "But Benedetto Croce has argued, not without reason, that any single event—let us say the assassination of Henri IV in 1610 or, to take an example outside our period, the arrival in power in 1883 of the Jules Ferry government—contains in embryo the entire history of mankind. To put it another way, history is the keyboard on which these individual notes are sounded" (II, 1243). This is pure Lévi-Strauss, both in the musical analogy and in the suggestion that *The Mediterranean and the Mediterranean World in the Age of Philip II* is only a "reference myth" with which all the others may be unlocked, a "key" in the sense of both locks and scores.

The ideology of structuralism claims that it is a universal science of the mind, man's reconquest of the reified, that is to say structured, world that has risen up against him. But, as the post-structuralists have repeatedly pointed out, structuralist activity is its own dismantling; for the relationship of structuralism to its structures may also be viewed structurally—ironically—thus displacing infinitely the central notion from which structuralism proper, the Saussurean tradition, proceeds. This deconstructive tendency in all structures, which I have signaled above etymologically as the "strewing" sense of the term (the structure of straw), has been indicated repeatedly by Derrida and others. All texts, they maintain, contain their own deconstruction: this deconstruction is not *done* to them—any more than the structuralist creates the structure that he identifies—it is already there. Consequently, the form

43. Jacques Derrida, *Glas* (Paris, 1974), 156.

of the structuralist venture is ironic, satirical, although it has not always been perceived as such.

Braudel's *The Mediterranean and the Mediterranean World in the Age of Philip II* is, to state the major claim of this chapter, the principal example of the anatomy, or Menippean satire, in this century. And, if I am not mistaken, this genre, above all others, most naturally voices both the ideology of the structuralist performance and the deconstruction that is always present in each such performance. Braudel, in contemplating his reference myth (which is evoked by the title of the work) has plunged into the in-terminable, endlessly subdividable, subjectless sea described by Lévi-Strauss and others. Unlike the school of structuralists proper, however, Braudel, for every structuring move he makes, self-consciously removes and scatters the objects of the structure. By the end, if such there be, of his book, he offers his reader a mystically imaginary construction, while the pieces lie like straw, strewn everywhere. It is a literary critic, Geoffrey Hartman, who has pointed out that the perpetual play or battle of post-structuralist activity has been "to disown language in order to own it,"[44] and it is in this sense that Braudel's text deconstructs itself in the interest of an ironic sense of mastery, and a dialectic reversal of the master-slave relationship of language to its users. Braudel's satirical sense creates that illusion of "mutual domination" and "interchangeable supremacy" cited by Wordsworth, without which "the idea of perfect history" may not be even entertained.

The principal movement of Braudel's book is from geography, where deep meaning and causation are most secure while language and naming are most insecure, to human events, where names fit things (Philip, Lepanto, Spain) but mean little or nothing. Meaning and language cannot fully coexist in Braudel's text: in this sense, he has recognized Saussure's principle that both words and things are arbitrary. This is a most radical assertion, and not even structuralism has fully exhausted the implications of it. For historical writing it is doubly challenging; it throws the burden of analysis upon words and things equally, displacing the center of attention from man to the systems of discourse that make "man" possible as an object of study. Foucault's work of the sixties and seventies was implicit in Braudel's work of the forties, but Braudel confronted the problem of "words and things" quite differently, although no less artfully and radically. Unlike Foucault, Braudel will not

44. Geoffrey Hartman, "The Recognition Scene of Criticism," *Critical Inquiry* 4, (1977), 414.

sacrifice "man," although he recognizes the illusory nature of human events. Braudel's "global history" requires both what is not man (for example, the mountains, which exist independent of man, but which exist *for history* only when they enter a system of discourse that is intrinsically flawed), and what is man but is without meaning (even the death of a great monarch, so secure as an event, but of no real import).

Braudel makes clear, at least in the second edition, that the two poles of his work are signified by Michelet, the geo-historian, *and* Ranke, the reporter of events. If events are so much "dust," why must they remain to hide the view? On this point *The Mediterranean and the Mediterranean World* is clear. "And yet [events] must be included, for there is more to history than the study of persistent structures and the slow progress of evolution" (II, 901). Global history, as history in its full phenomenological roundness, must have events as well as persistence; the latter "cannot provide the total picture" ("Mais cet essentiel n'est pas totalité"). When Braudel says "events," he *means* events—dust, ephemera, detail, the real stuff of Rankean history. His apology does not disguise a new kind of *histoire événementielle*; it justifies the old kind.

Traian Stoianovich's informative *French Historical Method: The Annales Paradigm* stresses the problem caused by the notion of event for the members of the school. For them, he writes *l'histoire globale* "does require discarding the notion of an *event* as a visible and tangible historical 'atom' that is given meaning by its chronological situation beside other historical atoms regardless of how these differ from one another."[45] Hexter has explained both this obvious contradiction and the practices of other *Annales* historians who do not follow the model of Braudel's *Mediterranean* in this regard by suggesting that the book has failed to "solve the historiographical problem that it poses: how to deal with the perennial historiographic difficulty of linking the durable phenomena of history with those that involve rapid change."[46] Responses to the book have tended again and again to boil down to this point.

In fact, Braudel treats this "historiographical problem" for what it is, a "graphic" problem, a linguistic problem. As the theorist of narrative Gerald Prince has written, no grammar exists "which would allow critics to relate explicitly and rigorously the semantic deep structure of any given text and the surface structures of its component sentences."[47] The real problem is one of "narrative grammar," as it is called today;

45. Stoianovich, *French Historical Method*, 102–3.
46. J. H. Hexter, *Journal of Modern History* 44 (1972), 533.
47. Gerald Prince, "Narratives with a Difference," *Diacritics* 6:2 (1976), 49.

Braudel, apparently, alone among modern historians (and this book alone among Braudel's works), has dared to use the linguistic solution to this deep linguistic dilemma—the solution is irony and satire, a homeopathic treatment that admits everything to the text at the cost of certifying nothing, not even the directionality of the syntax of the work. This aspect of *The Mediterranean and the Mediterranean World in the Age of Philip II* has been overlooked. Some may feel that the cure is worse than the disease, but no one can deny that Braudel has expended a great deal of art and energy to create a linguistic solution for a linguistic problem.

It seems to me that the reason for the continuing interest in Fernand Braudel has nothing to do with his historical conclusions, for it is not easy to say what the *thesis* of his works might be, or even his methods, for the source references, charts, graphs, lists, and so forth make their impact more by accretion than by argument. It is the immensity of the project that carries weight, particularly since Braudel has been described as a "bulemic" historian, a gargantuan gorger of history in company with Michelet (*mangeur d'histoire,* as Barthes called him).[48]

Ironically, it is Braudel's first major work that has attracted almost all the attention for theorists of history. If the worst thing that a scientific historian can do is to create a "masterpiece," with all of the attendant dangers that that entails, then Braudel's great book on the late sixteenth-century Mediterranean world may be seen as a magnificent miscalculation. Part of the essential quality of the master-text is its uncanny ability to undermine the ground on which it is built, but without falling, leaving itself at last as a sort of levitating structure, self-supporting. What Braudel's masterwork, *The Mediterranean and the Mediterranean World in the Age of Philip II,* has done is to pose a crucial formal problem: how to account for and represent significance in time from a perspective that makes of time in a certain sense the enemy of all significance. Consequently, it is *The Mediterranean* that is cited again and again in discussions of historical time and historical representation. In the wake of Braudel's *Mediterranean,* "narrative history" went into a long, slow decline, at least among members of the trend-setting French vanguard. Their reasons for this rejection are clearly enough stated. On the one hand, they hold a general sense that the *sort* of thing that can be narrativized—namely, human events like wars, revolutions, elections, strikes—are merely an entertainment, a diversion from the genuine,

48. François George, "Fernand Braudel face à l'histoire de France," *Critique,* nos. 469–470 (1986), 584.

unperceived, almost tectonic, movements in long-term economics, demographics, climatics, physiology, mentalities; on the other, many feel that only a form of knowledge produced by long-term statistical analysis made possible by the creation of comparable series of figures over centuries would have any serious scientific status.

Their authority for rejecting the story as a model for representing the past was Braudel himself, in practice and in theory. In an essay of 1950 from the *Revue économique,* calling for a new economic history, Braudel spelled out his three-tiered vision of time.

> The traditional historian is attentive to the brief time of history, that of biographies and events. That sort of time is hardly what interests economic and social historians. Societies, civilizations, economies, political institutions live at a less precipitous rhythm. It should not surprise the economists who have furnished us with our methods if in our turn we speak of cycles, intercycles, periodic movements whose phases go from five to ten, twenty, thirty, even fifty years. But even there, from our point of view, aren't we still talking about "short wave" history [*une histoire à ondes courtes*]?
>
> Below these waves, in the domain of *tendances* (the secular tendencies of economists), there spreads out in imperceptible slopes a history slow to change form and, therefore, slow to reveal itself to observation. It is what we designate in our imperfect language by the name of structural history, which is opposed less to a history of events than to a history of conjunctures with relatively short waves.[49]

The faith in the "sciences de l'homme" is here at its peak; in the influential collection of Braudel's essays, *Ecrits sur l'histoire,* published in 1969, the longest section is called "History and the Other Sciences of Man." The desire—I am speaking of desire in the sense in which the term is used by another Frenchman whose *Ecrits* were gathered about the same time, Jacques Lacan—of the historian for a place among the scientists of mankind is clear. This desire to make the "big time" translates into *la longue durée,* the long time-span, and dumping (or dumping on) the tools of small-timers, the narrative of events.

Note that in his essay on economic history, Braudel cannot escape—

49. Fernand Braudel, "Pour une économie historique" (1950), in *Ecrits sur l'histoire* (Paris, 1969), 128.

indeed, uses constantly—the aquatic imagery of waves, currents, depths, sea-bed slopes. This is quite typical of his style of that period and introduces us to the unique place of *The Mediterranean and the Mediterranean World in the Age of Philip II*. There is a tremendous irony in Braudel's rejection of the literary model found in the story and of the cult of the author-historian associated with the historical masterpiece in favor of a team *(équipe)* concept of historical discourse. Not only was Braudel himself, like his own master, Febvre, a fervid proponent of the greatest of author-historians, Jules Michelet, but, I maintain, Braudel's own reputation (despite "his" great output) rests on the qualities of one book that was not written with the help of a team and that invokes the most personal of solutions to the dilemmas of linguistic representation. *La Méditerranée et le monde méditerranéen à l'époque de Philippe II* stands, like *Les Misérables*, as a great French masterpiece, much admired, but little read because of its enormous length and frequent digressions; in a certain sense, perhaps, it is all digression, in the modernist vein.

To say that Braudel's *Mediterranean* is a work of *modernist*, rather than simply modern, historiography entails a considerable ambiguity. In *The Discourse of Modernism*, Timothy Reiss uses the word to describe the analytico-referential consciousness characteristic of scientific and rational knowledge since the sixteenth century. This is the modernist tradition with which the *Annales* school has sought to associate itself in its quest to bring history up to speed with the other "human sciences." The modernism I find in *The Mediterranean* is a very different one; it is the aesthetic modernism of Pound, Eliot, Joyce, Proust, and Mann. More than a modernism of form or a modernism of subject, it is a modernism of self-questioning representation, a continuous satire on the means available to historical comprehension. If, for example, the modernist work of literature cannot, properly speaking, be read, but only re-read, because of the essential simultaneity of presentation that demands an extratemporal perspective in the manner of Marcel Proust, *The Mediterranean* demands the same sort of readerly perspective. The lack of privilege accorded to position within the text is hinted at late in the second volume, when Braudel notes the reversibility of his text. It was Mallarmé, of course, who called for a language of absence, in which words negated their referents rather than affirming them; indeed, Maurice Blanchot's influential essay "Le mythes de Mallarmé" appeared in the same year that *La Méditerranée* was first published, 1949. I suggest that the intense referential irony in Braudel's *Mediterranean* makes it in one sense *the* Mallarméen history. Consider the catechreses, the displacements and proliferations of objects, the maps that dis-orient, the incessant defamiliarization that Braudel deploys throughout the book; these might lead a formalist like Victor Shklovsky to conclude that art, and art alone, is here at work. The title of the book foregrounds the environmental background of history; the structure of the book discredits what everyone could see at the time. Great events like the battle of Lepanto or the St. Bartholomew's Day Massacre are shown as dramatic events that led nowhere, as opposed, say, to the mid-century Turkish wheat boom, or the impact of American silver.

The general effect of Braudel's methods is not simply to re-orient the reader toward new and better perspectives. These antireferential referents make objects disappear at the level of *real* meaning (geo-history, in which things are always shifting in their representations because names and descriptions will not hold or cover their referents) and make meaning disappear at the level of *real* objects (the "dust" of events, swirling about in no evident direction because the intentions and outcomes of human events are always illusory, although language serves them fairly well); they present Braudel as a philosophical realist, offering the transcendent, the timeless, at the expense of the immanent.

If the spatialization of comprehension found in *The Mediterranean* is, in fact, the sign of Braudel's modernism, then a number of conclusions should follow.[50] Foremost among these would be a problematizing of time and its linguistic expression, narrative. As everyone knows, this is the case. The time *of* human experience and understanding is measure with little significance; the time *beyond* human experience possesses significance, but can never be grasped through language. Ideally, it would seem, eternity alone has true significance, being ineffable.

For Braudel, the death of Philip, allegorized as the disappearance of human events from the highest realm of historical significance, validates the rejection of narrative. Even the greatest actor understands little; his death changes little; the great events of his reign lead nowhere. However, if we choose to credit Braudel's hints about the reversibility of the book, viewing the round structure of the text as a mirror of the roundness of the sea so often stressed by its historian, a peculiar thing happens. As man disappears as actor at the conclusion of *The Mediterranean and the Mediterranean World in the Age of Philip II*, he reappears at the beginning. When we re-enter the book back in the realm of time-

50. Joseph Frank, "Spatial Form in Modern Literature," in *The Widening Gyre* (New York, 1966).

lessness, we find the deictic statement that opens the work, "I have loved the Mediterranean with passion, no doubt because I am a northerner like so may others in whose footsteps I have followed."

Having established an authority as narrator based upon his passion as a lover, Braudel embarks with his reader into geo-history, the analytical description of the Mediterranean environment. No historical events are represented, but a different sort of event fills the text. These are the textual events of the discourse itself, the narrative of comprehension that is inescapable as long as there is a narrative voice (or, perhaps, as long as there is any receiver at all for the message). Braudel, in a tradition that links him with Hugo and Michelet, emplots his tableau as a journey, circling concentrically round the mountains, then the plateaus, the plains, down to the sea (or rather seas) itself. The second section, on social and economic institutions, repeats this circularity (albeit in a peculiar way).

If we can accept Boris Tomashevsky's notion that "a story may be thought of as a journey from one situation to another," then we will want to ask: what are the situations, the outposts, of this journey? Clearly, the only answer to this question is found at the level of the text, since it is hard to imagine a narrative of historical events that would begin with mountains (even personified mountains who play "roles") and end with the death of Philip II, King of Spain, in 1598. The "situations" referred to by Tomashevsky are, for Braudel, different stages along the path of comprehending the relationship between words and things, *les mots et les choses*. The most scientific part of the story is the most allegorical; the most human part is the most literal.

Some commentators on the French historical scene—Paul Veyne or Paul Ricoeur, for instance—find themselves quite nervous at the apparent abolition of man from much of *Annales*-school history. For them, a narrative understanding is essential to all human comprehension, and *"all change enters the field of history as quasi-event."*[51] Ricoeur, who believes that without narrative the very value of human life will be lost, sees the three sections of Braudel's *Mediterranean* as a "quasi-plot."

> What frames the plot of the Mediterranean? We may say without hesitation: the decline of the Mediterranean as a collective hero on the stage of world history. The end of the plot in this regard is not the death of Philip II. It is the end of the conflict between the two

51. Paul Ricoeur, *Time and Narrative*, vol. I, trans. Kathleen McLaughlin and David Pellauer (Chicago, 1984), 214.

political leviathans and the shift of history toward the Atlantic and Northern Europe.[52]

Ricoeur sees the work as a three-part segmentation of a single story about the decline of the Mediterranean as world hero, a tale that Tolstoy might well have told as a single narrative. This is certainly a plausible reading, which emphasizes the scientific analysis inherent in Braudel's project. I think Ricoeur has missed the point, or the boat (as Braudel might put it).

Let us try to see *The Mediterranean* in another way. Rather than try to "naturalize" the narrative of comprehension as an expanded model of the narrative of events, so that all change enters the field of human understanding as a quasi event and the first two levels of Braudel's book become infrastructural props for the political trends of the third, I suggest that we try to reverse the hourglass (that topos of time and death) and to see even narrative of events as a narrative of comprehension, and equally allegorical. My reading of the allegorical death of Philip, that blind intersection (in traffic parlance), throws the reader back to the start of the book, to the amorous narrator, passionate lover of the sea that Philip did not even know. The end of the Mediterranean hegemony produces *The Mediterranean*, a text with its own hegemony, an object like the sea itself, difficult to know.

I quote Braudel in conclusion.

> I have sometimes compared models to boats. What is of interest to me, once the boat is built, is to put it on the water, to see if it floats, then to make it go up or down, as I wish, the waters of time. The shipwreck is always the most significant moment.[53]

Braudel's masterpiece may be read as such a shipwreck, and, like other great shipwrecks of French history, it finds whatever meanings it may have as art.

52. Ibid., 215.
53. Fernand Braudel, "L'Histoire et les autres sciences de l'homme," in *Ecrits sur l'histoire* (Paris, 1969), 71–72.

PART THREE

TROPOLOGY AND NARRATIVITY

When Hayden White published *Metahistory: The Historical Imagination in Nineteenth-Century Europe* in 1973, the most unconventional, and ostensibly unhistorical, part of the book was its use of the theory of tropes. Four classical figures of speech, well known since antiquity, were presented as the models for the "deep structures" of historical thought. Not only historians, but also historical eras, were dominated by one or another of these four ways of thinking. Further, these ways of thinking—metaphor, metonymy, synecdoche, and irony—also seemed to have lives of their own. By implication, they reflected upon each other; they explained a number of historical theories involving stages of development; they unified the overviews of historians with the stylistic peculiarities of their texts; they offered a model of comprehension itself; and a good deal more. Indeed, at a certain point these personified tropes reach a high level of self-awareness, which reveals itself as a keenly developed historical sense—a sense of the past as development, as narrative. The nineteenth century, in White's view, was the Golden Age of historical thought because it had attained for the moment a level of implicit tropological understanding that would soon collapse into ironic understanding-as-misunderstanding in the crisis of historicism at the end of the century. Tropology is the perfect embodiment of understanding-as-misunderstanding.

A renewed interest in tropes *as a system* began to develop, flowing back into the realm of literary studies from which it originated. As a model of narrative, implied but not spelled out in White's work, the theory of four tropes (metaphor, metonymy, synecdoche, irony) proved a powerful alternative to the two-trope structuralist orthodoxy, which presented metaphor and metonomy as the polar models of mental processes, the psychological existence of which could be scientifically demonstrated by their appearance in forms of neurological disease. The four-trope system has no such proof of its reality. It exists by revealing itself over and over again in certain texts that *allegorize* in some way a movement from trope to trope in a sort of would-be totalizing journey. As much as there is to say about the tropes, tropology itself remains a series of allegorical examples; it implies that there is, somewhere, a structure reflected in the examples, but it is never able to specify such a structure, except as another example. Each tropological allegory asks the question that it cannot answer: does this example reveal an essential form of thought, or rather a contingent mode of reading? The reason it cannot answer the question is simply that we can only know tropology as we "do" it, as a mode of readerly behavior. The tropology that derives from *Metahistory*, recently described in James Mellard's *Doing Tropology* (1987), has no essential connection with history. Anything can be read tropologically, and White may in fact have intended that the tropes would become a common ground for quite divergent discourses. Yet far from bringing together historians, literary theorists, philosophers, and others, tropology has been resisted by most of them. It causes anxiety even among its adepts because in its fullest form it is a form of analysis that deflects meanings and intention just at the moment of comprehension, of grasping. To *read* tropologically is a powerful thing, but *to be read* (or to read oneself) tropologically is unsettling.

In looking over the four admirable "shipwrecks" of Part II, I have come to the belated, slightly uncomfortable realization that they are arranged tropologically in sequence. That is, Guizot's social history of literature aimed at a metaphoric solution to the problem of cultural totality by presuming a formal, metaphoric analogy between the structure of society and the structure of artistic forms. Michelet, in his interruption of the narrative whole of the history of France, tried to constitute a whole nation from the mere parts of geography, but failed in this metonymic quest because no inner principle or spirit existed that could hold the whole together. For him, the trope of metonymy and its translation into geo-history was a failure, like the very middle ages that his "Tableau" inaugurates. Narrative and time were essential to figure the spirit of France. In Spengler's notion of cultures, the figure of synecdoche as essential inner spirit finds its purest expression, but cannot contain itself in its own embodiment, Faustian culture. Braudel, like Spengler, sees the inevitable breakdown of his historical grasp, but does not project this failure onto the culture, as Spengler does in *The Decline of the West*. Rather, it is the *text* of history that embodies Braudel's ironic ambivalence about language and meaning. I have discovered this tropology as a reader of my own text, rather than created it as an author-authority. Its presence surprises me. If someone were to explain to me the ways in which the four sections of the book as a whole also have a tropological sequence—as I suspect someone could do—I would be more anxious. It was not a part of my plan, or, if it was a part of my plan, then "I" (as controlling subject) was not fully present in the planning.

In *Prophets of Extremity: Nietzsche, Heidegger, Foucault, Derrida*, Allan Megill points to the way in which "fourthinking" functions for post-structuralism as a kind of antidialectic, throwing the Hegelian three-some of situation, response, countersituation into chaos by displacing it into a new moment that upsets the machinery. This post-structuralist "fourthought" certainly differs from the variety deriving from Augustine and culminating in Dante's famous letter to Can Grande della Scala, explaining the fourfold ways of *reading* the *Commedia*. It also differs from Fredric Jameson's newer version of Dante's vision, put forth in *The Political Unconscious;* for both Dante and Jameson, the fourth stage—whether seen as religious anagogy or historical totality—is the broadest understanding. Their foursomes arrive at an "ultimate" anagogic vision because they start at a level of "literality." With this as the first stage, their progression naturally leads to a synecdochic level as the highest vision. Irony is absent; if it had been present, no initial literal level could have been possible, because it is precisely the inability to establish the literality of the text that sets the tropological drive to comprehension in gear. Dante and Jameson seem to take as totality a synecdochic vision that unifies the levels of understanding.

The three chapters that follow flow away from strictly historical considerations concerning White's *Metahistory* to a more generalized, and technical, discussion of tropology, and finally to an account of the anxieties aroused by the "logic" of the tropes even in the great tropological thinkers, Freud and Kant. Since tropes seem, at least to me, the most powerful and general way in which language captures and creates reality, they seem to be the literal embodiment of "getting the story crooked." A trope, after all, is a *turn.* The key question involved has to do with the origin of tropes. Are they somehow "*a priori*" or even "natural" structures of understanding (as Kant or Freud would have it), or merely cultural "conventions" (as Hayden White or Roland Barthes would assert)?

The answer implicit in the chapters that follow—that tropology is an allegorical form and thus yet another "merely" human creation—is far from secure because it rests itself upon the tropological system it would evaluate. By this I mean that my tropological reflection has privileged Irony as the master trope, and this choice has dictated that all human forms be seen as in some degree allegorical. It also dictates its own allegorical status as a story that explains.

8

A BEDROCK OF ORDER

HAYDEN WHITE'S LINGUISTIC

HUMANISM

Ἄνδρα μοι'ἔννεπε, μοῦσα, πολύτροπον

(Tell me, O Muse, of the man of many turns)

The invocation of the Muse that opens the *Odyssey* does not, like that of the *Iliad*, identify its hero by name. He is called only *polytropos*, which is literally (although rarely) translated as "[the man of] many turns"—other renderings include "the adventurous man," "that ingenious hero," "the man of many devices," or (my own favorite) "skilled in all ways of contending." It was Odysseus who proposed the horse, given as a tribute, that opened the gates of Troy and ended a decade of futile, if glorious, slaughter. *Polytropos* seems an apt characterization of Hayden White, and *polytropic* of his book *Metahistory*. The issues raised by this book are bewildering. A language is scarcely available that will allow direct confrontation with a book so fully and openly about language. The historian, who is accustomed to more or less frontal attacks on his subject in the manner of Achilles, is frustrated by the "many turns" of the book, and by its ability to evade or absorb thrusts. In rhetoric, style of argument, authorial pose, and subject matter itself, *Metahistory* seems to dominate and control any discourse that might address it.

The book we are to consider is titled *Metahistory: The Historical Imagination in Nineteenth-Century Europe*, its subjects are historians, its course is diachronic; yet it specifically addresses literary criticism, philosophy, and history. The politics of academic discourse reflected in this situation must be the proper subject of preliminary inquiry, because cultural politics—the politics of historical, literary, and philosophical thought in America—have shaped both the book itself and responses to it. Furthermore, because Hayden White's own career as a historian and cultural critic has turned again and again to matters of cultural politics, the historian considering *Metahistory* is virtually compelled to examine the text as a political event and its writing as a political act.

This is not simple to do. The book is elaborately defended against interpretation because as a book about interpretation it not only gives a system of rules by which it might itself be interpreted, but also at many points carries out such an interpretation. One has scarcely begun to read *Metahistory* before learning that it is "cast in an Ironic mode" (xii), and that its method is "formalist" (3).[1] A few pages from the end of the book, we note that White takes this "purely formal way" of characterizing the interpretive strategies of the historians he discusses as a "value neutral" methodology (431). The strategy is explicitly announced shortly thereafter: "When it is a matter of choosing among these alternative visions of history, the only grounds for preferring one over another are *moral* or *aesthetic* ones" (433). By thus drawing its hermeneutic wagons into a circle, *Metahistory* assumes the posture of the "master-text" by forcing any prospective critic to address it—that is, to *name* it—on its own terms. It is perfectly possible to disagree with the contention that a "purely formal" approach (or any other) is "value neutral." White is clearly aware of all this, but he is also aware that any possible criticism of his text is already named and placed by the text itself. A confrontation with *Metahistory* cannot begin from without, because the book and its theory claim to comprehend and neutralize any such assault before it is made.[2]

Although the book is apparently impossible to outflank, it teaches a definite suspicion about the claims of any text and asserts that there is no escape from "indenture," whether to literary, epistemological, ideological, or linguistic forms. Despite the inoculation that *Metahistory* carries out on any critical reader by naming and placing itself within its own self-contained system, and equally by implicating possible readings of it within its own compass, the book also demands that it be mistrusted. It is perhaps even willing to authorize—to name and accept as classifiable—the grounds for its own rejection. If this is the case, "reading" in the classical sense of a voluntary communication between a fixed text and a relatively free mind becomes impossible: this permanent indenture seems to require either that one not read the book (by

1. All citations from *Metahistory: The Historical Imagination in Nineteenth-Century Europe* (Baltimore and London, 1973) are placed in parentheses.
2. On "master-texts," see Hayden White, "Review Essay: Leon Pompa, *Vico: A Study of the "New Science,"* *History and Theory* 15 (1976), 186.

which I mean that one not follow its premises to their conclusions, but rather reject the exercise in advance), or that one be read *by* it (that is, enter the text only to find oneself already in it). To escape this apparent impasse, or at least to avoid it for a while, one may proceed by indirection (as Odysseus rather than Achilles) to consider questions oblique to the text, choosing to forget that this polytropic attitude is also that of *Metahistory.*

The various assertions of *Metahistory* exist along two axes: one, a historical tradition that bequeaths and authorizes the basic direction of the book; and the other, a discourse of current cultural politics that shapes the tack of the book, its strategies and defenses, by enforcing certain prohibitions and presenting unavoidable confrontations. My intention in the first two sections of this chapter is to fix firmly the interaction of these axes, the traditional and the discursive. This done, I shall turn later to the relation of the book to its subject, the historical imagination in nineteenth-century Europe.

I

> *Valla is one of a long line of analysts of language who appear at that stage of any intellectual movement when it begins to question its values and terminology. He was an iconoclast who, in the interest of an intuited higher consistency, exposed the inconsistency in every contemporary form of cultural expression. As such, he is the prototype of the modern philologist as moral reformer.*
> Willson Coates, Hayden White, J. Salwyn Schapiro,
> *The Emergence of Liberal Humanism*

Metahistory is a book with no dedication or personal acknowledgments; its author makes few references to his own earlier works. The result is to obscure the relation of the book both to an intellectual tradition and to a professional career. But each of these extrinsic factors is of considerable importance in defining the meaning of *Metahistory,* either as an individual text or as a call for reformation in historical studies. The discontinuity that seems to place *Metahistory* in a different category from White's earlier work is illusive. To start with, the career itself has been filled with apparently discontinuous leaps. Beginning as a historian of the medieval Church, White turned to nineteenth-century thought in the early 1960s, and by the end of that decade his published work was ranging widely throughout Western cultural history: from the Greco-Roman tradition to contemporary philosophy of history, from Ibn Khaldoun to Foucault. The incoherence of this field of material is broken by repeated returns to two figures, Vico and Croce; but the interest that they hold for White does not in itself solve the problem. Nor does the fact that an interest in historical theory has been a part of this corpus of work from the bginning: not only does too much of White's work deal with other matters ("structuralism and popular culture," Darwin, the Noble Savage, literary theory) for historical theory to serve as the theme that unifies such a diversified field of inquiry, but historical theory itself is such an inchoate, unformalized concept that it seems as dispersive as White's thematic and chronological travels.

Two themes, nevertheless, consistently emerge throughout White's work. To name them is to define the intellectual path that leads to *Metahistory*, the "unacknowledgments." The first theme of White's work is *how a tradition elicits assent*, and what happens when a tradition ceases to define the rules by which important judgments are made. White's early writing notes how the Gregorian tradition of papal authority, with its emphasis on worldly power and canonical legalism, gave way to the new spirituality of the twelfth century, represented by Saint Bernard and his new set of criteria for papal authority. The two-volume intellectual history that White co-authored traced the emergence and ordeal of the tradition of "liberal humanism"; his interest in "cultural politics," the ways in which a tradition constrains the struggle of conflicting forces within it, has not flagged. At least a dozen articles deal with the subject in one form or another.

However, if the first of the major themes in White's work is an interest in cultural politics—how a tradition censors the debate it makes possible—the second is a pronounced fixation upon the force confronting the weight of tradition: *human choice*. Throughout White's work on the philosophy of history, he has consistently condemned pessimism and fatalism; the Ibn Khaldouns, Burckhardts, Spenglers, who see mankind walking a treadmill through time, the direction of which is occasionally reversed by forces outside human control, have struck him as antihumanistic, and *consequently* as wrong. His criterion is clear and simple: whatever reinforces the human sense of the possibility of mastery, the sense that the game has rules that make it worth playing, constitutes for White the precondition for a valid philosophy of history. Proper philosophy of history is thus humanistic because it provides the "tentative hypotheses necessary for action"; cyclical patterns of history, whether Greek, Arab, or tropological, are to be judged by whether they suggest some "essentially cumulative character of the human experience."[3]

White's insistence that historical writing should reinforce the sense of human mastery is complemented by an assertion that the greater course of history itself (as lived and as written) is based upon human choice. Men choose who they are by choosing who they were. Thus, Rome "fell" when "men *ceased to regard themselves as descendants of their Roman forebears and began to treat themselves as descendants of their Judaeo-Christian predecessors.*"[4] In this view, the true "fall" was an event in the minds of millions of men and women who "*act as if they could choose their own ancestors.*" To choose a tradition is to belong to it; the same is not true of genetic constitution. "And no amount of 'objective' historical work pointing out the extent to which this *chosen* ancestry is *not* the *real* ancestry can prevail against the choosing power of the individuals in the system."[5] The tradition, then, is the arena within which the battles of cultural politics are fought, but the nature of the tradition is not a dead hand of the past (a hereditary set of traits), but rather a continually chosen set of possibilities. If the tradition is exhausted or morbid, this too is a matter of human choice. *Metahistory* is a consistent step in this study of tradition and choice, but its identity remains obscure until we identify the tradition that it has implicitly chosen for itself.

The image of the renaissance humanist as founder of the modern and most fully "human" world-view is a topos of modern cultural historiography (shadowed, to be sure, by its counter-topos, which presents the renaissance humanist as a fundamentally medieval mind), but its particular appearance in White's work suggests his strong identification with the principal concerns of humanism. In White's vision of modern history, the renaissance begins "the culture of criticism," which is that of both the humanists and the humanities that derive from them. The collapse of religious restraints on various discourses during the

3. Hayden White, "Ibn Khaldoun in World Philosophy of History," *Comparative Studies in Society and History* 2 (1959), 122, 123.

4. Hayden White, "What Is a Historical System?" in *Biology, History and Natural Philosophy*, ed. Allen D. Breck and Wolfgang Yourgrau (New York and London, 1972), 239.

5. Ibid., 241.

renaissance liberated the "study of cultural artifacts as specifically _human_ creations," as phenomena rather than as epiphenomena of some deeper religious or metaphysical force. This process of secularization—from the "divinities" to the "humanities"—entails "the global process of demystification of culture which culminated in the foundation, at the end of the nineteenth century, of the social sciences."[6] Lorenzo Valla, as the quotation at the head of this section suggests, is seen as the prototypical humanist. Valla's best-known exploit was his exposure of the Donation of Constantine as a forgery through philological and textual criticism. Valla, the "philologist as moral reformer," attacked scholasticism where he found it most vulnerable, in its language, and, as was true of Ramus, much of his most important work was a philological reconsideration of Aristotelian categories. Paul Kristeller has noted that the sixteenth-century humanists effectively reduced logic to rhetoric; and White, in _Metahistory_, takes this sixteenth-century rhetoric as his authority for using a four-trope paradigm instead of the metaphor/metonymy dyad employed by the binary structuralists like Jakobson, Lacan, and Lévi-Strauss (31–33, n. 13).[7]

The replacement of a logic with a rhetoric in the interest of eliminating a host of false problems has been the task of a series of thinkers. Each of them reconfronts the same opponent—a spirit-deadening scholasticism that refuses innovation and leads discourse again and again into a series of debates that are known in advance to be impossible of resolution. Valla is the type, but Giambattista Vico is the incarnation, of a more self-conscious philologist; the latter has more than the former's "intuited higher consistency." In the fourfold theory of tropes, Vico forged the tools of a _human_ science that could make sense of events without appeal to divine will. Nietzsche is another apparition of this type and was thus wrong when he wrote of himself; "For the first time in history somebody had _come to grips_ with scholarship" (cited in _Metahistory_, 333). This procession of "philologist-reformers" includes Hayden White. White treats historical theory respectfully in _Metahistory_, but elsewhere has referred to "the trivia of my own discipline's internecine squabbles"[8] and has often maintained that "the conventional canons of historical scholarship" are unsuitable for judging work that he considers importantly innovative. Reading White and _Metahistory_

6. Hayden White, "The Culture of Criticism," in _Liberations: New Essays on the Humanities in Revolution_, ed. Ihab Hassan (Middletown, Conn., 1971), 55.

7. Paul Kristeller, _Renaissance Thought: The Classic, Scholastic, and Humanist Strains_ (New York, 1961), 101.

8. White, "What Is a Historical System?" 233.

into this tradition reveals that the nineteenth century plays a special role for it, acting out or "working through" its principal problems. White has identified the program of the sixteenth-century humanists with the formalization of the "human sciences" (from history to sociology, from historical philology to structural linguistics) in the nineteenth and early twentieth centures. Vico, whose profession was the study of renaissance rhetorical forms, not only seems a crystallization of these forms, but also "the nineteenth century in embryo," as Croce put it.[9] Untimely Nietzsche, embedded in his century, was struggling to get out, to get "above" it and its bewildering nihilism. And White makes of the nineteenth century an allegorical play, in which the tropes have finally learned their lines and delivered them properly, only to forget them at once.

Adrian Kuzminski has skeptically pointed out that *Metahistory* implicitly shares with Vico's work the claim to be the foundation of "a new science," a science that stresses the human power of institutional creativity against the oppressive force of sacred ordination. From Vico, White takes his tropology—the tools of "gentile," human creation. Vico, however, faces a human as well as a sacred barrier to his "new science"; the claims of logic to a truth beyond human power must be eliminated before Vico's science may operate.

> "Logic" comes from *logos*, whose first and proper meaning was *fabula*, fable, carried over into Italian as *favella*, speech. In Greek the fable was also called *mythos*, myth, whence comes the Latin *mutus*, mute. For speech was born in mute times as mental [or sign] language, which Strabo in a golden passage says existed before vocal or articulate [language]; whence *logos* means both word and idea. It was fitting that the matter should be so ordered by divine providence in religious times, for it is an eternal property of religions that they attach more importance to meditation than to speech. Thus the first language in the first mute times of the nations must have begun with signs, whether gestures or physical objects, which had natural relations to the ideas [to be expressed] [225]. For this reason *logos*, or word, meant also deed to the Hebrews and thing to the Greeks. . . .[10]

9. Hayden White, "What Is Living and What Is Dead in Croce's Criticism of Vico," in *Giambattista Vico: An International Symposium*, ed. Giorgio Tagliacozzo and Hayden White (Baltimore, 1969), 389; reprinted in *Tropics of Discourse: Essays in Cultural Criticism* (Baltimore and London 1978), 229.

10. *The New Science of Giambattista Vico*, trans. T. G. Bergin and M. A. Fisch (Ithaca, 1948), paragraph 401.

Tropology and Narrativity

That Vico's etymological deconstruction of "logic" is typically fanciful only underscores his desire to make the point that logic is not a truth behind events, but rather an event itself, a deed, a created thing. Before the advent of logical discourse is the age of "poetic" discourse, "the first wisdom of the gentile world."[11] The logic of ancient jurisprudence was a severe poem; the traces of figural residues are everywhere in Vico's creative etymology.

In Nietzsche's version of this tradition, the distinction between "truth and lie" (and even such uncontroversial notions as the principle of noncontradiction) is the result of a failure of nerve, a "peace pact" that man made with himself.

> This peace pact brings with it something that brings with it the first step toward the attainment of this enigmatic urge for truth. For now that is fixed which henceforth shall be "truth"; that is, a regularly valid and obligatory designation of things is invented, and this linguistic legislation also furnishes the first laws of truth: for it is here that the contrast between truth and lie first originates.[12]

Nietzsche, the professional philologist, lectured on Greek and Roman rhetoric (and tropes) at Basle. (He notes: "only two students enrolled, one of German and one of law.") His most frequently quoted words these days are his definition of truth as "a mobile army of metaphors, metonyms, and anthropomorphisms." Language, for Nietzsche, is the basic creative expression of a world of chaos; but when language congeals into a "legislation" that obscures its *made* nature, the way is clear for a tyranny of logic, "illusions about which one has forgotten that this is what they are."[13] And history, as White makes plain, is equally a *made* object, which becomes a "burden" when it claims a privileged weight of truth.[14]

That White belongs to this tradition is attested to by nearly every page of *Metahistory*. His initial (enabling) definition of the objects of his study makes the point.

I will consider the historical text as what it most manifestly is—

11. Ibid., para. 375.

12. Friedrich Nietzsche, "Of Truth and Lie in the Extra-Moral Sense," in *The Portable Nietzsche*, ed. Walter Kaufmann (New York, 1954), 44.

13. Ibid., 47.

14. Hayden White, "The Burden of History," *History and Theory* 5 (1966), 115–16; also in *Tropics of Discourse*.

that is to say, a verbal structure in the form of a narrative prose discourse that purports to be a model or icon of past structures and processes in the interest of *explaining what they were by representing* them. (2)

Representation (argument from similarity) subsumes explanation (argument from contiguity), which becomes a "moment" of representation, an attribute. White, in fact, suggests that explanation may well be an illusion, "a specifically Western prejudice." In the first section of *Metahistory*, White erects a quadruple tetrad of four sets, each containing four elements, which define the possibilities of Emplotment, Argumentation, Ideology, and "Deep Structure." In his discussion of "Explanation by Formal Argument," the logical component of his quadruple tetrad, White describes the nomological-deductive arguments that constitute the "laws" of historical explanation.

> This argument can be analyzed into a syllogism, the major premise of which consists of some putatively universal law of causal relationships, the minor premise of the boundary conditions within which the law is applied, and a conclusion in which the events that actually occurred are deduced from the premises by logical necessity. (11)

That this entire field of logical operations is undercut and subsumed by the rhetorical structure that authorizes it is made clear in White's characterization of Metonymy, which he presents as reductive in precisely the same way that formal arguments are.

> Once the world of phenomena is separated into two orders of being (agents and causes on the one hand, acts and effects on the other), the primitive consciousness is endowed, *by purely linguistic means alone*, with the conceptual categories (agents, causes, spirits, essences) necessary for the theology, science, and philosophy of civilized reflection. (35)

For White to italicize the already tautological phrase "by purely linguistic means alone" is indication enough of its importance to him. The laws of formal historical explanation may be "putative," but there is nothing in White's case to suggest that the "purely linguistic means" that authorize them are anything but genuine. The tropological structures of rhetoric consistently swamp the explanatory strictures of logic; logic is subsumed to Metonymy, a figure of rhetoric as figure of thought.

Tropology and Narrativity

White has described the move from literary theory to philosophy of history as a reflection of "the apprehension of imminent apocalypse."[15] His own move in the *opposite* direction equally bespeaks a despairing apprehension of *no* apocalypse—that little if any important change is likely to occur in historical reflection. To examine formalized historical reflection, or "philosophy of history," is to confront a literature without a field.

II

> *One can study only what one has first dreamed about.*
> Bachelard—
> epigraph of Hayden White, *Metahistory*

> *Doctrines must take their beginnings from that of the matters of which they treat.*
> Vico—epigraph of Edward W. Said,
> *Beginnings: Intention and Method*

White makes it clear that the trope is a beginning, that it happens *before* other things. He writes:

> I have maintained that the style of a given historiographer can be characterized in terms of the linguistic protocol he used to prefigure the historical field prior to bringing to bear upon it the various 'explanatory' strategies he used to fashion a 'story' out of the 'chronicle' of events contained in the historical record. (426)

This summary of the thrust of *Metahistory* identifies its major difference from the traditional images of history. These images name a variety of "beginnings"—the document itself, the ideological concerns of the historian, or her psychological predeterminations. "The linguistic protocol," however, is an odd point of departure; it cannot be naturalized by the discourse of historical thought.

Metahistory can scarcely be classified with works in the philosophy of history because it seems an implicit denial of the utility of the conclu-

15. Hayden White, "Ethnological 'Lie' and Mythical 'Truth,'" *Diacritics* 8 (Spring 1978), 2.

sions and disputes of recent philosophy of history. Since most philosophy of history is written by philosophers for an undefined audience, that genre has a strange, ethereal quality: indexes are almost entirely devoid of references to historians. When historians are cited, it is generally to focus on a well-known controversy or an explanatory vignette; "epistemic criteria," "decision procedures," "probabilistic concepts," "perceiving under a description," appear as members of the constituent set of historical procedures, but the set does not admit entire historical works, let alone the entire *oeuvre* of master historians. The philosophers of history prefer to discuss the literature of the philosophy of history, so the names of Collingwood, Danto, Dray, Gallie, Mandelbaum, and Morton White appear again and again. Historical arguments are cited as fragments to be analyzed piecemeal; their historicity seems an embarrassment to an Anglo-American tradition that feels most confident when confronted with a rather simple statement in common language. When historians write of the theory of history, they sometimes succumb to the temptation to be philosophical by reducing the problem at hand to the limited "common language" complexities of, for example, an athletic contest. In short, work in the philosophy of history tends to deal with neither philosophy nor history, but rather with other works in the philosophy of history.

At the risk of pointing out the obvious, I should note that if we judge such matters pragmatically, there is in fact no such field as philosophy of history or theory of historical narrative within the historical profession. Although nearly every history department, graduate or undergraduate, offers courses in historiography, philosophy of history, or introduction to historical thought, such courses are invariably taught by a historian from another area, often an intellectual historian or a senior scholar assumed to have a magisterial overview. I cannot recall seeing any history department advertise a job opening for any sort of historical theorist (while "U.S. Southern or South Carolina history" or "U.S. quantitative/behavioral, period not stipulated" and a surprising number of similar jobs appear regularly in the Employment Information Bulletin of the American Historical Association). If such an opening in historical theory, however defined, has escaped my notice, it is certain to attract applicants who were trained in other areas, and who simply reverse the first two lines in the "Fields of Specialty" section of the resume; "Philosophy of History" falls invariably in second or third place in this rubric, a sideline that may attract the attention of some department. To note the marginality of historical theory to the historical profession calls to mind that the situation is little better in departments of philosophy, and that nonfiction prose criticism remains a poor relation in comparative literature as well. In other words, despite the large number of works published in the philosophy of history, the power of that discourse is slight—it has few jobs to award, little direct influence on any other historical endeavor, and a set of conceptual concerns unique to itself (or borrowed from an equally problematic discourse, the "philosophy of science").

White's tactic has been to ignore both the principal problems of the philosophy of history since Collingwood and the debates carried on in the vast secondary literature on the individuals he discusses. The former problems (of the sort found in the standard anthologies of Meyerhoff, Dray, and Gardiner) White tends to dismiss as "essentially contested"; the latter writings he sets aside as too deeply implicated in the forms of thought that it is his purpose to characterize, and as too remote from the texts themselves. The texture of *Metahistory* is implicitly that of Erich Auerbach's *Mimesis;* extensive citations of texts are used directly to elicit a fully formed reading not visibly resting upon any secondary literature. Since White was not stranded, like Auerbach, in Istanbul without a research library, nor ignorant of the concerns of post–World War II philosophy of history, his tactic points to itself as an explicit move—the *refusal* of a discourse. By renaming a field and reclassifying its objects, White has, like the renaissance humanists, declared the existing edifice to be largely "scholastic," a round-robin of unresolvable questions and "merely" ideological debates.

The first move in White's rejection of the discourse of philosophy of history is his dismantling of the series of distinctions that have "enabled" that literature and its disputes. I have noted the subsumption of Explanation by Narration; a similar operation takes place with Tenor/Vehicle, Non-Fiction/Fiction, Science/Art, and History Proper/Philosophy of History. In each case, the first term of the paradigm becomes a "moment" of the second. White grants the distinction between "the historian's *investigative functions* on the one hand and his *narrative operation* on the other" (12) early in his text, but it quickly becomes clear that this distinction is not privileged. Since the basis of investigation is a preliminary *naming* of the field, a process that is poetic in its origin, the separation of research and writing also collapses.

White's second step in liberating himself from the discourse of Anglo-American philosophy of history is his sweeping use of W. B. Gallie's notion, "the essentially contested concept." Without honoring Gallie's qualifications of this term, White declares the essence of most historiographical discourse beyond debate. For example, the great historians "cannot be 'refuted,' or their generalizations 'disconfirmed'" (4); nor can one resolve the "questions which arise when two or more scholars, of roughly equal erudition and theoretical sophistication, come to alternative, though not necessarily mutually exclusive, interpretations of the set of historical events" (13); nor are there "extra-ideological grounds on which to arbitrate among the conflicting conceptions of the historical process" (27).

With these two basically defensive strokes, White has managed to evade the discourse of the philosophy of history since 1950, although in doing so his own discourse has been considerably affected. This theoretical ground-clearing re-enacts Lorenzo Valla's hope "to sweep the boards of culture clean and to show that beneath all contemporary confusion there existed a bedrock of order reflected in, and knowable through, formally pure language."[16] For White, this "bedrock of order" is the theory of tropes. But the matter of tropology itself is deeply implicated in the politics of discourse; White's quick deflection of the claims of binary structuralist tropology (31–32, n. 13) cannot dispel the internecine conflict of the contemporary tropological tradition. Furthermore, there is evidence of an anxiety of tropological influence throughout *Metahistory*. White is not Vico, in the simple sense that the discourse he enters with the four-trope Vichian tropology is thoroughly different from the Neapolitan's. Their circular strategy, however, is essentially the same. First, trope is inflated from a figure of speech into a figure of thought, making it "useful for understanding the operations by which the contents of experience which resist description in unambiguous prose representations can be prefiguratively grasped and prepared for conscious apprehension" (34). Thus, a surface structure (figure of speech) becomes a deep structure (figure of thought), *while remaining on the surface* and immune to the vagaries of "interpretation." A tropological reading is not an interpretation. It asserts with Oscar Wilde that "the mystery of the world is the visible, not the invisible."

Metahistory, therefore, challenges the discourse of both the philosophy of history (by impatiently brushing aside its distinctions and debates) and history itself (by dismissing the notion that the true causes of things are hidden or secret). But there are other matters at issue as

16. Willson Coates, Hayden White, and J. Salwyn Schapiro, *The Emergence of Liberal Humanism* (New York, 1966), 18.

well. The first is a matter of decorum, or "the appropriateness of style to content."[17] The epistemological and tropological tetrads of *Metahistory* are difficult for historians accustomed to the antijargon rule of traditional historiography; but the historical profession has of late welcomed both psychoanalytic and cliometric vocabularies and methods with relatively little struggle. "All this language stuff," however, is different. While econometric or psychoanalytic contributions to historical scholarship function exactly like other elements of the field, adding bits of insight or information to the ongoing process of amassing and digesting data, they do not make demands that have the universal scope of "deep" linguistic analysis as practiced by White. One can leave cliometrics or psychohistory to the specialists, since their research does not touch the bases of one's own work. Insofar as *Metahistory* is a work of intellectual history, containing interpretive readings of a set of nineteenth-century figures, the historians can respond normally, praising or condemning the various sections ("brilliant on Marx," "unfair to Burckhardt," or the reverse). But if the book is read as a "theory of the historical work," with nearly four hundred pages of illustrative material appended, then all are touched, including those who cannot identify Ranke or Croce. The anxiety of feeling oneself on trial in a court that, rather pointedly, uses a foreign language leads often enough to dismissal: "not historical."

Another matter of decorum derives from *Metahistory*'s choice of the largest issues involved in writing history—the "great" historians, the deep structure, emplotment. Most of what historians do is minute and rather tedious, as White is well aware. To find that the basic element of historical knowledge since Ranke is characterized as an "archival report" seems to suggest that whatever *Metahistory* is about, it is not about *what historians really do*. Furthermore, while historians have come to terms with "ideological skepticism" of the sort represented by psychological or sociological theory, "linguistic skepticism" is entirely another matter. Objectivity is not a fashionable term among historians today because of their sensitivity to the ideological implications of any position within a historical context. Once "value neutral" social science itself came under examination as a tool of domination, the universality of ideology came to be taken for granted. Yet this is not a disabling blow to historical writing; in fact, it has added to the feeling of security. Since ideological demystification of any given text or artifact is basic to both

17. Northrop Frye, *Anatomy of Criticism: Four Essays* (Princeton, 1957), 269.

A Bedrock of Order: Hayden White's Linguistic Humanism

marxist and nonmarxist practice today, and since the position of the scholar within society is also continuously scrutinized ideologically, the "ideological skepticism" really becomes a confrontation between two or more reasonably knowable positions. This dialectic is potentially unending (as suggested by the last chapter of Fredric Jameson's *Marxism and Form*), but it is secure in a (Newtonian) way that "linguistic skepticism" is not. In fact the loss of willed objectivity that followed the ideologizing of all thought and action offers the sense of a firmer grasp on a "reality," however complex and elusive that reality may be.

White addresses dialectics like the other surface elements of a text by subsuming it to language; any ideology that claims to represent some reality principle becomes epiphenomenal.

> In my view, it is no accident that the outstanding philosophers of history of the nineteenth century were, with the possible exception of Marx, quintessentially philosophers of language. Nor is it an accident that Hegel, Nietzsche, and Croce were all dialecticians. For, in my view, dialectic is nothing but a formalization of an insight into the tropological nature of all the forms of discourse which are not formally committed to the articulation of a world view within the confines of a single modality of linguistic usage— as the natural sciences became after their commitment to Metonymical usage in the seventeenth century. (428)

In White's view, history is a form of discourse without a "single modality of linguistic usage," as *Metahistory* fully demonstrates. He thus finds historical discourse inherently dialectical within its *possible* (four) fundamental modes of discourse. However, since language pulls the other levels of discourse into its own field—that is, since ideological forms may be resolved into linguistic forms, but linguistic forms are irreducible—dialectic between levels of discourse is impossible.

White has often maintained in his writings and especially in *Metahistory* that sciences are constituted by their vocabularies, and that history will remain at the level of a protoscience as long as it lacks such a vocabulary, a sort of "periodic table" of historical thought. What constitutes the bedrock vocabulary of scientific discourse is the *choice* of a common language by its practitioners. Despite the enthusiastic reception *Metahistory* has had among many historians, it seems doubtful whether tropology will become the periodic table of a new science of history (although a tropological science of language is quite conceivable). Historians mistrust language; to speak of it is disturbing.

It is tempting to reject this strain of criticism as old-fashioned, resistant to change, or just lazy, but that would be to miss an important point. Conservatives (as Eugene Genovese has shown of slaveholders) foresee the consequences of change more clearly than others because their "antennae" sense things before they can articulate them. This uneasiness before "the language thing" is a genuine fear of losing the heavy but comforting "burden of history" that has told us Westerners who we are for quite a while. Irenic readers, like Peter Munz, who cite *Metahistory* as an attempt to revive historical writing or to open the path to new ideas, fail to sense the issues as strongly as the troglodytes. Following a sort of tropological historicism that demonstrates the structural necessity for the existence of differing historical protocols and performances, White never challenges the bases of any significant past historical enterprise. He acknowledges both masterpiece and "archival report"; history is many things, but it is not bunk. However, his work is deeply subversive of professional historical endeavor in one important way—it replaces the traditional question, "Why write history?" with a very different question, "Why write?"

Historical events do not represent themselves, they are represented; they do not speak, they are spoken for. White asserts the freedom of the speaker, but leaves no basis for a responsibility to the subject (or, I should say, to the subject's voice, for it has none). This is a clash between one ethos and another; both see themselves as moral positions, and sources of hope. The ease (and credibility, at least to me) of White's subsumption of event and logic to writing and rhetoric and his quick glide over the vexed questions of traditional historical thought offend. They are indecorous.

Since history cannot begin with documents (the process is already well under way before a document is confronted), what is at the bottom of White's system? Where is its *beginning?* I have cited at the head of this section the epigraphs of both *Metahistory* and Edward W. Said's *Beginnings: Intention and Method*. To compare these two works, which both deal in their ways with how (or where) texts begin, is to note the point of obscurity, the mystery, of White's text. Said's book confronts the problem posed by post-structuralist thought and foreshadowed by Vico and Nietzsche: how can one make or identify a beginning within a discourse that is always already begun? His approach is to stress the act of will. *"The beginning, then, is the first step in the intentional production of meaning.*"[18] And, "beginnings inaugurate a deliberately other produc-

18. Edward W. Said, *Beginnings: Intention and Method* (New York, 1975), 5.

tion of meaning—a gentile (as opposed to a sacred) one."[19] White's theory, on the other hand, for all its emphasis on will and engagement, invokes an essentially sacred (that is, undialectical) source. His epigraph from Bachelard, cited at the beginning of this section, evokes "primary process" in the Freudian sense, but there are no corresponding gestures in *Metahistory* toward any psychoanalytic comprehension of the origin of the ethical or the moral. "A trope," as Disney's Cinderella might have put it, "is a wish your heart makes." But the refusal of a psychoanalytic dimension is, in my opinion, not merely a lack that can be remedied by simply referring to other tropologies that offer a dialectical dimension by relating tropes (if not precisely reducing them) to the processes of the dream-work. In other words, we cannot fill in the gaps of *Metahistory* by reading Jacques Lacan, or even Harold Bloom. To do so would make White's tropes "gentile" rather than "sacred," by *deferring* the origin to a set of processes from which the tropes may *differ* in order to establish the otherness of their status. This, I repeat, is what White has refused to do, not what he has neglected to do.

III

> *Geschrieben steht: "Im Anfang war das* Wort!"
> *Hier stock' ich schon! Wer helft mir weiter fort?*
> *Ich kann das Wort so hoch unmöglich schätzen,*
> *Ich muss es anders übersetzen,*
> *Wenn ich von Geiste recht erleuchtet bin.*
> *Geschrieben steht: Im Anfang war der* Sinn.
> *Bedenke wohl die erste Zeile,*
> *Dass deine Feder sich nicht übereile!*
> *Ist es der Sinn, der alles werkt und schafft?*
> *Es sollte stehn: In Anfang war die* Kraft!
> *Doch, auch indem ich dieses niederschreibe,*
> *Schon warnt mich was, dass ich dabei nicht bleibe.*
> *Mir hilft der Geist! Auf einmal seh ich Rat*
> *Und schreibe getrost: Im Anfang war die* Tat!

"In the beginning was the Word"—thus runs the text.
Who helps me on? Already I'm perplexed!
I cannot grant the word such sovereign merit,

19. Ibid., 12.

> I must translate it in a different way
> If I'm indeed illuminated by the Spirit.
> "In the beginning was the Sense." But stay!
> Reflect on this first sentence well and truly
> Lest the light pen be hurrying unduly!
> Is sense in fact all action's spur and source?
> It should read: "In the beginning was the Force!"
> Yet as I write it down, some warning sense
> Alerts me that it, too, will give offense.
> The spirit speaks! And lo, the way is freed,
> I calmly write: "In the beginning was the Deed!"
>   (I, 1224–1237)
>   Goethe, *Faust*, trans. Walter Arndt

One thing is certain: Faust knew his tropes. To trans-
late *logos* ("das heilige Original") into a natural language ("mein
geliebtes Deutsch"), Faust requires special aid ("Wer hilft mir . . .").
The fourfold articulation of the figures of thought displayed in this
famous passage culminates in the ironic solution that *die Tat* governs the
beginning, was always there. The exhaustion of the metaphoric
"word," of the metonymic "sense," and of the synecdochic "force"
reveals the constructed nature of any reality; consequently, no image of
a given, nonconstructed reality exists *in* which to act. Any possible
"background" of the "deed" *(die Tat)* is already a "deed," already
deeded, already owed to the *logos*.

But Faust does not stop with this momentous irony, the mention of
which brings forth physical metamorphoses in the poodle that has followed him to his study. To the fiery-eyed hippopotamus that arises
before him, Faust uses "the spell of the four" ("Spruch der Viere"); but
to no avail ("Keines der Viere / Steckt in dem Tiere"). With the ultimate
appearance of Mephistopheles, dressed as a "traveling scholar" ("Wie
ein fahrender Scholastikus"), we must infer that Faust's command of
troping, his unquestioned mastery of language protocols, has escaped
him, gotten out of hand. The irony *within* the system calls forth the irony
of the system itself; "the spell of the four" may exhaust the elements, but
not their interplay.

White preserves his figures of thought from dissolution into structures that claim to be deeper, but he also prevents the tropes themselves

from freely displaying their uncanny metamorphic power. In other words, *Metahistory* defends itself against both an external and an internal enemy. To identify tropology as the deep structure of historical writing, a depth whose foundations cannot be delved, is to confront the combined challenge of the fundamental determinisms of this century, psychoanalysis and Marxism. *Metahistory* permits the priority of neither class nor libido. "The best reasons for being a Marxist are moral ones, just as the best reasons for being a Liberal, Conservative, or Anarchist are moral ones" (284). By "best" here, White cannot mean morally preferable, or the statement becomes a tautology; he must mean "true" or "real," but as I have shown, "truth" and "reality" have already been unmasked as world choices, created and revealed through rhetoric. These well-intentioned "reasons" for being a Marxist are inherently anti-Marxist; and Marx turned his phrase of dismissal aptly in the *Manifesto:* "Bourgeois socialism attains adequate expression when, and only when, it becomes a mere figure of speech."[20]

Parallel to Marx's dismissal of trope ("a mere figure of speech") are the Freudian strategies of the dream-work, strategies that clearly reduce the "turnings" of tropes into primal workings of the Unconscious. Against Freud's claim to have unearthed a deeper irreducible "beginning," White unleashes Nietzsche, whose work as "historical psychologist" surpasses Freud's because it does not require a postulated "before."

> I say, "if not greater than Freud himself" because in his account of the origin of conscience in humanity, Nietzsche does not require, as Freud did in *Totem and Taboo*, the postulation of a generalized primal "crime" by which a socially conditioned experience such as the Oedipus complex is lived through by the entire species. He found the basis for the emergence of conscience is a purely aesthetic impulse in the strong and the similarly aesthetic response of the weak to this impulse, both of which were expressions of the single, shared will to power of the species. (365)

In Nietzsche, White finds a psychologist whose "depths" are always present in aesthetic, surface, impulse—no depths, in either the past or the mind, are needed here. The will to power is, after all, a will.

Thus, White has defended himself against the claims of the two con-

---

20. Karl Marx and Friedrich Engels, *Manifesto of the Communist Party*, in Karl Marx, *Political Writings, Vol. I: The Revolutions of 1848*, ed. David Fernbach (New York, 1973), 43.

tending powers in modern thought that confront structuralism: marxism and psychoanalysis. Each of the latter strategies names a "beginning"—the psychological unconscious, or the economic infrastructure.
One of structuralism's adaptive strengths has been its flexibility in
accommodating the requirements of psychoanalysis (by tropologizing
the dream-work) or of Marxism (as in the work of Goldmann or
Althusser). White's tropology is obviously not accommodationist. His
emphasis on *choice* (presented as both an aesthetic and a moral act) is
repeated unmistakably; despite his full awareness of the claims of Marx
and Freud, White persistently asserts human freedom. In this assertion, if I am not mistaken, an invisible presence, currently somewhat in
eclipse, appears. In Jean-Paul Sartre, White finds the element of choice
coexisting with necessity; he further finds an Ironic (absurdist) vision
that requires a continuously present choice of a future.

> Existentialism, Sartre argues, is essentially an analytical philoso-
> phy that disposes around the individual the various "possibles"
> open to him in his peculiar situation, enlivens the individual to
> the impossibility of not choosing, and then asks him to choose as
> if he were choosing for all mankind. The besetting sin of human-
> ity, or rather the one crime that the individual can commit against
> himself, is that of "bad faith," which is unwillingness to accept
> responsibility for his acts and ascription of this personal responsi-
> bility to something outside the self as the "cause" of its own
> servile condition.[21]

White's implicit use of the Sartrean "absurd" as his own privileged
vision derives from its emphasis on paradox, and its admission of "both
contingency and freedom within the same system."[22] The careful tack-
ing and yawing in White's use of tropes in *Metahistory* reveal his desire
to obscure this existential paradox and its absurdity; these are the costs
of his resolve to retain control of his linguistic weapons.

While historians may chafe at the excessive recognition of the power
of language in *Metahistory*—a recognition that threatens to dissolve
their basic categories and the entire syntagmic machinery that can be
built from them—the student of poetics may well sense quite the
reverse. For example, a very appreciative reviewer in *Comparative Liter-*

21. Willson Coates and Hayden White, *The Ordeal of Liberal Humanism* (New York,
1969), 370–71.
22. Ibid., 370.

ature notes the "procrustean" character of the tropological discussion; another critic has privately questioned the idea of a "dominant trope," suggesting instead that it is the nature of tropes to twist this way and that, changing kaleidoscopically. In short, if historians fear that White's move into the structural or "turning" depths of language draw him too far away from the intentional and extrinsic levels of his texts, critics may find his poetics too schematic. The consequences of this criticism are considerable; for, in suggesting that White has not gone far enough, or, in my own view, that he has drawn back from the consequences of his own work, this line of criticism delineates the path forward rather than backward from *Metahistory*. Since most of the historical citations of the book have been accommodative, using it either as a treatise on historiography or as a mere plea for free-form creativity in historical writing, it may be difficult to recognize just what "a new science" departing from *Metahistory* might look like. But we should try.

In the first place, one must come to terms with the power of tropes to spatialize time, and to temporalize space; in structuralist terms, tropes seem to collapse paradigm and syntagm into one another, leaving a deconstructive undecidability at the heart of things. In "Foucault Decoded: Notes from Underground," White notes that Foucault's characterization of modern cultural history (or archaeology of knowledge) makes each episteme the embodiment of a trope—the "classical episteme" is "dominated" by Metonymy and so forth.[23] Within each episteme the consequences of each trope's authorized strategy of order are worked out; and Foucault goes so far as to include in his schema ideas that were authorized by the trope, but which were never in fact produced, rather as Spengler maintained that Goethe's *Faust* would have existed without Goethe. Unlike Aristotelian "history," Foucault's "archaeology" includes "the kinds of things that might happen." But the course of these tropological strategies, for Foucault implicitly as for Vico explicitly, is strictly prescribed: Metaphor gives way to Metonymy, Metonymy to Synecdoche, and Synecdoche to Irony. Thus, the system gels into the very form that has given "speculative philosophy of history" a bad name in Anglo-American circles: a law of "stages." In *Metahistory* White backs away from this schematism but cannot escape it.

The theory of tropes provides a way of characterizing the dominant modes of historical thinking which took shape in Europe in

---

23. Hayden White, "Foucault Decoded: Notes from Underground," *History and Theory* 12 (1973), 23–54; reprinted in *Tropics of Discourse*.

> the nineteenth century. And, as a basis for a general theory of
> poetic language, it permits me to characterize the deep structure
> of the historical imagination of that period considered as a closed-
> cycle development. For each of the modes can be regarded as a
> phase, or moment, within a tradition of discourse which evolves
> from Metaphorical, through Metonymical and Synecdochic com-
> prehensions of the historical world, into an Ironic apprehension
> of the irreducible relativism of all knowledge. (38)

This passage seems designed to frustrate certain questions. What is
outside the "closed-cycle"? If the tropes are moments "within a tradition of discourse," what is the nature of such traditions? If Irony is the
fulfillment of the development, why is it not, for all its "apprehensions," the highest and final attainment, the end of history and of discourse? In short, how is it that tropes operate within such a safely
circumscribed set of parentheses? Hegel had described the course of
history, both Western and Oriental, as tropological stages (125–30);
Marx had done the same thing in his tropological analysis of the course
of economic history from Primitive Communism to the Ironic capitalism of his day. White, however, avoids the use of tropology as a philosophy of history in the speculative sense, despite all the open
indications in the text that such a use lies at the heart of his method.
White does not choose to recognize and exploit the available perception
that the "tradition of discourse" that *Metahistory* describes is dominated
by an *Over-Trope*, a trope that shapes and regulates the tropic differences and combats within it. It is a striking absence, striking because
its place is clearly framed by the adjoining "moments." White points
out that "the thought of the Enlightenment as a whole" is primarily "a
paradigm of historical consciousness in the mode of Metonymy, or of
cause-effect relationships" (66–67), which are served by the other tropes
in their various ways. He also notes that historical study since the end of
the nineteenth century, including his own, has been Ironic. *Metahistory,*
then, might well be subtitled "The Rise and Fall of Historicism in the
Age of Synecdoche." Instead, the tropes remain a "closed-cycle" functioning "within" a tradition; this definition tends to focus attention
away from the central historical issue of the book, which is "the crisis of
historicism into which historical thinking would be plunged by the
very success of nineteenth-century historiography" (270). The fundamental problem of nineteenth-century historians was to create a picture of the past that would be "realistic," to be sure; but it would be

realistic in a broadly Synecdochic sense, by seeing into the life of things through some form of what has come to be called *Verstehen*. Although Foucault, in White's readings, makes it clear that "the human sciences," as they developed in the nineteenth century, are Synecdochic in their fundamental strategies, White avoids more than a hint that the age he is describing might have an Over-Trope that would place it within a larger syntagm of historical tropic stages. Similarly, in part II of *Metahistory,* describing the work of four master historians, the chapter titles identify modes of *emplotment,* out of sequence but complete as a set of four. Part III identifies Marx, Nietzsche, and Croce by trope; the set is again out of sequence, but this time incomplete. Synecdoche is omitted, tempting the tropological reader to imagine a chapter between 9 and 10, perhaps titled "Dilthey: The Psychological Defense of History in the Synec-dochic Mode." But the philosopher of *Verstehen* and the Over-Trope of the century are missing; to have emphasized the importance of Synec-doche or of Historicism itself in any explicit form would have forced White to press the status of tropology farther than he wants to. White is willing to consider Synecdoche as the dream of Comedy, of which Michelet and Ranke are variations (190); but he has not gone forward to show how the specifically anti-Comedic historical visions of the Golden Age of History are regulated in their Tragic and Satirical realizations by Synecdoche-as-Over-Trope. By converting a trope (Synecdoche) into a mythos (Comedy), White has in effect eliminated the possibility that this figure may serve as a higher force. Of Tocqueville:

> The Comic conception of history, with its sanctioning Synec-dochic consciousness, he could not accept at all, because he did not inhabit a world of putatively reconciled social forces. The Comic vision was not even considered as a possible option by him, and, as his remarks on Fichte and Hegel suggest, to him it would have been immoral to foist such an idea of history onto an age as distracted as his own. (203)

This is a *reduction* of Synecdoche, a Metonymic rather than an Ironic awareness of the power of tropology. A more explicit example of confu-sion as to the level of trope being invoked is found in the Conclusion: "As thus envisaged, the history of nineteenth-century historical think-ing can be said to describe a full circle, from a rebellion against the Iron-ical historical vision of the late Enlightenment to the return to prominence of a similar Ironic vision on the eve of the twentieth cen-tury" (432). It is clear (at least to me) that these Ironic visions are in a basic sense not similar at all: the Irony of the twentieth century *is* the broad trope of the discourse itself, the Over-Trope, within which differing tropic visions may operate, including an Ironic moment within the Ironic discourse (which is, almost, *Metahistory*).

One can imagine a number of reasons why White might have avoided this neo-Vichian philosophy of history. The determinism of the system seems to contradict the sense of human freedom that I have suggested in the first section of this essay is White's primary goal in *Metahistory*. Further, the ingrained hostility of the professional historical community to such schemes would be a great hindrance to White's hope, described in the second section, to develop or at least suggest a vocabulary for historical thought that might eliminate the conceptual controversies of a protoscience. At the same time, it is clear that the very "dominance" of a dominant trope would be a seriously reductive force impeding anyone wishing to offer a fully figured image of the tropological possibilities of a given episteme; White's decision to play down (or forget, in Nietzsche's sense) the pressures of a dominant trope (Synecdoche), philosophy (historicism), psychology *(Verstehen)*, seems tactically justified—by an aesthetic and moral choice.

At a deeper level, White's ambivalence on the question of whether the tropes offer a set of "stages" of mind knowing itself through time (that is, as a diachronic syntagm related by contiguity) or a spatial "grid" of linguistic possibilities always already inherent in natural languages (a synchronic paradigm organized poetically) takes us back to a point made earlier. The traditional task of linguistic humanism since the Renaissance has been to transform a deadening scholastic logic into a rhetoric offering a freer and more vital form of thought. The theory of tropes offers White the means to do this. But the tropes may be construed Metaphorically, as the voice of Renaissance rhetoric, or Metonymically, as the logic (albeit a poetic logic) of an Enlightenment philosophy of history (albeit a Neapolitan Enlightenment). To avoid the danger that a logic of tropes would reconquer a rhetoric of tropes, White has carefully avoided the broad scheme of Foucault and the particular significance of Synecdoche, historicism, and *Verstehen*.

White's rhetorical use of tropes is complex and closely intertwined with the other elements of his quadruple tetrad. At certain points, for example, tropological and epistemological terms seem interchangeable. In the sentence "Marx's thought moved between Metonymical apprehensions of the severed condition of mankind in its social state and Synecdochic intimations of the unity he spied at the end of the whole historical process" (285), we may read Mechanistic for Metony-mic and Organicist for Synecdochic with little loss of meaning. Plot and trope seem confused at times, as when White writes, "Tocqueville began in an effort to sustain a specifically Tragic vision of history and then gradually subsided into an Ironic resignation . . ." (192). On the whole, however, White's tropological readings proceed by identifying a dominant trope in the thought of any writer or text, then demonstrating how the other, servile tropes order and marshal aspects of linguistic performance in order to form the structure of thought found in the writer or text. These aspects of language are the four levels of concep-tualization: lexical, grammatical, syntactic, and semantic. That these are analogues of the tropes is no surprise; they offer White another per-spective. For example, to say that Michelet's work is authorized by Met-aphor is to say that the lexical process of naming (creating new identifi-cations within the historical field) takes precedence over and exacts trib-ute from the grammar, syntax, and semantics of historical processes; the role of these latter aspects of language is to shape and carry along the mobile Metaphors that are predominant in Michelet's vision. Simi-larly, to say that Ranke repudiated romanticism (163) denotes his turn-ing away from a lexical treatment of language through his famous emphasis on documentary factuality; for Ranke, the proper role of the historian is that of the grammarian and syntactician. To place in the foreground either lexicographic or semantic aspects—that is, either the naming of elements or the extraction of meaning from the whole— would be to spoil the "reality effect" he wanted so hard to create. *Both* Michelet and Ranke, after all, ruined their eyesight in archives. In spite of this evidence that tropes may absorb and usurp the place of elements of argument, or of plot, or of linguistic structure, White maintains his scheme of levels as though it were stable; he presents his tropes as canny, structural, static. But they are not so easily controlled.

The passage from *Faust* that opens this section dramatizes the issue of Trope and Over-Trope; Goethe's position as a turning point, culminat-ing eighteen-century reflection on historical matters, and shaping the nineteenth-century pattern, is noted by Meinecke, whose classic *Histo-rism* ends with a 120-page chapter on Goethe, who wrote no history at all. "Without Goethe, we should not be what we are."[24] Meinecke's interest in Goethe derives from Goethe's resolution of the problem of

---

24. Friedrich Meinecke, *Historism: The Rise of a New Historical Outlook*, trans. J. E. Anderson (London, 1972), 373.

individual and universal. "His great idea was that of a creative divine nature, combining eternal being and eternal becoming, 'self-sufficient, living, creating from the highest to the lowest according to regular law,' disclosing itself in productive primal forms, types and individuals."[25]

This constitutes a Synecdochic Irony, the "no-fault" tropology, as found in *Faust*. Although the Irony of Mephistopheles ("Ich bin der Geist, der stets verneint!") handily manipulates Faust's Synecdochic striving, as well as the pedantic Metonymy of his assistant and the Metaphoric innocence of his beloved, this Irony within the world of discourse is not supreme. It serves a higher power, which is the system itself: the Synecdoche of the system is *Der Herr,* the Lord, who as Over-Trope makes a Comedy of the world. None can escape salvation, because all are part of a discourse in which each part is necessary to the whole, and cannot be lost. Thus even Mephistopheles is "Ein Teil von jener Kraft, / Die stets das Böse will und stets das Gute Schafft" ("Part of that force which would / Do ever evil, and does ever good" I, 1335–36).

That particular evil is a part of universal good is certainly a facet of the historicist vision. But Goethe's ability to fashion a tropological—that is, linguistically aware—picture of reality within the regulative discourse of Synecdoche demonstrates an awareness of the ability of *a moment within* the system to function as *the moment of* the system itself—as the Over-Trope. Goethe's tropological comprehension of the world is the Synecdochic, thus ultimately Comic, union of the One and the Many, the Universal and the Particular, the Tropology and the Tropes. The success of Goethe's answer to what Adrian Kuzminski has called "the paradox of historical knowledge"[26] makes him the capstone of Meinecke's *Historism.* White will not accept this in *Metahistory;* it would transform the rhetoric of choices within a discourse into a logical development of figural epistemes in history. Perhaps this represents for him the bad sort of cyclicality condemned in his essay on Ibn Khaldoun.

However, since White has suggested that Lévi-Strauss and his followers founder upon the dispersive "paradoxes" of their enabling postulates, by seeking a universal science of mind while asserting the uniqueness of all the forms of human meaning,[27] we might expect that he would follow the course of the *other* branch of the structuralist move-

25. Ibid., 493.
26. "The Paradox of Historical Knowledge," *History and Theory* 12 (1973).
27. Hayden White, "Foucault Decoded," 53; "The Absurdist Moment in Contemporary Literary Theory" *Contemporary Literature* 17 (1976), 397; both reprinted in *Tropics of Discourse.*

ment, whose integrative aim is to find the "structure of structures." White, I believe, has tried to avoid the dispersiveness of the former group; but he cannot do so and still accept the full implications of *his* structure of structures, at least not in *Metahistory*. So he ultimately sides with the "religionists of language" like Valla,[28] who today preach Mallarmé's gospel of the "Flesh made Word."[29] Yet by choosing to "forget" the dissolving force of trope (signaled as diabolical as early as the 1587 *Faust Book*), he refuses the fatalism of the modern idolators of the text. For him they have lost the true religion of language, which preaches freedom through human mastery. If language is irreducible, a "sacred" beginning, then human freedom is sacrificed. If men are free to choose their linguistic protocols, then some deeper, prior, force must be posited. White asserts as an existential paradox that men *are* free, and that language *is* irreducible.

IV

> *Consequently, "will to truth" does not mean "I will not allow myself to be deceived" but—there is no alternative—"I will not deceive, not even myself"; and with that we* stand on moral ground. *For you only have to ask yourself carefully, "Why do you not want to deceive?" especially if it should seem—and it does seem!—as if life aimed at semblance, meaning error, deception, simulation, delusion, selfdelusion, and when the great sweep of life has actually always shown itself to be on the side of the most unscrupulous* polytropoi. *Charitably interpreted, such a resolve might perhaps be a quixotism—a minor slightly mad enthusiasm; but it might also be something more serious, namely, a principle that is hostile to life and destructive. —"Will to truth"—that might be a concealed will to death.*
>
> Nietzsche, *The Gay Science*

Nietzsche, according to White, conceived of the historian as "the master of Metaphorical identifications of objects that

---

28. Coates, White, Schapiro, *Emergence of Liberal Humanism*, 19.
29. White, "Foucault Decoded," 53.

occupy the historical field" (353). I have identified Nietzsche and White metaphorically with a tradition of humanism represented by Lorenzo Valla and characterized by the reduction of logic to rhetoric. Nietzsche, who claimed that even the most primitive unarticulated utterance was already at least twice a metaphorical translation (from neurological perception to mental image, from mental image to neurological response), even before "the mobile army" of tropes could begin their campaigns, had, as we have seen, lectured on classical rhetoric at Basle; if Burckhardt's comment, "fundamentally of course you are always teaching history," is correct, we must conclude that history offered Nietzsche an escape from philology, once history itself had been liberated from the "prison" (or indenture, as White often puts it) that is language and the logic of signification. The fundament of logic, the principle of non-contradiction, is itself as completely subsumed by Nietzsche in metaphoric rhetoric as in human neurological response.

> The conceptual ban on contradictions proceeds from the belief that we *can* form concepts, that the concept not only designates [*bezeichnen*] the essence of a thing but comprehends it [*fassen*] . . . in fact, *logic* (like geometry and arithmetic) applies only to *fictitious truths* [*fingierte Wahrheiten*] *that we have created*. Logic is the attempt to *understand the actual world by means of a scheme of being posited* [*gesetzt*] *by ourselves, more correctly: to make it easier to formalize and compute* [*berechnen*].[30]

This passage suggests many things. Obviously, it states that logic is a tyrannical moment within the human power of rhetorical play. Designation must not take itself for comprehension, nor rhetoric for logic, since "comprehension" and "logic" are fictions. White notes that Nietzsche "held all 'truths' as perversions of the original aesthetic impulse, perversions insofar as they took the dream for the formless reality and tried to freeze life in the form provided by the dream" (332). Let us assume with White that neither the eternal recurrence nor the Dionysiac-Apollonian dualism is central to Nietzsche's task, but that this task begins with "a prior critique of historical knowledge." Valla and Vico had as their tasks the criticism of Aristotle, the New Testament, Homer—the privileged texts of their day. But Nietzsche, in White's view, aimed at *history* to save himself from "all forms of thinking that are not Metaphorical in nature" (337).

30. Nietzsche, cited in Paul de Man, "Action and Identity in Nietzsche," *Graphesis, Yale French Studies* 52 (1975), 17–18.

A Bedrock of Order: Hayden White's Linguistic Humanism

In his discussion of Nietzsche's attack on logic (and especially the principle of the noncontradiction of identities) as an adequate criterion of truth, Paul de Man turns Nietzsche's own strategy of tropological deconstruction back on its source.

> What has and will be shown, within the confines of this particular fragment, is the possibility of unwarranted substitutions leading to ontological claims based on misinterpreted systems of relationship (such as, for example, substituting identity for signification). The possibility of arousing such a suspicion suffices to put into question a postulate of logical adequacy which might well be based on a similar aberration. And since this aberration is not necessarily intentional but grounded in the structure of rhetorical tropes, it cannot be equated with a consciousness, nor proven to be right or wrong. It cannot be refuted, but we can be made aware of the rhetorical substratum and of a subsequent possibility of error that escapes our control.[31]

The relevance of this passage to *Metahistory* is clear enough. White, to be sure, is all too aware of his own position within language and points out unmistakably the "aberration" of his own Ironic vision, a vision that points out the misinterpretation ineluctably built into language. He cheerfully stresses that rational refutation is futile at all levels of analysis—that is, Romance is as valid a mythos as Tragedy *taken at the level of emplotment;* or, an Anarchic vision is as "realistic" as a Radical one, given one's ideological position in a social group. Irony, although "self-conscious" (or "sentimental" in Schiller's sense) compared with the other tropes, is not, for all that, superior to them, and in fact is seen as inherently debilitating, a trope to be overcome as quickly as possible. (Hegel is the model here.) However, the lack of a principle of disconfirmation, which is the price Irony pays for its enormous analytical strengths, leads us to the "substratum" of *Metahistory,* a substratum where much that is troubling lies forgotten.

That any tropology is basically Ironic, studying as it does the "turns" by which linguistic structures create meaning, is obvious; and the current interest in tropes is a clear indication of the Ironic stance of the structuralist/post-structuralist endeavor. However, it should also be noted that tropology's Ironic position within the system of hermeneutic engagements (epistemological, ideological, and the like) has itself been

31. Ibid., 20.

influenced (as *influenza* flows from the stars) by Over-Tropic hege-
monies. Renaissance rhetoric, for which the tropes are identifying categories used in *naming* the figures of speech and learning their uses,
plotted its field metaphorically, providing a tropological vocabulary
(rather too vast for later tropologies to exploit fully), but dominated by
the level of identification. Vico, by extending the figure of speech to the
status of a figure of thought, was able to use the system of tropes (carefully numbered at four) as cognitive categories through which the history of thought itself could be reduced to a series of stages that
constitute the foundation of the "new science." This dispersive, reductive, "scientific" tropology—which for all its power and depth ignores
the wholeness of the tropological system—is a Metonymic use of the
Ironic potential of the tropes. In the age of Goethe, implicit tropological
visions of the world of human meaning become fully aware that an individual trope and its claim to dominate a text or discourse are part of a
system itself, which is variable and which shapes the possibilities of any
tropological "choice" within it. This Synecdochic awareness of an
Over-Trope, however, stops short of a truly Ironic view of the Ironic
nature of tropologies. Although Goethe arrived at the consciousness of
one-in-manyness that Meinecke felt culminated in the rise of *Histo-
rismus*, the Synecdochic security of this view redeems *both* Faust and
every historical happening. The existence of the system within which
any meaning may be expressed is the justification of that meaning—this
is an Olympian, or Synecdochic, Irony.[32] But the security of trope

32. Meinecke notes in *Historism* (48): "Goethe was to be the first to acquire some deeper
understanding of the relationship between the type and the individual, that mysterious
problem of historical life that can never receive an entirely logical solution. The human
mind produces an abundance of recurring structures in state, society, religion, economics, and even in the human character; and these types partake of the essence of individuality to the extent that they, too, only reveal themselves through development. They
do not remain static, but are constantly changing, either advancing or decaying. A man
like Vico, who showed such power to break through the static thought based upon Natural Law and displayed such a deep and intensive grasp of the genesis, growth and decay
of a type, clearly also had the necessary background and capacities for understanding the
individual in history. Why did he never give his talents full play in this direction?" In my
opinion, it was because of the Metonymic Over-Trope of his episteme. Vico's tropological
rhetoric would "break through" the static logic based upon Natural Law, but the epistemological tenor of the age forced his rhetoric to become itself a logic. Thus, he could
handle types, their rise and decline, but his tropology, unlike Goethe's or Hegel's, was
Metonymic, truly a new *science*. Goethe's grasp of type and individual, found in *Faust*,
leads him to a comic Irony, a tropology above the tropes, found in the vision of *Der Herr*. In
this vision, evil is only a part of the whole which is good; there is no real division. "Alles
Vergängliche ist nur ein Gleichnis." Faust must be saved, because everything must be

comes under question only when its "turning" nature is asserted, when the structures emergent from an imaginary, stable tropology are dissolved by unnaming, releasing the original deconstructive fluidity of the figure of speech. In the essays of Jacques Derrida or Paul de Man, among others, reading is declared impossible, and writing too; the Mephistophelian *Geist, der stets verneint* is let loose with no back-up. This is the "absurdist moment."

The tendency of the syntagmic logic inherent in the four-trope system to swallow up other levels of analysis, which I have pointed out above, leads to an interesting unfolding of the quadruple tetrad. If we take tropology as the irreducible solvent, it becomes clear that the four levels of analysis are themselves tropological: Emplotment is a primarily Metaphoric process; Argument is inherently Metonymic; Ideology extracts coherent world-views in a Synecdochic manner; while Tropology is dissolutely Ironic. Furthermore, in extending this simple perception, we notice that each mode of explanation has privileged moments within it, related to its tropological analogue (see table 8.1). Thus

Table 8.1

Plot (mythos) (Metaphoric)	Argument (Metonymic)	Ideology (Synecdochic)	Tropology (Ironic)
Romance	Formist	Anarchist	Metaphor
Tragedy	*Mechanist*	Radical	Metonymy
Comedy	Organicist	*Conservative*	Synecdoche
Satire	Contextualist	Liberal	*Irony*

A different set of elective affinities emerges here, unsurprisingly. That emplotment is a fundamentally Romantic vision is the enabling premise of much of Northrop Frye's work. White alludes to the Metonymic mechanics of Argument, and the Ironic essence of troping. And Karl Mannheim places Ideology as the conservative opposition to Utopia. I do not mean this unfolding of the scheme to be a Metonymic elaboration of its logical potential; rather, I want to suggest one of a host of further "affinities" to be unpacked from within the workings of the scheme. The tropes can be "turned" onto each other within as well as

saved. In this Synecdochic tropology, even Mephistopheles (Irony) works for the Over-Trope, "The Lord," the Synecdoche.

from without the closed-cycle of the system, creating a poetics of nonfiction prose discourse as heady and unstable as any.

It is characteristic of White's safe tropology that his readings of texts are canny, secure in their extraction of meaning—these texts do not "differ" from themselves, in the sense, say, that Nietzsche's texts do in Paul de Man's readings. The single tension in the system is provided by the "elective affinities" (29) among the elements of the quadruple tetrad; violations of these affinities provide the individuality and complexity we expect from "classics." But who ordains these "elective affinities"? A hidden hand is at work here that seems to make the linguistic "level of engagement" as secure as the epistemological, aesthetic, and ethical. Perhaps this, White's sole (implicit) allusion to Goethe, is motivated by a Goethean impulse to save all from loss; for without the "elective" modifier, the "affinities" of tropology are indefinite, deconstructive, turning, uncanny. Derrida has put this with uncharacteristic clarity.

> This stratum of "founding" tropes, this layer of "first" elements of philosophy (let us suppose that scare-quotes are sufficient precaution here) cannot be subsumed. It will not allow itself to be subsumed by itself, by what it has itself produced, grown on its soil, or supported on its foundations. It is therefore self-eliminating every time one of its products (here the concept of metaphor) vainly attempts to include under its sway the whole of the field to which the product belongs. If we wanted to conceive and classify all the metaphorical possibilities of philosophy, there would always be at least one metaphor that would be excluded, or, to cut the argument short, the metaphor of metaphor.[33]

In the face of this abyss, in which the trope of trope has always escaped one's grasp, the electorate of affinities becomes clear: it is White's choice. His refusal of the "absurdist moment" lurking within his system, asking questions whose answers seem unimaginable, is a voluntarist rhetoric restraining a deconstructive antilogic.[34]

To write good history is a moral act because, as Kant wrote, to choose a past by constituting an image of it is to choose a future, to describe a model of how men ought to live, and to invoke an active sense of will. Good history is thus apocalyptic, an implicit vision of a world of desire,

---

33. Jacques Derrida, "White Mythology: Metaphor in the Text of Philosophy" ["La Mythologie blanche"], trans. F. C. Moore, *New Literary History* 6 (1974), 18.

34. Hayden White, "The Absurdist Moment," 403.

a release from "burdens." Following Plato, Richard Weaver has noted that "one's interest in rhetoric depends on how much poignancy one senses in existence."[35] White has identified *both* the myth of secure historical signification and the myth of "absurdist" deconstruction as elitist products of Western cultural and social life—that is, of a tradition that must be redefined, and thus rechosen. *Metahistory*, it seems to me, is his redefinition and rechoosing.

The paths from *Metahistory* will be quite divergent: on the one hand, the more canny historians will naturalize the elements of the quadruple tetrad, and incorporate them without difficulty into the tradition of professional discourse; on the other, the deconstructors will trope the turns and turn the tropes, unfolding their texts until they have arrived at their nondestination. What will *not* happen is a close approximation of White's own way. Its background, choices, and tradition are shaped by a constellation of influences that are unique. We may use the superb readings found in *Metahistory*, but to try to follow its method would be futile. It is the *possibility* of that method, of a "new science," that follows from the book. The existential center of *Metahistory*, however, the stress on human freedom *quand même, "sous rature,"* will be much harder to retain; I suspect that it cannot be "naturalized" by the discourse of historical studies in the late twentieth century. And if it cannot, the message of *Metahistory* will be lost, despite any flowering of tropological sophistication.

V

Socrates: *Rhetoric is the same case as medicine,*
don't you think?
Phaedrus: *How so?*
Socrates: *In both cases there is a nature that we have to*
determine, the nature of body in the one, and of soul in the
other, if we mean to be scientific and not merely content with
mere empirical routine when we apply medicine and diet to
induce health and strength, or words and rules of conduct to
implant such convictions and virtues as we desire.
Phaedrus: *You are probably right, Socrates.*
Plato, *Phaedrus*

35. Richard Weaver, *The Ethics of Rhetoric* (New York, 1954), 23.

It has been the single basic contention of this chapter that *Metahistory* represents an aggressive move to turn historical thought from a logical to a rhetorical form, and a defensive entrenchment against any countermovement from rhetoric to logic. The reasons for this move from logic to rhetoric are moral ones, stemming from a long tradition of linguistic humanism that stresses the ethical dimensions of rhetoric, and buttressed by an unspoken existentialist consciousness of human absurdity and the need to affirm choice against psychological and sociopolitical determinisms. A good deal of the evidence I have used to define these intellectual traditions has been drawn from Hayden White's early work, which shows a continuity with his writing of the 1970s *only* if seen, first, as a broadly based inquiry into the ways in which traditions gain assent and, second, as an ongoing study of human choice as the basis of both historical existence and historical writing.

Metahistory begins by denying the cogency of almost all of the basic distinctions, terms, and problems of "the philosophy of history" since the Second World War: these problems seem "trivial" and "essentially contested" to White, since their basis is a logical separation of "explanation" and "telling," however these two factors are weighed. By refusing this distinction in order to assert that the "telling" *is* the "explanation" (rather than its vehicle), White sets the stage for a rhetoric of historical writing—indeed, for writing of any sort. This rhetoric of historical writing in its deep structure is based upon Vico's tropology, but unlike Vico (and Foucault, and many others implicitly), White uses the "master tropes" synchronically (as a rhetoric) rather than diachronically (as a tropo-logic). Evidence of this defensiveness is apparent at many points of *Metahistory,* most notably in its refusal to place the entire period of its subject within the episteme (or Over-Trope, as I have called it) of Synecdoche. This omission, and the defense it reveals, is part of a willed "forgetting" of the sort that Nietzsche prescribes as necessary for any history that will not be another burden to humanity. By declaring the tropic structures irreducible to mind or society, and by denying that tropology entails a logic as well as a rhetoric, White has assumed his consistent, if absurd, stance. *Metahistory* is a moral text that can authorize itself only by declaring the freedom of moral choice in the face of the great determinisms of our times. In this final sense, White further resembles Lorenzo Valla, whom I have selected as the type of "philologist as moral reformer." Valla's assertion in his *Dialogue on Free Will*

A Bedrock of Order: Hayden White's Linguistic Humanism

that God's foreknowledge (the great determinism of his time) does not preclude human freedom foreshadows White's Ironic stress on choice.

At the beginning of this chapter I noted that *Metahistory* "places" any commentary on it, so that that commentary cannot attain an independent status, being already present within the master-text. I suspect that my position, although I have ignored it, is that of Metaphoric Ironist—Metaphoric, because I have placed *Metahistory* as one moment in a chain of recurring moments of liberation, reaffirming human freedom by pointing to the creative force of language; Ironic, because the rules of discourse in this century place any such affirmation "under erasure." To pose the issue of freedom is "to write [the] word, then cross it out, then print both word and deletion."[36] It is this willed Nietzschean "forgetting" that gives *Metahistory* its power. Within the tradition of linguistic humanism, the ethics of rhetoric emerge as the basis of philological moral reform. White's choice of tropology as a "bedrock of order" rather than *mise en abîme* is his own elective affinity. It will be interesting to see who will follow him in this, and how they will manage to do so.

36. Gayatri Chakravorty Spivak, "Translator's Preface" to Derrida, *Of Grammatology* (Baltimore and London, 1976), xiv.

9

THE INFLATABLE TROPE AS

NARRATIVE THEORY

STRUCTURE OR ALLEGORY?

From all this it follows that all the tropes (and they are all reducible to the four types above discussed), which have hitherto been considered ingenious inventions of writers, were necessary modes of expression of all the first poetic nations, and had originally their full native propriety. But these expressions of the first nations later became figurative when, with the further development of the human mind, words were invented which signified abstract forms or genera comprising their species or relating parts with their wholes. And here begins the overthrow of two common errors of the grammarians: that prose speech came first and afterward speech in verse.
Giambattista Vico, *The New Science of Giambattista Vico*

Language contains its own inner principle of proliferation.
Michel Foucault, *The Order of Things: An Archaeology of the Human Sciences*

As language has ascended into prominence well beyond literary studies, elevated in part by the broadly structuralist mood of the times, the various needs of different kinds of critics discussing different kinds of texts have put considerable pressure upon literary theory to provide some sort of "philosopher's stone," some key to the mystery of texts. The well-known problem of linguistic theories of prose narrative has been, and continues to be, the absence of any definitive link between the surface structures of sentences (or any other small segment of a text) and the deep or total structure of a work, including the structure of thought behind the work. The traditional strengths of literary and linguistic theorists have been in analysis of small, detailed matters; the thoroughness and elegance with which critics have discussed lyric poems have been envied by historians who regretted that such effective ordering and naming of parts and wholes could not be put to use with the work of Hobbes or Marx, or with the larger image of an "age," however defined. Without the critical tools of poetics, the historian is limited to the rather elementary and sterile figure periphrasis. Once the general strategy of "textualization" became fashionable, however, permitting the use of at least some linguistic tactics in the examination of virtually all meaningful cultural forms, the pressure to discover a "missing link" (which I take to be more like a philosopher's stone) has been intense. Paul Ricoeur has pointed out that the decision to look upon "meaningful action as a text" necessarily involves attention to the preconditions of meaning. "As the model of text-interpretation shows, understanding has nothing to do with an *immediate* grasping of a foreign psychic life or with an *emotional* identification with a mental intention. Understanding is entirely *mediated* by the whole of explanatory procedures which precede it and accompany it."[1]

Any synoptic view of current narrative theory must consider the surprising imperialism of rhetoric as the source of concepts that claim to dissolve and explain a wide variety of problems that have long been discussed in different terms. Tropes in particular have become a kind of *lingua franca* bridging linguistics, rhetoric, poetics, philosophy, criticism, and intellectual history; the descriptive power of tropes has extended itself into an explanatory power, and the solvent capability of these dual processes—description and explanation—seems to offer virtually limitless possibilities of analytical power in many different directions. To an extent, tropology has become the philosopher's stone sought by some critics and cultural historians influenced by structuralism. The attractions of tropology to these scholars are its transformational powers: the various and compound metals making up anything capable of being textualized (and there is little that is not) are transmuted tropologically into a form that is itself magical in its exchange value. It is not surprising that the influx of this new gold into critical discourse has been inflationary, a cause of both rapid expansion in the critical economy and the impoverishment of certain sectors of that

---

1. Paul Ricoeur, "The Model of the Text: Meaningful Action Considered as a Text," *New Literary History* 5:1 (1973), 116.

economy. The nature of the widespread inflation of tropological strategies is the subject of this chapter, which will focus primarily on the revival of one particular tropology—the four-trope series of renaissance rhetoric: metaphor, metonymy, synecdoche, and irony.

Gérard Genette has noted that the progressive reduction of rhetoric to tropology has resulted in an inflation of metaphor, an inflation that he finds debilitating to the many-sidedness of the rhetorical tradition. The narrative and elocutionary aspects of rhetoric have been subordinated in the work of the neo-rhetoricians of the 1970s to the inventive, which is itself reduced to a *figuratique*, a restricted sense of tropes.[2] This tropology is further shrunken to the metaphor/metonymy binary in the work of most structuralists, while both of these tropes are reduced in their turn to expressions of similitude or contiguity, following Jakobson's model. Finally, metaphor subsumes metonymy in the "last reductive moment" cited by Genette, to become, alone, "the trope of tropes," or the "figure of figures."[3]

This inflation of metaphor to the status of the trope of tropes is the symptom of a widespread desire to identify a dominant or germinal trope. Decio Pignatari has suggested that the traditional philosophic elevation of association by contiguity over association by resemblance is illusory, and that this "logical illusion" or "contiguity illusion," as found, for example, in the work of Hume or Peirce, has infected modern semiotics as a logocentric repression of the metasignic or intersemiotic aspect of any "translation from code to code."[4] Thus, where Genette deplored a triumphantly imperialistic metaphor, Pignatari laments the "contiguity illusion" in which "contiguity is even smuggled into similarity."[5] Further in this vein is the contention in the *Rhétorique generale* of *le Groupe μ* that synecdoche (to be sure, a synecdoche much altered in its adaptation by the group's redistribution of the modes of rhetorical figurality) is primal, and that metaphor is a product of two combined synecdoches.[6] This position, in turn, has been attacked by Nicholas Ruwet, again to defend the position of metaphor as the "fundamental trope."[7]

The claims of irony, the remaining member of the "four master

2. Cf. Groupe μ, *Rhétorique generale* (Paris, 1970), and Groupe μ, "Miroirs rhétoriques: sept ans de réflexion," *Poétique* (Paris) 29 (1977), 1–19.
3. Gérard Genette, "La Rhétorique restreinte," in *Figures III* (Paris, 1972), 21–40.
4. Decio Pignatari, "The Contiguity Illusion," in *Sight, Sound and Sense*, ed. Thomas Sebeok (Bloomington, Ind., 1978), 89.
5. Ibid., 87.
6. Groupe μ, *Rhétorique generale*, 108.
7. Nicolas Ruwet, "Synecdoques et métonymies," *Poétique* (Paris) 27 (1975), 187.

tropes" of renaissance rhetoric, to the status of trope of tropes have been less frequently championed, perhaps because it sits awkwardly outside the binary metaphor/metonymy tropology of the Jakobsonian model that has become structuralist orthodoxy. Irony has, however, been so put forth in the work of Hayden White, who views it as the "sentimental" trope (or the self-conscious one, in Schiller's sense) as opposed to the "naive" tropes, metaphor, metonymy, and synecdoche.[8] Thus, in White's view, irony merely expresses the self-awareness of all figural deviations from literality (or, in the work of the post-structuralist writers, of the absence of the possibility of literality inherent in the deconstructive antihermeneutic)—these deviations are the essence of the "turn" of trope, and hence always bear an ironic form, whether self-consciously or not. Irony, then, is for White implicitly the trope not only of tropes, but of all of language.

These disputes over priority among the tropes may seem singularly unenlightening, but they point to an interesting aspect of the rhetorical problematic—its tendency to turn inward upon itself, to discuss rhetoric in rhetorical terms, to discuss tropology (or *figuratique*) in tropological or figural terms. This rhetorical problematic, "restricted" as it has become (to use Genette's term) to a battle among tropes and their champions, has also often degenerated into an antiquarian conflict of "authorities"—as though the precise citation and elucidation of what Aristotle, Quintilian, Du Marsais, or Fontainer had to say about any trope or figure would settle the matter at once. What has sometimes been overlooked is the precise function of any tropology for literary theory in general—what it may be good for, wherein a given system fails.

The recent tropological discourse has been resolutely loose-constructionist in at least four ways. First, the terms themselves are freely treated and defined, with more attention to the needs of the individual critic than to any sort of discursive consistency or to classical or renaissance authorities. Consequently, Friedrich Schlegel's injunction applies: "The best way not to be understood, or, rather, to be misunderstood, is to use words in their original meanings, especially words from the ancient languages."[9] Second, the numbering of the "master tropes"—from Jakobson's celebrated binary set, to Kenneth Burke's or

8. Hayden White, *Metahistory: The Historical Imagination in Nineteenth-Century Europe* (Baltimore and London, 1973), 36, 37.
9. Friedrich Schlegel, *Lucinde and the Fragments*, trans. Peter Firchow (Minneapolis, 1971), 163.

Tropology and Narrativity

Hayden White's use of the foursome of Vico, to Harold Bloom's freestyle addition to them of hyperbole (or litotes) and metalepsis, bringing the total to six tropes as revisionary ratios—has been treated rather freely, since there seems to be no accepted criterion for establishing what would be their correct number. Third, the purposes to which these various tropologies have been put are divergent, and certainly far from anything envisioned by the classical or renaissance rhetoricians; whether seen by Roman Jakobson as analogues of linguistic capacities revealed in aphasia or by Jacques Lacan as substitutions for Freudian defenses, the tropes have become modalities of mind, and the natural indicator of the workings of mind in language. Finally, the levels at which tropes function have been magnified (or, as I suggest in the title of this chapter, "inflated") in a number of ways beyond the chaste trope of Quintilian, so carefully distinguished even from "figure." Without entering too deeply into the debate about the number of master tropes, their "proper definitions," or the boundaries of their legitimate uses as hermeneutic devices, one notices that the fourfold tropology has generated a striking number of strategies of analysis, including self-analysis. This four-trope system, "conventional" since the renaissance, seems implicitly to authorize so many ways of ordering experience that it merits special attention.

One of the most striking and least examined aspects of the four-trope series—the "master tropes" of Vico and Kenneth Burke—is their inherent movement through a fixed course: from metaphor, and preliminary naming operations, to metonymy, the process of reductive manipulation and formalization, to the integrative, macrocosm/microcosm relationships of synecdoche, to the final awareness within the series that all of its processes have been relativizing turns, the whole process ironic. On this view, the tropes become "moments" of the tropology itself, which is seen less as a set of forms or categories than as a system, indeed *the* system, by which mind comes to grasp the world conceptually in language. The order in which the tropes present themselves in this system is strictly and logically entailed. That is, to speak of the "four master tropes" as a tropology necessarily invokes the sequence of the series, which thus represents a narrative curriculum with its own propulsive forces. Consequently, it is clear that the statement by the seventeenth-century rhetorician Vossius that the customary order of the tropes among the rhetoricians may be attributed to their frequency of appearance—with metaphor the most frequently used, and for this reason first, and irony the least often employed, and so listed last—is nonsense.[10] It is the precise order of the four-trope system that constitutes, in a suitably inflated form, the narrativity of mind that has been implicitly exploited often in the past, and is being examined increasingly today. A brief consideration of examples of the tropological narrative curriculum will indicate how it is used in its largest inflations.

We have already noted that Goethe, in the translation scene from *Faust*, thought his way through the notion of the *logos* by a stage-by-stage tropological rendering of the term. Goethe was also drawn to the four-stage philosophy of history of Gottfried Hermann, which he summarized in his brief essay "Geistesepochen" ("Epochs of the Human Spirit"), cited by Spengler. In "Epochs of the Human Spirit," Goethe elaborated on Hermann's theory that humanity had emerged from chaotic, formless, preverbal beginnings into a first age of poetry, myth, and imagination, followed by an age of theology, in which intellectual constructs and reason dominated. The third era is that of philosophy and enlightened intellect (*Verstand* replaces *Vernunft*), which gives way, in turn, to an age of prose, the dissolution into the everyday knowledge of the senses, and, characterized by intermixture and contradiction, the return in a degraded form of the chaos of the *Uranfänge*, the "primeval beginning."[11] It is certainly unlikely that the source of such a sketch of human history was a dispassionate meditation on the past, let alone an exhaustive compilation of the documentary record. The principles that directed Faust in the translation scene are at work here; it is the dynamic of the four-trope system.

According to Hayden White, the identifying mark of Karl Marx's conception of historical and economic process—indeed, of almost every process unfolding in time—is the use to which he put the same set of implicitly tropological processes employed by Faust.

> No matter what Marx undertook to analyze . . ., whether it was stages in the evolution of society, forms of value, or forms of socialism itself, he was inclined to break down the phenomenon under study into four categories or classes, corresponding to the tropes of Metaphor, Metonymy, Synecdoche, and Irony.[12]

Thus, Marx discusses four basic social forms in Western history: Primi-

10. Gérard-Jean Vossius, "Rhétorique de l'ironie," *Poétique* (Paris) 30 (1978), 497.

11. Goethe, "Geistes-Epochen nach Hermanns neuesten Mitteilungen (1817)," *Sämtliche Werke* Jubiläums-Ausgabe, vol. XXXVII (Stuttgart and Berlin, 1902–7), 102–5. The essay is discussed by Erich Heller in *The Disinherited Mind*, (New York, 1959), 91–93.

12. White, *Metahistory*, 317.

tive Communist, Slave, Feudal, and Capitalist. In this series he plots a complete cycle of consciousness corresponding to the changing modes of production. The Capitalist economic system, as the ironic culmination of the course of history fully grasped as a conceptual whole, represents the meaningful conclusion of history's self-narration. The social curriculum relates to the four "forms of value" outlined in the well-known first chapter of *Capital*.

The four basic forms of value identified by Marx are the Elementary, Total, Generalized, and Money. White has pointed out the tropological nature of the steps of analysis. The Elementary form of value is a simple metaphorical relation of whole/whole equivalences between any two particular commodities.

> In the elementary form, the value of commodity A is expressed in terms of only one other commodity. It does not matter what this other commodity may be, whether coal, or iron, or wheat, or what you will. Thus for any one commodity there are numerous elementary expressions of value, according as it is brought into the value relation with this or that or the other commodity. The number of possible expressions of value is restricted only by the number of kinds of commodities differing from the first.[13]

Similarly, the Total, or Extended, form of value is a metonymically conceived reduction, in which the value of any commodity is related to an extended system of relative equivalence, based upon ratios or "labour which is essentially the same as all other human labour." However, as these relationships are not integrated by any deeper principle, this form has the defect of dispersive part/part relationships. "Since the bodily form of each individual commodity has now become a particular form among countless other particular equivalent forms, we have nothing left but fragmentary equivalent forms, which are mutually exclusive."[14] The Generalized form, unlike the series of disparate relationships in the Total form, symbolizes the essence of value in the single commodity, the form of which is "the visible incarnation, the generalized social chrysalis form (temporary resting form) of all human labor." The relation of this "social chrysalis" to the economy for which it identifies value is that of microcosm/macrocosm, a synecdoche. Finally, with the emergence of Money, gold, as this form of value, the ironic

13. Karl Marx, *Capital*, vol. I, trans. Eden and Cedar Paul (London, 1962), 34.
14. Ibid., 36.

preconditions of capitalism arise; this, Marx says, "is a very queer thing," "the enigma," "the mystery," "manifestly absurd." "We are concerned only with a definite social relation between human beings, which in their eyes has here assumed a semblance of a relation between things" (45). It is this "semblance of a relation between things" that Marx wishes to unmask. As White puts it: "The second half of the first chapter of *Capital*, then, is an exercise in Irony, consisting as it does of the exposure of the purely fictional nature of all conceptions of the value of commodities which do not begin from the apprehension of the truth of the labor theory of value."[15] We should also note that Marx's grasp of the meaning of the course of economic history depends upon his own ironic position, a position that enables him to perceive the deceptiveness of each of the categories he describes. In short, this tropological reading of history is itself an ironic one.

The largest scope of narrative is found in metahistories, which unite in themselves a consideration of the past and a consideration of consideration of the past—that is, which self-consciously integrate the *gnostic* (or more specifically the diagnostic) with the *narrative* that descends from the same linguistic root. While the notion that the course of history has been fundamentally tropological has been the discovery of many thinkers implicitly (as White makes clear in *Metahistory*), the two most explicit and ambitious tropological metahistories have been those of Vico and Foucault, the one explicitly a rhetorical principle of narration, the other implicitly a telling conditioned by a tropologic.

Giambattista Vico, in his *On the Study Methods of Our Time* (1709),[16] sounded a note that seems to foreshadow Genette's lament about "restricted rhetoric." Vico wrote: "In our days, philosophical criticism alone is honored. The art of 'topics,' far from being given first place in the curriculum, is utterly disregarded."[17] In fact, however, Vico's own use of topics in *The New Science* (3d ed., 1744) is a tropology: "The first founders of humanity applied themselves to a sensory topics, by which they brought together those properties or qualities or relations of individuals and species which were, so to speak, concrete, and from these created their poetic genera."[18] This poetic logic informs the historical

---

15. White, *Metahistory*, 296.

16. Giambattista Vico, *On the Study Methods of Our Time*, trans. Elio Gianturco (Indianapolis, 1965).

17. Ibid., 14.

18. *The New Science of Giambattista Vico*, trans. T. G. Bergin and M. A. Fisch, 2d ed. (Ithaca, 1970), paragraph 495.

consciousness of all purely human events—that is, events that are not informed with revealed truth—and prescribes a pattern of recurrences directed in their courses and recourses by an analogy to the linguistic movement from metaphor, through metonymy and synecdoche, to irony and a re-beginning. Vico's admiration for this strictly human, if always deceived, knowledge shows through in his striking assertion that figurative noncomprehension seems truer, or at least by implication nobler, than metaphysical understanding.

> So that, as rational metaphysics teaches that men become all things by understanding them *(homo intelligendo fit omnia)*, this imaginative metaphysics shows that man becomes all things by not understanding them *(homo non intelligendo fit omnia)*; and perhaps the latter proposition is truer than the former, for when man understands he extends his mind and takes in the things, but when he does not understand he makes the things out of himself and becomes them by transforming himself into them.[19]

The essence of these "sensory topics" that constitute the "imaginative metaphysics" of pagan society is the course of the tropes. The primary informing process in *The New Science* is described by White as "the dialectic of the exchange between language on the one side and the reality it seeks to contain on the other."[20] The ages that Vico identifies—of Gods, of Heroes, and of Men—are not merely fanciful and arbitrary divisions of human history but the result of a narrative principle based upon the progressive course of linguistic protocols from metaphor, through metonymy, to synecdoche, all observed from an ironic point of view. In each of these periods, Vico casts the forms of society, language, law, reason, writing, and politics in tropological terms. For instance, the age of heroes is metonymically constituted by the fundamental division of the world into the higher and lower orders. The epic, which is based upon the recognition and development of the differences of the divinely sired heroes from ordinary men, and the laws, which are concerned primarily with the privileges of the nobility, are the cultural products of this reductive and divided world. To quote White: "And all this in accordance with the principle that the most vivid objects of experience, in this case the strongest and most terrifying men in the group,

19. Ibid., para. 405.
20. Hayden White, *Tropics of Discourse: Essays in Cultural Criticism* (Baltimore and London, 1978), 209.

are treated as the primitive data of consciousness to which all extrinsic apprehensions of human experience must be referred for determination of their significance."[21]

If Vico's poetic logic of the origins of nonsacred history seems remotely quaint to us, and appropriately characteristic of an age obsessed with categorization, he has a modern counterpart in Michel Foucault, whose work has implicitly followed the logic of tropology in tracing (or unearthing, to follow Foucault's preferred archaeological metaphor) the strata of Western thought. Foucault describes a sixteenth-century *episteme* caught in a web of similitudes and contraries, a metaphoric consciousness that finds in language a perfect, although obscure, match with the book of nature.

> In its raw, historical sixteenth-century being, language is not an arbitrary system; it has been set down in the world and becomes a part of it, both because things themselves hide and manifest their own enigma like a language and because words offer themselves to men as things to be deciphered. The great metaphor of the book that one opens, that one pores over and reads in order to know nature, is merely the reverse and visible side of another transference, and a much deeper one, which forces language to reside in the world, among the plants, the herbs, the stones, and the animals.[22]

The age of resemblances draws to a close when the critique of the senses, the work of Bacon and Descartes, brings about the metonymic apprehension of the order of things as a gridlike system of representative order.

> What makes the totality of the Classical *episteme* possible is primarily the relation to a knowledge of order. When dealing with the ordering of simple natures, one has recourse to a *mathesis*, of which the universal method is algebra. When dealing with the ordering of complex natures (representations in general, as they are given in experience), one has to constitute a *taxinomia*, and to do that one has to establish a system of signs.[23]

It is this system of signs that replaces the correspondence of language

21. Ibid., 211.
22. Michel Foucault, *The Order of Things: An Archaeology of the Human Sciences* (New York, 1970), 35.
23. Ibid., 72.

and nature found in the metaphoric stage of knowledge. In the nineteenth century, the system of signs that constitutes the linguistic form of the Classical episteme was demoted, to be replaced by organic forces that overrule the dispersive orderings of the gridded knowledge of the eighteenth century. No longer will plottable species, categories, or classes constitute the reality of things, but rather deeper, synecdochic processes—the *force* rather than the *mind*.

> Thus, European culture is inventing for itself a depth in which what matters is no longer identities, distinctive characters, permanent tables with all their possible paths and routes, but great hidden forces developed on the basis of their primitive and inaccessible nucleus, origin, causality, and history.[24]

Foucault's ironic status is brought forth in the series of "questions to which it is not possible to reply" that he poses at the end of *The Order of Things*. "Since man was constituted at a time when language was doomed to dispersion, will he not be dispersed when language retains its unity? And if that were true, would it not be an error—a profound error, since it would hide from us what should now be thought—to interpret our actual experience as an application of the forms of language to the human order?"[25] When Foucault suggests that the disappearance of man must accompany the concern with language of our own day, he seems to replicate Faust's conclusion that the *act* was always already there, before word, mind, or force—or, by implication, even actor. With this ironic sensibility to the implications of a tropological vision of Western thought, Foucault seals his book with the image of the erasure of man, whose conceptuality had been exhausted by the curriculum of tropic "grasping."

It is not surprising, then, that in his great *Bildungsroman, The Magic Mountain* (1924), the ironic Thomas Mann would cast the curriculum of his hero-pupil Hans Castorp as a tropological conceptualization, a seven-year self-grasping, concluding in a return from a world of illness and death, the tuberculosis sanitorium of the Berghof, to the world of alleged health and life, itself refashioned as the "universal feast of death" that was World War I. The first part of Hans Castorp's story consists of his naming and identifying the routine of the ill, by first relating it to life in the flat-land. His momentous identification of Clavdia Chau-

---

24. Foucault, *The Order of Things*, 251.
25. Ibid., 386.

chat with a childhood acquaintance, Pribislave Hippe, leads, in the section "Walpurgis-Nacht," to a metaphorical reenactment of the "return of the pencil," the long-prepared affair. The only souvenir of this love is the glass chest x-ray that Clavdia gives to Hans Castorp on her departure; this *portrait transparent* represents the collapse of metaphor into a reductive, scientific consciousness. The metonymic turn of Hans Castorp's *Bildung* emerges when the newcomer Naphta comes to confront the humanist Settembrini in their unforgettable contests for the young man's soul. These debates are presented as the inevitable result of a stimulus-response process inherent in the permanent and irreconcilable Settembrini/Naphta opposition; each plays upon his knowledge of the other, while the course of their discussion traces an exhaustive analytic. However, at a certain point, the end of the section *"Operationes Spirituales,"* these distinctions and counterdistinctions, so clear at first, begin to blur. "But there again were distinctions that tended to disappear in the process of definition."[26] This dead-end ("There were no limits to the subject—but they could not go on forever") leads directly to the great synecdochic section, "Snow," the microcosmic vision of the whole course of Hans Castorp's education. In this vision, while the hero's will battles to survive the narcosis of a blizzard, he sees integrated the meaning of his stay on the mountain.

> It is meet and proper, I hereby declare that I have a prescriptive right to lie here and dream these dreams. I have wandered lost with Settembrini and Naphta in high and mortal places. I know all of man. I know mankind's flesh and blood. I gave back to the ailing Clavdia Chauchat Pribislave Hippe's lead-pencil. But he who knows his body, life, knows death. And that is not all; it is, pedagogically speaking, only the beginning. One must have the other half of the story, the other side. For all interest in disease and death is only another expression of interest in life, as is proven by the humanistic faculty of medicine, that addresses life and its ails so politely in Latin, and is only a division of the great and pressing concern which, in all sympathy, I now name by its name: the human being, the delicate child of life, man, his state and standing in the universe.[27]

But the synecdochic grasp of the wholeness of things was momen-

26. Thomas Mann, *The Magic Mountain* (1924), trans. H. T. Lowe-Porter (New York, 1953), 468.
27. Ibid., 495.

tary: by dinner that night, the dream "was already fading from his mind." The irony of the last two hundred pages of *The Magic Mountain* begins with the death by disease of Hans Castorp's military cousin, Joachim ("Als Soldat und brav," in Mann's allusion to Goethe's Valentin), and ends with the most civilian of heroes disappearing on the battlefield. The return of Clavdia Chauchat to the mountain, but not alone, and the horrifying duel of Settembrini and Naphta (in which the latter, infuriated that Settembrini has fired his shot into the air, blows his own brains out) pointedly dismantle any possibility of a return to an earlier stage of consciousness. Hans Castorp is complete, tropologically, ready for death. "Farewell, honest Hans Castorp, farewell, Life's delicate child! Your tale is told. We have told it to the end, and it is neither short nor long, but hermetic." Hermetic—"magical," as well as "completely sealed."[28]

From all of the above, it is clear that if there is any coherence and validity to the progressively inflated use of tropes, either implicitly or explicitly, this coherence must somehow come from the system of tropes itself. The implicit tropologies found in a wide variety of Western thinkers and noted explicitly today by a number of critics point to a remarkable narrative process at work here. The tropes unfold upon themselves, projecting their paradigmatic dimension as a rhetorical system of categories onto a syntagmatic plane that represents their self-explanation. This tropological urge to "explain themselves" leads them conceptually through the stages corresponding to the levels of linguistic organization above the morpheme. The lexical process of creating conventional whole/whole correspondences that lend meaning to both the sounds and the concepts that are thereby joined is a metaphorical transfer. The reductive categorization of these words into "parts" of speech, categories governed by grammatical rules of combination that create cause-effect entailments (as, for example, a preposition entails an object), is a metonymic process. The rules of combination regulating these parts, inadequate in themselves to create any wholeness of meaning, are the rules of syntax, which serve as the synecdochic

---

28. "Eine hermetische Geschichte": ibid., 715. Mann's conclusion may suggest the meaninglessness of all that has gone before, but in Nietzsche's *Also sprach Zarathustra*, another tropologically ordered work, the "Fourth and Last Part" further serves to decentralize the parts that have gone before, and to frustrate any hope of grasping Zarathustra himself. His meetings with the "higher men" offer Zarathustra nothing but "parodies, misunderstandings, and fragments of himself." Cf. Gary Schapiro, "The Rhetoric of Nietzsche's Zarathustra," in *boundary 2* 8:2 (1980), 165–89.

integrative force lending to mechanical parts the organic status of sentences. Finally, the study of meaning itself, seen from above its elements, components, and rules of combination—the study of semantics—is the ironic level of language studies.

The basic levels of what I have called tropological inflation also present themselves as a tropological sequence. The trope itself, or figure of words in which a single word (or several, in some views) is substituted for another, is patently a metaphorical transference; to this extent, metaphor *is* the trope of tropes. At the first level of inflation, however, that of the figure of thought, a change of meaning and of form occurs on a larger scale than in the figure of words. The nature of this change of thought is a compressed logical syntagm (rather than the analogical paradigm produced by the figure of words), and is thus analytical rather than synthetic. To view this level of tropological inflation as metonymic is an inevitable consequence of the reductive appeal to logical, cause-effect contiguity made by the form of the figure of thought. Thus, while the content of the figure may be any one of the entire set, the nature of the inflation to a figure of thought is metonymic. The synecdochic inflation of trope is the symbol, which has in fact moved beyond the notion of figure in its proper sense, as figure has moved beyond that of trope. The symbol stands in a microcosm/macrocosm relationship to some aspect of its surroundings, and serves as a sort of syntactic regulator by which the elements (conceivable as mere elementary figures, or as lexical and grammatical units) are brought into a rule-governed, integrative comprehension. Paul de Man has noted: "The symbol is the product of the organic growth of form; in the world of the symbol, life and form are identical: [citing Coleridge] 'such as the life is, such is the form.' Its structure is that of the synecdoche, for the symbol is always part of the totality that it represents."[29]

At the next level, the use of a full tropology as a figurology of discourse—that is, as the key to a semantic structure of thought in a full text or even in the oeuvre of a writer—is the allegorical inflation of trope. When Hayden White, for example, identifies the dominant trope in the thought of Jakob Burckhardt as Irony, or suggests that Nietzsche wanted to "break the power of the will to consistency, which all forms of thinking that are not Metaphorical in nature impose upon man,"[30] he is identifying tropological figures of discourse, full semantic identifica-

29. Paul de Man, "The Rhetoric of Temporality," in *Interpretation: Theory and Practice,* ed. Charles Singleton (Baltimore, 1969), 176.
30. White, *Metahistory,* 337.

tions of texts and thinkers, ranging beyond the symbolic into a level that we must call allegorical. Allegory, "speaking otherwise than one seems to speak," identifies precisely the ironic inflation of tropology into the philosopher's stone alluded to at the beginning of this chapter. Just as metaphor appears to be the trope of tropes (as figures of words), metonymy the trope of figures of thought, and synecdoche the trope of symbol, so irony presents itself to us as the *trope of tropology,* the figure that authorizes the deployment of the narrative logic of tropes as the allegorical "telling" of a sequential set of "moments" of thought. As de Man has put it: "Allegory and irony are thus linked in their common discovery of a truly temporal predicament. They are also linked in their common de-mystification of an organic world postulated in a symbolic mode of analogical correspondence or in a mimetic mode of representation in which fiction and reality could coincide."[31]

We may formalize these suggestions about the tropological sequence of the inflation of tropology itself in the accompanying chart, which suggests the course of movement upward from the elementary "turn" of a single word to the largest figure of discourse, the hermeneutic turn of allegory (see table 9.1). These stages of inflation seem again like Faust's solutions to his problem of translation; we might put *das Wort, der Sinn, die Kraft,* and *die Tat* in a column of their own.

Table 9.1

Trope	Levels of Linguistic Order	Levels of Figural Inflation	Figure of Tropological Inflation
Metaphor	Lexical	Figure of word	Trope
Metonymy	Grammatical	Figure of thought	Figure
Synecdoche	Syntactic	Figure of comprehension	Symbol
Irony	Semantic	Figure of discourse (tropology)	Allegory

At the same time, these figures of tropological inflation are a neo-Kantian expression of the stages of comprehension. I say "neo-Kantian" because it seems clear to me that the use of a renaissance fourfold tropology corresponds in essential respects to the Principles of Pure Understanding (*Grundsätze des reinen Verstandes*) that lie at the heart of the *Critique of Pure Reason:* (1) Axioms of Intuition; (2) Anticipations of

31. De Man, "Rhetoric of Temporality," 203–4.

Perception; (3) Analogies of Experience; and (4) Postulates of Empirical Thought in General.

The "Axioms of Intuition" establish the "extensive magnitude" of appearances—in other words, the thinghood of things. When an appearance is apprehended (and not the *representation* of an appearance, which is the material of the "Analogies of Experience"), the existence of a wholeness must be intuited, metaphorically, from "the manifold and homogeneous." Unlike the "Analogies of Experience," the "Axioms of Intuition" pertain directly to appearances and not to their already mediated mental forms; both principles, however, involve the process of a "synthetic" unification that integrates, respectively, appearances and representations of appearances.

Defining the "Anticipations of Perception," Kant describes the principle that enables the understanding to distinguish *parts* within the intuited *wholes* of experience. "In all appearances, the real that is an object of sensation has intensive magnitude, that is, a degree."[32] Since the continuum between reality and negation consists of "possible smaller perceptions," it is the "Anticipations of Perception" that permit the understanding to establish *a priori* the existence of parts, if only in the sense of degree within continuity.

> Consequently, though all sensations as such are given only *a posteriori*, their property of possessing a degree can be known *a priori*. It is remarkable that of magnitudes in general we can know *a priori* only a single quality, namely that of continuity, and that in all quality (the real in appearances) we can know *a priori* nothing save [in regard to] their intensive quantity, namely that they have degree. Everything else has to be left to experience.[33]

Realities, in short, always have perceivable degrees; to understand this is to constitute the existence of parts, which in turn make possible the reductions and ratios, the analyses and distinctions, characteristic of metonymy in general.

Kant defines the principle of the Analogies of Experience as "the representation of a necessary connection of perceptions." "Representation" is the precise word used by Kenneth Burke to describe synecdoche, and when Kant later writes of a "synthetic unity" necessary for

32. Immanuel Kant, *The Critique of Pure Reason*, trans. Norman Kemp Smith (New York, 1965), 201.
33. Ibid., 208.

the experience of objects of the senses, the synecdochic nature of the analogies becomes clear. Similarly, the Postulates of Empirical Thought in General (which correspond to the Category of "Modality") establish the possibility, actuality, and necessity of an object of knowledge, and conform to that dialectical view of irony shared by Burke and White. Kant notes that the question here is "only how the object, together with all its determinations, is related to the understanding and its empirical employment, to empirical judgment, and to reason in its application to experience."[34] In other words, the Kantian Postulates guard against the possible misuse of the understanding in the same way that, according to White, irony is "deployed in the self-conscious awareness of the possible misuse of figurative language."[35]

Kant's arrangement of his Principles suggests a few further points about the narrativity of the four-trope system, which I should like to develop here. In the first place, Kant positions the Principles on his page in a peculiar and unexplained form (see Figure 9.1).

1
Axioms of
Intuition

2
Anticipations
of Perception

3
Analogies
of Experience

4
Postulates
of Empirical Thought in General

Figure 9.1

To note that this arrangement follows and is clearly dictated by the earlier arrangement of the Table of Categories only defers the question. Kant's Categories (I. Of Quantity; II. Of Quality; III. Of Relation; IV. Of Modality) are "an exhaustive inventory" of the powers of the understanding. But he himself further defers the question of their arrangement.

> For that this table [of Categories] is extremely useful in the theoretical part of philosophy, and indeed is indispensable as supplying the complete plan of a whole science, so far as that science rests on *a priori* concepts, and as dividing it systematically

34. Ibid., 239.
35. White, *Metahistory*, 37.

according to determinate principles, is already evident from the fact that the table contains all the elementary concepts of the understanding in their completeness, nay, even the form of a system of them in the human understanding, and accordingly illustrates all the *momenta* of a projective speculative science, and even their *order,* as I have elsewhere shown.[36]

This "elsewhere" is the "Introduction" to the *Metaphysical Foundations of Natural Science,* at which level Kant notes that the "concept" *(Begriff)* of matter had to be carried out through all the four functions of the concepts of understanding (in four chapters), in each of which a new determination of matter was added.[37] At this point, however, Kant typically displaces the whole business once again into yet another tetrad—*Phoronomie, Dynamik, Mechanik,* and *Phänomenologie.* And so forth.

Kant's diagram (Figure 9.1) is not a list, nor a row, nor a (baseball-style) diamond. This arrangement is a displacement of the Table of Categories, itself a displacement of the four parts of the "Logical Function of the Understanding in Judgments" *(Von der logischen Funktion des Verstandes in Urteilen);* let us displace it with four tropes (see Figure 9.2).

1
Metaphor

2   3
Metonymy   Synecdoche

4
Irony

Figure 9.2

In this form we notice that there is a vertical axis of whole/whole relationships (positive in the case of Metaphor, negative in the case of Irony) and a horizontal axis of part/whole relationships. Further, the tropes in the odd-numbered positions, metaphor and synecdoche, are clearly *integrative* in their operations, while the even-numbered metonymy and irony are equally *dispersive* of the field they strive to command. (I avoid using the obvious terms "synthetic" and "analytic" here, because the special Kantian usage of them elsewhere might lead to confusion.) Kant alludes to this matter much later in the first *Critique,*

36. Kant, *Critique of Pure Reason,* 15–16.
37. Immanuel Kant, *Metaphysical Foundations of Natural Science,* trans. James Ellington (Indianapolis, 1970), 13.

when, speaking of the "Regulative Employment of the Ideas," he writes, "Thus, one thinker may be more particularly interested in *manifoldness* (in accordance with the principle of specification), another thinker in *unity* (in accordance with the principle of aggregation). Each believes that his judgment has been arrived at through insight into the object, whereas it really rests entirely on the greater or lesser attachment to one of the two principles."[38]

Kant adds to his Principles another distinction. The first two moments of the understanding, the Axioms and Anticipations, Kant designates as *constitutive*, while the latter components, the Analogies and Postulates, he calls *regulative*. This distinction provides a remarkable clue to the tropologist. Constitutive principles deal with the *objects* of intuition, whether empirical or pure; regulative principles deal with the existence of the objects as they relate either to each other or to the understanding itself. Kant's description of the "Analogies of Experience" clarifies the distinction.

> An analogy of experience is, therefore, only a rule according to which a unity of experience may arise from perception. It does not tell us how mere perception or empirical intuition in general itself comes about. It is not a principle *constitutive* of the objects, that is, of the appearances, but only regulative. The same can be asserted of the postulates of empirical thought in general, which concern the synthesis of mere intuition (that is, of the form of appearance), of perception (that is, of the matter of perception), and of experience (that is, of the relation of these perceptions). They are merely regulative principles, and are distinguished from the mathematical, which are constitutive, not indeed in certainty—both have certainty *a priori*—but in the nature of their evidence, that is, as regards the character of the intuitive (and consequently of the demonstrative) factors peculiar to the latter.[39]

In other words, this distinction, which Kant elsewhere states "must have some ground in the nature of the understanding," sets apart two separate binary paradigms. The constitutive pair, corresponding to the "Axioms of Intuition" and the "Anticipations of Perception," is the *structuralist binary* of metaphor and metonymy; the regulative pair, which displaces the "Analogies of Experience" and "Postulates of Empirical Thought in General," are synecdoche and irony, the *romantic binary*. For

38. Kant, *Critique of Pure Reason*, 537; emphasis in original.
39. Ibid., 211.

if we conceive of Symbol and Allegory as tropological inflations of synecdoche and irony, as I have suggested above, then the passionate concern of the romantics with these forms may be viewed as a tropology in
its own right, just as genuine—and just as incomplete—as the structuralist binary.

The definitions and relationship between metonymy and synecdoche
are problematic; in general, both are recognized as particular forms of
part-whole relationships. Although Roman Jakobson's essay "Parts and
Wholes in Language" makes no mention of tropes, noting instead the
"rich scales of tensions between wholes and parts . . . involved in the
constitution of language,"[40] his work has done the most to suppress
that tension by forcibly subsuming a certain idea of synecdoche to a
certain idea of metonymy in his "Two Aspects of Language and Two
Types of Aphasic Disturbances."[41] Jakobson's metaphor/metonymy
binary is displaced in that essay by similarity/contiguity, alternation/
alignment, and so on, while his binary tropology itself is a displacement of "two basic types of aphasia." That these two basic types, the
well-known "similarity disorder" and "contiguity disorder," are not, in
Jakobson's words, "the classical distinction (not discussed in this paper)
between EMISSIVE and RECEPTIVE aphasia" reveals a repressive displacement typical of his procedure. Although the point of Jakobson's
bipolar system is ostensibly its analogy to the processes of mind, and
although a good deal of its relentless prestige rests upon its scientific
basis and the scientific claims made for it by its practitioners, Jakobson's
own stated standard is "suggestiveness," a term that seems to mean
subject to an indefinitely large number of displacements. Clearly the
suggestiveness of the structuralist binary is enormous, and my discussion of the Kantian Principles owes much to it; but it can go only half-
way toward the grasping of a concept.

What I have called the *romantic* binary, that is, the familiar Symbol/
Allegory opposition construed as versions of synecdoche and irony, is
the regulative complement to the constitutive *structuralist* pair, metaphor and metonymy (see Figure 9.3). The extensive discussion of
symbol and allegory (and the definite rejection of the latter) by the
romantics amounts to a tropological literature needing exploration.[42]

40. Roman Jakobson, "Parts and Wholes in Language," in *Parts and Wholes*, ed. Daniel
Lerner (New York, 1963), 162.

41. In Roman Jakobson and Morris Halle, *Fundamentals of Language* (The Hague, 1956).

42. It is no surprise that our own century, tired of symbolisms, tends to champion allegory; *vide* theorists from Walter Benjamin to Paul de Man.

Again it is Goethe who initiates the debate in his essay of 1797, "On the Subjects of the Plastic Arts."[43] Because Goethe is discussing the *subjects* of artistic representation in relation to the kinds of feeling proper to them, his considerations address regulative, rather than constitutive, issues. Like Kant's "Analogy of Experience," which generates unity from perception, Goethe's *symbol*, caused by "deep feeling," also brings manifold perceptions into a signifying, universal ideality. "Subjects represented in this way only seem to stand naked by themselves but are freshly and deeply significant on account of the ideal, which always carries universality with it."[44] Finally, in his characterization of allegorical forms, Goethe notes that "they destroy the interest in the representation itself and drive the spirit back into itself, so to speak, and remove the eyes from what is actually represented."[45] Certainly, for Kant the function of the "Postulates of Empirical Thought in General," which, as we have seen, must attempt to synthesize intuition, perception, and experience, can only be to reveal the artificiality of the work of experience in relating perceptions, an ironic operation. Removing the eyes from what is repre- sented in order to perceive the mode of representation is getting the story crooked, as it were, using the visual metaphor of understanding to underscore its own artifice. Jeffrey Mehlman has pointed out that the word "theory" not only has the familiar meaning of a mental scheme of something, but also signifies a solemn procession sent forth on a religious rite.[46] The procession (or "going forward") above is thus a the- ory, with the tropes serving as *theors*, ambassadors or go-betweens.

Although Kant, like Hobbes and Locke, shows himself to be rou- tinely suspicious of the use of tropes and figures by philosophers in his discussion of the epistemology of rhetoric in *The Critique of Judgment*,[47] his principles in the first *Critique* offer an implicit tropology of understanding.

> Granted, then, that we must advance beyond a given concept in
> order to compare it synthetically with another, a third something

---

43. A translation of this essay is found in an appendix to Hazard Adams, *Philosophy of the Literary Symbolic* (Tallahassee, 1983), 395–97. My citations are from Adams' translation.

44. Ibid., 396.

45. Ibid., 397.

46. Jeffrey Mehlman, *Revolution and Repetition: Marx/Hugo/Balzac* (Berkeley, 1977), 84. Mehlman cites the Robert *Dictionnaire:* the *OED* is more informative on "theory" and "theor."

47. See Paul de Man's discussion in "The Epistemology of Metaphor," *Critical Inquiry,* 5:1 (1978), 13–30.

The Inflatable Trope as Narrative Theory: Structure or Allegory?

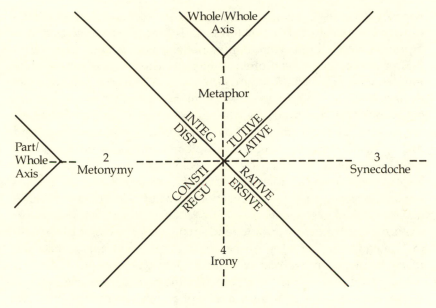

Figure 9.3

is necessary, as that wherein alone the synthesis of two concepts can be achieved. What, then, is this third something that is to be the medium of all synthetic judgments? There is only one whole in which all our representations are contained, namely, inner sense and its *a priori* form, time.[48]

This "third something" that makes experience possible is analogous to the "mediator" cited by Ricoeur; and time, which Kant calls "nothing but the form of inner sense, that is, of our intuition of ourselves and of our inner state," is also Thomas Mann's theme in *The Magic Mountain*: "Can one tell—that is to say, narrate—time, time itself, as such, for its own sake [*an und für sich*]? That would surely be an absurd undertaking." Experience presupposes time; to know is a narrative course.

My principal contention here has been that the four-trope system of renaissance rhetoric, far from assuming its arrangement from frequency of use, represents a form of knowing, of grasping a concept—the German terms *begreifen* and *Begriff* seem useful here—that not only accords, whether loosely or strictly, with many theoretical systems of knowing, or coming to be known, as in Vico, Kant, Hegel, Marx, Croce,

48. Kant, *Critique of Pure Reason*, 192.

Foucault, Goethe, and many others, but also possesses an inherent narrativity. In familiar structuralist terms, these tropes are paradigmatic as figures of words, but become syntagmatic when they are inflated into figures of thought or even philosophies of history. The curriculum of mind thus becomes a diachronic course as it strives to grasp its concepts by re-rendering them in succession, metaphorically, metonymically, synecdochically, and ironically. The nature of these successive changes seems unmediated, catastrophically sudden and discontinuous; and this radical discontinuity between tropic renderings, while it helps to explain the necessity faced by essentially tropological thinkers like Foucault or Marx to cast their narratives in "archaeological" or "revolutionary" terms, also suggests that some sort of "catastrophe theory" may be devised to elucidate the nature of these discontinuities. The literature on the tropes is vast (and tends to proceed tropologically—naming, categorizing, inflating, unnaming), but the concept of the *intertropes* has not been grasped or named. Only one "inter-trope" has a name: that great catastrophe that marks the cyclicality of the system, the space-event from irony toward metaphor that Vico calls *ricorso*. This notion has hardly been discussed, let alone the catastrophes that signal the turns from metaphor to metonymy, metonymy to synecdoche, and synecdoche to irony. My use of the word "catastrophe" is more than a mere reference to recent catastrophe theory, which represents the fullest attempt to explore the nature of "discontinuous and divergent phenomena" mathematically; in my own opinion, the claims of this theory to "provide a mathematical language for the hitherto 'inexact' sciences" are far from demonstrated.[49] The catastrophic nature of tropology is also suggested etymologically; the words stem from separate roots meaning "turn." Each trope itself is a turn, by definition; and the course from trope to trope in thought, diagnostically as it were, is a series of turns, tropes troping themselves. And these turns, in turn, are catastrophic, as in *strophe*, the turning of the chorus in Greek drama from one side of the orchestra to the other.

To refer to the curriculum of the tropes as narrative similarly leads us back to the root of narrate, /gno/, "to know." The well-known etymological identity of narration and *gnosis* is nowhere clarified as fully as in the narrativity of the tropological grasp. This knowledge is diagnostic, as Faust's translation of *logos* is dia-gnostic, a "knowing through." The tropology, then, *is* a narrative theory; the trope cannot

49. E. C. Zeeman, "Catastrophe Theory," *Scientific American*, Apr. 1976, 65.

restrain itself from self-explanation. From the small transference of trope itself (a metaphoric process) to the full semantic figurology of discourse that judges and measures each turn of meaning, the tropological movement is the "movement of ironic consciousness." The ironic narrative movement of consciousness is described by Paul de Man: "The whole process happens at an unsettling speed. Irony possesses an inherent tendency to gain momentum and not to stop until it has run its full course; from the small and apparently innocuous exposure of a small self-deception it soon reaches the dimensions of the absolute."[50] To allegorize irony like this is to underscore the status of irony as the trope of tropology, but it also points to the allegorical nature of any inflation of the tropes into figures of thought, comprehension, or discourse. Whether it is an allegory of the conventions of language, or of the deep structures of reason, the inflatable trope provides a narrative diagnostic that is distinctly alchemical.

50. De Man, "The Rhetoric of Temporality," 197.

TROPOLOGY VERSUS

NARRATIVITY

FREUD AND THE FORMALISTS

I

The question of tropology and narrativity broached in the previous chapter is a troubling one. Such abstract and capacious literary terms cry out for some specific textual discussion, yet because no text is unimplicated somehow in these terms, any such exemplary discussion is likely to seem not quite germane to the topic. There is no solution to the quandary, but if the text involved were somehow a privileged one, with a large theoretical literature crystallized around it, an allegorical discussion might emerge that could resituate the terms. At the risk of entering a minefield, or wandering through several minefields, I shall venture such an allegorical discussion here.

The standard histories of rhetoric state that the formal study of rhetoric in the West died out in the late nineteenth century, when the primary (albeit waning) source of vitality in the rhetorical tradition was the study of style and oratory. They rarely note (in fact, they never note) that 1899 saw the publication of the great rhetoric of the coming century (our own—the book is dated 1900), disguised as a book on dreams. Freud's "dream-work" presents a full system of subversive rhetoric, geared to persuasion through denial, existing only through deep mystification; it is a rhetoric, we might say, of resistance to totalitarianism. The generalization of this totalitarianism into language itself has certainly been a main theme of the century from Karl Kraus and Hofmannsthal to Heidegger and the current hermeneutics of suspicion.

The Interpretation of Dreams is the rhetoric of our century, and has often been implicitly recognized as such, in various ways. Its focus on inner discourse parallels the decline of public man and the rise of the private realm as the most significant and most signifying of human arenas.

The "dream-work" is the labor process of the private, and tropology is its "means of production." That the dream-work is fundamentally a renaming of the tropes of antiquity has been a commonplace for three decades, although the terms have never been explicitly agreed upon (as they rarely are, where tropes are concerned). Indeed, the question of whether the term "trope" is appropriate at all is often at issue: I personally feel that "trope" is sometimes used where "topos" would be more appropriate. However, since much of the history of rhetoric is little more than a dispute over which term goes where, it is better to clarify my own usage.

Let us review a little of the bidding in this game. In 1956 the linguist Emile Benveniste noted in his essay "Remarks on the Function of Language in Freudian Theory" the striking analogies that Freudian discourse suggests.

> The unconscious uses a veritable "rhetoric" which, like style, has its "figures," and the old catalogue of tropes would supply an inventory appropriate to the two types of expression. One finds in both all the devices of substitution engendered by taboo: euphemism, allusion, antiphrasis, preterition, litotes. The nature of the content makes all the varieties of metaphor appear, for symbols of the unconscious take both their meaning and their difficulty from metaphoric conversion. They also employ what traditional rhetoric calls metonymy (the container for the contents) and synecdoche (the part for the whole), and if the "syntax" of the symbolic sequences calls forth one device of style more than any other, it is ellipsis.[1]

To be sure, Jacques Lacan had broached this matter several years before Benveniste in his notorious *Discours de Rome* (and Kenneth Burke, not surprisingly, had raised the question two decades before, but that is another issue), but it was not until "The Insistence of the Letter in the Unconscious," a lecture of 1957, that Lacan began to map the dream-work specifically.

Entstellung, translated as distortion, is what Freud shows to be

1. Emile Benveniste, "Remarks on the Function of Language in Freudian Theory" (1956), in *Problems in General Linguistics,* trans. M. E. Meek (Coral Gables, Fla., 1971), 75. It is conventional to begin this discussion with Benveniste; it is inescapable to note that Kenneth Burke broached the matter long before in his essay "Freud—and the Analysis of Poetry," in *The Philosophy of Literary Form* (Baton Rouge, La., 1941).

the general precondition for the functioning of dreams, and it is what we described above, following Saussure, as the sliding of the signified under the signifier which is always active in speech (its action, let us note, is unconscious).

But what we called the two slopes of the incidence of the signifier on the signified are also found here.

The *Verdichtung*, or condensation, is the structure of the superimposition of signifiers which is the field of metaphor, and its very name, condensing in itself the word *Dichtung*, shows how the process is connatural with the mechanism of poetry to the point that it actually envelops its properly traditional function.

In the case of *Verschiebung*, displacement, the German term is closer to the idea of that veering off of meaning that we see in metonymy, and which from its first appearance in Freud is described as the main method by which the unconscious gets around censorship.[2]

From here, Lacan goes on to suggest that these privileged forms of representation differ from the homologous forms in normal speech because they are limited, defined, and placed by other aspects of the system, namely the *Rücksicht auf Darstellbarkeit*, or considerations of representability, and later by elaborations, which are secondary. Lacan's tropology is the two-trope model proposed by Roman Jakobson in his famous essay on aphasia; Anthony Wilden's explications of Lacan's use of this tropology serve as a classic introduction to the structuralist work of the 1960s.[3]

Tzvetan Todorov took up the question in his *Theories of the Symbol* of 1977. His primary focus was on Freud's study of the *Witz*, the verbal joke, but Todorov inevitably moved on to the tropology of the dream-work. Initially, Freud divides the joke (for Todorov, the *mot d'esprit*) into the spirit of the word *(esprit des mots)* and the spirit of the thought *(esprit de la pensée)*. The inevitable inflation of this process by which the joke moves between the signifier and the signified, pointing, as it were, to their mismatch, leads Todorov to consider the claims of the binary Freudian tropologists, and to note that Freud's metaphor and metonymy cannot

2. Jacques Lacan, "The Insistence of the Letter in the Unconscious," in *The Structuralists: From Marx to Lévi-Strauss*, ed. Richard and Fernande DeGeorge (Garden City, N.Y., 1972), 305.

3. See Anthony Wilden's notes to Jacques Lacan, *The Language of the Self* (New York, 1968); and Anthony Wilden, *System and Structure* (London, 1972), chaps. 2 and 16.

be clearly distinguished from one another and that, besides, there are other tropes unaccounted for.

> We propose, then, in place of "condensations," "multiple uses," "double meaning" and "puns," four other groups founded on the opposition between resemblance and identity, unique and multiple occurrence: *antanaclases, paronomasias, syllepses,* and for the fourth case, in which the second signifier is partially or totally absent, *contaminations* or *puns.*[4]

Todorov's decision to make the book on verbal jokes his basic Freudian rhetoric text led him away from *The Interpretation of Dreams* into a fourfold tropology, and a very idiosyncratic one. Suffice it to say that he questions the idea of a tropological *system* at work in Freud's primary process while acknowledging the fundamental necessity of recognizing a set of tropes as the core of its functions.

By the 1970s, however, the binary tropology of the early structuralist era was being rebuilt. Hayden White, following Kenneth Burke's work of thirty years before, revived the four-trope system of the renaissance, as inflated by Vico into a skeletal philosophy of history. White's initial work used the tropes on historical texts, but in a series of later essays others were tropologized, including Freud. For White, citing Roman Jakobson, but without confronting the enormous differences in their uses of tropes, the process of *die Traumarbeit* corresponds, more or less, to the "master tropes" of metaphor, metonymy, synecdoche, and irony, which Freud would have known from the standard educational curriculum of his youth.

> His "discovery" of the processes of "condensation," "displacement," "representation," and "secondary revision" might seem to be undermined by the suggestion that he had only rediscovered in, or unconsciously imposed upon, the psychodynamics of dreaming, transformative models already explicated fully, and in much the same terms as those used by Freud, as the tropes of rhetoric.[5]

White is careful to point out that there is no diachronic aspect to these processes, with the rather minor exception that "secondary revision"

4. Tzvetan Todorov, *Théories du symbole* (Paris, 1977), 311. Translation mine.
5. Hayden White, *Tropics of Discourse: Essays in Cultural Criticism* (Baltimore and London, 1978), 13–14.

implies something *prior* to revise. He also modestly states that the four-trope system could hardly be claimed to be a "law of discourse," but is rather only an available "convention" that reappears regularly within Western thought.

In *Rhetorical Poetics*, Peter Schofer and Donald Rice work a new variation on this four-trope reading of Freud's dream-work; they locate all four tropes in *displacement* and *condensation*. Metaphor and synecdoche tend to dominate, although irony is the basic process by which "sense is produced from nonsense."[6] They find powerful implications for reading in these processes, which suggest that the "naive" reader's tropological imagination will produce readings attuned to his or her own fantasies, while the critic must be more disciplined.

> It is quite often after this pleasurable free reading that the critic returns to confining, decondensing, and replacing the fantasy of traces in order to construct an ordered text on literature.[7]

I am not sure what a decondensation looks like (although if it is analogous to milk, it would be a watering-down), but tropology is both the cause of and cure for literature in this poetics.

Now, all of this sounds like a marvelous episode in cultural history, in which a brief glimmer of understanding grows and grows under various hands until a fuller comprehension of its subject is attained—with more to come, of course. For all I know, such an account may even be true. This is not to deny that certain problems have arisen. For one thing, I have not mentioned the considerable post-structuralist literature on tropes and Freud in places like *Diacritics*, *Poétique*, and *Yale French Studies*—Freud being so French these days. Further, it is not entirely clear that all of the participants in this cheerful, if tedious, allegory are dealing with the same tropes, or even the same Freud. But this is the great commonplace in the long history of rhetoric. Inevitably, at some point, we will want nothing more than to cite Butler's old saw:

> For all a rhetorician's rules
> Teach nothing but to name his tools

Mis-naming and un-naming are more to the point; the elegance and clarity of tropologies often seem a pretext for a wild and unbounded

---

6. Peter Schofer and Donald Rice, *Rhetorical Poetics: Theory and Practice of Figural and Symbolic Reading in Modern French Literature* (Madison, 1983), 105–6.

7. Ibid., 107.

play of *will*. And why should it be any other way, if tropology is to claim for itself a privileged spot in human understandings? In a science of rules—and that is what tropologists after Nietzsche often claim to have created—there are, ostensibly, no final rules.

II

Except insofar as I have invented an elementary historical narrative about tropological readings of the dream-work, narrativity itself has not yet made an appearance here. Freud, however, expresses a clear attitude toward narrativity in chapter 6 of *The Interpretation of Dreams*, the chapter on the dream-work. Narrativity, at least a certain narrativity, is a fraud, and a trope.

Let me first clarify what I mean here by narrativity. In Paul Ricoeur's definition, which seems heavily influenced by Freud, as well as by earlier Freudians like St. Augustine, narrativity is the process by which the dissonant is made consonant, so to speak. Through emplotment, a text finds its "dynamic identity." Narrativity is thus the mediator that synthesizes the heterogeneous.[8] Narrativity is the "grasping together" that constitutes the Kantian faculty of judgment; for Ricoeur, no human understanding proper is possible without it. Thus, Ricoeur takes seriously the etymological connection of narrative and *gnosis;* to narrate is to know. Without it things are meaningless.

What Freud says of dreams is quite similar to Ricoeur's notion of narrative: dreams must create unities of their materials, despite the disparate nature of these sources "er gehorcht einem *Zwang, eine Einheit aus ihnen zu gestalten*"[9] (191). Freud's comments on this unifying, narrative process, succinctly stated in *On Dreams*, published in 1901 as a virtual summary of *The Interpretation of Dreams*, are in line with Ricoeur's definitions.

I shall not deal exhaustively with this part of the dream-work, and will therefore merely remark that the easiest way of forming an idea of its nature is to suppose—though the supposition probably

8. See Paul Ricoeur, "The Text as Dynamic Identity," in *Identity of the Literary Text*, ed. Mario Valdés and Owen Miller (Toronto, 1985). Also idem, *Time and Narrative*, vol. I, trans. Kathleen McLaughlin and David Pellauer (Chicago, 1984).

9. German citations from Sigmund Freud, *Die Traumdeutung*, in *Studienausgabe*, vol. II (Frankfurt, 1972); English citations are from the *Standard Edition* of Freud's works (London, 1953).

does not meet the facts—that *it only comes into operation AFTER the dream-content has already been constructed.* Its function would then consist in arranging the constituents in a dream in such a way that they form an approximately connected whole, a dream-composition. In this way, the dream is given a kind of façade (though this does not, it is true, hide its content at every point), and thus receives a first, preliminary interpretation, which is supported by interpolations and slight modifications.[10]

In this process, dreams mimic waking thought—all too well, it seems, for the dream goes too far in the direction of waking thought. Comparing this process to "an adept in sleight of hand" (499; "Kunststücke der Taschenspieler," *Traumdeutung*, 480), Freud notes that our intellectual habit of understanding all things in a unified—that is, a narrative—way is turned against us, so that we are misled by our most trusted ally, our narrative understanding.

The process to which I have been referring is, of course, "secondary revision" *(die sekundäre Bearbeitung)*, the ironic moment of the dream-work tropology construed as a four-trope system, although it is perhaps mistaken here to refer to the four tropes as "moments" of the entire tropology, as I have done elsewhere. If narrative is always implicated in time, somehow—a fact that Ricoeur relates to our difficult human placement vis-à-vis eternity—Freud denies, or at least wants to deny, even the mitigated narrativity of his ironic trope. Let me explain what I mean. As noted in the previous chapter, the fourfold tropology possesses a strong, in-built narrativity: the naming features of metaphor precede and entail the classifying (grammatical) powers of metonymy, which necessitate—according to this allegorical system—the textualizing, unifying syntagmic trope of synecdoche. All of which leads in a dizzying whirl to the semantic, interpretive stance assumed by irony as master trope. Seen from this perspective, irony serves as the trope of tropology or, as Hayden White put it, as the "sentimental" trope, set against the other, "naive" three. And as he suggests, it is logical to assume that "secondary revision" *follows* the other parts of the dream-work, which are primary. Freud acknowledges that this assumption is a natural one, as St. Athanasius might have acknowledged as merely "natural" the position held by Arius and his followers in the third century A.D. that the Father is prior to the Son. Then Freud, like Athanasius, *denies* what seems natural. Secondary revision is

10. Freud, *On Dreams, Standard Edition,* vol. V, 666.

cotemporal (to use the theological term), if not consubstantial, with the rest of the dream-work. Freud, unlike Athanasius, seems none too dogmatic about this, saying things like "We must assume," "probably," and "In any case." It is *time,* and thus *narrative,* that he must keep out of the tropological machine.

I am suggesting that Freud's anxiety about the tendency of a foreign agent, narrativity, to creep into his stable dream tropologies shows itself in parts of his discussion of the dream-work, and shows itself in his selection of examples, which seem, at least to me, to reveal as much about his textual concerns as about the subjects they purport to illustrate. No Freud discussion would be complete without a dream, and he offers us one from a male patient as an example of secondary revision.

> The dream—it is the only one of which I possess no careful notes—ran roughly as follows. The dreamer, a young unmarried man, was sitting in the restaurant at which he usually ate and which was presented realistically in the dream. Several people then appeared, in order to fetch him away, and one of them wanted to arrest him. He said to his companions at table: "I'll pay later; I'll come back." But they exclaimed with derisive smiles: "We know all about that; that's what they all say!" One of the guests called out after him: "There goes another one!" He was then led into a narrow room in which he found a female figure carrying a child. One of the people accompanying said: "This is Herr Mueller." A police inspector, or some such official, was turning over a bundle of cards or papers and as he did so repeated "Mueller, Mueller, Mueller." Finally he asked the dreamer a question, which he answered with an "I will." He then turned around to look at the female figure and observed that she was now wearing a big beard.[11]

Freud quickly determines that the dream contains a *phantasy of marriage* disguised as a *phantasy of arrest.* Freud's last two sentences sum up the dream thoughts:

> In fact, all kinds of qualms were evidently preventing the dreamer from throwing himself into the phantasy of marriage with any enjoyment. One of these qualms [*Bedenken*], a fear that marriage might cost him his freedom, was embodied in the transformation into a scene of arrest.[12]

11. Freud, *Standard Edition,* vol. V, 494.
12. Ibid., 495.

Tropology and Narrativity

Let us note that this dream, the only dream in the section from Freud's own practice, appears in a section on secondary revision that Freud hedges about with many qualms of his own. The function of secondary revision is, in effect, to "marry" the coded elements of the dream together; the danger to Freud's tropology is that a subsequent process *within* the dream-work, standing on a different temporal level from the other aspects of the dream tropology, would "arrest" (or capture) the process. The public official shuffling through the bundle of papers is behaving very like the censor embodied in the revisionary trope, repeating the proper name as if to emphasize (while undercutting in Freudian terms through reiteration) the identity of the dreamer. This dream begins to look a bit like an inserted comment on, as well as an example of, the problem at hand, which is not so much "secondary revision" as Freud's qualms that dream narrativity might prove an "imprisoning" "marriage" for the analyst.

There is one other example of any length in this section (section I) of chapter 6. In this example, not a dream but an experiment, Freud cites a Herbert Silberer, who demonstrated that one set of ideas could overcome another, replacing them with coded but related images, by forcing himself to maintain complicated trains of thought while in a sleepy or exhausted state. Silberer tried to compare Kant's notions of time with those of Schopenhauer, but found that he could not keep both in mind at the same time while exhausted. At last, unable to recall the Kantian system, Silberer got an image of an uncooperative, disagreeable secretary, who refused to do what was requested of him.[13] That Freud should select this meditation on the inner forms of time, which Kant bequeathed to nineteenth-century philosophy, as an example of "secondary revision" suggests to me his own problems in keeping these things in mind, and perhaps his resentment against the uncooperative and uncomplying recording secretary in the dream-work—that is, secondary revision. If my suggestions are to be as much as considered, then his selection of just this example from his reading, and its placement at just this point, become splendid examples of "secondary revision" in waking thought, hiding the purpose of the selection from Freud himself—this purpose being to deny that the tropology he has described as the essence of the all-important dream-work may be a system of knowledge with its own systematic principles, an inner form, and that narrativity within the sequence of tropes is the expression of this.[14]

13. Ibid., 503.

14. Thus, Shlomo Breznitz's attempt to clean up "secondary revision" (in "A Critical

III

The reference to the Formalists in the title of this chapter may now seem itself a ruse. (Indeed, it is questionable whether we should call them by a single name at all; and if we can do so, whether we may use the name "Formalists" instead of the "Specifiers" suggested by Boris Eichenbaum.)[15] In a few final comments, I would like to contrast the positions some of them have taken on the general matter of tropology and its apparently antagonistic implication in narrativity which I have suggested in my discussion of Freud and secondary revision. The so-called Formalists are the proper starting place for any discussion of tropology and narrativity whatever because both modern tropology and modern narratology spring directly from this source. This does not make it easier to use their work, even casually. Peter Steiner's and Victor Ehrlich's admirable guides to the Formalists are enormously helpful, but the diversity and range of the work of the Formalists remain as problems.

However, my use of the Formalists (or "Specifiers") here is simple: I want to note how, for all their differences, they tend to generate narrative from tropes. I shall do no more than indicate a few of the many ways in which this is done, granting that the circumstances differ, that the terms used are naturally not the ones I employ here. The trend, however, is clear and suggestive. Boris Tomashevsky put a minimal definition of narrativity into his remark that a story is a journey from one situation to another.[16] That this road is a crooked road, as Viktor Shklovsky said of the road of art, is taken for granted; it is a road full of turns, that is to say, literally, of tropes.[17] This turning story-road formed the basic model of Formalist narratology (it is, after all, quite an ancient topos), but despite the disputes over details, the essential poetics of

Note on Secondary Revision," *International Journal of Psycho-Analysis* 52 [1971], 407–12), far from helping matters, seems to compound the confusion. By analyzing Freud's "secondary revision" into three different processes (primary revision, secondary revision, tertiary revision), which apply to three different stages of the dream-work, Breznitz is at the mercy of the ironic process, about which, he notes, Freud was "completely unreliable."

15. "We are not 'Formalists,' but if you will *specifiers (specifikatory)*." Boris Ejxenbaum (Eichenbaum), cited in Victor Ehrlich, *Russian Formalism: History—Doctrine*, 3d ed. (New Haven, 1981), 171.

16. Boris Tomashevsky, "Thematics" (1925), in *Russian Formalist Criticism: Four Essays*, trans. Lee T. Lemon and Marion J. Reis (Lincoln, Nebr., 1965), 70.

17. "The road on which the foot senses the stones, the road which turns back on itself—that is the road of art." Viktor Shklovsky, "The Connection Between Devices of *Syuzhet* Construction and General Stylistic Devices (1919)," in *Russian Formalism: A Collection of Articles and Texts in Translation*, ed. Stephen Bann and J. E. Bowlt (Edinburgh, 1973), 48.

narrative was not in question. Indeed, Shklovsky will state that the essential methods of "plot" *(syuzhet)* formation are identical with poetics, "even with acoustic instrumentation."[18] Juri Tynjanov's discussion of the "temporal simultaneity" of prose and the "atemporal successivity" of verse, described in Peter Steiner's book on the Formalists, strikes me as another example of this problematic, although, to be sure, it is rhythm more than tropology that marks the essence of verse for this Formalist.[19] He elsewhere defines form as the ongoing creation of equivalents, a dynamic process that explicitly foreshadows Ricoeur's notion of the dynamic plot.[20]

To see the plot thus as a part of poetic language, one of the theses of Formalism, is to celebrate the tropology of narrativity.[21] When Tynjanov and Roman Jakobson wrote the brief "Problems in the Study of Literature and Language" in 1928, they stressed the breakdown in the opposition between synchrony and diachrony, their mutual implications, but the precise reformulation of this opposition as tropology and narrativity remained to be drawn.[22] Jakobson, whose reputation as a generator of ideas would already have been secure if he had done nothing more than state his ideas about how the paradigmatic axis collapses onto the syntagmic, would elaborate this characteristic formulation of later structuralist poetics about the relation of tropology and narrativity.[23] For him, narrative is tropological, but tropology, being binary, has no recognized narrativity.

The response to these attempts, and the many others inaugurated by these great inaugurators, has a certain pattern. One name reappears to damn them as a blot on their lineage—the name of Immanuel Kant. We note, for example, Lev Trotsky's discussion in *Literature and Revolution* of 1924, which accuses them of neo-Kantianism unawares, or Julia

---

18. Shklovsky, "Connection," 70.

19. "In verse, with its dynamized verbal material, the goal sought is not a simultaneous meaning but the sequence itself, the rhythmical unfolding of the verbal material. Such speed is perceived as a process—a continuous correlation of different facts of language whose heterogeneity resists any final semantic summation." Peter Steiner, *Russian Formalism: A Metapoetics* (Ithaca, 1984), 192.

20. Juri Tynanov, cited in *Formalist Theory*, ed. L. M. O'Toole and Ann Shukman, (Oxford, 1977), 30.

21. Ibid., 40.

22. Jurij Tynyanov and Roman Jakobson, "Problems in the Study of Literature and Language," in *Readings in Russian Poetics: Formalist and Structuralist Views*, ed. Ladislav Matejka and Krystyna Pomorska (Cambridge, 1971), 79–70.

23. Ehrlich, *Russian Formalism: History—Doctrine*, 75; Elmar Holenstein, *Jakobson ou le structuralisme phénomènologique* (Paris, 1974), 35–61.

Kristeva's essay of 1970 on Bakhtin, "The Ruin of a Poetics," which followed Trotsky in citing Kant as forerunner of the Formalists, but also noted that their debt to German aesthetics "remained something shameful, unavowed, repressed."[24]

The name of Kant was to be repressed, and this repression carries us back to Freud and his dream-work. What is it about Kant that prompts his intrusion, whether as tacit self-criticism or emphatically political public criticism as the case may be, into discussions relating tropology and narrativity? In a broad sense, it is perhaps his notion of time as an inner form of consciousness that tends to render time atemporal. But it is also the case that Kant's four Principles of Pure Understanding are not only a splendid four-trope system, but contain within themselves their own narrative curriculum. Or is it because his name evokes (and calls into question) the faculty of will that informs all allegorical tropologies?

In any case, all of this is to say that while tropology and narrativity are fundamentally opposed activities, they are deeply implicated in one another; *to study one is to defend one's discourse against the other because each seems to want to become the other, as dialectic.*

In the *Prolegomena to Any Future Metaphysics*, Kant wrote:

> These are then the transcendental Ideas, which, in accord with the true but hidden ends of the natural destiny of our reason, aim not at extravagant concepts, but at an unbounded extension of their empirical use, yet seduce the understanding by an unavoidable illusion to a transcendental use, which, though deceitful, cannot be restrained within the bounds of experience by any resolution, but only by scientific instruction and with much difficulty.[25]

The labyrinthine syntax of this sentence cannot quite hide the tonal words within it: illusion, seduction, hidden, deceitful, difficulty. But the source of all this trouble has not yet been named—that is, the identity of the author-censor whose coding of his text is so effective as to impede its reading totally. In the *Critique of Pure Reason,* Kant names the villain Dialectic, "the logic of illusion" (*Logik des Scheins*).

> There exists, therefore, a natural and inevitable Dialectic of pure reason, not one in which a mere bungler might get entangled

24. Trotsky is discussed in Victor Ehrlich, *Russian Formalism: History—Doctrine,* 103; Kristeva, in Bann and Bowlt, *Russian Formalism,* 102–3.

25. Immanuel Kant, *Prolegomena to Any Future Metaphysics* (New York, 1950), 81.

> from want of knowledge, or which a sophist might devise to
> confuse rational people, but one that is inherent in, and insepara-
> ble from, human reason, and to precipitate it into momentary
> errors, such as require to be removed again and again.[26]

The Kantian "logic of illusion," as I have suggested in my earlier discussion of the Principles of Pure Understanding, is tropology, which he
names Dialectic.[27] Thus, Dialectic functions tropologically as an ironic
mediator of concepts; it privileges none of them, but dominates their
presentation to reason so impressively that reason quite naturally
accepts these presentations as transcendental reality, rather than
empirical appearance.

Like Freud's secondary revision, Dialectic functions both as the disease, so to speak, and as the model for the cure. It is an "imprisoning
marriage" because it unifies the terms of the dream or the principles of
understanding in a system that cannot be escaped, either for analysis or
for critique. The system is dangerous because it threatens to inflate
itself to such an extent that any higher-level discussion becomes part of
the system. Kant's defense is his familiar positing of things-in-them-
selves (which might be called things-without-tropes), impossible to
know in a precisely human way. Freud's defense against tropology was
to insist that his ironic trope, secondary revision, had no higher status
as Over-trope. That is, while secondary revision has a "regulative function" (in the Kantian sense), it is not allowed (however natural or logical
it may seem) to exist *after,* on a more knowing temporal plane, the other
facets of the dream-work. The Freudian dream analysis, after all, is but
another secondary revision, just as the Kantian critique is yet another
Dialectic. Each is threatened by the existence of its own model within
the logical system of mistaken appearances (dialectic, *Logik des Scheins,*
dream-work, tropology) that it seeks to set right. Kant's reference to
repeated errors that must be removed "again and again" seems a fore-
cast of analysis interminable.

26. Immanuel Kant, *Critique of Pure Reason,* trans. Max Müller, (Garden City, N.Y.,
1966), 224.

27. Cf. the preceding chapter, "The Inflatable Trope as Narrative Theory: Structure or
Allegory?"

PART FOUR

ALLEGORY AND ANXIETY

The anxieties described up to now epitomize the resistance to rhetoric mentioned in the first chapter of this book. For most historians pure rejection, using the classic defense of the specialist ("that's not my field," or "it's not really history") has sufficed, but when a Kant, a Freud, or Hayden White shows concern about the status and power of language over his constructs—which are devoted to displaying the power of dialectic, rhetoric, or tropology in all verbal representations—then this anxiety must be taken seriously. The chapters that conclude this book take up the concern about the allegorical nature of historical discourse, and attempt to situate it in current discourses both inside and outside the world of professional historians.

A description of what "historians" are currently "doing" (i.e., producing a history of recent historical work) is the sort of thing that evokes surveys, statistics, polls, content analyses, enrollment reports by field, job listings, salaries, pages published per field, fellowships granted, dissertations in progress, and so on. The nature of this evidence is constituted in advance by the processes of *definition, categorization,* and *division*—what historians like to call "asking the right questions." Once the evidence is constituted (as "findings"), analysis (usually implicit and self-explanatory) begins: *comparison* (for example, page production is *better,* enrollments are *worse,* fellowships the *same:* the situation is *like* the 1970s, *unlike* the 1960s): *degree* (for example, *more* Japanese, *fewer* British job listings); *relationship* (for example, more social history *causes* lower or higher enrollments; change in student ethnic composition is the *antecedent,* pressure to change course offerings the *consequence*). And so on. Will the future be *like* or *unlike* the present; what is *possible* and what *impossible?* How should we evaluate the relative *authority* of the evidence (whether personal testimony or statistics)? What *precedents* appear to cast light on the situation? Are there *maxims* that are worthy of mention with regard to the evidence, perhaps even as explanation?

That this plausible, by no means exhaustive, group of historical considerations comes directly from the list of "common topics" of classical rhetoric, at base the source of all "historical questions" and "models," does not in any way devalue them as historical concerns. (Future possibilities, I grant, are traditionally touchy ground for historians, but more so in *theory* than in *practice*—to cite yet another topic, that of contraries.) These topics are an essential part of our way of knowing, whether they formulate the inquiry behind a computer program, a political speech, or historical research. Far from being a late process that puts the evidential "findings" in literate form, the rhetorical categories of invention are basic to the initial stages of definition and generation of evidence. Still, it is the *ways* in which they are or are not used that create communities of people, such as historians.

Historians as a guild have little in common with each other, making surveys and projections such as the one imagined above highly complex and contradictory. What they seem to share is a certain set of anxieties that constitutes their professionalization and their differentiation from scholars in other fields. This is neither good nor bad; it is certainly not unique to history. Chapter 11, "Triangular Anxieties: The Present State of European Intellectual History," plots anxieties in one subfield of history. Because this area of study contains as an important part of its subject matter the major social, psychological, and linguistic influences on historical thought in the twentieth century, the study of European intellectual history is uniquely placed in historical studies. Because it cannot ignore challenges to historical thought as easily as other specialties, it must deal with a complex of anxieties that define the possibilities of a modern historical approach. At their most extreme, the challenges to historical thought sketched briefly at the beginning of Chapter 12, "Narrativity and History: Post-Structuralism and Since," accuse history of being a purely ideological form, dependent upon a discourse that enforces orderly representation, which in turn mandates a vision of an *order* in *what* is represented, stereotyping general terms (of which universal "humanity" is the most oppressive), and tendentious hierarchies of experience (the public over the private, the mind over the body, the content over the form). It strikes me that these objections cannot be overcome, even if it were agreed that they should be, which it is not. They can, however, show us how to be better crooked readers, more inquisitive and suspicious than before about the foundations of historical writing, as the examples of Ankersmit, Ricoeur, and White demonstrate.

11 TRIANGULAR ANXIETIES

THE PRESENT STATE OF EUROPEAN

INTELLECTUAL HISTORY

> *When I contemplate the present age with the eyes of some*
> *remote age, I can find nothing more remarkable in present-*
> *day humanity than its distinctive virtue and disease*
> *which goes by the name of "the historical sense."*
> Nietzsche, *The Gay Science*

I

> *The historian looks backwards; eventually he also*
> *believes backwards.*
> Nietzsche, *Twilight of the Idols*

When historians ponder the future, even the future of their own trade, the time is, at least in some small and very literal sense, out of joint; the future, that great *generator* of insecurity, must be defused, turned into a special variety of the past, a new sourcebook in the "lessons of history." Since the question "Where are we going?" almost invariably covers the question "Where are we?"—itself a surrogate for the question "Where have we just been?"—our logic or direction of inquiry will doubtless bear out the truth of Nietzsche's sarcasm about believing backwards.

The origin of inquiry into the future of anything is found in an apprehensive desire to grasp something that seems to be unraveling or slipping away; and concern for the future of academic disciplines is not to be found in a merely healthy curiosity about the opinions of one's colleagues. But what precisely is the nature of these anxieties? What are their origins? What forms do they assume? How do changes in the way intellectual historians perceive the challenges to their traditional tasks influence the kind of intellectual history that is being written? To ask such questions is to suggest a unanimity of voice and direction among historians that is clearly nonexistent. Furthermore, it is all too clear that to label a group of thinkers as the vanguard is to assume as proven the case one is about to test. Nevertheless, certain trends are becoming apparent. The pages that follow will focus on some of the issues that European intellectual history is addressing at present and will increasingly address in the future.

Areas of formal study are, in my view, complexes of defenses against particular anxieties, anxieties whose kaleidoscopic changes shape and blur the entire discourse of the field. This assertion can be made as relevant to biochemistry or astrophysics as to historical study, but it is the last that is the subject here. The classic theory of anxiety, scattered and developed throughout Sigmund Freud's writings, follows the course of many of his ideas, from an early hydraulic model of sexual disorders to the later psychological subtleties of defenses and defenses against defenses. A brief survey of his notions on this matter will provide a clue to the problem at hand in intellectual history.

In an early undated draft, Freud speaks of anxiety as a "damming-up" of accumulated sexual tension, which is converted into a neurosis resembling coitus in its symptoms.[1] Soon after, he noted that the "psyche finds itself in the *affect* of anxiety if it feels unable to deal by appropriate reaction with a task (a danger) *approaching from outside*."[2] This "affect," however, may lead to an anxiety attack as described above, or it may become a neurotic symptom, usually a phobia. The function of the symptom, Freud added in *The Interpretation of Dreams*, is "to avoid an outbreak of anxiety; the phobia is erected like a frontier fortification against the anxiety."[3] Anxiety is a response to the *perception* of external danger, of an "expected and foreseen" injury. As such it is related to instincts of flight for self-preservation, but it is by no means merely a fearful response to imaginary troubles. Although Freud points out that there *is* an anxiety based upon ignorance, such as a savage's fear of solar eclipses, there is also an anxiety based upon "superior knowl-

1. Sigmund Freud, "Extracts from the Fliess Papers," in the *Standard Edition of the Complete Psychological Works of Sigmund Freud* (London, 1966), I, 191, 195.
2. Freud, "On the Grounds for Detaching a Particular Syndrome from Neurasthenia Under the Description 'Anxiety Neurosis,'" in *Standard Edition*, III, 122.
3. Freud, *The Interpretation of Dreams*, in *Standard Edition*, V, 581.

edge," such as the same savage's terror of the signs of a wild animal on a trail, signs that would tell a civilized observer nothing.[4] He concludes that the preparedness for anxiety (the apprehension that leads to action) is the expedient element, while the generation of anxiety (the onset of the attack itself) is inexpedient.[5] To abbreviate Freud's lengthy discussion of anxiety in the *New Introductory Lectures* of 1933, we note that the origin of anxiety, in his late opinion, is the fear of castration.[6] It is worth noting here that while the older Freud criticized Otto Rank's notion that the act of birth was "the model of all later situations of danger,"[7] he had put forth such a notion himself—no mention of Rank—in his discussion of anxiety in the *Introductory Lectures on Psycho-Analysis* of 1916–1917. In sum, anxiety is *both* the prophylactic defense against a psychic attack *and* the attack itself, should the defense fail; it is also the general term for the condition under which the anxiety-as-neurotic-defense and the anxiety-as-hysterical-attack may take place. The etiology is a fear of castration, the loss of identity and definition provided by differentiation—and, lingering beside it perhaps, in Freud's mind, a repressed birth trauma. Anxieties about identity and origins, the sublimated descendants of castration and birth traumas, haunt intellectual history today.

Harold Bloom has described the "anxiety of influence" experienced by the poet who fears that competition with the great poetic fathers will render him speechless, without an identity.[8] Intellectual historians face a different problem. In a sense, the historian's anxiety today is "an anxiety in expectation of *being flooded*," to cite Bloom—flooded not by the past, but by the methodological competitors of our own day. Questions arise without answers; new developments seem only to confuse matters. Yet repression, the continuation of old ways, seems increasingly ineffective, that is to say, unrewarding. Adaptations must be made.

The traditional problem of intellectual history has been that almost none of its subject matter has ever been peculiar to it. While geneticists study genes, political theorists study governments, epigraphers study epigraphs, intellectual historians study—what? Not ideas as such, for these are the traditional fiefs of the philosophers. With one exception, intellectual historians have had to study the ideas of members of other

---

4. Freud, *Introductory Lectures on Psycho-Analysis*, in *Standard Edition*, XVI, 594.
5. Ibid., 595.
6. Freud, *New Introductory Lectures on Psycho-Analysis*, in *Standard Edition*, XXII, 86–87.
7. Freud, *New Introductory Lectures*, 88.
8. Harold Bloom, *The Anxiety of Influence: A Theory of Poetry* (New York, 1973).

discourses, whether philosophers, witch-hunters, economists, or poets. The exception has traditionally been the study of historians themselves; that is, historiography has "belonged" to historians, if only as a questionable form of inbreeding. Recently even this preserve has been lost, as literary critics, theorists of narrative, poeticians of prose, and the like have begun to swarm over nonfiction texts of all sorts, spoiling the last refuge of "proper intellectual history"—that is, the historian writing about another historian's writing. In the hands of critics like Roland Barthes, Lionel Gossman, and Linda Orr, the historical text becomes a text among others, to be studied for the art of its composition, the devices required by the discourse of historical writing, and the means by which it claims to represent reality.[9] Historical writing thus becomes an instance of *writing*, historical representation an instance of *representation* in general, historical truth an instance of rhetorical *figuration*. The "historical" identity of the text becomes as secondary as that of a patient in a hospital gown; the name may be on the wristband, but what matters is on the chart. If, at the level of language, there is nothing to differentiate the historical text from other forms of "realistic" representation, the problem of identity becomes even more perplexing.

This question of identity—perhaps "legitimacy" is a better word—was taken up by Leonard Krieger in an article called "The Autonomy of Intellectual History."[10] Although the title suggests Louis Mink's essay "The Autonomy of Historical Understanding,"[11] Krieger hardly inspires confidence in the assertion of his own title by calling intellectual historians "cuckoos in the historical nest," nor by enumerating a bewildering series of schools of intellectual history past and present, varieties of method, divergent definitions, and so forth. The confidence of the essay's tone is undercut by the briar-patch complexity of its struc-

9. See Roland Barthes, "Le Discours de l'histoire," *Social Science Information* 6:4 (1967); Lionel Gossman, "Augustin Thierry and Liberal Historiography," *History and Theory*, Beiheft 15 (1975); and Linda Orr, *Jules Michelet: Nature, History, Language* (Ithaca, 1976).

A linguistic approach to these matters is Roberto Miguelez, "Théorie du discours et théorie de l'histoire," *Dialogue* 13 (1974), 53–70. See also the literary critics on historical writing: Geoffrey H. Hartmen, "History-Writing as Answerable Style," in *The Fate of Reading and Other Essays* (Chicago, 1975), 101–13; Paul Hernadi, "Clio's Cousins: Historiography as Translation, Fiction, and Criticism." *New Literary History* 7 (1976), 247–50; and J. Hillis Miller, "Narrative and History," *English Literary History* 41 (1974) 455–73.

10. Leonard Krieger, "The Autonomy of Intellectual History," *Journal of the History of Ideas* 34 (1973), 499–516.

11. In *History and Theory* 5 (1966), 24–47.

ture. If intellectual history is "autonomous"—that is, possesses the right to make its own laws—Krieger has, quite correctly, noted the absence of a definable polity. In fact, in his later study of Ranke he suggests, on the basis of some comments on the role of ideas in the *History of the Popes*, that the "ostensibly scientific and political Ranke, then, leaves us with the intriguing thought that the only scientific universal history is intellectual history."[12] To cite Ranke as an unexpected ancestor in the family tree of intellectual history is to suggest that the lineage is as insecure as are the current family relationships, since Ranke has long been conventionally considered the founder of an archive-centered study of diplomatic politics.

While Krieger's essay was optimistic in its positive tone, but depressing in its elusive content, Hayden White in a 1969 article addressed the same subject in a funereal voice, only to find a new source of hope for intellectual history outside the "profession." Noting that "as historical reading, intellectual history is rather like vicarious sex: neither satisfying nor, ultimately, very helpful as a guide to action,"[13] White states quite bluntly that the most fruitful intellectual history of recent times has been done by philosophers, art historians, literary critics, scientists—scholars like E. H. Gombrich, Thomas Kuhn, Michel Foucault, Roland Barthes, or Lucien Goldmann.[14] White, who has written some of the most significant work to date on the nature of historical discourse, now calls his own field "cultural criticism" and teaches in a program in the "history of consciousness." Similarly, a thesis on, say, Diderot and Hegel is today more likely to be written in a department of comparative literature than in a department of history; and one may pick up a book with the title *Gödel, Escher, Bach*, written by a professor of computer science.

Yet another indication of this loss of definition is the emergence of new journals to prominence, journals that are by no means historical in the traditional academic sense, yet that publish some of the best thought today about figures of longstanding canonical interest to intellectual historians. Titles such as *Diacritics*, *New Literary History*, *New German Critique*, and *Telos*, to name but a few, are much more likely, in any given issue, to provide fresh insight into major cultural texts than is the true-blue *Journal of the History of Ideas* or the true but no longer blue *American Historical Review*.

12. Leonard Krieger, *Ranke: The Meaning of History* (Chicago, 1977), 158.
13. Hayden White, "The Tasks of Intellectual History," (1969), 608.
14. Ibid., 616–23.

Allegory and Anxiety

The traditional rhetorical figure of intellectual history has been periphrasis, the circumlocution of an essential position. Central to this tactic is the prior extraction of a vital core in the text or corpus of texts to be studied, and the focusing of all aspects of these texts back upon this core. This assumption of unity, which has been just as tyrannical for historians as it *used* to be for critics, dominates the method of intellectual history; it is not easy to conceive of an intellectual history without it. In approaching a figure like Rousseau, a figure whose stature is preselected and focused by that great lens, the canonical tradition, we assume a fundamental meaning, an *Ur*-Rousseau, which must be found either in the texts or, more likely, in the tradition of Rousseau scholarship. Once this center has been hypothetically identified (that is, chosen), the *possibility* of "reading" Rousseau is secure despite the variety of available strategies:[15] the center may be questioned by revisionists; or isolated aspects of Rousseau's corpus may be found to contradict it; or certain divergences from the core meaning may be posited either before or after the core in the form of developmental stages or degenerative lapses; or the meaning of the core itself may be found to be demonstrably ambiguous, inconsistent, or self-contradictory. None of these tactics denies or in any way compromises the assumption of the unity of meaning in a text—the meaning of Rousseau's identity, to put it another way. They are rather the poses that this prior assumption makes possible; this is what "interpretive" intellectual history is all about. Because this attitude privileges the *communicative* (and particularly the *referential*, to use the terminology of Roman Jakobson) model of a text, at the expense of other possible facets, it has been accused by recent critics and philosophers of making "an unwarranted presupposition of coherence."[16] Jonathan Culler describes these presuppositions: "The work tries to express an essence which presides over it as its source and its purpose. To capture the truth of the work is to recapture that essence and make it present to consciousness."[17] Surely, this "nostalgic desire to recover essences" has been a hallmark of the

15. A notable example of interpretation that systematically questions the possibility of reading is the work of Paul de Man, especially *Allegories of Reading* (New Haven, 1979), in which Rousseau is discussed at length.

16. Jakobson's influential essay "Linguistics and Poetics" may be found in *The Structuralists: From Marx to Lévi-Strauss*, ed. Richard and Fernande DeGeorge (Garden City, N.Y. 1972), 85–122. A full discussion of modern trends in literary structuralism is Jonathan Culler's *Structuralist Poetics: Structuralism, Linguistics, and the Study of Literature* (Ithaca, 1975).

17. Jonathan Culler, *Flaubert: The Uses of Uncertainty* (Ithaca, 1974), 17.

general anxiety of the intellectual historian. Whether or not we wish to view the nostalgia for essences as a desire for a more secure—that is, prenatal—fantasy state, this presumption of coherence remains the primary historical defense. Indeed, history itself is the existential projection of this anxiety. But challenges have appeared fairly recently that call so much into question that new adaptations and accommodations have arisen, different, but no less anxious.

The questions must inevitably arise: What is a historical treatment of a source? Where may we draw a line to distinguish between treatments of past texts that are historical and those that are not? May the historically trained, those of us who were trained to share historical anxieties, ignore those whose anxieties are different when they confront the texts with which we are, as a group, familiar? If we do not ignore them, what imitative symptoms must be adopted in order to defend ourselves against the dangers they pose—most particularly the striking loss of differentiation and definition that they represent—without succumbing to *their* anxieties?

II

> We cease to think when we refuse to do so under the
> constraint of language; *we barely reach the doubt that*
> *sees this limitation as a limitation.*
> Nietzsche, *The Will to Power*

The anxieties about intellectual history's loss of identity, both as a field and as a method, have led its practitioners to pay a great deal of attention to matters that were until recently relatively unproblematic. Language and hermeneutics have become virtual obsessions, although there is certainly no developing consensus about what the proper role of linguistic or hermeneutic studies ought to be. In most cases, to be sure, historians' responses to the "dangers" of language studies or hermeneutic method have been rather cheerful suggestions that aspects of those methods may be profitably incorporated into the ever-flexible methodology of intellectual history, so that the traditional goals may be more effectively pursued.

Historians' awareness of language as a general focus of interest and as a special and pressing problem is no secret. Nancy Struever notes in her essay "The Study of Language and the Study of History" the "early and brazen case of poaching" on the territory of intellectual history found in Noam Chomsky's *Cartesian Linguistics*, but suggests that Chomsky's "rather threatening humanism" must be confronted in the forms of structural linguistics and sociolinguistics by the "modestly equipped historian."[18] Although her treatment is sympathetic overall to the projects and accomplishments of the linguistic tendencies she discusses, Struever notes rather sharply that the most challenging approaches—those of Foucault and Chomsky, for instance—have all failed in one way or another. History itself, in her complex recounting of this recent work, is defined as the mediator, that which recognizes the challenge from formal linguistic theory, but which, like Dürer's knight, remains steadfastly on course.

The final message Struever brings to historians on the subject of language is: fear not. She writes: "The Humanist portents of contemporary linguistics cited at the beginning of this paper need not be threatening, then, but cheering. And historians should feel not only cheered, but braced."[19] Because of the nice balance found among the range of structuralists, hermeneuticists, sociolinguists, and grammarians, the field has divided itself into "incompatible and inseparable" approaches—the extralinguistic and the endolinguistic—and because historians have long specialized in straddling these aspects, we may cheerfully note that we straddlers are adequate to history, while *they*, despite great descriptive or theoretical virtues, are not. A bit of imitation, protective coloration as it were, will dispel the anxieties provoked by these threatening poachers who fail to respect historical obsessions. However, as often as Struever suggests that historians should be recognized as active participants in the discourse that they form, the thrust of her essay suggests the reactiveness of recent thought; it is difficult to determine whom history as a form of thought has threatened, challenged, or even braced in recent years.

Far more formal and less speculative than Struever is Nils B. Kvastad in his essay "Semantics in the Methodology of the History of Ideas." Stressing the need for careful categories of definition (such as narrative, descriptive, or real) and for precise methods of determining such vital issues as synonymity and ambiguity, Kvastad wants to establish

18. Nancy Struever, "The Study of Language and the Study of History," *Journal of Interdisciplinary History* 4 (1974), 401.

19. Ibid. 415.

historical semantics as a bedrock of interpretation that will attain a formally logical state, a sort of translation to the history of ideas of the
"covering law" notions of Hempel and Popper. To his credit, Kvastad
repeatedly stresses the importance of ambiguity, a flexibility of interpretation, and the difficulty of establishing definiteness of intention
while "dealing mostly with dead authors."[20] Nevertheless, he concludes with the familiar apprehensions. Lagging behind general history, "the history of ideas is in its infancy." Semantic studies must
become part of the historical discourse. "The reason is that when the
foundation of a house is shaky, it does not make much sense continuously to add new stories to it."[21] The only evidence for the immaturity,
inadequacy, or illogic of intellectual history is the absence of consensus
in the historical interpretation of texts. The presumption that interpretive agreement is the standard of academic maturity mirrors the
general assumption of univocal coherence in the texts themselves. "Textuality," the sensitivity to the way in which texts generate alternative
meanings, is ignored. This rather alarming suggestion of imminent
architectural collapse has not prompted, to my knowledge, any widespread cessation of work in historical construction; however, the anxiety that historical writing has been seriously undermined by its
inattention to language has not been quite repressed.

Arthur Danto, in an essay titled "Historical Language and Historical
Reality," has followed a more philosophical path than Kvastad, but a
path toward the same goal. The philosopher quicky trims the sails of his
subject by stating at the outset that the "philosophy of history is just
philosophy writ small."[22] In the same vein, he writes that the "deep but
easily sloganized intelligences of the past, Hegel, Marx, Nietzsche, or
Freud," seem destined to live on, reduced to "what men smaller and
sillier than they believe them to have said."[23] The "historically real x"
decays into the "historically apparent x." Danto proceeds to clarify matters by blasting "shallow naturalism," "stale games" (of continental
philosophers, naturally), "dumb oscillations and proto-paradoxes"—in
short, he gives a small dose of philosophical salts to purge the small
problem of historical reality. Danto, with his philosophical belief in the

20. Nils B. Kvastad, "Semantics in the Methodology of the History of Ideas," *Journal of the History of Ideas* 38 (1977), 168.

21. Ibid., 274.

22. Arthur Danto, "Historical Language and Historical Reality," *Review of Metaphysics* 27 (1973), 219.

23. Ibid., 244.

fundamental triviality of the problem of representation in language and his confidence that the difference between the "historically real x" and the "historically apparent x" disappears when causal and semantic information are analytically distinguished, never addresses the problem of representation itself, nor the structural slippage of signifieds beneath signifiers, nor any of the other "stale games" played by the perfidious continentals. Nevertheless, he finishes his essay with an evocation of historical anxiety as frightening as any: "our actions lose their point and, in dramatic cases, our lives their purpose," when our belief in *real* history is shattered. "For when the past is in doubt, a question mark blurs the present, and, since we cannot will falsehood, our lives persist unclearly until history-as-science has had its say. The present is clear just when the relevant past is known."[24] Ignorance of the present, we should recall, is the cursed situation of the shades in Dante's *Inferno*, and the anxiety of Danto's.

Language studies seem to have no clear, single place in historical methodology. Philosophers want a highly restricted protocol for reading; some semanticists want a formalized understanding of the linguistic processes of definition that lead toward a full semantic dimension; some historians want to use the work of socio- and structural linguistics as broadly as possible in forming models. Even as traditional and antitheoretical a historian as J. H. Hexter sees himself as a student of historical language, of the changing meaning of words, and of the emptiness of most of the generalizing terms we use. What is shared by these people is an anxiety that the meaning of the past (and with it so much more) is lost (or remains uncaptured) by misnaming or misreading. Whether or not Ranke is to be considered a father of intellectual history (a dubitable paternity, to say the least), we must note that he *was* first of all a philologist, a student of language. However, the nineteenth-century philological concern with authenticity of texts and editions and Ranke's own skills at recognizing the intentions of their creators do not address the modern problems of reading, the density or supplement of meaning created by the reader or the language or the act of writing itself. For this sensitivity, the work of Ranke's contemporaries Schleiermacher, Droysen, and Humboldt seems more to the point. It is hermeneutics rather than philology, interpretation rather than verification, that defines the anxiety of intellectual history these days.

Quentin Skinner has described the turn from empirical and positivist

24. Ibid., 259.

theories of meaning toward more hermeneutical approaches to texts in "Hermeneutics and the Role of History."[25] He cites the revival of a hermeneutical tradition in the work of Gadamer, Ricoeur, and Habermas, as well as the current interest in Wittgenstein's study of language games rather than verification procedures, as signs of a challenge to the traditional practice of intellectual history, which attempts to capture and restate the correct meaning of a text in terms of extrinsic (biographical, social, political, etc.) information. Skinner is nonetheless very much the historian (that is, his anxieties are traditional historical anxieties) in his optimistic conclusion, which greatly softens the confrontation between the two approaches. His tactic uses two standard distinctions. The first and more crucial is between text and context. Once one grants this distinction, which has been severely challenged by recent literary criticism from a number of directions, a system of reciprocal hermeneutical relationships—the famous "circle"—may be posited, leading to a second distinction between "autonomous" and "heteronomous" texts. Skinner makes the telling point that the interpretive approach based upon contextual study (and this includes most traditional histories of various sorts) "is based on a misleading overstatement which consists (in effect) of assimilating all works of literature to the category of strongly heteronomous texts."[26] The reverse of the contextual approach, however, the privileging of the autonomy of the text and a consequent emphasis on textual or internal interpretive strategies, is only a mirror image of the problem of the first approach. To assimilate all texts into the category of "autonomous" texts fails, in Skinner's view, as much as their assimilation into the category of "heteronomous" texts. While the relationship of autonomous and heteronomous texts derives rather obviously from the prior distinction between text and context, and while these distinctions have been standard among historians for a long time, it is not clear to me how such distinctions can be made except on the basis of prior interpretive decisions. Skinner's sensible spirit, like Struever's, takes the conciliatory position that both approaches should be followed (ritually, as it were), even if "such a process of checking adds little to our original sense of the text."[27] The anxiety about the loss of "text and context," the strong contrast of foreground and background, which has been essential to histor-

25. Quentin Skinner, "Hermeneutics and the Role of History," *New Literary History* 7 (1975), 209–32.
26. Ibid., 227.
27. Ibid., 228.

ical study, is overcome by Skinner through an *a priori* assumption, which he implies is self-evident, but which is not.

The easy generosity of spirit shown in Skinner's essay is challenged somewhat by Frank Kermode's study of the regulation of interpretation by institutions. Using the example of the early Christian fathers as a model of the development of institutional control of texts and their interpretation, Kermode compares the establishment of a canon of sacred books—a long, bitter, and momentous task—with the establishment of a canon of secular, intellectual, and literary texts. It is this canonicity, established by the "profession," which designates what is a "text"—that is to say, what is worthy of foregrounding and study in the first place.[28] To be sure, the canon does change as the institution which designates it (and which issues the "licenses for exegesis" that one must possess to enter discussions such as this one) responds to external pressures, enthusiastic movements, and the like. (These comments obtain, of course, only in those places where a reasonably open intellectual life is possible.) Surely, the institutional control of hermeneutic possibility, which Kermode guardedly approves, responds to an anxiety similar to that of the early Church. It is anxiety before these multiple historical interpretations that leads Kvastad to call intellectual history an infant, while Danto merely notes the smallness and silliness of some historians. The vision of a similar profusion of sacred texts, a profusion of orthodox readings, and a profusion of accredited interpreters is as academically frightening as it is theologically disturbing, and for similar reasons: both anxieties dread the loss of a truth or meaning necessary for saving something, whether a soul or the past.

Yet the past *is* lost, of course, in the sense of its unrecoverability as present; we recall it not as living memory, but as a series of catalogued signs, the archive, the canon. This loss of living memory is a very old anxiety, but as Paul Ricoeur notes in his essay "History and Hermeneutics," this very loss, and the separation of knowledge and history, may also be taken as opportunity, the hermeneutic opportunity.

> It is still possible to argue with Plato that the perversion of the historical bond begins with recourse to external marks which come to serve as traces for subsequent generations. This primary misfortune is the externalization of memory in such marks. Plato's famous argument against writing in the *Phaedrus*

28. Frank Kermode, "Institutional Control of Interpretation," *Salmagundi* 43 (1979), 72–86.

(274e–277a) applies to historical objectification to the extent that it sets in opposition two forms of memory, the one internal and based on the requirements of true reminiscence, the other external and submitted to the condition of marks and imprints. History, after all, is a particularly explicit case of remembrance by means of traces and imprints. Plato's sharp attack against externalization in marks and his ringing defense of reminiscence without external mediation forbid our simply recognizing the fact of temporal distance. It is why we need to introduce a principle of distantiation, which is a form of putting something at a distance rather than the mere fact of being at a distance.[29]

Rather than concede Plato's ancient case against writing, a case that makes our entire tradition and our profession in particular seem diseased in its essence, Ricoeur finds the "distantiation" or "externalization in marks" to be the augmentation of reality, and the mediation that "gives temporal distance its true significance."[30] Because this gap may be seen itself as textual, a hermeneutic arises that may claim ultimately to undermine the text/context dualism of traditional historical method, as well as undermining the distance between past and present. The "paradox of historical methodology" in Ricoeur's view arises from the double interest it serves: the interest for knowledge (which implies a naturalistic, scientific history) and the interest for communication (which implies an evaluative, interpretive history). However, Ricoeur's view of this dualism is as irenic in a practical sense as Struever's or Skinner's; the paradox is not paralyzing, because "the two interests do not exclude each other, but mutually imply each other."[31]

The hermeneutic interest demonstrated by current historiography and philosophy of history, like the interest in language described above, is a symptom, a defense against a primal anxiety—ironically, fear of *the domination of the past by the present*. The traditional defenses against such anxieties, which threaten a loss of identity through a loss of origin, have been a nostalgia for lost essences, the desire to abolish or deny the textual slippage inherent in writing, and the attempt to control the dangerous "intrinsic" of a text by appealing to the allegedly more secure "extrinsic" of its context. These hermeneutics share with seman-

29. Paul Ricoeur, "History and Hermeneutics," trans. David Pellauer, *Journal of Philosophy* 73 (1976), 691.

30. Ibid., 692.

31. Ibid., 695.

tics and analytical philosophy a desire to rediscover a past-as-reality, without repressing the ever-urgent (almost libidinal) pressure of the present-as-interest. In privileging the past, even in so circuitous a way as suggesting that we cannot know our own present without a dose of the past-as-reality (an ethnocentric suggestion that arrogantly dooms vast numbers of societies and individuals to self-ignorance), one proves one's loyalties and demonstrates that one's anxieties are in the right place. The dualisms of textual and contextual, autonomous and hetero- nomous, endolinguistic and extralinguistic, all of which history is sup- posed to encompass with humanistic virtuosity by using "distantiation" to overcome distance, are never relinquished. At most a "transcendence" into a metalanguage is posited, but the cheerful admission of small homopathic doses of various approaches into the body historical seems to aggravate at least two disquieting matters noted above—the loss of an identity, a differentiation for historical stud- ies; and the ingress of ideas, methods, inspirations, and fads into his- torical thought without a corresponding egress.

III

> Historia abscondita.—*Every great human being exerts a*
> *retroactive force: for his sake all of history is placed in the*
> *balance again, and a thousand secrets of the past crawl out of*
> *their hiding places—into his sunshine. There is no way of*
> *telling what may yet become part of history. Perhaps the*
> *past is still essentially undiscovered! so many retroactive*
> *forces are still needed!*
> Nietzsche, *The Gay Science*

Thus far I have noted that the anxieties inevitably con- stituent of any formal study have recently been focused upon a loss of identity in intellectual history. The incursion of a powerful movement in literary criticism, which has increasingly chosen to treat all texts as *formally* equivalent and responsive to the same rules of "textuality," has led historical thought, and intellectual history in particular, to study in self-defense the roles of language and of hermeneutics to an unprece- dented extent.

Triangular Anxieties: The Present State of European Intellectual History

For the past century, historical method has uneasily faced principles of interpretation that challenged the "commonsense," periphrastic, and antijargon rules that have been the basis of "gentlemanly" history, and has sought to demystify ideological obfuscations, to analyze latent forces, or to excavate deep structures. These hermeneutic tendencies, the tradition of Marx, Freud, and Saussure, do not claim the majority of intellectual historians as party members or even as fellow-travelers. Nevertheless, I believe that marxism, psychoanalysis, and structuralism create a triangular field of forces, with each point exerting a powerful magnetic pull on all within. To be pulled toward one point is to be pulled away from the others; to "belong" to one point of the triangle creates an ironic sense of loss (for what is "reductionism" if not a loss of scope and flexibility?) that leads increasingly to anxious defenses and adaptations. The new anxieties, which have seemed especially pronounced during the past decade, derive from this triangular field of interpretive strategies. These trends affect the books published in the field, the substance of academic debates, and the vocabulary that all must use in addressing texts.

One significant aspect of the emergence of the hermeneutic movements of the past two decades has been a struggle within each complex of ideas to establish just the sort of power relationships described by Kermode. The issue of canonicity, for example, has come to the fore as the groups scramble to decide the authority of texts. Who, for example, may be admitted into the canon of the Freudian tradition, and who expelled? Who will be assigned to apocrypha or to heresy? Is Foucault a structuralist? How are we to reread Hegel so as to admit the Frankfurt School (both echt and neo-) into a marxist mainstream? These and innumerable related questions will proliferate in the absence of a professional or an extraprofessional tribunal of judgment or intimidation. Indeed, we may hypothesize that the weakness of the "profession" as a secure reward-and-penalty-dispensing agency in the past decade has encouraged the creation and collision of new canons. What we are dealing with here is a politics—that is, a struggle for power—without much in the way of stakes beyond the profession itself. This creates a great deal of surface movement and engenders a sort of nervous agility that does not disturb the fundamental shape of things.

Reports of summaries of recent work have become a new genre. Americans, in particular, seem hungry for news of the fortunes of English psychoanalysis after Winnicott, or how the French go about "forgetting" Foucault, or the extent of Habermas' accommodations to liberal democracy. Of course, one of the great practical uses of such reports is to sum up and digest difficult and scattered work in a field; historians tend to prefer predigested summaries to grappling with difficult texts. The primers on structuralism and semiotics, or existential marxism, or French Freud, or the Frankfurt School, all serve to overcome the necessary concern of an American academic audience that it cannot be on the spot in the still-vital theater of European ideas. But they also carry with them a certain privilege for their authors, who gain from them the right to speak both about the figures within a tradition and about the tradition itself.

A second notable trend in recent scholarship in European intellectual history has been the spate of works on already canonical figures, written with the clear intent of rereading them "into shape." Just as a scientist must, in Thomas Kuhn's view, return to nature and "beat nature into shape" after a paradigm shift, so the recent studies of thinker after thinker have reflected the need to reinterpret the canon in the light of Derrida, or Habermas, or Erikson. Freudians write about Freudians, marxists write about marxists, and structuralists about structuralists, as well as about their putative intellectual ancestors. The point of this work is not quite to establish the canonicity of these figures, although in some cases (that of Walter Benjamin, for example) the status of the writer has been rapidly elevated. Rather, the interest served by the extensive writing *of* the converted *to* the converted has been that of establishing a right to speak with authority from within the tradition. As such, these works serve the same political purpose as the ones I have discussed above. However, because they are more strictly retrospective, they also serve to reshape the traditions with which they deal. As the post-Derrideans reread Descartes and Kant, as Habermas (and countless others) reread Benjamin and Dilthey, the shape of these figures changes, *their* field of force changes in direction and amplitude. To mention their names is thereafter to invoke a new problematic. The anxious contention of the old canon with the new hermeneutics produces, among other things, a lot of discourse, as it is meant to do.

There is a third element to the hermeneutic wave, however, and it is upon this element that I would like to focus attention here. I refer to the "triangular anxieties" shown in the mutual confrontation of the Freudian, structuralist, and marxist camps. In general, I should note that anxieties arise in historical thought when something is perceived to be lost or excluded, and that the triangle of hermeneutic camps divides the field—context, intention, and textuality—between them. Freudians will, to be sure, continue to write their form of psychohistory; marxists, their form of contextual history; and so forth. But when they begin to desire the "lost" territory of the others, a situation arises in which the marxist, for instance, can grasp at the desired psychological richness of the Freudian only by imitating or adapting in some way to the problematic or terminology of the other. My use here of the terms "desire" and "triangularity" is borrowed loosely from René Girard; a few examples will suggest what I mean. Girard notes that the desire of a subject for an object is always mediated by a third point, the other who already possesses or also desires the object.[32] Consequently, in the perfect case of triangular desire, the approach of any two points of the triangle must be mediated by the third. Although I suspect that this pure form of triangulation will become more frequent as the virtuosity of hermeneutic rapprochements increases, at the moment most efforts of this sort involve a single encounter, a recognition of the importance of one other part of the triangle.

The amount of attention given today to spelling out these encounters is considerable. I shall mention only a few examples. Russell Jacoby's work, which seeks to identify "the radical core of psychoanalysis," and to read out of the true canon those followers of Freud whose writings reflect their "social amnesia"—that is, who are reduced by their failure to navigate the forces of the triangle—certainly may stand for many similar attempts to transcend the longstanding hostility (or at least mutual indifference) of Marxism and psychoanalysis.[33] The French, whether Althusserians, Lacanians, Girardians, or Derrideans, are adept at this sort of triangulation, producing structuralist marxism, linguistic psychoanalysis, universal structural strategies of desire, and a deconstructive technique that calls into question the basis of meaning itself. Habermas has sought to reconcile an interest-oriented hermeneutic of marxist tendency with a certain view of the psychoanalytic dialogue in the last section of *Knowledge and Human Interests*; the fact that this reconciliation is brought about by translating both into a rather structural pattern of exchange serves to remind us of the triangular model that

32. René Girard, *Deceit, Desire, and the Novel: Self and Other in Literary Structure*, trans. Yvonne Freccero (Baltimore, 1965), 1–52.

33. See Russell Jacoby, "The Radical Core of Psychoanalysis," *Queen's Quarterly* 86 (1979), 105–9, and *Social Amnesia: A Critique of Conformist Psychology from Adler to Laing* (Boston, 1975). See also Robert A. Pois, "Historicism, Marxism, and Psychohistory: Three Approaches to the Problem of Historical Individuality," *Social Science Journal* 13 (1976), 77–91.

these accommodations more or less resemble. When he notes, for example, that "Freudian theory can represent a structure that Marx did not fathom,"[34] he is using the third point of the triangle—the linguistically based structures of communication that he derives from the work of Alfred Lorenzer—to mediate the other two, which appear to be primary for him.

The varieties of triangular anxiety may range from the utter rejection of the real existence of the other approach to its amicable incorporation into one's own methodology. In the first case, which corresponds to a phobia, one may deny the ability of a given hermeneutic stance to confront reality in any adequate way, as when Galvano Della Volpe cites the "essential philosophical, *gnoseological* poverty" and the "radical evaluative impotence" of Russian formalist developments in criticism.[35] Literary studies may bear fruit, we are told, only when the literary work is rooted in the " historical humus, with all its ideologies or moral or human ferments—according to the modern materialist conception of poetry."[36] While the ascription of impotence and the concern for fertility remind us of an anxiety based upon the fear of an event that may call both potency and fertility to a halt, this case is a bit extreme. Other tactics are a good deal more subtle. I have in mind the work of Fredric Jameson, whose *Prison-House of Language* represents a marxist confrontation with the structuralist tradition that does not fall into Della Volpe's "reductive" strategy of preemptive castration. Jameson laments the loss of diachronic sensibilities in traditional structuralist thought, but never fails to recognize the importance and utility of structuralism's ordering virtuosities. Remarking that the French structuralists "know Marx so well as to seem to constantly on the point of translating him into something else (the same is true of Freud . . .)," Jameson suggests that the inability of structuralism to overcome the Kantian dilemmas inherent in its static categories has led to the post-structuralist counterpart of nineteenth-century Hegelianism—that is, the Derrideans and the *Tel Quel* group, whom Jameson calls "Left-Heideggerians."[37] Similar confronta-

34. Jürgen Habermas, *Knowledge and Human Interests*, trans. Jeremy Schapiro (Boston, 1971), 282. See also idem, "History and Evolution," trans. David Parent, *Telos* 39 (1979), 5–44; and Werner Marx, "Habermas' Philosophical Conception of History," *Cultural Hermeneutics* 3 (1976), 335–47.

35. Galvano Della Volpe, "Settling Accounts with the Russian Formalists," trans. John Mathews, *New Left Review* 113–14 (1979), 139–41.

36. Ibid., 145.

37. Fredric Jameson, *The Prison-House of Language: A Critical Account of Structuralism and Russian Formalism* (Princeton, 1972), 176. See also idem, "Marxism and Historicism," *New Literary History* 2 (1979), 41–74.

tions of interpretive systems are becoming frequent. When Benveniste or Todorov reveals the functions of the Freudian dream-work to be essentially psychic versions of the linguistic tropes beloved of the structuralists, or when Hayden White points out that Marx's sketch of the history of commodity forms in the first chapter of *Capital* follows the same pattern, or when we read a book by a literary critic titled *Revolution and Repetition: Marx/Hugo/Balzac*, we must realize that the most urgent anxieties today, as well as the most productive ones, are the triangular anxieties.[38]

IV

> *I am afraid we are not rid of God because we still have faith in grammar.*
>
> Nietzsche, *Twilight of the Idols*

As intellectual history becomes increasingly hermeneutical, with the erstwhile "annalists of ideas" becoming "analysts of ideas," to cite the title of an article by Morton White,[39] a yet deeper anxiety emerges along with the growing confidence in commentary. Because "all commentary is allegorical interpretation," in Northrop Frye's words, the basic structure of historical explanation in the modern period is also allegorical. Allegory, which "says one thing and means another," is the essential genre of interpretation; to speak of hermeneutics is to speak of allegory. To speak of *class* or of *instinct* or of *structure* is to speak allegorically; references to infrastructure, displacement, or liminality are allegorical. In fact, pushed to or at least toward its limit, allegory may be said to encompass the act of reading itself. The distantiation lauded by Ricoeur as the hermeneutical space, the tension of text and context traditionally seen as the space of historical explanation, or the "backward" (*rückwärts*) reading identified by Nietzsche as

38. Emile Benveniste, *Problems in General Linguistics,* trans. M. E. Meek (Coral Gables, Fla., 1971), 65–75; Tzvetan Todorov, *Théories du symbole* (Paris, 1977), 285–321 and 361–69; Hayden White, *Metahistory: The Historical Imagination in Nineteenth-Century Europe* (Baltimore and London, 1973), 287–97; and Jeffrey Mehlman, *Revolution and Repetition: Marx/Hugo/Balzac* (Berkeley, 1977).

39. Morton White, "Why Annalists of Ideas Should Be Analysts of Ideas," *Georgia Review* 29 (1975), 930–47.

the source of the indefinite freshness of the past, all these are the terrain of allegory. The characters of allegory are timeless; when placed in a diachronic narrative—as they inevitably must be—they create, in Paul de Man's phrase, the "rhetoric of temporality," which mediates symbol and time. In *The Transformation of Allegory*, Gay Clifford writes:

> The several strands of the narrative, and the multiplex figures and images which provide texture and meaning locally, anatomize the concepts and emotions and beliefs which concern the author. Particular events or places then provide a culmination to this process. They focus through metaphor and so have the essential open-endedness intrinsic to that figure, but by virtue of providing a culmination, a focus, imply the possibility of perceiving coherence in the world, and the viability of a total conception of life. The values and structures revealed are natural components of an interpreted world.[40]

The ability to represent and transmit "values and structures" is the traditional test of historical writing. Without the former, it would be an idle morbidity, a preoccupation with the past for its own sake, which is itself a value of sorts, however useless; without the latter, it would represent a chaos of discrete events (if chaos may be represented), and thus be equally useless either as an explanation of anything or as a stimulus to action in the world. It is the need for value and structure that leads histories to interpret, to generalize, to compare, and to dramatize—all these processes lead toward the allegorical.[41]

The strengths of allegory make it the "natural" mode of historical explanation. A leading authority on allegory, Angus Fletcher, puts the matter as follows: "It allows for instruction, for rationalizing, for categorizing and codifying, for casting spells and expressing unbidden compulsions, for Spenser's pleasing analysis, and, since aesthetic pleasure is a virtue also, for romantic storytelling, for satirical complications, and for sheer ornamental display. To conclude, allegories are the natural mirrors of ideology."[42] The characteristic weakness of allegory, however, is its tendency to "overmanage" events, to know too

40. Gay Clifford, *The Transformation of Allegory* (London, 1974), 105.

41. In *Metahistory*, Hayden White stresses the "moral and aesthetic" choices that must be made existentially by the historian, without provable grounds. I believe that these "moral and aesthetic" choices correspond to the "values and structures" transmitted in allegory. See above, Chapter 8, "A Bedrock of Order: Hayden White's Linguistic Humanism."

42. Angus Fletcher, *Allegory: The Theory of a Symbolic Mode* (Ithaca, 1964), 368.

much.[43] In history, this leads to what Nancy Partner has called the "overplotting" of modern historical texts, which use a rigorous principle of selection to eliminate everything not "significant to the major themes of the work."[44] This leads, in turn, to an anaesthesia that incessantly calls attention to our inability to apprehend reality directly. Perhaps it is more accurate to say that the self-awareness of allegorical interpretation *is* merely the apprehension of the inability to apprehend reality directly.

The *anxiety* before allegory comes from the heightened awareness of the distance between what we mean and the texts we produce, or of the uncertainty whether we *can* mean without producing a text, the existence of which always already undercuts the grounds of meaning. The anaesthesia that sometimes accompanies allegory stems from the distantiation necessary to hermeneutic (or allegorical) interpretations. This distance extends to the rupture between our readings of the texts of the past and our "readings" of other times, as well as that between our construction of systems of discourse and our desire to signify, or to "mean" (made particularly explicit in French as *vouloir-dire.)* Hints of this anxiety, which I am suggesting here is the deepest and most "affective" of historical anxieties, are to be found in the discussions of "language" or "semantics" in history; and in the simple realization that language possesses its own density, a dimension far more broadly significant than the conventions of past historiography have recognized. Further indications are revealed by the widespread interest in historical hermeneutics, which was not so long ago one of those terms that historians, the last defenders of "common language" against jargon (which usually means words with Greek, rather than Latin, roots), used only at the risk of violating historical decorum. Even the dread inspired by the deconstructive "terrorists" among all those who read texts for a living pales in my judgment before the allegorical anxiety. After all, deconstruction in the by-now classical Derridean sense is reassuring in the same (allegorical) way that marxism or Freudianism is reassuring: the goal of the quest is Grail-like, known in advance. It is the quest itself, always renewable, that is the thing.[45]

43. Stephen A. Barney, *Allegories of History, Allegories of Love* (Hamden, Conn., 1979), 49.

44. Nancy F. Partner, "Making Up Lost Time: Writing on the Writing of History," *Speculum* 61:1 (1986), 102.

45. Fredric Jameson has pointed to allegorical aspects of Jacques Derrida's philosophical technique, noting that "the very structure of the sign is allegorical, in that it is a perpetual

288

Allegory and Anxiety

If we grant that the most notable characteristic of recent intellectual history is its lack of autonomy—that is, its increasing use of ideas and systems borrowed from nonhistorical sources—and that these sources (including the three I have identified as defining the triangle dominating the current scene) rest upon assumptions and vocabularies elaborated long before in other texts but shared by the reader and the historian, the nature of history-as-allegory becomes clearer. The naming of characters is the most familiar aspect of explicit allegory; the Red Cross Knight, or Everyman, or Ahab alerts the knowing reader to possible meanings behind the tale even before the tale is told. Similarly, the vocabularies of the marxist, Freudian, and structuralist place and order the evidence before any full consideration of it is possible. However, allegorization is by no means limited to specific ideologies. The *"Annales* school" of historical scholarship is a good example of fertile allegorization disguised as quantitative objectivity of the most rigorous sort. A large variety of special terms has entered its vocabulary; these terms have often created (as an object of study) the concepts that they denote. *Mentalité, la longue durée, l' outillage mental, conjoncture,* are among the many terms invested with allegorical authority; when we have agreed to deal with these questions in these terms, we have acknowledged the same distance from phenomena that we note in the allegorical characters Good Works or Fellowship.

The traditional movement of defense against the claim that allegory is the basis of discourse in intellectual history has been to insist upon the possibility of semantic equivalence (that is to say, paraphrase) as the foundation of an elementary form of intellectual history. If, for example, it is possible to paraphrase Rousseau adequately, then it follows that it is at least possible to assemble a string of adequate paraphrases to form a sort of intellectual biography, or to "place" these paraphrases among paraphrases of Rousseau's contemporaries to form an elementary "life and times." I have cited above the work of the semanticist Kvastad and the philosopher Danto, each of whom, through improved analysis of language, wants to ensure more perfect paraphrases. The ability to paraphrase and summarize is valued highly among historians, as it should be. However, even at the most microscopic levels, the possibility of semantic equivalence is questionable.[46] At the level of

movement from one 'level' of the signified to another from which it is expelled in its turn in infinite regression." *Prison-House of Language,* 180.

46. A discussion of the linguistic problems in the concept of semantic equivalence is found in Oswald Ducrot and Tzvetan Todorov, *Dictionnaire encyclopédique des sciences du*

intellectual history, which involves large corpuses of difficult texts, it is even harder to grant. The only semantic equivalent of a complex text is the text itself. What the allegorist does, and what the historian does as well, is to create a *counter*discourse that confronts the chosen "evidence" with the real meaning of the latter, a meaning that is different from or presumed to be hidden in the evidence. The counterdiscourse is thus dependent upon *both* the evidence *and* the system of understanding that makes a counterdiscourse necessary. All forms of historical *explanation* as such thus make use of allegorical devices to mediate between the evidence and the history created from it.

Although the politics of a given allegorical system may be radical, the structure of explanation is not.

> Allegory is, in literary terms, conservative because it relies on special knowledge of language and it alludes to old literature. As the poet says, it must be abstract. Allegory loses in coldness and intellectualism what it gains in freedom and knowledge. All fiction works by indirection, but allegory refuses to conceal its artifice and its scheming. After all, allegory may be considered relatively artless.[47]

The relative artlessness of the allegorical aspect of historical texts has hidden it from scrutiny until fairly recently; but in various guises, the awareness of the linguistic or allegorical nature of historical writing has become an important anxiety.

Properly speaking, the allegorical anxiety that has emerged as a major theme in writing on history and culture occurs when one unmasks the allegorical nature of a given discourse from within a counterdiscourse that is equally allegorical, whether or not it is aware of itself as such. Michel Foucault's work has been a model of this sort of thing.[48] In *Orientalism*, Edward Said notes the tendency of the orientalist discourse to overmanage reality to the extent that Arabic (an important

langage (Paris, 1972), 565–67. A different position, offering the necessity of synonymy, is E. D. Hirsch, Jr., "Stylistics and Synonymity," *Critical Inquiry* 1 (1975), 559–79.

47. Barney, *Allegories of History*, 49.

48. For a discussion of the linguistic and allegorical principles at work in Foucault's writings, see Hayden White, "Foucault Decoded: Notes from Underground," in *Tropics of Discourse: Essays in Cultural Criticism* (Baltimore and London, 1978), and idem, "Foucault's Discourse: The Historiography of Anti-Humanism," in *The Content of the Form* (Baltimore, 1987).

See also Allan Megill, "Foucault, Structuralism, and the Ends of History," *Journal of Modern History* 51 (1979), 451–503.

character in the orientalist's allegorical discourse) "*speaks* the Arab Oriental, not vice versa."[49] Similarly, Said believes the failure of Orientalism to be its inability to recognize human experience in "the Orient";[50] this is an example of the anaesthesia mentioned by Fletcher as allegory's weakness. Yet Said is keenly aware that he himself speaks from within a universe of discourse that sanctions representation (or misrepresentation) only "for a purpose, according to a tendency"[51]— or, in the terms I have been using, allegorically.

Hayden White expresses a version of allegorical anxiety in an essay on René Girard, in which he criticizes Girard for assuming that history—as "background" or "context"—affords a secure base on which to stand in the tricky business of interpreting literary texts. Because this tacit claim that the individual text, which is problematic, may be explained by the allegedly more secure "historical context" has been essential to critics and historians, the explicitness of White's statement is instructive.

> But it must be pointed out that it is one thing to interpret literary texts and quite another to purport to construct a comprehensive philosophy of history and theory of society, laying claim to the authority of science, as Girard has done. This is not because literature inhabits a realm of fantasy and history is comprised of facts, or because art is one thing and society another. It is because our interpretations of history and society can claim no more authority than our interpretations of literature can claim.[52]

This passage certainly makes plain the illegitimacy of using the *product* of an allegorizing process as the scientific foothold for another allegorizing process. White's point here is not that interpretation is inherently flawed, or utterly without standards of choice; it is rather that Girard has failed to face the consequences of allegory, and instead is trying to escape into a "reality" of "context." In accusing Girard, as well as Freud and Lévi-Strauss, of explaining too much, White has indicated that what they assume to be their secure base is itself an allegorical construction.

Today, theories of "reading," of interpretation, are not only prob-

49. Edward W. Said, *Orientalism* (New York, 1978), 321.
50. Ibid., 328.
51. Ibid., 272–73.
52. Hayden White, "Ethnological 'Lie' and Mythical 'Truth,'" *Diacritics* 8 (Spring 1978), 9.

lematic, but are drawn not infrequently from theological sources by writers who call upon us not to believe, but rather to consider and, in considering, to draw an allegorical lesson about matters that are, in René Girard's phrase, *cachées depuis la fondation du monde.* Harold Bloom's excursion into medieval Jewish mysticism in *Kabbalah and Criticism* took Gershon Scholem's history of the kabbalist tradition and made of these ideas an "extended metaphor" of textual creation. Frank Kermode's *Genesis of Secrecy* uses early Christian sources in a similar project, while Edward Said has recently described a dispute between eleventh-century Islamic linguists as anticipating the major critical debates of today.[53] What seems most striking about all this work is the use of theological speculation—which can be presented today *only* as an allegory—as an almost explanatory procedure. That is, if Bloom had ignored Isaac Luria, or if Said had ignored the Cordovan Zahirites, and each had presented his critical stances at once in the language of Freud or Lukacs, the allegorical *gesture* would be missing, although the allegory would not. Instead, each chose a metaphorical model that calls attention to its figurative nature; unlike Girard, they self-consciously demonstrated the allegorical base upon which they envision the process of interpretive reading erecting itself.

The need for self-consciousness in recognizing the fundamentally figurative or allegorical nature of our images of history is the explicit theme of Hayden White's *Metahistory* and *Tropics of Discourse.* Whether or not one finds the tropes, emplotments, explanatory procedures, and ideological stances that he plots of interest, one must, I think, address his major assertion, which resides in none of these. For White, the major problem behind historical writing is the question of *will* expressed in the choice of principles of representation; allegory is precisely the existential projection of our will upon the given field of historical artifacts—meaning as *vouloir-dire,* as the will to say. At its most extreme, the focus on allegorization comes from an awareness of the artificiality of distinctions in the undifferentiated, but indefinitely differentiable, continuum of "reality," in particular the distinctions that lie behind words. When we speak of the renaissance and give to it both a name and a body so that it can enter the lists of historical periods, we are behaving as allegorically as when we speak of the libido (whose promptings, it has been noted, often differ little from those of Aphro-

53. Harold Bloom, *Kabbalah and Criticism* (New York, 1975); Frank Kermode, *The Genesis of Secrecy* (Cambridge, Mass., 1979); Edward W. Said, *The Text, the World, the Critic* (Cambridge, Mass., 1983).

dite), or of a social class, rising or struggling, falling or decadent. The canonical tradition in history offers a cast of allegorical characters—the idea of the renaissance, the notion of class, or *la longue durée*, or anxiety—from which one must choose in interpreting texts. From these and other choices originate the "values and structures" that a history will impart.

V

> *Every idea originates through equating the unequal.*
> Nietzsche, *The Will to Power*

This chapter has delineated the current state of European intellectual history by stressing the role of anxiety in defining the goals, strategies, and defenses of both the field in general (an increasingly difficult field to identify) and the major trends within the field. The general anxiety has, perhaps, come from the blurring of distinctions among the various traditional ways of dealing with texts and the breakdown of the traditional professional decorum that has in the past decided which kinds of texts were legitimately part of which canon. Intellectual history is no longer merely political, social, and philosophical thought, nor are literary studies now limited to belles-lettres. "Historical discourse," the means by which historians create a verbal icon representing the past, has come under the same scrutiny that has traditionally been applied to novels; and this scrutiny must generate a certain anxiety in a profession whose identity is based upon precisely the distinction between its own prose and that of the writer of fiction. The results of this blurring of the edges of intellectual history have been a growing interest in language study in historical method, and a renewed and explicit interest in hermeneutics.

In effect, the turning of historians toward linguistics and hermeneutics is more than simply an expression of the desire to assume imitatively some of the remarkable powers of modern linguistic and hermeneutic models. It also corresponds, I think, to the breakdown in confidence in semantic equivalence, which is the foundation both of paraphrase and of traditional intellectual history. Synonymy, the ability to say the same thing in other words, has come under attack in literary theory in a number of ways; in historical study, it is giving way to a self-consciousness about the "distantiation" that impedes the attainment of semantic equivalence. As the process takes place, an awareness of the allegorical heart of historical representation emerges.

Hayden White, who has noted in passing the allegorical nature of the forms of representation discussed above,[54] has also signaled for us the psychological faculty to which it corresponds. He suggests in the Introduction to *Tropics of Discourse* that the neglected Kantian faculty of *will* should be re-examined as the source of both our decisions about the nature of the past and our goals for the future. However, this Kantian belief that a chosen, allegorical past is morally necessary for projecting a chosen, better future confronts a problem posed by Nietzsche's *Zarathustra.* "Nicht zurück kann der Wille wollen; dass er die Zeit nicht brechen kann und der Zeit Begierde—das ist des Willens einsamste Trübsal" ("The will cannot will backwards; and that it cannot break time and time's covetousness, that is the will's loneliest melancholy").[55] Yet the will can and does will backwards in the form of historical writing itself; this is the "believing backwards" that Nietzsche found to be the "distinctive virtue and disease" of his contemporaries. It is a disease insofar as it serves as a "revenge," "the will's ill will against time and its 'it was.'" It is a virtue insofar as it is a willing forward in the service of a chosen future. The problem of the will to allegory is, in my opinion, the specific anxiety that will in large part define the future of European intellectual history.

54. White, *Metahistory*, 15n.
55. *Also Sprach Zarathustra,* part II, "Von der Erlösung," trans. Walter Kaufmann, in *The Portable Nietzsche*, ed. Walter Kaufmann (New York, 1954).

12 NARRATIVITY IN HISTORY

POST-STRUCTURALISM AND SINCE

I

Recent debates among historians on narrative often suggest that what is at issue is a simple decision: should the historian tell a story (i.e., narrate the material in a chronological, cause-effect way) or not. To choose not to tell a story is to be more "modern," following the social and economic sciences in presenting synchronic, and quantitative if possible, models of past affairs. New historical methods and recently explored kinds of documentation often deal with the general and the mass, rather than the particular and the individual; modeled on computers and lacking in "events," this "new" history, which flourished in the 1960s and 1970s, established the basis for a nonnarrative history that challenged the traditional core of historical knowledge. Even the turn to storytelling by certain prominent nonnarrative historians only served to mark the distinction; tales of personal life in heretical medieval villages, or of returning husbands with uncertain identities, were distinctly *different* from the earlier work of these historians. The stories seemed to be luxury articles, earned as indulgences after the drudgery of economic, social, climatological, family, demographic, history. Indeed, the stories were often by-products of such research.

During the same period of time, roughly the twenty years from 1965 to 1985, another movement of thought emerged, which looked at forms of knowledge from quite an opposite perspective. While historians were confidently processing larger and larger quantities of information, producing broader comparisons and wider conclusions, and in general extending the historical domain toward a goal of a "total history," the countermovement sought, like Penelope, to unravel the weaving of texts and to question wherever possible both the meaning and the tactics and conditions that made meaning possible in written texts of all sorts. History was for some of them a special target; they considered it both dependent upon and supportive of the oppressive and inescapable atmosphere of "humanism."

Both movements, at first, found their theoretical inspiration in France; both found essential practical support in the large and varied world of American academia. The postwar *Annales* "school" of historians has by now seen three generations, each with its own style and interests. The movements once marked as "structuralist" have similarly changed and developed to such an extent that the term "post-structuralist" is conventionally used, in the Unites States at least, to designate the idiosyncratic and difficult thinkers who have challenged the primacy and security of meaning, of history, of narrative, and of the idea of "man" that is constructed by these practices.

To study the writings of the "unravelers," the opponents of the extensive and totalizing forms of reading that information technology has made into the tacit current model of knowledge, is to suspect that the debate over narrative history is a good deal more complex than the recent debates among historians might suggest. My purpose here is to present an image of post-structuralist thinking on narrative and its intricate relationship with history and to sketch the work of three writers on historical narrativity. I am looking for common threads that might serve as guides for those studies of historical writing that desire neither to dissolve history into the area of pure textuality, in which it will have little or no identity, nor to accept the representationality of historical writing on its own traditional terms of "getting the story straight."

At the risk of bringing down on my head the objection that "argument by selective example is philosophically unpersuasive, a rhetorical device not a scientific proof,"[1] I shall sketch an image of post-structural thought about narrative and history by discussing briefly a few quotations from prominent figures. These figures might reject the term "post-structuralist," which is current primarily in the United States; even the small group of writers sampled here differ in more ways than they might agree. A properly post-structuralist reading might well find important ways in which each passage differs from itself, offering a play of contending voices repressed by readings that stress their meaning and their essence. This said, I can only add that a survey of post-struc-

---

1. This observation is made by Lawrence Stone, "The Revival of Narrative: Reflections on a New Old History," *Past and Present* 85 (1979), 3–24.

turalist thought is a project that runs against the grain of post-structuralism. What follows is meant, therefore, as a point of departure, not a conclusion.

> (182) *He reaped the fruits of his genius by winning the sculpture prize,*
> *ACT. "Career": 4: to win a prize.
> (183) *established by the Marquis de Marigny, the brother of Mme de Pompadour, who did so much for the arts.* *REF. History (Mme de Pompadour).
> (184) *Diderot hailed the status of Bouchardon's pupil as a masterpiece.*
> *ACT. "Career": 5. to be praised by a great critic. **REF. History of literature (Diderot as art critic).
>
> > (Roland Barthes, *S/Z*, trans. R. Miller
> > [New York, 1974], 101)

So much of Roland Barthes's work has dealt with history and historical texts that it seems absurd to enter this corpus by way of a quotation from *S/Z*, Barthes's unique and meticulous decoding of a story by Balzac. The quotation itself requires decoding: the parenthetical numbers refer to the numbered segments (quoted in italics) into which Barthes has divided Balzac's text; the abbreviations marked by an asterisk (e.g., "REF," "ACT") designate the five codes that Barthes traces through the tale in his search for the conditions that give rise to the creation of meaning in this text. In *S/Z*, as we can see, "History" figures within a single code, the Referential, among the five that constitute this version of narrative poetics. What makes this instance important for a consideration of post-structuralist considerations of history and narrative is that it signaled a change in Barthes's way of approaching narrative.

In his work of the 1960s, heavily influenced by the formalism of early structuralism, which he had done much to articulate, Barthes presented narrative as "international, transhistorical, transcultural; it is simply there, like life itself."[2] Naturally, the model Barthes used to describe narrative was that of language; it follows that for him mimesis or realistic representation is a matter of codes that are largely conventional. At about the same time, Barthes wrote related essays on "Historical Discourse" and "The Reality Effect" that spelled out in the structuralist terms of the mid-1960s how the illusions of reality are achieved in the realistic texts of both history and fiction. Certainly, nar-

2. Roland Barthes, "Introduction to the Structural Analysis of Narrative," in *Image—Music—Text*, trans. Stephen Heath (New York, 1977), 79.

rative and the narrative competence of readers were essential parts of the referential and rational illusion. "In fully constituted 'flowing' discourse the facts function irresistibly either as indexes or as links in an indexical sequence; even an anarchic presentation of the facts will at least convey the meaning 'anarchy' and suggest a particular philosophy of history of a negative kind."[3] This flowing narrative discourse carries its own message independent of its subject matter: the gist of this message has to do with the meaningful relatedness of the facts in the discourse. Even meaninglessness or anarchy is meaningful in this view. Narrative is irresistible.

Returning to the quotation from *S/Z* cited above, we see that history serves there merely as one of the systems of reference that generate the "effect of reality" in narrative, just as, in a different way, it is narrative that creates the possibility of historical discourse. Both history and narrative have for Barthes a mythic dimension, in the sense of myth developed in his work of the 1950s. The essence of this myth is the conversion of history into nature, and the essence of the myths of our own day is the process by which the dominant cultural forces transform the reality of the world into images of that world.[4] Myth is a metalanguage, an

3. Roland Barthes, "Historical Discourse," trans. Peter Wexler, in *Introduction to Structuralism*, ed. Michael Lane (New York, 1970), 153.

4. Roland Barthes, *Mythologies* (Paris, 1957), 215, 229. Yet these political writings of the 1950s (which maintained that, yes, the left also made myths, but that these myths were "inessential"), although they seemed to herald a career trajectory of historical demystification, led in fact to Barthes's great battle with the establishment of literary history in France over his book *On Racine*. At the beginning of the last chapter of this book, he cited a "naive and touching" program on French radio that sought to suggest to its listeners that art and history are interconnected by introducing musical selections— "1789: Convocation of the Estates General, recall of Necker, concerto for strings #4 in c minor, by B. Galuppi."

In his *Sade, Fourier, Loyola* (1971), Barthes would produce a reply to chronological history by treating three figures from disparate areas of endeavor and different centuries, organizing his discussion without regard for chronology (going so far as to divide his discussion of Sade into two sections separated by Loyola and Fourier, thus repeating in his text the "mania for cutting up" that he describes in his subjects). The final section, a dozen pages long in the English translation, is called "Lives" and presents a series of unconnected statements ("biographemes") about Sade and Fourier (but not Loyola). These fragments are not only unconnected, but pointedly lack any consistency of narrative voice: some are bare statements of fact ("4. Fourier hated old cities: Rouen."); some pointedly imitate the stupidities of Flaubert's "received ideas": ("2. Fourier was contemporary with the two greatest events of Modern History: the Revolution and the Empire. Yet in this social philosopher's work, no trace of these two cataclysms . . ."); some suggest the histories that might be made from such fragments ("7. Inter-Text: Claude de Saint-Martin, Sénancour, Restif de la Bretonne, Diderot, Rousseau, Kepler, Newton."); the last,

allegory in that it structures a gap between its surface and its content, and history is mythologized by its subservience to "irresistible" nar- rativity.[5]

> What can a science of writing begin to signify, if it is granted
> . . . that historicity itself is tied to the possibility of writing; to the possibility of writing in general, beyond those particular forms of writing in the name of which we have long spoken of peoples without writing and without history. Before being the subject of history—of an historical science—writing opens the field of his- tory—of historical becoming. And the former (*Historie* in German) presupposes the latter (*Geschichte*).
> The science of writing should therefore look for its object at the roots of scientificity. The history of writing should turn back toward the origin of historicity. A science of the possibility of science? A science of science which would no longer have the form of *logic* but that of grammatics? A history of the possibility of history which would no longer be an archaeology, a philosophy of history or a history of philosophy?
>
> (Jacques Derrida, *Of Grammatology*, trans.
> G. C. Spivak [Baltimore and London, 1976], 27–28)

The characteristic prose of Jacques Derrida, with its personified sub- stantives, its inquisitory nominatives ("A science of the possibility of science?"), semantic conundrums ("a science of science"), passive modalities ("if it is granted"), implied assertions (". . . which would no longer have the form of . . ."), mixed concretes and abstractions ("the roots of scientificity"), ambiguous relationships ("in the name of which"), and so on, is easier to identify and even describe than to pene- trate. But this is not because Derrida does not write well—his prose is clearly an inextricable part of his thought, like Milton's no less difficult prose—but because, like Lacan and other modern writers, he takes great pains to perform the rigors of his thinking in his work. Derrida's project is a science of sciences that will delve the roots of the generalized writ- ing that he takes to be the unacknowledged and repressed counterpart of the privileged voice of centered and locatable meaning that has domi- nated the "history of metaphysics."

which ends the book, notes: "12. Fourier had read Sade."—a fact of no more importance for Barthes than the fact that Loyola had not read Sade.

5. Barthes, *Mythologies*, 200, and Louis-Jean Calvet, *Roland Barthes: un régard politique sur le signe* (Paris, 1973), 39–44.

Those who follow this project find that reading even the rational, commonsense world of historical writing is fraught with dangers and pitfalls.[6] The contradictory voices brought forth by deconstructive readers are generated by the fact that writing for them is constituted by a system of negative "traces" that mark an absence; the negative hermeneutics of Derridean analysis arrives at a dispersed, even chaotic, field of signifiers posed against the meaning-oriented, false coherence always sought (and always found, even in paradox and error) by the "logocentric" reading of the tradition. That this tradition supports itself as a discourse of morality and a discourse of power by means of its images of itself, its history, is clear. The "origin of historicity" referred to above is not, or is not only, the origin of history-writing as the histories of historiography locate it; it is the origin of the possibility of historicity, of being in history, which is a vital part of the creation of "humanity" as our culture represents it. Thus, Derrida is usually taken to be one of the radically antihistorical inheritor-critics of the structural linguist Ferdinand de Saussure.

The fundamental concepts that make history possible, that is to say, orderly, are undermined by Derrida and dispersed by a discourse that confesses it must make use of these concepts at every turn (hence the importance of Derrida's style, which calls attention to its inevitable implication in language by what has been called "sawing off the branch on which you are seated"). This process of reading, well described as the "careful teasing out of warring forces of signification within the text itself," strives to leave no essential concepts unexamined, while welcoming the paradoxes, problems, and intricacies that are routinely overlooked by less rigorous readings.[7] The material assumptions of totality, identity, self-agreement, and so forth yield before this analysis; all of the logocentric human sciences of western metaphysics come under scrutiny—history most of all, perhaps.[8] Cause, in particular,

6. Among many examples of post-structuralist readings of historical discourse, see Linda Orr's *Jules Michelet: Nature, History, Language* (Ithaca, 1976); "Tocqueville et l'histoire incompréhensible," *Poétique* 49 (1982), 51–70; "L'Autorité 'populaire' de l'historiographie romantique," *Romantic Review* 73 (1982), 463–72. See also Dominick LaCapra's readings of Allan Janik and Stephen Toulmin's *Wittgenstein's Vienna* in LaCapra's *Rethinking Intellectual History: Texts, Contexts, Language* (Ithaca, 1983), and of Carlo Ginzburg's *The Cheese and the Worms* in LaCapra's *History and Criticism* (Ithaca and London, 1985).

7. Barbara Johnson, *The Critical Difference* (Baltimore and London, 1980), 5.

8. An interesting survey of these issues is found in "Text and History: Epilogue, 1984," an essay added to the expanded edition of Robert Weimann's *Structure and Society in Literary History* (Baltimore and London, 1982). Here (277) Weimann takes issue with the con-

Allegory and Anxiety

which can be seen as merely the product of narrative structures once the world is considered as a text, is a trap, always to be questioned.[9]

> As to the problem of fiction, it seems to me to be a very important one; I am well aware that I have never written anything but fictions. I do not mean to say, however, that truth is therefore absent. It seems to me that the possibility exists for fiction to function in truth, for a fictional discourse to induce effects of truth, and for bringing it about that a true discourse engenders or 'manufactures' something that does not yet exist, that is, 'fictions' it. One 'fictions' history on the basis of a political reality that makes it true, one 'fictions' a politics not yet in existence on the basis of a historical truth.
>
> (Michel Foucault, "The History of Sexuality" (an interview), in *Power/Knowledge: Selected Interviews and Other Writings, 1972–1977*, ed. C. Gordon, trans. C. Gordon, L. Marshall, J. Mepham, K. Soper [New York, 1980], 193)

Michel Foucault's importance for historical theory scarcely needs mention; it was his "revolutionization of history" that led many to the desire to "forget" him.[10] Although his earlier work, especially *Madness*

---

tion in Michael Ryan's *Marxism and Deconstruction* (Baltimore and London, [1982], 57) that there is "a radical concept of history in Derrida." He grants, however, that Derridean philosophy offers a "certain mode of textual analysis which, by analogy, can prove potentially helpful in dismantling any monistic, mechanical, or idealist approaches to historical data, events, and gestures" (278). I take this to mean that deconstruction is appropriate to everything except dialectical materialism.

9. Examples of the sort of assumptions questioned by Derrida are easy to find; the assumptions seem perfectly "natural." For example, in a review of Lynn Hunt's *Politics, Culture, and Class in the French Revolution*, Robert Darnton writes: "Split by incompatible arguments, the book pulls the reader in opposite directions—toward sociology on one side and hermeneutics on the other" (*New York Review of Books*, 31 Jan. 1985, 23). That arguments should be compatible, that readers should be pulled in only one direction, that the author is in charge of the reader's performance, and that sociology and hermeneutics (or any forces in a text) should be "connected" somehow at the end of a responsible work are all epistemological and (primarily) aesthetic assumptions built into the discourses analyzed by Derrida.

10. For example, Paul Veyne's "Foucault révolutionne l'histoire," in *Comment on écrit l'histoire* (Paris, 1978). "Is Foucault still a historian? There is no true or false answer to this question, since history itself is one of those false natural objects: it is what we have made of it, it has not ceased to change, it does not survey an eternal horizon. . . ." (242).

See also Allan Megill's "The Reception of Foucault by Historians," *Journal of the History of Ideas* 48 (1987), 117–41.

and Civilization and *The Order of Things,* put forth a highly rationalized image of modern Western history implicitly based upon the sequentiality of the ordering principles found in rhetorical tropes, the work of the 1970s (reflected in the theory of historical "fictions" above) extends his scope in such a way as to call these very presuppositions into question as constructs toward a goal.[11]

When Foucault asserts that our enlightening, demystifying liberators actually repress us with their scientific authority, based on surveys, experimentation, and research, the open-endedness inherent in the critique expressed in the quotation above becomes manifest. In beginning his *History of Sexuality,* for instance, he posits as a problem, not the repression of sexual practices, but rather the discourse surrounding the discovery and attack on such alleged repressions. "The question I would like to pose is not, Why are we repressed? but rather, Why do we say, with so much passion and so much resentment against our most recent past, against our present, and against ourselves, that we are repressed?"[12] Foucault's emphasis on the *discourse* about repression rather than the alleged repression itself is characteristic of his work. He repeatedly examines authoritative "discourses," particularly the meliorist and value-free discourses of enlightened modern social improvers (medicine, psychiatry, penology, etc.) in such a way as to unearth, "genealogically," the will to power embodied by *all* appeals to authority. For this reason, I stress the emphasis on "fictionality" and "truth" in his own work expressed above.

"Truth" and "reality" are, of course, the primary authoritarian weapons of our time, an era characterized by nothing more than the debate over what is true of reality. Despite the obviously constructed nature of these twin concepts, which Foucault, like other post-structuralists, points up again and again, he will not dispense with them, but rather examines the way in which discourse creates reality, as reality creates discourse. His own fictions, therefore, are true because they are based upon a certain reality; this reality is real, in part, because it has been figured by his fictions. Insofar as Foucault is the opponent of what is "natural" and "commonsensical," insofar as he unmasks these as merely the *doxa,* the dominant opinion of our time, he links himself with Barthes as a radical historicist who surveys the past "under the

---

11. On the tropology in Foucault, see Hayden White, "Foucault Decoded: Notes from Underground," in *Tropics of Discourse: Essays in Cultural Criticism,* (Baltimore and London, 1978), 230–60.

12. Foucault, *The History of Sexuality,* vol. I, trans. R. Hurley (New York, 1978), 9.

sign of the Other," confronting (that is, creating) a stark sense of repressed differences in history.[13]

> If it were to come out in a new day that the logocentric project had always been, undeniably, to *found* (fund) phallocentrism, to insure for masculine order a rationale equal to history itself?
> Then all stories would have to be told differently, the future would be incalculable, the historical forces would, will, change hands, bodies; another thinking as yet not thinkable will transform the functioning of all society.
>
> (Hélène Cixous, "Sorties," in *New French Feminisms*,
> ed. E. Marks and I. de Courtivron [Amherst, 1980], 93)

The de-naturalizing that seems so much a part of post-structuralist practice appears most complex, contradictory, and provocative among feminists who are concerned with the dilemmas of entering a discourse that they assert, by its very structure as rational, sequential thought, excludes a certain notion of *woman*, as body, freedom, Other. Among these modes of masculine, phallocentric writing, history is particularly indicted not only because it is the substance of a story that has, to a large extent, excluded women from its scope, but, far more important from a post-structuralist perspective, because its alliance with narrative has indentured it to hidden forms of authority that are far more repressive to *woman* than being nameless in histories. "Nearly the entire history of writing is confounded with the history of reason, of which it is at once the effect, the support, and one of the privileged alibis" (249).

The problem confronted by Hélène Cixous is how to speak, to find a voice within a discourse of reason and representation that has not only failed generally to speak of woman, but has more generally repressed the possibility of speaking as a woman from our very imaginations. Only an occasional poet, the foe of representationalism, has managed briefly to open a crack in which for a moment, woman might appear. "Woman un-thinks the unifying, regulating history that homogenizes and channels forces, herding contradictions into a single battlefield" (252). Logocentrism, the term that denotes Derrida's concept of the word-centered, conceptual history of Western metaphysics, is equated with phallocentrism, the need to claim authority by defining, clarify-

13. Paul Ricoeur, *The Reality of the Historical Past* (Milwaukee, 1984), chap. 2.

ing, making sequential points, leading to conclusions.[14] The danger is the theoretical, the authority of the signified, of essentialized meaning and definitions themselves. All of these traps are encased in a form of writing that leads through text-time to a goal, like histories, and that we may call narrative.[15]

If the attentions of structuralism and its aftermath to history have a coherent direction—that is, if we choose to make plausible historic sense out of them—then it seems to me that this direction must lead toward a thoroughgoing examination of the process of reading. It is reading that is the key, that has been redefined by post-structuralist practice and revealed as a process far more elusive and problematic than was recognized before. In a sense, reading has been reinvented.

While formalist structural narratology seems to have reached a state of near-technical perfection, offering an array of useful tools for foregrounding and examining aspects of texts, or of any phenomena that may be treated as though they were written texts, its treatment of the essential concept of the reader has, in general, been limited to matters of competence and how readers are constituted by texts. Post-structuralism has produced a practice of reading that has enacted the difficulty, even the impossibility, of trusting readings based on a simple, communicative model.[16]

14. The notion of the phallus referred to here is central to an understanding of Jacques Lacan. It is not a human organ of any sort, but rather a reference to the ancient processions in which a veiled phallus was carried about. For Lacan, the phallus is a signifier that creates desire for the unveiling of a signified, of meaning and truth; since this is always deferred by the nature of desire, it is desire of the phallus that is the basic motor of the intersubjective economy because of the universality of castration. Jacques Lacan, "The Signification of the Phallus," in *Ecrits: A Selection*, trans. Alan Sheridan (New York, 1977), 281–91.

15. Post-structuralist consideration of narrative from a feminist perspective tends to conflate the weight of history and the ends-oriented exchange value of narrative. Maria Minich Brewer writes: "We [interpreters of twentieth-century texts] read and describe with relative ease texts of fiction that contain a multiplicity of narrative voices, dissolution of characters, and perturbations in the logic of events and temporal developments. The challenge to narrative constraints in modern texts may seem to stem from a discontinuity created between essential terms: process without assigned Finality; multiple textual effects without an identifiable Cause; Writing that possesses neither a simple Origin nor End; signifiers without immediate access to a privileged Signified." "A Loosening of Tongues: From Narrative Economy to Women Writing," in *MLN* 99 (1984), 1141.

16. The narratological literature is already vast. Useful introductions in English are Shlomith Rimmon-Kenan, *Narrative Fiction: Contemporary Poetics* (London and New York, 1983); Gérard Genette, *Narrative Discourse: An Essay in Method*, trans. J. E. Lewin

The post-structuralist trajectory continues Roland Barthes's project of demythologizing; the myth is the conversion of history (the contingent, the force of the letter, human discourse) into nature (what is absolute, commonsense, beyond doubt, universally granted). As more and more of the accepted and inevitable components of human life are revealed as construction, no particular perspective can claim to be a privileged, secure basis. Although the post-structuralist thinker might point to a term, a scheme, a tactic, as a master viewpoint at any given moment, it is more than likely that the next work will discard that term or scheme and erect an entirely new one. Their creation of jargons and specialized, neologistic vocabularies is authorized precisely by subsequent rejection and replacement by other jargons and vocabularies; the perils of language require that it be treated as scaffolding, always waiting to be taken down. One might say, with Hélène Cixous, that the chaos of reality occasionally peeps through a crack, a poetic moment; but narrative and history, for the post-structuralist, are guilty until proven innocent.

II

Not all recent thought about history and its relationship to narrative has privileged the story as the single index of nar-

---

(Ithaca, 1980); and Wallace Martin, *Recent Theories of Narrative* (Ithaca, 1986). The classic statement of a communications model of poetics, which was a starting-point for structuralists and a system to be dismantled by post-structuralists, is Roman Jakobson's "Linguistics and Poetics," in *The Structuralists: From Marx to Lévi-Strauss*, ed. Richard and Fernande DeGeorge (Garden City, N. Y., 1972), 84–124.

In stressing the importance of reading as a category of research for historians, I am not referring primarily to the "history of reception," as the Germans and Swiss have pursued it, nor the "sociology of literature," as the French have pursued it, nor to histories of publishing and printing à la Robert Darnton and Elizabeth Eisenstein, nor to attempts to discover whether more Renaissance readers were reading Plutarch or Polybius. These unquestionably respectable pursuits all deal with an essentialized view of the book, of context, and of society, and, with the partial exception of *Rezeptionsgeschichte*, have little sense of reading as process, nor of the reciprocal construction of text and reader, nor of conflicting voices within the text, nor of codes that make reading possible, nor of narratological categories.

That such a pursuit of signs, codes, and the like need not be a formalist exercise conducted in a "historical vacuum"—such exercises, to be sure, are often of great value—is demonstrated by Hayden White's essay on Droysen and on how his *Historik* functions to construct a particular kind of bourgeois reader. "Droysen's *Historik*: Historical Writing as a Bourgeois Science," in *The Content of the Form: Narrative Discourse and Historical Representation* (Baltimore, 1987), 83–103.

rativity. The work of Paul Ricoeur, F. R. Ankersmit, and Hayden White recognizes in various ways that narrativity is a world-view, within which story-history is a genre. Narrativity, as explored and defined by Ricoeur, appears to authorize the historical enterprise itself in all its forms; it is the meaningful representation of human beings in time, or as Paul de Man put it from a linguistic perspective, a sense of the irreversibility of tropes. With the acceptance of the logic and the rhetoric of temporality, history is constituted. That is to say, regardless of the *form* of representation, history rejects a dissociation of cause from effect, rejects the idea that cause can "follow" from effect through processes of *Nachträglichkeit,* or *après coup,* ideas that are commonplaces of the poststructuralist critique of the essentialized cause-effect paradigm.

The distances are vast between the post-structuralist critique of historical reason and the essentially defensive theorizing of Ricoeur, Ankersmit, and White. Ricoeur locates narrativity in the human soul as its fundamental way of comprehending the fact of death. Although Ankersmit maintains that reality cannot be translated into discourse, he also posits for historical writing the fundamentally humanistic goal of broadening our scope of "vision." Hayden White has named poststructuralism an "absurdist moment," but White, long influenced himself by existentialism, will not dismiss the absurd out of hand.[17] Instead, he seeks to account for it historically, by suggesting, through a virtual crack in his own text, that the possibility of an absurdist, "sublime" historiography was institutionally repressed during the last century in favor of a safer, "beautiful" form, narrativity. Although from a post-structuralist point of view they often leave unexamined essentialized concepts, notions of the unified human subject and the centered text, the studies of historical narrativity that I shall discuss below nevertheless share one vital aspect of post-structuralist activity— namely, a consciousness of the *allegorical* nature of narrativity, and thus of history itself.

RICOEUR AND THE SOUL OF NARRATIVE

If one is to reject "story" as the identifying mark of narrativity, then what will replace it? Paul Veyne's *Writing History* makes the point quite clearly that history is the comprehension of *plots* and that theories are in

17. Hayden White, "The Absurdist Moment in Contemporary Literary Criticism," in *Tropics of Discourse.*

fact plot summaries (*résumés d'intrigue*).[18] His nominalist position rejects science as a goal for history for reasons that involve a responsibility to the past. History has not the right to reject all that has been, in order to address only what can be studied scientifically.[19] Besides, Veyne suggests that scientific theories (especially the economic) are too abstract to explain history.[20] Veyne's position has the considerable virture of being couched in terms that are specifically *moral* and *aesthetic;* it calls attention directly to questions about the purpose of historical study that are overlooked, avoided, or trivialized in many discussions, which are too often interested in "what shall we teach the graduate students?" or "what will the historian of the 1990s have to know (to get ahead)?" It also draws attention to the vast disparity in standards of knowability for various periods, areas, and kinds of history; for Veyne, the historian of classical antiquity, the stakes are quite different from those of the historians of early modern Europe, whose methods and materials seem to have provided a new model and agenda to a surprising degree.

In *Time and Narrative,* Ricoeur accepts Veyne's elevation of plot in history, but he feels that Veyne fails to explain how narrative remains the essence of history when history ceases to be about events.[21] This is the key problem for all "narrativist" understandings of history, particularly in the face of the French historical accomplishment.[22] Ricoeur addresses the issue in terms of time. In discussing Augustine's treatise on time in the *Confessions,* Ricoeur sketches the terms of the debate over the question "What is human time?" Time is experienced primarily as an absence, because only the present can ever be experienced except in the form of memory and expectation. Memory and expectation, however, are the central modalities of time, to the extent that one may speak of human time as a threefold present: a present of past things (memory), a

18. Paul Veyne, *Writing History: Essay on Epistemology,* trans. M. Moore-Rinvolucri (Middleton, Conn., 1984), 118.

19. "The reason for this separation between history and science is that history has as a principle all that has been, is worthy of it; it has not the right to choose, to limit itself to what is susceptible of scientific explanation. The result is that in comparison with history, science is very poor, and repeats itself terribly." Veyne, *Writing History,* 254.

20. Ibid., 255.

21. Ricoeur, *Time and Narrative,* vol. I, trans. Kathleen McLaughlin and David Pellauer (Chicago, 1984), 174.

22. "This question today must be addressed to all holders of a 'narrativist' theory of history. English-speaking authors have been able to avoid it because their examples usually are naive and do not surpass the history of events." *Time and Narrative,* I, 174. Cf. also Ricoeur, *The Contribution of French Historiography to the Theory of History* (Oxford, 1980).

present of present things, and a present of future things (expectation). The neatness of this threefold present dissolves with the endless and unavoidable "slippage" of the present of the future into the present of the present and of the past. It is "Augustine's inestimable discovery" to have linked this slippage with the *distensio animi*, the stretching of the mind in different directions by the structure of temporal experience itself. Citing the example of reciting a psalm from memory, Augustine reviews the mnemonic itinerary through the three modes of time.

> What is true of the whole psalm is also true of all its parts and of each syllable. It is true of any longer action [in actione longiore] in which I may be engaged and of which the recitation of the psalm may only be a small part. It is true of a man's whole life, of which all his actions [*actiones*] are parts. It is true of the whole history of mankind, of which each man's life is a part. (XI;28:38)[23]

Augustine's meditation on eternity provides Ricoeur with another important clue about human time. Instead of merely abolishing time, the concept of eternity, which cannot be grasped by human minds except as absence, provides the elements for an internal hierarchization that deepens our experience of time itself. This, for Ricoeur, provides the key to understanding the attempts of historiography and literature to "de-chronologize narrative." Far from being the denial of temporality, this de-chronologization deepens it. "Chronology—or chronography—does not have just one contrary, the a-chronology of laws or models. Its true contrary is temporality itself."[24]

This temporality has an element of order and intelligibility, which is Ricoeur's subject in *Time and Narrative*; succession itself comes from this order, not from experience. Carefully following Aristotle's discussion of *muthos* (plot) as *mimesis* (imitation) of human action, Ricoeur emphasizes *muthos* as the key to a threefold mimesis that follows the "destiny of a prefigured time that becomes a refigured time through the mediation of a configured time" (54). The prefigured time (Mimesis 1) is the human experience of temporality itself, with its intense preoccupation with Care and being-toward-death, in Heidegger's terms. Configured time is the text in its formal, narratological state (Mimesis 2), which leads to our historical understanding, the analogical faculty that comes from our narrative competence (Mimesis 3).

23. Cited in Ricoeur, *Time and Narrative*, I, 22.
24. Ibid., I, 30.

Ricoeur's central point regarding history and narrative is that *"all change enters the field of history as a quasi-event."*[25] He has, in effect, reversed the hierarchy of terms that places the long time span over the event, by demonstrating how fully any understanding of long time spans must be saturated with forms of human understanding based upon human time as understood in particular by Augustine as a three-fold present. For Ricoeur the danger inherent in forgetting that events also populate the temporality of the long time span is not historiographical, but epistemological and moral.

> For the discovery of the long time-span may simply express the fact that human time, which always requires the reference point of a present, is itself *forgotten*. If the brief event can act as a screen hiding our consciousness of the time that is not of our making, the long time span can, likewise, act as a screen hiding the time that we are.
>
> This disastrous consequence can be avoided only if an analogy can be preserved between the time of individuals and the time of civilizations: the analogy of growth and decline, of creation and death, the analogy of fate.[26]

Ricoeur is aware that much Anglo-American discussion of history and narrative has foundered on the event-orient history that populates its examples; his appreciation of the French historians of the past four decades is great. The example of Braudel, Chaunu, Le Goff, Duby, Ariés, and others leads Ricoeur to an understanding of event that is produced by his concept of plot, rather than the other way around. Events are not the brief and nervous motions described by Braudel, but "variables of the plot," which literally *comprehends*, "grasps together," as an "intelligible whole, circumstances, goals, interactions, and unintended results."[27] It is the extension of human temporal understanding in the form of what Ricoeur (following Paul Veyne) calls "quasi-plots," "quasi-characters," and "quasi-events" that points to the analogical character of historical categories.[28]

25. Ibid., I, 224.
26. Ibid.
27. Ibid., I, 142.
28. In *The Reality of the Historical Past* (25–36), Ricoeur stresses the "analogue" in the form of the tropology described by Hayden White in *Metahistory* and elsewhere. The tropological element in refiguration (Mimesis 3) centers the question on its goal, which is the human understanding; in *Time and Narrative*, this aspect becomes subsumed in the whole structure of threefold mimesis governed by plot, not trope.

Ricoeur suggests that the recent works on the history of death may represent the farthest point reached by all history.[29] In a long endnote, Ricoeur surveys the literature on death and its relation to the history of the long time span; he cites Michel Vovelle's comment that although "the death of a certain historizing history is today an accomplished fact," the event has not really disappeared from the historical field. This citation from a leading historian of death to the effect that the "death" of a certain sort of history, although a "fact," may not be final casts an interesting light on Riceour's own thesis. Even in the face of the possible "death of narrative," narrativity cannot die precisely because it is the symbol of human immortality, or at least of the understanding of human life afforded by the contemplation of eternity. *History,* far from turning away from narrativity with the ostensibly antinarrative French contribution to twentieth-century historiography, has experienced a deepening and broadening of the sense of temporal emplotment, but Riceour notes that *literature* may yet give in to the discord between truth and consolation, a discord generated by the narratological precision of recent literary studies and by the sort of post-structuralist critique of humanism that gives rise to the notion that common sense itself is merely the sum of the fictions that we accept as part of human nature.

> The result is that the book ceaselessly oscillates between the invincible suspicion that fictions lie and trick insofar as they console, and the equally invincible conviction that fictions are not arbitrary insofar as they answer a need of which we are not the masters, the need to put the seal of order on chaos, of sense on non-sense, of concord on discord.[30]

Ricoeur cites Walter Benjamin's pessimistic suggestion that the end of the era of narration may come because human beings no longer have experience to share.

Ricoeur's tracing of Care (a character from the second part of Goethe's *Faust,* adopted philosophically by Heidegger) and Death (who needs no introduction) toward the limits of history and narrativity, and his fear that we may lose our humanity if we discount the sense-making essence of narrativity, in certain ways reblazes the overgrown trail of Oswald Spengler's *Decline of the West.* Spengler, like Ricoeur, notes the deep link between the study of a culture's behavior before death (including dis-

29. Ricoeur, *Time and Narrative,* I, 111.
30. Paul Ricoeur, *Temps et récit,* vol. II (Paris, 1984), 45 (my translation).

posal of the dead) and its idea of the historical past.[31] For Spengler, however, history (and implicitly narrativity) is a purely Western (that is, Faustian) ideology; for Ricoeur, it is "trans-cultural." And while Ricoeur cannot envision a proper humanity without a sense of time made possible by narrativity,[32] Spengler concludes that our image of history (and of the death that it embodies) also entails the birth of the new.[33] Both Spengler and Ricoeur see historical writing as a consoling way of disposing of the dead and of situating human beings in their peculiar relationship with time, but Spengler foresaw, like Cixous, "another thinking as yet unthinkable," like Derrida, "a science of science which would no longer have the form of *logic*," like Foucault, "a politics not yet in existence." In other words, Spengler could contemplate the possibility of a radically different life-form in which the solace of history would play a different part, or no part at all. Ricoeur also contemplates such a life-form, but with deep regret.

F. R. ANKERSMIT AND THE SUBSTANCE OF THE NARRATIO

In *Narrative Logic: A Semantic Analysis of the Historian's Language*, F. R. Ankersmit has put forth a theory of historical logic and practice that reverses the traditional way in which historians and philosophers of history have looked at the relation of the historical text and the historical past.[34] Narrative logic, as Ankersmit describes it, is found, not in relation to time, but in the *narratio*, the narrative text taken as a whole; this logic is characterized by a strict attention to the conditions of existence of narratios and an avoidance of the "material assumptions" that have caused a great deal of the confusion in both philosophy of history and the social sciences.[35] Narrative logic relates the narratio only to other

31. Oswald Spengler, *The Decline of the West*, vol. I, trans. C. F. Atkinson (New York, 1934), 13.

32. Ricoeur, *Time and Narrative*, I, 52.

33. "Every great symbolism attaches its form-language to the cult of the dead, the forms of disposal of the dead, the adornment of the graves of the dead. The Egyptian style begins with the tomb-temples of the Pharaohs, the Classical with the geometrical decoration of the funerary urns, the Arabian with catacomb and sarcophagus, the Western with the cathedral wherein the sacrificial death of Jesus is re-enacted daily under the hands of the priest. From this primitive fear springs, too, historical sensitiveness in all its modes. . . ." Spengler, *Decline of the West*, I, 167.

34. *Narrative Logic: A Semantic Analysis of the Historian's Language* (The Hague, 1983).

35. Indeed, most reviews this book has received, particularly in *History and Theory*, the *Journal of Interdisciplinary History*, and *Historische Zeitschrift*, are based upon precisely the material assumptions that Ankersmit wishes to put aside.

narratios; it does not assume that the narratio "represents" anything but itself.

Although he believes that history cannot become a social science (since social science has more to learn from history than history from social science), Ankersmit also makes clear at the outset that we must avoid associations with belles-lettrism and storytelling in speaking of narratios; indeed, he asserts that nonstorytelling historiography is most clearly in conformity with his narrativist philosophy. The narrative substance that is contained in narratios is the complete image contained in a historical work; it is these narrative substances that Ankersmit analyzes rather than the statements contained in them.[36] The essence of historical thought (and the key to how historical works are evaluated and how historical debates take place in practice) is to be found in the nature of narrative substances. To look elsewhere is to be lost in a sea of relativism.

Modernism and structuralism, which was in many ways the end of modernism, stressed the scientific knowledge of "out there," whether in the sciences of nature, the sciences of man, or the sciences of the text. Nature, man, texts, are all portrayed as observable, knowable, and describable because discourses about them may be repeatedly compared with the original object, using the analytico-referential method that provides a means of translating reality into discourse about reality, based on the visual model of the telescope.[37] Citing the explosion of conflicting discourses about reality (especially historical reality), Ankersmit espouses a postmodern attention to the discourse itself, and its relation to other discourse. The historical discourse (or narratio) exists only because of other discourses, not because of the past, which is always absent by definition.

The three theses of narrative logic are (1) that there are no translation rules for reality, (2) that it is the *whole* of a narratio, rather than the sum of its narrative sentences, that gives us an interpretation of the past, and (3) that there is a similarity between historical and metaphoric statements. Although Ankersmit reiterates Huizinga's anti-Rankean statement that there exists no "*es*" to correspond to history "*wie es eigentlich gewesen ist*," he is nevertheless the champion of *historism*—with a dif-

36. Examples of historical narrative substances might be Vovelle's description of early modern death (as opposed, say, to that of Ariès), or Baron's "Renaissance" (as opposed to Burckhardt's), or Stephen Bann's "nineteenth-century historical imagination" (as opposed to that of Hayden White).

37. Cf. Timothy Reiss, *The Discourse of Modernism* (Ithaca, 1982).

ference. The historism Ankersmit embraces is not the historicism of the grand speculative philosophers of history; it is rather the historism that stresses the uniqueness of the historical moment and the error of comprehending it other than on its own terms. (The question of judgment is a separate one.) Almost all historical writing is to some extent historist in practice, but Ankersmit maintains that historical disputes are regularly caused by our historist attribution to the "past" that which is *only* true of narrative substances. "Not what is explained but what explains is unique."[38] It is not the "past" (or time, eternity, the soul, reality), but rather our understanding of narrative substances, that has a narrative structure; even if the "past" did have a narrative structure, we could not know this because there are no translation rules that might verify some correspondence between the "past" and the narrative substances that offer our only knowledge of it.

In a most memorable metaphor, Ankersmit speaks of the narrative substance as a "black hole" that draws into itself all meaning and objects, while remaining monad-like in its inability to express true statements about other things. The "Louis XIV" in Voltaire's *Le Siècle de Louis XIV* and Goubert's *Louis XIV et Vingt Millions de Français* have nothing to do with each other *from the point of view of narrative logic*. This startling statement may be explained as follows: assume that both Voltaire and Goubert have made only true (that is, conventionally documented) narrative statements in their narratios; because of their different interests, their statements are rarely the same and present different understandings of "Louis XIV." To what, then, do these statements relate? To assume that they are true and that they relate to a "real" Louis XIV creates misleading problems of evaluation. In fact, in Ankersmit's view, they refer only to the narrative substances in which they appear. While narrative *statements* may be true or false, narrative *substances* should not be spoken of in these terms. The "incompatibility of narratios" (say, Voltaire's and Goubert's) does not mean that one is true and the other false. Ankersmit prefers the terms "subjective" and "objective"—but here again with a difference. Texts, but not people, can be "subjective," by which Ankersmit means much more than "influenced by moral values."

> Moreover, a historiography may be "subjective" for a number of reasons other than that its author was influenced by values.
> Indeed, aesthetic preferences, stylistic habits, lack of imagination

38. Ankersmit, *Narrative Logic*, 249.

or congeniality with a certain subject-matter or just sheer incompetence may also make an author's historiography "subjective." As a matter of fact, it is quite astonishing that the term "subjective" should always have been linked so exclusively with ethical and political values.[39]

The fundamental theorem of narrative logic, therefore, is that "all statements expressing the properties of Nss [narrative substances] are analytical." We are speaking correctly, I presume, as long as we make clear that we are talking about narrative substances and not about the past. What makes historical discussion possible is not references to specific statements, but rather "points of view," a commonplace word that Ankersmit believes is the historian's greatest tool.

> The "point of view" of a narratio is comparable to a belvedere: the scope of the "point of view" we get access to after having climbed all the steps leading to the top is far wider than just the staircase of the belvedere: from the top we look out over a whole landscape. The statements of a narratio may be seen as instrumental in our attaining a "point of view" like the steps of the staircase of a belvedere, but what we ultimately see comprises much more of reality than what the statements themselves express. Whatever the weakness of historical knowledge may be—and in many respects the historians' cognitive equipment is far less impressive than what his colleague in the exact sciences has at his disposal— we have here found one of the most formidable assets of the historian's methodological inventory.[40]

How then do we decide between the "points of view" that are embodied in narrative substances? It is wrong to suggest that the most "objective" narratio is the one that best corresponds to reality, because the first premise of narrative logic is the absence of translation rules. Further, according to Ankersmit, if one view of the past prevails, there is *no* view of the past, because only a multiple play of perspectives provided by a variety of narratios can enable us to "see" at all the contours and specificity of each view of the past.[41]

Consistent with Ankersmit's visual metaphors (point of view, belvedere), he cites "scope-maximalization" as the goal of narrative

39. Ibid., 235.
40. Ibid., 223–24.
41. Ibid., 240.

substances.[42] Because narratios are ways of seeing an image of the past, what narratios on roughly the same topic have in common (their "conventionalist" part) is not part of the individuation of any particular narratio. What presents the greatest scope, and hence the most objective narratio, is the least conventional and most original, daring one. "Thus, the essential duty of the historian is to be original and to refrain as much as possible from repeating what his predecessors in the investigation of a particular topic have said."[43]

The metaphors of vision employed by Ankersmit would lead his readers to suspect that the visually dominated discourse of modernism is at the basis of his narrative logic, but he makes it clear that the past cannot be seen from the historian's belvedere. It is a masquerade of narrative structures that we "see" from the belvedere; behind this masquerade is something that has no narrative structure, and thus cannot be properly "seen" at all.[44] Citing Wilhelm von Humboldt's statement that historical ideas cannot be grasped by mere logic, but only by a subtle, hidden disposition of the mind, Ankersmit maintains that within narratios familar concepts like "the Renaissance" or "the Cold War" are not "seen" but rather "smelled" or "heard."[45]

The narratio, then, has its uniqueness, its identity, only through its existence in a world of other narratios. It possesses as its own only what it does *not* share with them. Without this world of narratios, we could have no "apprehensions" of the past at all. The traditional historist term used to describe how the historian grasps the historical idea is *Ahnen* (premonitions, apprehensions); Ankersmit, I think, might say that the historian "catches a whiff" of them. When Ankersmit remarks that human "self-identity"—far from depending on our sense of time and eternity as in Ricoeur's rendering—is another narrative concept, and that classic mental disorders are often problems of narrative constructions, which are treated by historiographic-linguistic methods such as psychoanalysis, his reader scents the post-structuralist critique of the subject.[46]

42. Although there are many different ways of putting the matter, some form or other of "scope-maximalization" has, with the tacit decline of "realism," become a standard criterion of excellence in history and other fields these days. See, for example, Paul Veyne's "Lengthening the Questionnaire," in *Writing History*.

43. Ankersmit, *Narrative Logic*, 239.

44. Ibid., 88.

45. Ibid., 196.

46. "Psychological disorders such as depersonalization, schizophrenia or anxieties can probably be described as uncertainties and inconsistencies in the way the Ns "Iint" is

HAYDEN WHITE AND THE NARRATIVE SUBLIME

In the recent work of Hayden White, we find a distrust of narrative that is based neither on hostility to story-history nor on the idea that the new social history has somehow managed to escape narrative constraint. White sees narrativity itself as a potentially repressive force, especially once rhetoric and the possible visions of history it engendered have been rejected, as happened when history became a discipline in the early nineteenth century. In those fields of study, like history, seeking the newly elevated title of "scientific disciplines" in the nineteenth-century mold, the armatures of power or appeals to political authority that lie beneath all forms of interpretation as such could not be revealed. Interpretation had to be either hidden or purified to resemble the interpretations of the physical sciences—that is, either repressed or sublimated by dissolving the authority to interpret into the interpretation itself. Among the most important and permanent consequences of this sublimation of authority in the constitution of professional historical studies was the deep and lasting distinction between philosophy of history, with its metahistorical goal of articulating the modes of authority and centers of power in historical discourses, and "proper" history, with its disciplinary mandate to ignore the analysis of the deep, implicit choices in presentation and configuration, and the relative merits of these choices in opposition to other possible choices.

The question White poses is: "What is *ruled out* by conceiving the historical object in such a way that *not* to conceive it in that way would constitute prima facie evidence of want of 'discipline'?"[47] His answer is *rhetoric*, which he describes, following Kant, as the awareness of a variety of ways of configuring a past that in itself exists only as a chaos of forms. By de-rhetoricizing history, thus creating a discipline, historical studies in fact chose a certain stylistic mode (the middle style of declamation), which excludes from its scope the possibility of expressing or imagining all that does not pass for the common sense of socially

constructed by human beings." Ankersmit, *Narrative Logic*, 191. The French psychoanalyst Jacques Lacan is the key figure in the post-structuralist dissolution of the human subject into an Unconscious modeled on language, but Foucault (who presents the subject as an intersection of pre-existing discourses) and Derrida (who places the subject in an uncentered play of substitutions) have found their own ways of dealing with human identity. Good treatments of this matter are Kaja Silverman, *The Subject of Semiotics* (New York, 1983), and Allen Megill, *Prophets of Extremity: Nietzsche, Heidegger, Foucault, Derrida* (Berkeley, 1985).

47. Hayden White, "The Politics of Historical Interpretation: Discipline and De-Sublimation," *Critical Inquiry* 9 (1982), 120; collected in *The Content of the Form*.

"responsible" individuals at a given moment. This rhetoric of anti-rhetoric configured the past in the form of "science," a meaningful representation of a reality that was assumed to have an order that could be expressed.

In other words, White argues that in electing a certain mode of rhetoric, which found its natural expression in the realistic narrative forms of other nineteenth-century prose fictions, history became a "discipline" precisely by indenturing itself to those modes of thinking (and writing) so invisibly woven into the existing structures of power and discourse that their existence could either be denied or taken for granted as the indisputable foundation of enlightened, educated, or at least professional opinion.

The "beauty" of orderliness, which Edmund Burke put forth in his conservative assault on the "strange chaos" of the French Revolution, finds its true opposite in the "sublime" vision of history in Friedrich Schiller, who deplored the "counterfeit harmonies" of the effeminate historical vision. With Hegel's demolition of the concept of the "sublime," in favor of a rationality (hence, beauty) in history, the stage is set for the "aestheticism" of modern historical consciousness, which asserts with Ranke that the confusion of the historical scene is not essential to it, but rather a product of the accidents of sources and scholarly error, and can be set straight by historians "endowed with the proper kind of understanding."[48]

This desublimation of the historical field, which is as well the repression of the possibility of calling to consciousness radically different ways of conceiving the past and the human role in creating such conceptions, politically domesticates history in ways that White considers unfortunate.

> In my view, the theorists of the sublime had correctly divined that whatever dignity and human freedom human beings could lay claim to could come only by way of what Freud called a "reaction-formation" to an apperception of history's meaninglessness.[49]

The sublime view of history as a chaotic field, and of human freedom as the power to make of it and of our place in it what we will, is what impels human beings to change their lives, like the sublimity of Rilke's "Archaic Torso." Instead, the ideologies of the last two centuries, both capitalist

48. White, "Politics of Historical Interpretation," in *The Content of the Form*, 71.
49. Ibid., 72

and communist, have based their notion of morality and responsibility on a vision of history constituted as a discipline by the suppression of the historical sublime.

To grasp White's notion of the role of narrative in this suppression, we should first note his discussion of the value of narrativity as a form. Unlike other recent commentators on the status of narrative in history, who focus on distinctions discussed above in Chapter 5, White chooses to return to the classic historiographic genealogy: annal, chronicle, history. His suggestion is that in this apparent progression in human consciousness of the past, we see a growth of narrativity, which can only exist in a social world that recognizes some corporate entity that might serve as the organizing principle for a narrative selection of facts. The annal, with its discontinuous gaps between years, its lack of any theme or subject that can be followed, and its variety of annalists, can be seen at best as a record of time that might be meaningful only to God, who alone can comprehend the chaos (narrative absence) recorded by the annalist. Thus, narrative appears with a social consciousness, and carries with it the burden of representing that consciousness to its members, with all the political and ideological baggage that the construction of social consciousness entails.[50]

By now we can perceive the roots of White's distrust of narrative, a distrust that he shares with post-structuralist writers like Roland Barthes and Julia Kristeva. The narrative that White distrusts is not that speciously essentialized narrative that tells nineteenth-century stories about people and such, as opposed to the nonnarrative forms found in the work of the *Annales* school or the cliometricians. He recognizes that *all* of these forms are narrative, easily analyzed by the narratological tools of modern criticism, well honed as they are by the study of modernist literature.

What White calls into question is the unfailing ability of narrative to make sense out of things, and to present them in a form that *seems* natural. This is the "mythic" aspect of narrativity itself, both in the Aristotelian sense that narrative always gives things a plot (*muthos*) of some sort, and also in Barthes's sense that narrative turns the chaos of the past into an illusion of the immediacy and order of nature. Narrativity is virtually inescapable, but it is not natural, in White's view.

And one of the things that you learn from the study of the study of

50. Hayden White, "The Value of Narrativity in the Representation of Reality," in *Critical Inquiry* 7:1 (1980), collected in *The Content of the Form*.

history is that such study is never innocent, ideologically or otherwise, whether launched from the political perspective of the
Left, Right, or Center. This is because our very notion of the
possibility of discriminating among the Left, Right, or Center is in
part a function of the disciplination of historical studies which
ruled out the possibility—a possibility that should never be ruled
out of any area of inquiry—that history may be as meaningless "in
itself" as the theorists of the historical sublime thought it to be.[51]

What has been ruled out, in other words, appears to be what Ricoeur
fears may reappear: the sense of the possible meaninglessness of history, and thus of human life. White, however, adds the words "in itself"
to history, alluding to a sort of past that Ankersmit, for one, believes is
essentially unrepresentable, and consequently meaningless "in itself."
The past is the "thing in itself," which is beyond our direct apprehension, although we may create a world of appearances through our narrative abilities to create meanings. Kant's categorization of historical
forms named the third one (after eudaemonistic optimism and ter-
roristic pessimism) the abderitic or farcical; this approach maintained
that humanity had neither advanced nor decayed through time (as the
other modes, respectively, asserted), but rather that nothing had essentially changed. Any number of interpretations or meanings could be
generated from such a chaotic, directionless field. Kant wrote: "It is a
vain affair to have good so alternate with evil that the whole traffic of our
species with itself on this globe would have to be considered as a mere
farcical comedy [als ein blosses Possenspiel]."[52] It would seem from this
quotation that an optimistic or pessimistic history always precedes the
farcical. After all, it is the appearance of differences within the vision of
the past that calls its form into question. Marx, then, was apparently
thinking in a perfectly Kantian way when he noted (vaguely citing
Hegel) that all significant facts and personages appear twice in history,
first as tragedy, then as farce. As Ankersmit would suggest, it is only
the second appearance that creates the perspectival contours necessary
to create historical significance. On this view, the rule-governed, scientific structuralism of the 1960s may be regarded as a tragic moment in
the light of the farcical, but very serious, post-structural critique that
has followed it. The possibility of this abderitic, "absurdist moment" is

51. White, The Content of the Form, 82.
52. "The Strife of the Faculties," trans. Robert Anchor, in Kant on History, ed. L. W. Beck
(New York, 1963), 141, cited in White, The Content of the Form, 227.

what must never be ruled out of any theoretically justified inquiry, including historical study.

Ankersmit, Ricoeur, and White all reject, in their different ways, historical realism as it is usually understood. At the same time, each makes explicit a *moral* basis for his arguments, in what is perhaps the sharpest departure from standard procedure in building historical or philosophical positions. Ankersmit believes that what might be called his narrative perspectivism is precisely what *in practice* enables historians—indeed, people in general—to compare, evaluate, and understand images of the past (and of the present and of the self). When he notes that "the all-pervasive anti-narrativism of the 20th Century mental climate strongly stimulates solipsism," he is in fact attacking the modernism that posits that our knowledge is of reality rather than of accounts of reality.[53]

For twenty years the thrust of White's inquiry into the nature of historical thinking has been to single out the values—both moral and aesthetic (in the Kantian sense of that which validates judgments) in the choices underlying historical images.[54] His recent discussions of narrative, which show the influence of Sartre and Foucault as well as Roland Barthes, question the ideological weight of narrative as the "common sense," "natural" mode of presentation for all serious formulations, including his own, within a discipline. That the orderly meaningfulness of narrativity is implicated in the repression of meditations on the potential sublimity of the field of history as an unprocessed and essentially meaningless chaos (as if such a meditation were not already processed and, so to speak, narrativized in its very conception!) cannot imply a call for some sort of antinarrativism that might escape the ideology, discipline, and constraints of linguistic and social productions like history. White insists that it is our awareness of the human power to construct realistic images, such as histories, and of the choices involved in doing so, that he wants to foster. Possible visions of the past far outnumber those sanctioned by the historical discipline based upon its highly restrictive rhetoric, always in the interests of some "order."

Ricoeur sees the stakes somewhat differently, since it is the human experience of time itself that is deepened by narrativity. When Ricoeur

---

53. Ankersmit, *Narrative Logic*, 252.
54. On this, cf. Chapter 8, "A Bedrock of Order: Hayden White's Linguistic Humanism."

states that the end of the era of narration might come because we no longer have any experiences to share, he makes explicit the idea that we *experience* the world as narrative and that this form of experiencing is based on social forms that are precarious. What history and the novel share is the ability to configure heterogeneity in a unified form. Since most of the knowledge that humans have of the world comes in the form of "hearsay" (*ouï-dire*), the narrated report is the normative symbolic mediation between world and action. (As Ankersmit might say, our knowledge of the world is always a knowledge of narratios.) It is emplotment that enables humans to turn the heterogeneity of narrative statements into the monadic unity of narrative substances.[55] Consequently, Ricoeur's work offers a phenomenology of plot as the essence of our being in the world. However, I agree with David Carr's statement that Ricoeur, far from suggesting that reality has a narrative form, instead points to our ability to narrativize the essentially "pre-narrative" elements of "the real world."[56] Ricoeur's defense of narrativity against the potential loss of human experience is aimed at the same solipsism mentioned by Ankersmit. The tension between truth and consolation, however, is not resolved.

Ankersmit, Ricoeur, and White stress the figural and figured nature of historical representations; each sees analogic process embodied in tropes as the key to the realism claimed by historical discourse. However, metaphor functions in different ways in their theories. White's work since *Metahistory* is widely known, so I shall not spell it out too laboriously here. Suffice it to say that White points to metaphor (that is, to tropes) as the prefiguring protocol ordering our apprehension of the historical field from the start. In Ricoeur, on the other hand, metaphor (the sign of the analogue) is what can overcome the clashing visions of the past as either radically the Same (endlessly repetitive) or radically Other (chaos—Ricoeur does not share White's sympathy with the historical sublime). No reality can come from either view, but tropological imagining shifts the accent and makes a sense of "reality" possible: *really* has meaning only in terms of *such as*.[57] Ankersmit's third thesis of "narrative logic" states the similarity of metaphoric and historical statements. Unlike Ricoeur, however, Ankersmit specifies the value of metaphor as its ability to individuate a point of view, and hence to create the

55. Ricoeur, *Temps et récit*, II, 230–31.
56. David Carr, "Narrative and the Real World," in *History and Theory* 25:2 (1986), 119.
57. Ricoeur, *The Reality of the Historical Past*, 35.

play of perspectives without which our understanding of the world would fall apart. For White, tropes are a faculty of mind; for Ankersmit, a model of narrative substances; for Ricoeur, the way in which our experience of the concordant discord of time is expressed.

The link, or at least *a* link, between the post-structuralist critique of historical thinking and the narrativity that makes historical writing "historical" in a disciplinary sense is their sense of the *allegorical* nature of historical writing. One virtue of quantitative history, cliometric history, theory-oriented history, and psycho-history is that they are far more openly and self-consciously allegorical than more traditional narrative histories. By this I mean that the narrative form is much more clearly separable from the discourse itself than in less explicitly theoretical histories; a computer program, for example, resembles the narrative grammars of the formalists far more obviously that does, say, *The Decline of the West*. Ultimately, allegory questions its own authority by inescapably drawing attention to the *will* exerted in its creation; this will to represent is revealed as a human need, the product of desire or "Care," and can be understood only within the authoritative confines of—another allegory.[58]

The allegorical will, which seeks to "master" the "sources" and, for history at least, has the goal of referring to some form of "totality," creates problems that prove insuperable, except when revealed ironically as problems. It is this final insuperability that keeps history in its narrative business; as has often been observed, narrative continues to forestall death, while narrativity assures us in advance that it will all make sense, someday. Walter Benjamin noted that allegorical figures that express the "will to symbolic totality" always stare out at us as something incomplete and imperfect.[59] However, by thematizing this imperfection, satirizing the contents of the book, and foregrounding the elements of will and desire, a historian like Fernand Braudel reveals the allegorical in his *The Mediterranean and the Mediterranean World in the Age*

58. In this regard, allegory "becomes the gesture of an obsessive player who knows that the game is already lost, but who continues to play." Paul Smith, "The Will to Allegory in Postmodernism," *Dalhousie Review* 62 (1982), 113.

Hayden White has written that "the moral implications of the human sciences will never be perceived until the faculty of the will is reinstated in theory." *Tropics of Discourse: Essays in Cultural Criticism* (Baltimore, 1978), 23.

59. Walter Benjamin, *The Origin of German Tragic Drama*, trans. John Osborne (London, 1977), 186.

of Philip II, and adds to its authority as a human creation by calling into question its authority as an allegorical representation.[60]

Quantitative history, with its mathematical short-cut to referential realism, offers the most explicitly allegorical of genres. One is tempted to say that an appeal to figures is naturally an appeal to the figural. The self-conscious distance between the representation and what is represented, the willful blindness of the quantification in focusing on the one aspect of the evidence that affords a series, the explicit references to values and scientific authority that reside elsewhere, in other discourses—all of these factors are characteristic of allegories because "it is the nature of allegory to stress discontinuity and to remark the irremediable distance between representation and idea."[61] The founder of our modern view of allegory, Goethe, put things in rather the same way.

> Allegory changes a phenomenon into a concept, a concept into an image, but in such a way that the concept is still limited and completely kept and held in the image and expressed by it.
>
> The symbolic changes the phenomenon into the idea, the idea into the image, in such a way that the idea remains always infinitely active and unapproachable in the image, and will remain inexpressible even though expressed in all languages.[62]

To the extent that the narrative substances presented by histories are conceptual, displaying the distance between the historian and the phenomena in the explicit manner of the "social scientific" historian, the allegorical nature of their images is foregrounded. Hence, Ankersmit's comment that quantitative history in particular exemplifies his narrative logic. In story-history (*l'histoire événementielle*) the narratological devices correspond more clearly to the human sense of *muthos* as a *mimesis* of action, but a great deal is obscured, as both Ricoeur and White

60. Thematizing: "History becomes many stranded once more, bewilderingly complex and, who knows, in seeking to grasp all the different vibrations, waves of past time which ideally ought to accumulate like the divisions in the mechanism of a watch, the seconds, minutes, hours, and days—perhaps we shal find the whole fabric slipping away between our fingers" (II, 893).

Satirizing: "No sooner does a historian think he has isolated the particular quality of a civilization than it gives proof of the exact opposite" (II, 757).

Foregrounding: "I have loved the Mediterranean with passion. . . ." (beginning of vol. I).

Citations are from the English translation of Siân Reynolds.

61. Paul Smith, "The Will to Allegory in Postmodernism," 106.

62. These citations of Goethe's *Maximen*, 1,112 and 1,113 are taken from Hazard Adams' *Philosophy of the Literary Symbolic* (Tallahassee, 1983), 56–57.

admit. For Ricoeur, the "lies and tricks" of *récit*, relying on and using our narrative competence, have been unmasked; thoroughly familiar with the work of modern narrative theory, Ricoeur agrees that the *Annales* history inspired by Braudel and others has deepened our sense of time by building on analogies between human time and forms of the longer time spans. But he fears the loss of narrativity, so far exhibited in literature alone, because for him narrativity alone responds to the human power of communication. White distrusts even this human "need" to communicate, and notes that it, like every other essential quality of human nature, has an ideological, socializing dimension masking some appeal to power. This may be good or bad, but only for specific human purposes. "If one is going to 'go to history,' one had better have an address in mind, rather than go wandering around the streets of the past like a *flâneur*."[63]

In his famous essay, "Meditations on a Hobbyhorse," E. H. Gombrich has pointed out that a representation is not to be looked upon as an imitation of something (by which criterion a broomstick hobbyhorse would fail to represent a horse in almost any way), but rather as something capable of substituting for the object represented *for a particular purpose*. The decision about what is "capable of substitution" in a situation is obviously conventional and, at least to a certain extent, social. What I have stressed here is the element of will and choice in the representation of reality, even to the choice of the point of view that reality is representable in a coherent (narrative) way at all.[64] It is clear that not all histories are *narratives*, that they do not all offer a representation of events taking place in time. But it should be equally clear that virtually all histories are founded on a *narrativity* that guarantees that what they represent will "contain" meaning. The foundational narrativity of modern disciplinary history precludes exactly the sort of inquiry pursued by the post-structuralists. For this reason, historians generally feel them to be anti-historical. Yet this is only another way of saying that they suggest a vision of history that has been repressed, one that can recognize in all historical representations an allegorical creation for a human purpose.

63. Hayden White, "Getting Out of History," in *Diacritics* 12 (1982), 11, collected in *The Content of the Form*, 164.

64. On allegory and representation, see Morton W. Bloomfield, "Allegory as Interpretation," *New Literary History*, 3 (1972), 301–17; and *Allegory and Representation*, ed. S. J. Greenblatt (Baltimore and London, 1981). Stephen Bann's recent book *The Clothing of Clio: A Study of the Representation of History in Nineteenth-Century Britain and France* (Cambridge, 1984), has explored the changing criteria for adequate historical representations.

CONCLUSION

In his paean to the "facts" in the lectures on the *History of Civilization*, Guizot refers to them as "the immortal part" of history. By this he implies that while opinions, theories, fads, ideologies, classes, and regimes may come and go (and themselves become facts), the facts endure. Their number may be and should be augmented through research (and Guizot's role as minister in editing and publishing historical documents is well known), but once established by critical methods and accepted by the community of historical scholars, a fact was in principle immortal. If the immortal Greek deities could spawn mortals, the mortal, modest historical researcher could make a lasting, even immortal, contribution to the enterprise. Now, Guizot was no positivist, and his definition of "fact" was so broad as to undermine his apparent intention; nevertheless, this distinction between the mortal and immortal parts of history has retained its force. It stands as the authorization of the separation of form from content in historical work, a separation that enables books like Peter Gay's *Style in History* or essays like Trevelyan's "Clio—A Muse" to celebrate those historians with a certain literary flair and to assert that historians in general should look to their styles, the better to communicate their findings and ideas. As John Clive notes in a passage discussed in the first chapter of this book, all historians must put their work into a readable form; he adds that by this he means "a certain manner of literary construction and presentation." With this triviality I quite agree, yet it is profoundly misleading. The problematic word is "literary." Whether "literature" is taken to mean any body of writing in prose or verse (as in German or Latin literature), or writing of a belles-lettristic sort (as in Samuel Eliot Morison's dictum: "A few hints of literary craftsmanship may be useful to budding historians"), it always denotes a certain type of finished thought, a verbal icon, the result of prior processes that are nonliterary. In a sense they *are* nonliterary; the literary component of history is usually designed to erase the signs of the prior processes in the interest of communicating pure content—that is, "getting the story straight."

If the processes of the historical imagination are specifically *literary* only in the final stages of creation, however, I have argued in this book

326

that they are everywhere *linguistic*, shaped and constrained from the start by rhetorical considerations that are the "other" sources of history. The immortality of facts is dependent upon the conventions of discourse governing the culture that accepts their authority, which is to say the authority of the process by which they are constituted. This authority is an important form of cultural power, to be sure, and the basis of the human sciences, but it is a tenuous sort of immortality indeed. In the first place, facts themselves are invariably constituted by communities through defining, naming parts, sorting these designated objects, devising conceptions of the relations between them, distinguishing oppositions and contraries, selecting beginnings and endings, eliding gaps, evaluating relative importance among objects or categories, creating hierarchies, finding or creating new objects that will differ from existing objects in detail while resembling them in kind (as evidence), and so forth. The thoroughly rhetorical character of the process that decides what can and cannot stand as an immortal fact becomes more elaborate as the historical enterprise develops. Within a profession, careers (and research) are implicitly guided by the rhetorical topoi. A conventional career will be made (where there is room and opportunity) by following the *same* technique in *different* territory, a revisionist career will arrive at *different* conclusions in the *same* territory. These distinctions seem to be so natural as to be unworthy of notice, but *natural* is precisely what they are not. They are thoroughly cultural, encoded in and by language. Entire visions of the past can also be divided into those which see it as essentially the *same* as the present, and thus open to our understandings of human nature, economic behavior, causes of aggression, forms of belief, and so on, and those which assert the *difference* of the past, which is thereby rendered a mystery, an otherness beyond our categories, and knowable only by a considerable, ultimately doomed, act of imagination.[1]

Not only individual careers and historical imaginations are pre-figured by the elementary rhetorical categories I have just described. Metahistorical judgments also make instructive use of the same/different opposition. Whether a theorist finds essential the differences that characterize the professional historical enterprise or the considerable sameness within it is a crucial factor in determining how he or she reads history. Some theorists emphasize the differences between the work of

---

1. When Paul Ricoeur, in *The Reality of the Historical Past* (Milwaukee, 1984), posits a third position beside the past-as-same and the past-as-other, he call it the *analogue*. This category corresponds to the third rhetorical topos, that of degree.

historians equipped with much the same evidence and techniques; their concern for these differences leads them to consider the historical imagination as a set of choices that must be determined by other than historical considerations. In the extreme, this attitude may suggest that any matter on which there is no room for disagreement has ceased to be properly historical.[2] There is, however, the opposite point of view, based, predictably, on the topos of sameness. This position, subtly presented by Leon Goldstein's *Historical Knowing*, is a modern form of Guizot's notion of the immortality of the fact. Goldstein's argument grants that historical knowledge in no way observes or represents reality in any form recognizable to science or philosophy. He is, however, impressed by the extent of the agreement among professional historians, and seeks to account for it by a revealing appeal to the metaphor of "superstructure" and "infrastructure."

> By the "superstructure of history" I shall mean that part of the historical enterprise which is visible to nonhistorian consumers of what historians produce. That means the literary product of the historian's work, the final form in which his conclusions are cast, which may take the form of a narrative but need not and does not always. And by the "infrastructure of history" I shall refer to the aspect—actually, a whole range of aspects—of historical work which, for the most part, remains beneath the visibility lines of most nonhistorian consumers of what historians produce.[3]

Superstructure/infrastructure, visible/invisible, producer/consumer, are paradigms that escort us into the rhetorical realm of contraries, meaning through opposition. Each of these sets is redolent with cultural significance. Marx's relegation of the superstructure of sociocultural forms to the status of epiphenomena to the "base" infrastructure of technology and economics establishes a one-way flow of signification (the topos of cause/effect) upward. The visible/invisible pair suggests the classic message of Western literature that things are not what they seem to be, that a gnostic message exists for the initiated. Finally, the choice of the word "consumer" to designate the nonprofessional reader of history not only identifies Goldstein's concept of reading as an activity, but also implies a particular concept of modern society. Each of the conceptual oppositions from which this case is constructed con-

---

2. This position is F. R. Ankersmit's. Cf. Chapter 12.
3. Leon J. Goldstein, *Historical Knowing* (Austin, 1976), 141.

tains a member that is dominant, "marked" as the linguists would say. Infrastructure is conceptually *prior* to superstructure (as cause is to effect); the producer is prior to the consumer in a sequence of exchange; the invisible is prior to the visible in the process of discovery. The prior is privileged, naturally.

Once the priority of the infrastructure has been established through its constitution in marked pairs, Goldstein turns to definition.

> The infrastructure is that range of intellectual activities whereby the historical past is constituted in historical research; it involves treatment of evidence and thinking about evidence and is preoccupied with the determination of what conception of the historical past makes the best sense given the character of the evidence at hand. One of the most interesting and important consequences of work at the level of history's infrastructure is the way the very domain of historical evidence has been expanded from the reports of eye-witnesses, to which the ancient historians were largely limited, to the wide variety of things from which present-day historians have learned to extract such a variety of historical truth.[4]

Again marked pairs prevail: "activities" characterize the infrastructure, as opposed to the implicit "passivity" of the historical consumer—indeed, the definition of the superstructure is in the passive voice ("is visible," "are cast"). Actions abound in the infrastructure: treatment, and thinking, and determination. Also good sense, even "the best sense." To the processes of the infrastructure Goldstein attributes the attainment of a wider domain of evidential variety, cast in the evaluative topos of few/many. Although the ship metaphor of superstructure/infrastructure comes from Marx, the "infrastructure" that actually constitutes Goldstein's argument comes directly from Aristotle (*Rhetoric*, bk. I, chap. 7). It is the rhetoric that seems to be the immortal part of the case here.

It would be unfair to Goldstein to imply that his notion of the infrastructure is a philosophical version of the realm of absolute fact beloved of the typical positivist (who has always been easier to describe in theory than to locate in practice). On the contrary, Goldstein's notion of the infrastructure is a broad one; it is both a form of activity and a body of "historical truth" extracted by that activity. The contradiction

4. Ibid.

between the nature of the activity and the truth is resolved by a circular definition.

> The impressive thing, then, is that, for all the rivalries and jealousies with which historians are affected, for all the spite and pettiness which sometimes mar their disputes, a large and growing body of established historical truth, while always subject to correction, is nonetheless widely agreed to.[5]

This body of truth is perhaps better named "historical knowledge," as implied by the title of Goldstein's book; the notion of correcting truth, after all, does pose certain problems of definition. The key to historical knowing is *agreement* within a certified group, and agreement among historical producers is what Goldstein finds.

This definition of historical knowledge bears a resemblance to the theories of the literary critic Stanley Fish in a number of respects. Fish suggests "that the fact of agreement, rather than being a proof of the stability of objects, is a testimony to the power of an interpretive community to constitute the objects upon which its members (also and simultaneously constituted) can then agree."[6] Both Goldstein and Fish concede that the object itself, whether the past or the literary text, is not directly observable, but that secure meanings, which Goldstein goes so far as to call truth, arise when groups define the object, the proper mode of interpretive treatment, and the boundaries of the "interpretive community." For Goldstein the opposition of historical producer and historical consumer is the key to the interpretive authority of the former; the infrastructure belongs to the producer, the superstructure facilitates the consumer. In contrast to the eighteenth-century situation, in which historian and reader were conversing in a shared realm of cultural experience and understanding (see Chapter 1); the consumer-reader gains acknowledged competence only by accepting the prior authority of the producer-historian. This is the reality of academic history today and for Goldstein is the guarantee of continued progress in infrastructural "historical knowing."

The matters of the historical infrastructure are not predominantly *literary;* matters of "style in history" rarely appear at this level. However, they are *linguistic* throughout, entirely answerable to rules and con

---

5. Ibid., 200.

6. Stanley Fish, *Is There a Text in This Class? The Authority of Interpretive Communities* (Cambridge, Mass., 1980), 338.

straints that have been conventionally studied through literary texts, as I have emphasized in various ways throughout this book. The processes of rhetorical judgments, choices of tone, categorizations, decorum, definition of events, selection of textual boundaries, and on and on are what we bring to the task of writing history and to the task of reading history. Once linguistic considerations are recognized as the "other" sources of historical thought and its representation, the (never very clear) opposition of superstructure and infrastructure becomes problematic, as does the distinction between producer and consumer. The distinctions themselves will not disappear, however. The "other" sources are not the only sources; each body is reciprocally dependent upon the other for its constitution. In classical rhetoric, a tiny category accounts for all the traditional historical evidence. Called "nontechnical" means, they are briefly listed as a particular component of forensic rhetoric, which has traditionally afforded historical thought many of its dominant judicial metaphors of testimony, evidence, authority, objectivity, verdicts, and the like. These nontechnical means are five: laws, witnesses, contracts, tortures, and oaths.[7] The brevity of the treatment of "nontechnical" material in a large treatise on rhetoric seems to us absurd (which is to say rhetorically indecorous through disproportion); we can excuse it only by recalling the very limited existence and availability of evidential sources in Aristotle's time, and a general unfamiliarity with their potential uses. Yet it is precisely a mirror image of the place of rhetoric in modern historical studies.

Is there a "zero degree" of evidence, some statement of fact so universally acknowledged that it can stand as a model of "established historical knowledge" at the infrastructural level? Offhand, anyone can think of thousands of examples, such as "George Washington was born 256 years before these words were written." Or: "The first president of the United States was born before these words were written." Or even: "George Washington was born." I grant that there are plenty of cultural and linguistic forces in the constitution of these statements, but they are safe enough for my purposes here. As Fish puts it: "A sentence that seems to need no interpretation is already the product of one."[8] That is not my point. What I want to ask is, is this *historical* knowledge?

F. R. Ankersmit notes that the prevalence of any one view of the past renders impossible any view of the past, because such a view requires a perspective and that perspective can come only from diverse points of

7. Aristotle, *Rhetoric*, bk. I, ch. 14.
8. Fish, *Is There a Text*, 284.

view. I would suggest that universal agreement within a community about any "established" "fact"—to conflate Goldstein's and Guizot's language—takes the statement out of the realm of the historical and places it in that of the *chronicle*. It has fallen below the level of specifically historical knowledge into an area of elementary linguistic products, such as the statements above about Martha Washington's husband. From the "chronicle" it may serve historical knowledge in any number of ways, but it will remain in itself subhistorical unless it is for some reason called into question or redefined. Let us say that the date of Danton's death is a piece of relatively "immortal" knowledge, but not fully historical knowledge, while Burke's image of the French Revolution *is* properly historical, and very mortal. What I am getting at here is certainly analogous to the allegory suggested by my reading of Braudel's *Mediterranean:* that which is linguistically secure (although only within limits) must exist at a lower level of significance and signification than that which is more intricately and problematically enmeshed in rhetorical and cultural forms from its inception. It is the latter that is properly historical. While establishing and extending the chronicle are vital parts of the modern historical enterprise, the study of historiography suggests that long ages found this concern irrelevant to their historical requirements. Bossuet, for example, discussed in Chapter 3, certainly felt no such need while fulfilling his moral purpose of instructing a future monarch in God's plan for human events.

It is *meaning* that is missing from zero-degree historical facts like the date of Washington's birth, and by no means entirely missing, since no pure chronicle can exist, even in annalistic parish birth records, which exist after all for precise legal and religious purposes. "A sentence is never not in a context," notes Fish.[9] In my text the birth of the owner of Mount Vernon is used as an example of a decontextualized statement; that is its context. Or rather, one of its possible contexts. I say "one of its possible contexts" because the notion of a prior, unified, definable context (such as *fin de siècle* Vienna, or the professional historical community, or the concluding argument of this book) is not a plausible one.[10]

9. Ibid.

10. "The systematic defect of much traditional historiography has been the attempt to employ the simplest documentary texts—or documentary texts subjected to a simplistic interpretation—as the basis for an understanding of the past or the 'context' to which complex texts are made to conform. A fruitful reversal of perspectives would propose the complex text itself as at times a better model for the reconstruction of the larger 'context.' The relationship between text and context would then become a question of 'intertextual' reading, which cannot be addressed on the basis of reductionist oversimplifications that convert the context into a fully unified or dominant structure saturating the text with a

Conclusion

Contexts are allegorical, interpretive representations erected for specific functions from available materials in order to lend these materials meaning by relating them to one another. The issue of narrative has powerfully reappeared in historical theory of recent years, and the study of tropology in various forms occupies a growing place in literary studies. Both of these endeavors deal with the creation of contexts, how they are constructed, why they appear to be inevitable or natural, what choices exist among contextual models. Tropes serve as the elementary model of context formation by specifying how elements may be related; tropological analysis always points to the other existing possibilities. Narrative, as discussed in Chapter 5, is itself a context, and narrativity an inescapable means of contextualizing the discontinuous fragments from the chronicle into a fully bound, framed representation. Just as every sentence will be heard or read within some context (with as many potential meanings as there are possible contexts), every historical statement, however elementary, will be comprehended by even a minimally competent reader of history (Goldstein's imaginary "consumer") as part of some narrative field that affords the context of meaning for that statement.

The early nineteenth century saw at once the rapid decline of rhetoric as the master study of human affairs, and the equally rapid rise of history as an authoritative mode of understanding and explanation. They passed each other on the staircase of ideas, one young and ascendant, the other ageless and declining. It is a truism that the constitution of history as a professsion and formal study is closely linked to its elimination of traditional ties to rhetoric, thereby appropriating for the historical "producer" the power that had once been shared by writer and reader as part of a community. Over and over again, this primal scene has been repeated, as every generation sends forth a "new history" that makes just the same claim as the one before—that its predecessor was hopelessly implicated in the toils of linguistic forms and illusions, and that it has found a method that masters and dominates representation. The romantic historians made this claim as they opened and created the archives of Europe, the positivists as they rejected romantic enthusiasms, the social and economic "new" historians of the turn of the twentieth century as they cast aside the sagas of nationalist history;

certain meaning. Meaning is indeed context-bound, but context is not itself bound in any simple or unproblematic way." Dominick LaCapra, *Rethinking Intellectual History: Texts, Contexts, Language* (Ithaca, 1983), 117.

and, of course, the new quantitative historians make the claim again, hoping to escape the toils of narrative itself.[11]

The archive is revered as the locus of the pure "sources" of history; the latest monograph is the most authoritative statement on the subject. What is lost is the "dusty tomes in between," always doomed by their age to the merely literary status to which they had once consigned the histories before them.[12] They are given over, as often as not, to the "consumers" of history, who will judge them by the power of their vision and the effectiveness of their representative force, rather than by their relation to the ever-fluctuating, yet ostensibly immortal, chronicle. It has become clear that the dualities mentioned here are all highly dubitable. The processes that find their literary form in the "superstructure" (that part of a ship—or text—which is visible above the surface) are fundamentally the same as those of the structures of discovery and judgment in the "infrastructure." What is visible in language sometimes obscures the invisible rhetorical choices of historical research and thinking, but hardly differs in kind. And if the "consumer" of history can derive meaningful conclusions from a reading of the historical text, such understanding must be based upon the same mental processes that directed the creating of the text. The representation of history (*pace* Wordsworth) is in consequence "both what they half create, / And what perceive."

The "shipwrecks" of historical representations are never to be understood as failures. Like Braudel, I feel that the bold venture that pushes an idea to its limits and experiences the constraints of the "other" sources is the most valuable product of the historical imagination, not as a tutelary lesson nor as a guide for further research nor as a literary masterpiece, but as a creative act that exercises and extends the possibilities of representation. By the same token, the reader of history—of which the first and most important exemplar is the historian—must push the act of reading farther, looking for the shoals where the craft, the historical text, will founder and reveal its "other" sources, hidden but permeating historical representations. These are the *crooked* readings; they show the deepest respect for reality by recognizing and probing the tense and contradictory double sources of history, each striving to enforce its right as the immortal part.

11. On this Oedipal procession of "new histories," see Linda Orr's brilliant essay, "The Revenge of Literature: A History of History," in *New Literary History* 18 (1986), 1–22.

12. Ibid., 8–9.

INDEX

Acton, J. E. Dalberg, Lord, 7
Adorno, Theodor W., 149
Allegory, x, 14–20, 68, 76, 81, 89, 91–94,
    100, 117, 120, 124, 151, 185–87, 189–92,
    199, 241, 247–48, 251–52, 256, 258, 263,
    265, 285–93, 298, 305, 321–23, 331–32
Althusser, Louis, 212, 283
Andrews, Richard M., 159–160
Ankersmit, F. R., 7n6, 39, 75, 266, 305,
    310–14, 318–22, 330
Annales school, 8, 17, 104, 106, 108–9,
    119–20, 154, 159–60, 164, 176–77, 181,
    184, 186, 288, 294, 317, 323
Aquinas, Saint Thomas, 146
Ariès, Philippe, 308
Aristophanes, 23
Aristotle, 9, 122, 150, 220, 231, 307, 317,
    328, 330
Arius, 258
Athanasius, Saint, 258–59
Auerbach, Erich, 204
Augustine, Saint, 191, 257, 306–8

Babbitt, Irving, 81
Bachelard, Gaston, 170, 202, 209
Bacon, Francis, 23, 237
Bagehot, Walter, 79
Bailyn, Bernard, 153, 158, 160
Bakhtin, Mikhail, 21, 88, 117, 263
Balzac, Honoré de, 296
Bann, Stephen, 3, 4, 7n6, 16, 107
Barante, Prosper, baron de, 6
Barthes, Roland, 7n6, 21, 58, 65, 104, 115,
    117, 174n36, 175, 182, 191, 270–71,
    296–97, 304, 317, 319
Bayle, Pierre, 23
Benjamin, Walter, 282, 309, 321
Benveniste, Emile, 21, 253, 285
Berkeley, Bishop George, 42, 156
Bernard of Clairvaux, Saint, 196
Bertalanffy, Ludwig von, 37, 137
Blanchot, Maurice, 184
Bloch, Marc, 30, 32, 44, 65, 119

Bloom, Harold, 209, 232, 269, 291
Boniface VIII, pope, 11, 14
Bossuet, Bishop Jacques-Bénigne, 69–72
Boswell, James, 46, 55
Bracciolini, Poggio, 9
Bradley, F. H., 31
Brahms, Johannes, 42
Braudel, Fernand, viii, ix, x, 18, 65–70, 72,
    76–77, 119–20, 153–87, 190, 308, 321,
    323, 333
Brewer, Maria Minich, 303n15
Breznitz, Shlomo, 260n14
Broadbent, D. E., 38
Brown, Norman O., 2, 47, 49, 54
Bruner, Jerome, 39
Burckhardt, Jakob, 60, 115, 196, 206, 220,
    241
Burke, Edmund, 316, 331
Burke, Kenneth, 231–32, 243–44, 253, 255
Burton, Richard, 163
Byron, George Gordon, Lord, 55

Carr, David, 320
Catherine of Aragon, queen of England,
    45
Chateaubriand, François-René, vicomte
    de, 86
Chaunu, Pierre, 308
Chomsky, Noam, 274
Churchill, Winston, 62
Cixous, Hélène, 302, 304, 310
Clausius, Rudolf, 142
Clement V, Pope, 14
Clifford, Gay, 286
Clive, John, 22–23, 325
Coleridge, Samuel T., 241
Collingwood, R. G., 136, 203–4
Columbus, Christopher, 13
Conze, Werner, 157
Corneille, Pierre, 82, 85, 92
Croce, Benedetto, 31, 49, 179, 196, 199,
    206, 215, 249
Culler, Jonathan, 272

335

Index

Index

Lying Down Together: Law, Metaphor, and Theology
Milner S. Ball

Shaping Written Knowledge: The Genre and Activity of the
Experimental Article in Science
Charles Bazerman

Politics and Ambiguity
William E. Connolly

Machiavelli and the History of Prudence
Eugene Garver

Language and Historical Representation: Getting the Story Crooked
Hans Kellner

The Rhetoric of Economics
Donald N. McCloskey

Therapeutic Discourse and Socratic Dialogue: A Cultural Critique
Tullio Maranhão

The Rhetoric of the Human Sciences: Language and Argument in
Scholarship and Public Affairs
John S. Nelson, Allan Megill, and Donald N. McCloskey, eds.

The Politics of Representation: Writing Practices in Biography,
Photography, and Policy Analysis
Michael J. Shapiro

The Legacy of Kenneth Burke
Herbert Simons and Trevor Melia, editors

The Unspeakable: Discourse, Dialogue, and Rhetoric in the
Postmodern World
Stephen A. Tyler

Heracles' Bow: Essays on the Rhetoric and the Poetics of the Law
James Boyd White